Late Soviet Britain

Why has the United Kingdom, historically one of the strongest democracies in the world, become so unstable? What changed? This book demonstrates that a major part of the answer lies in the transformation of its state. It shows how Britain championed radical economic liberalisation only to weaken and ultimately break its own governing institutions. The crisis of democracy in rich countries has brought forward many urgent analyses of neoliberal capitalism. This book explores for the first time how the 'governing science' in Leninist and neoliberal revolutions fails for many of the same reasons. These systems may have been utterly opposed in their political values, but Abby Innes argues that when we grasp the kinship in their closed-system forms of economic reasoning and their strategies for government, we may better understand the causes of state failure in what remains our inescapably open-system reality.

ABBY INNES is Associate Professor of Political Economy in the European Institute at the London School of Economics and Political Science.

Late Soviet Britain

Why Materialist Utopias Fail

ABBY INNES
London School of Economics and Political Science

CAMBRIDGE
UNIVERSITY PRESS

Shaftesbury Road, Cambridge CB2 8EA, United Kingdom

One Liberty Plaza, 20th Floor, New York, NY 10006, USA

477 Williamstown Road, Port Melbourne, VIC 3207, Australia

314–321, 3rd Floor, Plot 3, Splendor Forum, Jasola District Centre, New Delhi – 110025, India

103 Penang Road, #05–06/07, Visioncrest Commercial, Singapore 238467

Cambridge University Press is part of Cambridge University Press & Assessment, a department of the University of Cambridge.

We share the University's mission to contribute to society through the pursuit of education, learning and research at the highest international levels of excellence.

www.cambridge.org
Information on this title: www.cambridge.org/9781009373623

DOI: 10.1017/9781009373647

© Abby Innes 2023

This publication is in copyright. Subject to statutory exception and to the provisions of relevant collective licensing agreements, no reproduction of any part may take place without the written permission of Cambridge University Press & Assessment.

First published 2023

A catalogue record for this publication is available from the British Library

Library of Congress Cataloging-in-Publication Data
Names: Innes, Abby, author.
Title: Late Soviet Britain : why materialist utopias fail / Abby Innes, London School of Economics and Political Science.
Description: Cambridge, United Kingdom ; New York, NY : Cambridge University Press, 2023. | Includes bibliographical references and index.
Identifiers: LCCN 2023006815 | ISBN 9781009373623 (hardback) | ISBN 9781009373647 (ebook)
Subjects: LCSH: Great Britain – Economic conditions – 1997– | Soviet Union – History – 1953–1985. | Great Britain – Economic policy – 1997– | Neoliberalism – Great Britain.
Classification: LCC HC256.7 .I56 2023 | DDC 330.941–dc23/eng/20230309
LC record available at https://lccn.loc.gov/2023006815

ISBN 978-1-009-37362-3 Hardback
ISBN 978-1-009-37363-0 Paperback

Cambridge University Press & Assessment has no responsibility for the persistence or accuracy of URLs for external or third-party internet websites referred to in this publication and does not guarantee that any content on such websites is, or will remain, accurate or appropriate.

The aims of the system reveal its most essential characteristic to be introversion, a movement towards being ever more completely and unreservedly itself, which means that the radius of its influence is continually widening as well. This system serves people only to the extent necessary to ensure that people will serve it. Anything beyond this, that is to say, anything which leads people to overstep their predetermined roles is regarded by the system as an attack upon itself. And in this respect it is correct: every instance of such transgression is a genuine denial of the system …

'The Power of the Powerless', (October 1978)
(translated by Paul Wilson), East European Politics
and Societies 32 (2) (2018): 353–408, p. 361.

Václav Havel

We always knew that everything the Party told us about communism was a lie. What we didn't know was that everything they told us about capitalism was true.

A post-Soviet joke

Contents

List of Figures	page viii
Acknowledgements	ix
Introduction: The Gods That Failed	1
Part I The Materialist Utopias	**21**
1 Rationality and Closed-System Reasoning	23
2 General Equilibrium and the Balanced Plan	51
3 On Bureaucracy	77
4 On 'Organised Forgetting' in the Governing Science	105
Part II Britain's Neoliberal Revolution	**125**
5 The New Public Management, *or* Enterprise Planning in Capitalist Form	127
6 Quasi-markets in Welfare, *or* the Non-withering State	173
7 Tax Competition, *or* the Return of Regulatory Bargaining	221
8 Efficient Markets and Climate Change, *or* Soviet Cybernetics 2.0	272
Part III The Rise and Fall of the Neoliberal 'Movement Regime'	**325**
9 Neoliberalism: The Brezhnev Years	327
10 A Politics for the End of Time	371
Index	392

Figures

7.1 The 2013 HMRC CGE model *page* 235
7.2 Channels through which a reduction in corporate taxation affects GDP 257

Acknowledgements

I would not have had the quiet time to explore the questions discussed in this book were it not for the generous financial support of the British Academy, whose Mid-Career Fellowship funded the sabbatical that started this project. My heartfelt thanks go to Peter Hall, Jonas Pontusson and Anke Hassel, who vouched for that all-important application.

For their kindness in commenting on chapters-in-progress I am indebted to Saul Estrin, Robert Falkner, Sam Fankhauser, Simon Glendinning, Howard Glennerster, Sam Greene, David Hall, Merryn Hutchings, Sian Jones, Jeffrey Kopstein, Tim Lankester, William Lazonick, Adam Leaver, Brendan O'Leary, Lorenzo Marvulli, Mark Philp, Rupert Read, Quentin Reed, Martin Rhodes, Rory Stewart, Dustin Voss, Veljko Vujačić, Richard Ward and Jonathan White. I can still scarcely believe my luck in being able to draw on their exceptional expertise. My thanks too to Alexander Clarkson for his cheerfully allowing me to pinch his phrase 'Late Soviet Britain' for the title. I would also like to thank two very dear friends, Wade Jacoby and Denis Gromb, posthumously. They were brilliant scholars, generous and encouraging, and like everyone who knew them, I miss them terribly.

Within my academic home, at the European Institute of the London School of Economics and Political Science, I owe a particular debt of gratitude to Nick Barr, Richard Bronk, Robert Hancké and Waltraud Schelkle, who I tend to think of as my long-standing partners in crime. Richard's work on imagination and uncertainty in economics was also an important inspiration. Through the years it has taken me to write this book, they have been there as debaters, jokers, senders of articles and true friends. This project has been altogether more enjoyable for their wonderful company along the way.

As I became more confident in this Soviet and neoliberal comparison I ran a master's course entitled 'The Political Economy of the Neoliberal State', and I would like to thank all those students who braved this rather counter-intuitive discussion with their characteristic curiosity and brilliance. Those conversations were hugely valuable to me on every level. My sincere thanks also to the European Institute's exceptional professional services team, who enabled us all to thrive.

I was helped by extremely constructive reviewers and editors at the *Review of International Political Economy*, where the argument on outsourcing was first aired in A. Innes, 'The Limits of Institutional Convergence: Why Public Sector Outsourcing Is Less Efficient than Soviet Enterprise Planning', 28 (6) (2021): 1705–1728, www.tandfonline.com/. I am grateful for the permission from Taylor & Francis to reprint a significant part of that argument here.

When it came to the full book, draft chapters were sent to anonymous reviewers at Cambridge University Press, and I was beyond fortunate in their thoughtful observations. I am particularly grateful to Martin Rhodes, who not only did the hard work of complete manuscript review but also then re-read the whole text to suggest sympathetic edits for the final cuts: an extremely generous act that I experienced like a fireman's lift over the flames of indecision. For their patience and consistent kindness throughout this entire process, my heartfelt thanks to John Haslam, my editor at Cambridge University Press, and the hugely supportive team of Carrie Parkinson, Chloe Quinn, Balaji Devadoss and their colleagues who have produced this book with such care.

On the home front, I want to thank my father, Michael, his wife Veronika, my siblings, Hannah and Simon, their partners Adrian and Jo, and their wonderful families for their love and support. Finally, my partner, Vic Long, has lived with this book scarcely less than I have, and I cannot thank him enough for being such a nurturing, funny, safe haven of a man through this entire adventure. This tome is dedicated to him, and to my late mother, Jean, with love.

The responsibility for the thesis that follows is nevertheless mine, and like all arguments about the political economy, it should stand or fall on its merits.

Introduction
The Gods That Failed

The bad news:
Dreams don't come true
The worse news:
Yours might[1]

Why has Great Britain, historically one of the strongest democracies in the world, become so unstable? What changed? This book demonstrates that a major part of the answer lies in the transformation of its state. It shows how Britain championed radical economic liberalisation only to weaken and ultimately break its own governing institutions. This history has direct parallels not just in the United States but across all the advanced capitalist economies that adopted neoliberal reforms. The shattering of the British state over the last forty years was driven by the idea that markets are always more efficient than the state: the private sector morally and functionally superior to the public sector. But as this book shows, this claim was ill-founded, based as it was on the most abstract materialist utopia of the twentieth century. The neoliberal revolution in Great Britain and Northern Ireland – the United Kingdom – has failed accordingly, and we are living with the systemic consequences of that failure.

The rise of nationalist populism in some of the world's richest countries has brought forward many urgent analyses of contemporary capitalism. What this book offers, by contrast, is the explanation of a dark historical joke. It explores for the first time how the Leninist and neoliberal revolutions fail for many of the same reasons. Leninism and neoliberalism may have been utterly opposed in their political values, but when we grasp the kinship between their forms of economic argument and their practical strategies for government, we may better

---

[1] Eric Jarosinski, *Nein: A Manifesto* (Melbourne: Text Publishing, 2015), p. 42.

understand the causes of state failure in both systems, as well as their calamitous results.

Britain's neoliberal policies have their roots in neoclassical economics, and Part I begins by comparing the neoclassical and Soviet economic utopias. What emerges are mirror images – two visions of a perfectly efficient economy and an essentially stateless future. These affinities are rooted in their common dependence on a machine model of the political economy and hence, by necessity, the shared adoption of a hyper-rational conception of human motivation: a perfect utilitarian rationality versus a perfect social rationality. As the later policy chapters demonstrate, these theoretical similarities produce real institutional effects: a clear institutional isomorphism between neoliberal systems of government and Soviet central planning.

When it comes to the mechanics of government, both systems justify a near identical methodology of quantification, forecasting, target setting and output-planning, albeit administrative and service output-planning in the neoliberal case and economy-wide outputs in the Soviet. Since the world in practice is dynamic and synergistic, however, it follows that the state's increasing reliance on methods that presume rational calculation within an unvarying underlying universal order can only lead to a continuous misfit between governmental theory and reality. These techniques will tend to fail around any task characterised by uncertainty, intricacy, interdependence and evolution, which are precisely the qualities of most of the tasks uploaded to the modern democratic state.

The Soviet and neoliberal conceptions of the political economy as a mechanism ruled by predetermined laws of economic behaviour were used to promote pure systems of economic coordination, be that by the state or the market. Leninism, as it evolved into Stalinist command planning, dictated the near-complete subordination of markets to the central plan. In neoliberalism, the state has been more gradually stripped of its capacity for economic government and, over time, for prudential, strategic action, as its offices, authority and revenues are subordinated to market-like mechanisms. Both Soviet and neoliberal political elites proved wildly over-optimistic about the integrity of their doctrines, even as they demonised the alternatives.

For all their political antipathy, what binds Leninists and neoliberals together is their shared fantasy of an infallible 'governing science' – of scientific management writ large. The result is that Britain has

Introduction: The Gods That Failed 3

reproduced Soviet governmental failures, only now in capitalist form. When we understand the isomorphism between Soviet and neoliberal statecraft, we can see more clearly why their states share pathologies that span from administrative rigidity to rising costs, from rent-seeking enterprises to corporate state capture, from their flawed analytical monocultures to the demoralisation of the state's personnel and, ultimately, a crisis in the legitimacy of the governing system itself. This time around, however, the crisis is of liberal democracy.

After setting out the philosophical foundations of these ideologies, the book's policy chapters in Part II explore how the neoliberal revolution has transformed the British state's core functions in the political economy: in administration, welfare, tax and regulation and the management of future public risk. In Part III I examine the political consequences of these changes, and demonstrate how Britain's exit from the European Union has played out as an institutionally fatal confrontation between economic libertarianism and reality. The final chapter considers how the neoliberal revolution, like its Leninist counterpart, has failed within the terms by which it was justified and instead induced a profound crisis not only of political and economic development but also of political culture.

I use different periods of Soviet history as an analytical benchmark throughout the book, but the Brezhnev years (1964–1982) were those of the fullest systemic entropy: the period of ossification, self-dealing and directionless political churn. Under 'late' neoliberalism we can see a similar moment of political hiatus, as neoliberal governments likewise resort to nationalism and the politics of cultural reaction to forestall public disillusionment and a shift in paradigm. I use the United Kingdom as the case study because it was both a pioneer of these reforms and, in many respects, has gone furthest with them. If neoliberalism as a doctrine had been analytically well-founded, it was in the United Kingdom, with its comparatively long and strong liberal traditions, that we should have seen its most positive outcomes.

To be clear, Britain's neoliberals were never totalitarians of the Soviet variety. They never used revolutionary violence to create a one-party state, deployed ubiquitous intelligence agencies to enforce repression or used systems of mass incarceration and murder for political ends. Britain's neoliberal consensus has nevertheless favoured a one-doctrine state, and the violent suppression of specific, typically economy-related, protests has been a periodic feature of its politics since 1979. Britain's neoliberal governments have also developed an increasingly callous attitude to social hardship and suffering. Most troubling of all is that the more neoliberalism has been implemented, the more the country has been driven to the end of its democratic road. By the early 2020s the Conservative government of Boris Johnson had sought to criminalise peaceful protest, to constrain media independence and to insulate the political executive from parliamentary and public scrutiny. In short, it had abused its authority to disable legitimate political opposition. What I hope to explain is why any regime that commits itself to neoliberal economics must travel in this direction or abandon this ideology.

What follows is an argument about the collapse of the empiricist political centre and its replacement by utopian radicalism. Specifically, this is a story of how the pioneering and socially progressive philosophy of liberalism is being discredited by utopian economics and the practically clientelist methods of government that follow from it, just as the politics of social solidarity essential to a civilised world was undermined by the violence and corruption of the Soviet experiment. As the old Soviet joke had it, 'Capitalism is the exploitation of man by man. Communism is its exact opposite.' There are, of course, many challenges distinct to neoliberalism and I pay attention to them, but my purpose here is to see what we can learn about the political economy of the neoliberal state when we look at it through the lens of comparative materialist utopias.

Critical Realism

Part I of the book begins with an analysis of the Soviet and neoclassical economic conceptions of reality and the methods they chose to understand it. My purpose here is to explain why the forms of justification used are so problematic as a basis for government strategies in any system, but most particularly in a democracy. To do this transparently, however, I must begin by setting out my own philosophical assumptions about the nature of reality (the problem of ontology) and what any of us can reasonably claim to know about it (the problem of epistemology).

All theories about the social world inescapably have their own philosophical underpinnings. It follows that the most important decision any government or social scientist makes at the start of their analysis is how they conceptualise the world they think they are in. The foundations of my argument are 'critical realist',[2] and what distinguishes a critical realist account is an explicit interest in how a given theory, or body of beliefs, conceives of the nature and structure of social reality, the forms of justification it uses in its claims 'to know' a particular thing and the reasonableness of those beliefs, given the limits we face in acquiring knowledge.[3]

Some background may be helpful here. Critical realism emerged in the 1970s in response to an extreme pendulum swing in the philosophy of knowledge. In research that transformed conventional 'positivist' understandings of scientific progress, Thomas Kuhn had demonstrated in the early 1960s that as a matter of historical fact scientific progress had not developed in a nice straight line. Kuhn showed that reality has not unfolded itself to us like the pages of a Book of Truth: as something we can simply read to answer our inquiries. He demonstrated that scientific knowledge has moved instead through periods of conformity to existing theories and assumptions, followed by episodes of rapid and revolutionary disagreement and change. Anomalies and new insights confronted those theories, fuelled their critical contradiction and built towards periodic 'paradigm shifts' in how we understood the world around us. These new paradigms had gone on to create new questions for further research, and so it continues.[4]

In reaction, the philosophical debate about what we can know veered rather drastically from the 'naïve empiricism' that Kuhn had just refuted towards arguments for a humanistic philosophical pragmatism, or, to its critics, 'relativism'. Thus, for example, the philosopher of mind Richard Rorty suggested that there is no objective reality at all outside of the forms we construct in language. In this view, it is a fool's errand to search for general knowledge or general truth, as distinct from realities that we apprehend purely through our mental constructions.[5] This interpretivist approach said, 'we cannot establish

---

[2] Roy Bhaskar, *A Realist Theory of Science* (Hassocks: Harvester Press, 1978).
[3] Roy Bhaskar, *The Possibility of Naturalism: A Philosophical Critique of the Contemporary Human Sciences* (Hassocks: Harvester Press, 1989).
[4] Thomas Kuhn, *The Structure of Scientific Revolutions* (Chicago: University of Chicago Press, 1962).
[5] Berth Danermark, Mats Ekström, Liselotte Jakobsen, Jan Ch. Karlsson and Roy Bhaskar, *Explaining Society: Critical Realism in the Social Sciences* (New York and London: Taylor and Francis, 2001), pp. 16–17.

anything definitively'. Physicists or economists might search for eternal verities, but they are essentially theatre critics, absorbed in the narrative performances that interest them most. As Rorty concluded, "True" resembles... a compliment paid to sentences that seem to be paying their way and that fit in with other sentences which are doing so.[6] His apparent intention was to radically 'de-divinise' the world so that, no longer justifying our actions and conflicts through some supposed Truth beyond ourselves, we might focus instead on imagining the solutions to our common problems and so learn to describe our relationships to each other and our environments more harmoniously.[7]

As a way out of this polarisation between an over-optimistic positivism and this notably humanistic but radically destabilising interpretivism, critical realists stepped in and observed that some forms of knowledge are demonstrably more reliable than others. They further noted that relative reliability is more characteristic of the natural than the social sciences. To take just one compelling example, the accuracy of weather forecasts within short time frames has improved significantly as the quality and quantity of observations have increased, along with the computing power to manage them. Financial forecasts in the meantime have repeatedly failed to anticipate imminent financial losses, let alone the rising frequency and intensity of financial crises since the 1970s, those same increases in computational sophistication notwithstanding.

To help explain this contrast, critical realists observed that all science, both natural and social, is socially defined. We cannot transcend the history of our own curiosity to gain unmediated access to the 'world-as-it-really-is'.[8] But they also drew attention to the fact that to acquire useable knowledge we need to know the mechanisms that produced the empirical events we are observing, and those underlying generative mechanisms are often harder to discover in the social world, as distinct from the natural, physical world. This is because

---

[6] Richard Rorty, *Consequences of Pragmatism: Essays, 1972–1980* (Minneapolis: University of Minnesota Press, 1982), p. 13.

[7] Peter Reason, 'Pragmatist Philosophy and Action Research: Readings and Conversations with Richard Rorty', *Action Research* 1 (1) (2003): 103–123, pp. 105–109.

[8] Richard Bronk and Wade Jacoby, 'Uncertainty and the Dangers of Monocultures in Regulation, Analysis and Practice', MPIfG Discussion Paper 16/6 (2016), pp. 11–12.

it is often harder to isolate specific causative factors in society from other unstable but highly interdependent factors, and the outcomes are rarely stable in themselves.[9]

To elaborate on both points, critical realism has its roots in Kantian epistemology, as indeed does Kuhn's work on the scientific revolutions.[10] It has been widely accepted since Immanuel Kant that we have no choice but to interpret the world in ways that are structured by our operating concepts, and this is as true for the natural as for the social sciences. There is no Archimedean point where we can stand to observe the entire universe of causal mechanisms that led to a given situation. The facts we discover are framed by the theories we construct and apply.[11] This is not to say that we know nothing but to accept that all knowledge, including all science, is contingent on the frameworks of interpretation we have already developed. Even in today's data-rich world, the data analyst is inescapably like Narcissus who, confronted with a pool of information, is also transfixed by their own reflection.

Why is it often harder for the social sciences to identify causation than it is for the natural sciences? As critical realists point out, the causal mechanisms at work in the social world tend to be less stable and less open to analytical isolation than many phenomena in the natural world. Roy Bhaskar drew a valuable distinction between the intransitive objects of knowledge that don't depend on human activity, such as death, and transitive phenomena that are the 'artificial objects fashioned into items of knowledge by the science of the day',[12] such as taxes. This distinction helps us understand why the natural sciences, with their greater focus on the intransitive, manage more often to repeat experiments around underlying causal factors and confirm their findings in diverse environments, even, in some realms, to establish robust 'general laws', for example, around gravity, or thermodynamics, or chemical compounds. Such findings have created relatively secure foundations for further discovery in particular fields, not least around changes in weather patterns and climate

---

[9] Danermark et al., *Explaining Society*, p. 87.
[10] Tony Lawson, 'A Realist Theory for Economics', in R. E. Backhouse, *New Directions in Economic Methodology* (London: Routledge, 1994): 257–286, p. 271.
[11] Danermark et al., *Explaining Society*, pp. 5, 31.
[12] Roy Bhaskar, *A Realist Theory of Science: With a New Introduction* (London: Routledge, 2008), p. 11.

change more broadly. By contrast, while social scientists can productively look for the causal relationships behind trends and events, they must struggle to transcend the dynamic contingencies of social reality. This leads critical realists to emphasise the fact that while the social world is demonstrably structured, differentiated and stratified it is also *changing*.[13]

One of the key implications of this observation is that we can lay claims to predict outcomes only in essentially closed systems, where generative mechanisms can operate under conditions of isolation and independent of other mechanisms and/or where there are 'natural laws' in operation with demonstrably consistent effects.[14] It is only in such environments that we can reasonably hope to account for the causal mechanisms at work to the point of prediction, and such environments are peculiarly hard to find in the social world.

Short of being actively poked by an analytical stick, the objects of study in the natural sciences tend to be indifferent to our investigation. By contrast, the objects of study in social science are constantly manifesting, reviewing and reinventing the terrain the social scientist is trying to understand. Social scientists themselves are part of that constant process of social 'becoming'. Thus, where the objects of study for the natural science researcher are *naturally* produced but socially defined, the objects of study for the social analyst are thus both *socially* produced and socially defined.[15] Economists, political scientists and sociologists are consequently interpreting a world full of people who are themselves constantly interpreting the world.[16] As individuals within communities, we adapt our behaviour based on those frames of interpretation, and in our evermore informationally connected world these frames emerge from a huge variety of sources. These include political ideologies, religious and other cultural narratives and, of course, the sciences. We all act interdependently, and we do this at the individual, collective and institutional level, even as we try to generate a purely personal understanding of our own, unique, existence. For the social scientist, as for governments, this produces an inalienable problem of causal instability, not to mention an entirely understandable desire to

---

[13] Danermark et al., *Explaining Society*, pp. 16–17.
[14] Ibid., pp. 205–206.   [15] Ibid., p. 16.
[16] Richard Bronk, *The Romantic Economist: Imagination in Economics* (Cambridge: Cambridge University Press, 2009), pp. 263–264.

make it all go way by deciding that a given thinker, or a given ideology, has hit upon the definitive answer, so that we can exchange an exhausting curiosity for a more relaxing conviction.

Critical realists consequently understand knowledge as neither wholly objective nor subjective but as the result of interaction between subject and object, and when that object is other people, the grounds for certainty are narrowed.[17] These insights form a key working assumption for this book's argument, and they are highly consequential for anyone who claims to have discovered 'the' science of government. They warn us, to take just one example, that it is analytically treacherous to fixate on a single account of the 'real' nature of human motivation. From the critical realist perspective, analytical and normative frames, cultural practices and emotional interactions will alter our motivation, often significantly and unpredictably. It follows that even if we were to encounter consistent motivational properties at the individual level of behaviour in a controlled environment, we could hardly rely on their constancy when the individual steps outside into the evolving social world. The same is obviously true in reverse: to draw inferences about individual motivation from mass behaviour is equally fraught.

To admit all this, however, is emphatically not to say that the social sciences are useless. Reasoned comparison and triangulation can produce practical knowledge about distinctive trends within our complex reality. To revisit that point about death and taxes, the consequences of certain forms of social pressure have proved remarkably consistent over time and across cultures. It is a consistent social fact, for example, that social inequality causes disparities in mortality, morbidity and life chances in every society with high and even moderate income inequality, as confirmed by centuries of observation. The causes and character of that inequality have evolved, however. Policies and technologies change, and as a result, so do the underlying causes of social harm. You may fix one source of damaging human exploitation only for new sources of exploitation to emerge. What all this implies is that the story of social causes and effects cannot simply be solved once and for all. At best, as Richard Bronk points out, when it comes to the

---

[17] James D. Proctor, 'The Social Construction of Nature: Relativist Accusations, Pragmatist and Critical Realist Responses', *Annals of the Association of American Geographers* 88 (3) (September 1998): 352–376, p. 361.

political economy, all economic models and all paradigms are 'fragments in the search of a unified understanding...they create an ordered vision that is complete and systematic in one sense, while necessarily partial and provisional in other respects... They cannot provide us with a complete vision; and the tendencies they reveal are abstracted from complicating factors'.[18] To analyse the political economy, let alone to govern it, is consequently an exercise that begs for analytical humility and analytical pluralism,[19] at least for any government that claims to govern in the public interest.

Why are social environments quite so changeable? It is not just that we are constantly dealing with interpretation, reinterpretation and error, it is also that we are imaginative and tend to act upon it. We consequently live in a world of 'ontological indeterminacy'.[20] New ideas, radical policy reforms, technological innovations, changing preferences and emergent novelty in complex systems guarantee that the future cannot be like the past.[21] We all consequently face what Frank Knight called 'uncertainty' rather than measurable 'risk'.[22] None of us can know how the future will differ from the past, not just because we can't know definitively how we got to the present but because every time we apply our imaginations, or someone has a new response to a given stimulus, the future is going to be different anyway.[23] Innovation and novelty imply a break with past regularities, and this creates inescapable barriers to complete knowledge of the future. As George Shackle put it, 'What does not yet exist cannot now be known.'[24] The novelty, and hence uncertainty, implied by one innovation is compounded by the fact that we cannot know what the creative reactions of others to the new situation will be.[25]

The combination of epistemological uncertainty, dynamic interdependence and ontological indeterminacy carries devastating consequences

---

[18] Bronk, *The Romantic Economist*, pp. 292–293.   [19] Ibid., p. 11.
[20] Bronk and Jacoby, 'Uncertainty and the Dangers of Monocultures', pp. 8–11.
[21] Richard Bronk, 'Epistemological Difficulties with Neo-classical Economics', Southern Economic Association Conference Paper, 19–21 November 2011, Washington, DC, p. 7.
[22] Frank Knight, *Risk, Uncertainty and Profit* (Boston: Houghton Mifflin, 1921).
[23] Bronk, 'Epistemological Difficulties', pp. 8, 14.
[24] George Shackle, *Epistemics and Economics: A Critique of Economic Doctrines* (New Brunswick: Transaction Publishers, 1992), p. 3.
[25] Jens Beckert and Richard Bronk, *Uncertain Futures: Imagination, Narratives and Calculation in the Economy* (Oxford: Oxford University Press, 2018), p. 6.

for the materialist utopias discussed in this book, because it follows that the unvarying, predetermined economic laws of motion they claim to have mastered do not, in fact, exist. Indeed, they cannot exist. Not only does epistemological uncertainty render such 'laws' mere assertion, their existence would require the end of the human imagination, not to mention a biosphere of infinite capacity and stability, regardless of human activity. Even at our most mundane, we exercise real choices that go beyond those that can be described by theories and, by extension, by ideologies.[26] This is an inalienable feature of societies made up of people who think, love, fight, learn, get frustrated and have a laugh, and create coping mechanisms for our worst fears.

The history of science is a history of shifts in paradigm. Properly understood, the scientific method is one of evidence-based justification, review and adaptation. It is not the assertion and heedless projection of one set of ideas. An 'open system' can be understood as one in which the causes of things operate in combination with each other and in which both the constitutive elements and their interactions evolve in an unpredictable but not entirely random way.[27] Human society shows every sign of being an open system. To accept this is also to notice that it is the unique virtue of liberal democracies that they are built on procedures for making continuous, adaptive choices in an inclusive way. It is precisely the democratic principles of openness and fairness *in procedure* that provide the highest potential to accommodate society as a changing entity and that allow for this essential self-critique.

By contrast, the assumption that we have found a good-for-all-time, scientific blueprint for government is the distinguishing feature of totalitarian regimes. It is the defining element of totalitarian, as distinct from authoritarian, regimes that the state's laws, narratives, institutions and constitution are given over to the fulfilment of that blueprint, so that society may attain a fixed, idealised form. What twentieth century history and epistemology duly taught us is that faith in such blueprints is intellectual hubris, and we know from Greek tragedy that nemesis will inevitably follow in its wake. For any political

---

[26] Lawson, 'A Realist Theory', p. 269.
[27] Tony Lawson, 'Cambridge Social Ontology: An Interview with Tony Lawson, Erasmus', *Journal for Philosophy and Economics* 2 (1) (Summer 2009): 100–122, p. 105.

economic orthodoxy to claim that it has closed the epistemological gap between science and reality would require that all the mechanisms behind transitive social phenomena have been discovered, isolated, tested, found to be intransitive in fact, unvarying and fully understandable. For the resulting system not to become a system of oppression, we would have to live in a social world as simple as a watch, and each of us would have to possess the watchmaker's knowledge and be motivated by the pristine logic of that machine alone.[28] Both Soviet and, it turns out, neoliberal economic thought are guilty of this conceit. My analytical starting point is that we do not live in such a closed-system world, we do not and cannot have such knowledge and our motivations are far more complicated than what these materialist utopias allow.

Logical Reasoning from Assumption versus the Scientific Method

Most natural and social sciences apply 'the scientific method', often referred to as 'hypothetical deduction'. Broadly speaking, this is a process of assessment and theory-building that starts with an empirical observation. The scientist will observe something and notice a discrepancy between what they see and the existing theoretical accounts of it. They will make further observations and, having refined their understanding, both by confirming what they saw and comparing it with the relevant cases and theories, they will develop a new hypothesis about what they think is going on. Depending on the nature of that hypothesis, the scientist will then try to come up with a plausible way to test, confirm or disconfirm their new theory. Over centuries the scientific method has thus developed as a process of critical observation, trial, theoretical error correction and continuous review. The goal is to update our understanding of what is happening around us and why it is happening.

As we will see, both Soviet economics and the neoclassical economics that formed the basis of British neoliberal policy did something else entirely. Both asserted the existence of a system of political economy

---

[28] Alain Supiot, *Governance by Numbers: The Making of a Legal Model of Allegiance*, translated by Saskia Brown (Oxford: Hart Publishing, 2017), pp. 19–25.

dynamics based on arguments from *axiomatic* deduction. In other words, their arguments and the strategies that follow are based on logical deduction from certain propositions or postulates, the utopian nature of which I explore in the next chapters. In essence, neoclassical and Soviet economists engaged in closed-system reasoning, based on arguments from theoretical *assumption*. Of the two, only the Soviets were working from concepts derived from observations about an identifiably human history.

The concept of 'isomorphism' in sociology refers to the idea that there are similarities in the processes or structures of one organisation to those of another, as the result of either deliberate imitation or independent development under similar constraints.[29] I will argue that the failures in both Soviet and neoliberal systems of government originate in their shared insistence on a closed-model or 'complete' political economy ontology: in their shared beliefs that social reality is governed by predetermined economic laws and that like God the watchmaker we know how these work.[30] This is not to argue that closed-system reasoning is a pathological form of reasoning per se. For an engineer, such reasoning is the entirely appropriate analytical approach to everything from a car engine to a power station, but that's because the mechanical, chemical and physical processes involved in these systems are isolated and governed by known and demonstrably predictable properties. By contrast, the application of closed-system reasoning to the human political economy is doomed to become dysfunctional in practice, because it is neither a watch nor an engine nor a cybernetic system but is open-ended. Also, for better or worse, our freedoms live in that openness.

The neoclassical economics at the root of British neoliberal policy began life as a purely academic project. Using mathematical formalism instead of empirical observation followed by hypothesis-testing, neoclassical economists aspired to explanations that should be valid for any type of economic phenomena in any country. As Ada Marinescu explains, for the neoclassical economist, it is less important that a specific model corresponds with a specific or even general observable

---

[29] Paul DiMaggio and Walter Powell, 'The Iron Cage Revisited: Institutional Isomorphism and Collective Rationality in Organizational Fields', *American Sociological Review* 48 (2) (1983): 147–160.
[30] Supiot, *Governance by Numbers*, p. 21.

reality. The goal is to build a coherent and convincing system from which, as a matter of *logic*, we can observe the pure, essential dynamics of 'the system', unsullied by local empirical noise. The resulting models are supposed to offer a simplified but fundamentally true version of that reality. The models may be obviously reductive, but the supposedly universal truth of their findings is put forward as the only way to achieve a unitary interpretation of economic events.[31]

The Soviets shared the same underlying fascination with rationalisation – the same 'high modernist' confidence in science and technical progress – and they too abandoned the scientific method while seeking to retain its legitimising stamp.[32] Karl Marx had opposed attempts to foreclose the future with exact specifications of the socialist society,[33] but what distinguished Vladimir Ilyich Lenin, the founding father of Soviet socialism, was, precisely, his treatment of Marx as justifying a deterministic governing science. Ergo, 'by following the path of Marxist theory we shall draw closer and closer to objective truth (without ever exhausting it)'.[34] Lenin's real innovation in Marxist theory was consequently epistemological – specifically, his view that left to itself the working class under capitalism would only succumb to bourgeois ideology as the prevailing interpretation of their own condition. Instead, he argued, a body of professional revolutionaries, armed with scientific Marxism and committed full-time to the study of class conditions and revolutionary work, could drive the socialist revolution forward. It was the revolutionary party's task to supply the people with a scientific politics,[35] and though the events of 1905 and 1917 would make Lenin review the role of workers'

---

[31] Ada Marinescu, 'Axiomatical Examination of the Neoclassical Model: Logical Assessment of the Assumptions of Neoclassical Economics', *Theoretical and Applied Economics* 23 (2) (Summer 2016): 47–64, p. 48.

[32] James Scott, *Seeing Like a State: How Certain Schemes to Improve the Human Condition Have Failed* (London and New Haven: Yale University Press, 1999), Chapter 6.

[33] Roger Paden, 'Marx's Critique of the Utopian Socialists', *Utopian Studies* 13 (2) (2002): 67–91, pp. 89–90.

[34] Vladimir Ilyich Lenin, 'Materialism and Empirio-Criticism: Critical Comments on Reactionary Philosophy', in *Collected Works*, Vol. 14 (Moscow: Progress Publishers, 1972) (first published in 1909), Chapter 2, Section 6, 'The Criterion of Practice in the Theory of Knowledge'.

[35] Vladimir Ilyich Lenin, 'What Is to Be Done?', in *Collected Works*, Vol. 5 (Moscow: Foreign Languages Publishing House, 1961) (first published in 1902), Chapter 1, 'Dogmatism and Freedom of Criticism'.

democratic participation in that party, the argument for a 'scientific socialism' was set.[36] The terminal point of analytical closure in Soviet economic thought comes with Stalinism, however. By the late 1920s, Joseph Stalin had asserted that the Communist Party need not seek cooperative forms of economic development as the incipient socialist consciousness was formed, but instead it should drive industrialisation forward through command planning and the forced collectivisation of agriculture[37] – a process he would later define in *The History of the Communist Party of the Soviet Union* as a 'revolution from above'.[38]

In his 1902 essay, 'The Application of Mathematics to Political Economy', Vilfredo Pareto had observed that as a matter of mathematical reasoning, the socialist economy operated by an idealised social planner and the idealised free market are formally identical. In principle, both are equally capable of offering the 'conditions that are necessary for maximum welfare'. Thus, the coefficients that yield maximum economic satisfaction ('ophelimity') 'can be determined by free competition among entrepreneurs, as well as by socialist state measures, if the latter are aimed at giving everybody the maximum ophelimity compatible with the rules of distribution prevailing in that state'.[39] At the beginning of the twentieth century this insight was purely theoretical. What Pareto had noticed, however, was the kinship that would come to haunt first the Soviet East and then the neoliberal West, as Stalinist and then neoliberal regimes embarked on the implementation of a perfectly planned state and, half a century later, its free market twin.

By stepping onto the path of economic determinism, both doctrines abandoned an open-minded investigation into the complex causal mechanisms of political economic development and claimed to know their essence as a matter of economic metaphysics. The result in both systems was a revolution to replace politics with economism. Where these economic philosophies had built abstractions, economism

---

[36] Anthony Polan, *Lenin and the End of Politics* (London: Methuen Ltd, 1984), p. 140.
[37] David McLellan, *Marxism after Marx*, 2nd ed. (London: Macmillan Press, 1979), pp. 131–134.
[38] Joseph Stalin, *History of the Communist Party of the Soviet Union: Short Course* (New York: International Publishers, 1939), Chapter 11.
[39] Vilfredo Pareto, 'The Application of Mathematics to Political Economy', *History of Economic Ideas* 17 (1) (2009): 158–179, p. 178.

took them literally. As David Fleming pointed out, 'The scale of this category error is so large that it tends to capture all our judgement. Everything but the principle of the competitive market [or socialist state] is assumed away, leaving economics disconnected from the texture and purposes of society, ecology, and culture which it exists to serve.'[40]

Research Strategy

To be clear from the start, I will use the term 'neoliberalism' as synonymous with neoclassical economic theory and its policy correlates, though I will also include the contributions of the 'Austrian school' where relevant. The neoclassical paradigm, explored in Part I, has occupied an increasingly dominant position in Western economics from the 1970s to today, and as I will show, it is neoclassical economic theory that has formed the basis of Britain's political economic strategies over the last forty years. I am interested not just in the theory, however, but in its unanticipated consequences in practice, and to explore these I apply two forms of critique throughout the policy chapters in Part II.

The first form of critique is from within neoclassical economics itself – specifically, I set out what even the acknowledgement of market failures as defined from within the neoclassical paradigm implies for neoliberal policy. My second line of critique is drawn from the lessons of the Soviet economy that prove salient given the isomorphism between neoliberal and Soviet forms of reasoning and statecraft. I think it is illuminating to highlight the internal debates *within* neoclassical economics because it is important to acknowledge that neoclassical economists can choose from a spectrum of assumptions that range from the utopian to the relatively plausible. Apply the more sceptical, so-called second-best-world neoclassical approaches that focus on market failures and it becomes easier to see how truly utopian the neoliberal promises based on 'first-best-world' models are and hence how untenable they must prove once applied. However, even if we understand this more critical neoclassical economics as a heuristic device for understanding how far the reality is

---

[40] David Fleming, *Lean Logic: A Dictionary for the Future and How to Survive It* (Vermont: Chelsea Green Publishing, 2016), p. 123.

from the ideal, the ideal itself is deeply misleading. In fact, as we shall find, even the more critical neoclassical economics introduces a systematic analytical bias that leads governments to increasingly mistake the closed-system map for the open-system terrain over which they govern, and it is this profound analytical introversion that invites the Soviet comparison.

Neoclassical economics can operate only in two dimensions in the sense that it considers purely material values that are assumed to be commensurable, that is, measured on a single plane of values. But human society and its institutions operate in three dimensions and, contrary to the 'world' that can be depicted in mathematics, human society is not sociologically flat and the values people hold are frequently conflicting.[41] Society also operates in historical, as distinct from logical, time.[42] It follows that to understand not just why but how neoliberal policies tend to fail we must also examine how these policies evolve and the new, unanticipated institutional dynamics that emerge. When we notice the analytical solipsism that follows from this closed-system reasoning in neoliberalism, it turns out that the Soviet system, with its increasingly chronic and largely unanticipated institutional syndromes, becomes informative.

One of the simple but important insights from a political economy approach known as 'historical institutionalism' is that public policies themselves should be understood as politically and economically consequential structures.[43] Policy results, or legacies, can be seen to feed back into, and may even dictate, subsequent policy choices and options. They may thus produce 'path-dependencies': a distinctive trajectory that might tend to reinforce itself. This tendency is all the more likely when the governing ideology is based on closed-system reasoning. By tracing the evolution of neoliberal policies, the book's policy chapters examine why these reforms failed in the terms by which they were justified and why remedies drawn from the same doctrine only compounded those failures. This basic intuition about institutional feedback can thus help us understand why new and systematic pathologies have arisen within the neoliberal political economy that were

---

[41] Bronk, *The Romantic Economist*, Chapter 7.
[42] Joan Robinson, 'Time in Economic Theory', *KYKLOS* 33 (1980): 219–229.
[43] Paul Pierson, 'When Effect Becomes Cause: Policy Feedback and Political Change', *World Politics* 45 (4) (July 1993): 595–628, p. 624.

never anticipated by the theories that motivated them.[44] We can then explore what it is about their forms of reasoning that makes both Soviet and neoliberal systems peculiarly susceptible to these dynamics of self-reinforcing dysfunction. The history of British neoliberalism is open to this approach because we can trace both the theoretical and the practical political genesis of reforms and the new institutional rules and tangible resources that followed, and hence, to a useful degree, the results.[45]

Scholars have already set out the intellectual roots of neoliberalism and its utopian qualities. They have also explored the conditions that account for its political rise and its varieties, most notably the contrast with Germany's post-war ordoliberalism, which sees an effective state as essential to maintain the virtues of market competition. This literature has taught us about the theory behind neoliberal reforms,[46] Britain's transformation towards the 'regulatory state',[47] the reforms to its welfare state,[48] the shifts towards delegated governance,[49] the rising power of the large business corporation,[50] the development in Britain of a systematically parasitic, 'rentier' form of capitalism,[51] and, finally, how neoliberalism is diffused differently within different political economies.[52] My own exploration has also been made

---

[44] Peter Hall and Rosemary Taylor, 'Political Science and the Three New Institutionalisms', *Political Studies* 44 (1996): 936–957.

[45] Pierson, 'When Effect', p. 602.

[46] See Patrick Dunleavy, *Democracy, Bureaucracy and Public Choice* (Hemel Hempstead: Harvester Wheatsheaf, 1991); Peter Self, *Government by the Market?* (Basingstoke: Macmillan International, 1993).

[47] See Michael Moran, *The British Regulatory State: High Modernism and Hyper-innovation* (Oxford: Oxford University Press, 2007).

[48] See Jane Gingrich, *Making Markets in the Welfare State: The Politics of Varying Market Reform* (Cambridge: Cambridge University Press, 2011); Anton Hemerijck, *Changing Welfare States* (Oxford: Oxford University Press, 2012).

[49] See Matthew Flinders, *Delegated Governance and the British State: Walking Without Order* (Oxford: Oxford University Press, 2008).

[50] See Paul Pierson and Jacob Hacker, *Winner Take All Politics: How Washington Made the Rich Richer and Turned Its Back on the Middle Class* (New York: Simon and Schuster, 2010); Colin Crouch, *The Strange Non-death of Neoliberalism* (Cambridge: Polity Press, 2011); Stephen Wilks, *The Political Power of the Business Corporation* (Cheltenham: Edward Elgar, 2013).

[51] See Brett Christopher, *Rentier Capitalism: Who Owns the Economy and Who Pays for It* (London: Verso, 2020).

[52] See Cornel Ban, *Ruling Ideas: How Global Neoliberalism Goes Local* (Oxford: Oxford University Press, 2016).

possible by the rich descriptive and theoretical literatures from public finance, forensic accounting, public administration, social policy, economic sociology and environmental economics that explore the individual policy reforms examined here. But to these I add insights from the history of the Soviet economy. Standing on the shoulders of these many colleagues, therefore, my aim is to develop an understanding not just of the revolutionary scale of these changes but also of why the core functions of the British state have become so compromised and in such consistent and systematic ways

My working definition of 'the state' is from Colin Hay, who argues that it is more productive to investigate the changing practices of state power than to fixate on essential qualities of 'the state' itself, an approach that is surely apt in this era of the state's hyper-innovation.[53] There would be a serious risk of redundancy if we were to assert some fundamental definition or ontology of the state today – some essential conception of what the state *really* is – when the British state's most striking characteristic is its accelerating institutional transformation and disintegration. As Hay puts it, '[T]he state serves to define and construct a series of contexts within which political agency is both authorised (in the name of the state) and enacted / institutionalised; and the state is a dynamic institutional complex whose unity is at best partial and the constantly evolving outcome of unifying tendencies and dis–unifying countertendencies.'[54] As a definition this is open to the changeability of state institutions without being conceptually empty. At its core, it recognises the continuing capacity of state actors to authorise administrative and functional agency in the name of the democratic polity but also to command its resources: it indicates a complex, shifting but nevertheless uniquely powerful agency.

I know that economic theory can make for a jargon-infested read, and I will try to clear this thicket as we go by explaining concepts in what I hope is relatively plain English. There is no avoiding a technical debate, however, because it is on the pseudo-scientific character of these Soviet and neoclassical economic debates that this history

---

[53] Michael Moran, 'The Transformation of the British State: From Club Government to State-Administered High Modernism', in Jonah Levy, *The State after Statism* (Cambridge, MA: Harvard University Press, 2006), p. 31.
[54] Colin Hay, 'Neither Real Nor Fictitious, but "as if Real"? A Political Ontology of the State', *The British Journal of Sociology* 65 (3) (2014): 459–480, p. 477.

turns. As late-stage neoliberalism induces a level of political economic upheaval that threatens the existence and political stability of the United Kingdom itself, it is more important than ever that we stop being bamboozled by the technocratic language of neoclassical economics and that we identify continuities in neoliberal policy as Britain's Conservative governments in particular seek to de-couple their rhetoric from their actions. As we shall see, the assumptions behind neoliberal policies typically have a perfect, super-refined intellectual neatness and, as it turns out, a staggering lack of common sense that betrays their source in the imaginations of academic theoreticians on a roll. As I explore in Part III, what is remarkable is how completely the leaderships of Britain's political parties were then seduced by these ideas, beguiling in their essential simplicity as they are.

This book concludes that until we challenge the theory and practice of the neoliberal revolution root and branch Britain's rolling political economic crises will only intensify. The effectiveness of the state as a referee within the capitalist system has historically been essential to the credibility of liberal democracy as a practical idea. As the state fails, so will liberal democracy, and with it the chance for some of the richest economies in the world to learn from their mistakes. And learn they must, to manage the unprecedented ecological emergency that they have wrought, not just upon themselves but upon the rest of the world that carries but a fraction of the responsibility for the devastation to come. The critical threats to planetary systems are such that we need to take the facts of ecological limits and place them at the centre of a new political economy. We live in genuinely frightening times, and if, like me, you are British, you may add to the realisation that it is at this point that we have elected to govern a succession of the most extreme devotees of the twentieth century's most abstract materialist utopia. Before we can harness the actual virtues of markets and states in the cause of a genuinely sustainable economy, therefore, we need to understand how neoliberal business-as-usual has become a recipe for disaster.

PART I

The Materialist Utopias

1 | Rationality and Closed-System Reasoning

The Cold War and its aftermath taught us that Soviet socialism and neoliberalism were ideological opposites, and who could disagree? The everyday political values of these doctrines could not have been further apart. Ask how they understood the nature of economic reality, however, and this dichotomy proves false. On closer inspection, we find that both Soviet socialism and neoliberalism conceived of the political economy as a closed system, governed by predetermined economic laws and dependable behaviours. Both presumed that their belief system alone reflected the objective economic reality. The epic historical irony is that these shared conceits in the face of an uncertain reality led Soviet and neoliberal governments to converge on similar forms of statecraft. We should not be surprised, therefore, that their strategies failed for essentially similar reasons.

There are several historical reservoirs of neoliberal thought in addition to neoclassical economics, from the Austrian school to German ordoliberalism, and they are often at odds with each other.[1] As we will see, however, Britain's neoliberal policies have been drawn almost exclusively from the neoclassical source, and the fact that neoliberal governmental practice in the Anglosphere has an essentially neoclassical economic basis is well established. A large body of scholarship has traced the influence of key neoclassical economists and their sponsors in the neoliberal project; the hegemony of neoclassical economics within academic economics; its dominance in international financial institutions with global reach; and the centrality of these ideas at the root of the Global Financial Crisis and in the policies of austerity that followed. But these analyses have tended to 'write out' the fact that neoclassical economics did not develop as an argument for capitalism

---

[1] Philip Mirowski and Dieter Plehwe, *The Road from Mont Pelerin: The Making of the Neoliberal Thought Collective* (Cambridge, MA: Harvard University Press, 2009), pp. 1–2.

alone. It has always contained those who made the case for 'mixed' as well as 'free' markets, and even those who argued for radical economic democracy via workers' ownership within competitive markets.[2]

As Johanna Bockman shows, many of the most influential neoclassicists in the first half of the twentieth century were committed socialists, and the Soviet experiment in command planning was a key reference point. Neoclassical ideas evolved in support of, in conversation with and in opposition to socialist economics, though the Union of Soviet Socialist Republics (USSR) itself only flirted periodically and unsuccessfully with neoclassical methods.[3] My aim here is to explore their unacknowledged affinities and to understand why Soviet and neoliberal economics fail so dismally in the terms by which they are justified. I argue that Soviet and neoliberal regimes implemented strategies and policies rooted in arguments about the universal truths of the political economy that are not just utopian but tautological – circular – in their reasoning. Their axiomatic assumptions and actions are valid, as distinct from true, by virtue only of their logical formulation, and their end goals are as impossible to realise as they are to refute. In striving to outdo each other in creating the system of supreme economic efficiency, they shared the same ontological and epistemological fallacies. Britain has pursued the neoliberal revolution longest, deepest and, given its liberal traditions and relative wealth, under the most favourable possible preconditions. I will turn to British policy in detail in Part II. But before we look at the application of these ideas, we need to understand their philosophical foundations.

The Neoclassical Path

The classical liberal economists of the eighteenth and nineteenth centuries had been strongly empiricist and transparent in their moral judgements. They believed that to preserve virtuous behaviour you needed to identify its sources.[4] It was in this light that Adam Smith built the case for the disciplinary value of competition in encouraging

---

[2] Johanna Bockman, *Markets in the Name of Socialism: The Left-Wing Origins of Neoliberalism* (Stanford: Stanford University Press, 2011), Introduction, pp. 1–17.
[3] Ibid., Chapters 1–4, pp. 17–133.
[4] Ryan Patrick Hanley, *Adam Smith and the Character of Virtue* (Cambridge: Cambridge University Press, 2009).

virtue, but also for a state that would regulate financial markets, prone to speculation and failure as he found them to be.[5] The classicists preferred descriptive histories and accounting statistics as they tried to understand what combinations of institutions tended to produce what combination of effects. They sought to explain states of affairs by observing trends and developing practical knowledge, and one might argue they were critical realists by instinct. The conclusions of the economic science John Stuart Mill hoped to define were valid only in the abstract sense.[6] While he believed political economists could run thought experiments that featured a purely wealth-seeking subject, he stressed that 'no political economist was ever so absurd as to suppose that mankind are really thus constituted'.[7] What the histories of neoclassical and Soviet economic thought demonstrate, by contrast, is that if you want to make claims for the predetermined economic laws of society you have to adopt an altogether more instrumental attitude towards metaphysical argument.

Thorstein Veblen coined the term 'neoclassical' to describe the efforts of Stanley Jevons, Leon Walras (a socialist) and others in the late nineteenth century who promoted mathematics as the basis for a more formal economic science.[8] Attempts to mathematise economics dated back to the Enlightenment,[9] but it was through the neoclassical turn that these aspirations gained traction, as thinking about thermodynamics and economics developed in conversation. The neoclassical pioneers would come to depend on mathematical physics for their theoretical framework.[10] As both Philip Mirowski and Theodore Porter describe in detail, they proceeded to lift wholesale the empirically robust axioms of energy physics and statics onto a terrain where

---

[5] Adam Smith, *An Inquiry into the Nature and Causes of the Wealth of Nations (1776)* (Charlottesville: Intel Ex Corporation, 2009), Book 2, Chapter 2.
[6] Richard Bronk, *The Romantic Economist: Imagination in Economics* (Cambridge: Cambridge University Press, 2009), pp. 263–264, p. 53.
[7] John Stuart Mill, *Essays on Some Unsettled Questions in Political Economy (1844)* (New York: Perennial Press, 2016), p. 116.
[8] Tony Lawson, 'What Is This "School" Called Neoclassical Economics?', *Cambridge Journal of Economics* 37 (5) (September 2013): 947–983.
[9] Tony Lawson, 'Reorienting History (of Economics)', *Journal of Post-Keynesian Economics* 27 (3) (Spring 2005): 455–470, pp. 459–560, www.tandfonline.com/doi/abs/10.1080/01603477.2005.11051445.
[10] Theodore Porter, *Trust in Numbers* (Princeton: Princeton University Press, 1995), Chapter 3.

they had no such foundation – a criticism made by physicists at the time, who wondered at so pointlessly abstract an exercise.[11]

The only model of human motivation simple enough to fit these borrowed mechanical metaphors was that of 'utilitarian' man.[12] The core idea of the new moral philosophy of utilitarianism was that we should understand what was morally right or wrong by what caused us pleasure as opposed to pain. An act was morally virtuous if it produced a net gain in pleasure. Moral decision-making could thus be reduced to a cost–benefit analysis. But as Mirowski and Edward Nik-Khah explain, the neoclassical economists were attracted to utilitarianism not as a theory of mind or moral philosophy but because it filled a technical gap. A formal, 'scientific' system of economic analysis that depended on mathematics required a universal economic agent with consistent properties, because without a predictable agent there was no hope of building consistent statements about economic behaviour. Fix the nature of human motivation and you could derive equations about the dependable motions of consumers and firms. What mattered was to be able to equate the formalisms of energy with 'utility', for only then could you portray the market as a system determined by natural laws.[13]

It was a fateful decision. The idea of the rationally selfish individual who sits at the core of contemporary British politics originates in a pragmatic device that let neoclassicists operationalise basic concepts from Newtonian mechanics. The analogy allowed economists to treat individuals as particles moving in a defined commodity space, where, as Frank Ackerman explains, 'the spatial coordinates are quantities of different commodities. Utility was the vector field indicating the direction in which individuals would move, to the extent allowed by budget constraints'.[14] Using mathematics, neoclassical economists purport to show how we will navigate our way through a given economic space.

---

[11] Ibid., pp. 71–72.
[12] Philip Mirowski, *More Heat than Light: Economics as Social Physics, Physics as Nature's Economics* (Cambridge: Cambridge University Press, 1989), p. 3 and Chapter 5.
[13] Philip Mirowski and Edward Nik-Khah, *The Knowledge We Have Lost in Information: The History of Information in Economics* (Oxford: Oxford University Press, 2017), p. 25.
[14] Frank Ackerman, 'Still Dead after All These Years: Interpreting the Failure of General Equilibrium Theory', *Journal of Economic Methodology* 9 (2) (2002): 119–139, Section 4.1.

There is no meaningful subjectivity here, no agency or morality as we would usually understand it. The 'individual' in this scheme is merely a vehicle for the theoretical analogy. Utilitarianism swept aside the likelihood that individuals would behave with mixed, irrational or even contradictory motives, and *homo economicus* was born.

By the end of the nineteenth century, rational economic man was a solitary figure forever calculating his utility and apparently insatiable in his wants. From the 1870s, Walras had worked on a hypothetical 'general equilibrium', in which all demand and all supply were continuously reconciled, but for this to be possible you would need a perfect competition, and by the 1920s Frank Knight was objecting that neoclassical economic man would need two further traits if this imaginary was to be coherent.[15] To engage in such a perfect competition, economic agents would have to operate with perfect knowledge and perfect foresight, with 'practical omniscience on the part of every member of the competitive system'.[16] Such a society 'would demand a community of immortal individuals who would never learn or forget or change their minds'.[17] By the 1930s, a neoclassical economic man had been duly constructed who was 'rational' (i.e., self-interested) and benefit (i.e., 'utility') maximising and perfectly well informed. Super-empowered, rational economic man became the central actor in neoclassical economic theory: an agent who reliably employed a cold, deductive and instrumental logic to maximise their gains within what was necessarily assumed to be a closed system of given factors and preferences.[18]

To be free in this narrative is to have the freedom to choose, with choice conceptualised in primarily material terms through a conscious rank ordering of individual preferences. It conjures a world in which we are the masters of our fates within the limits set by taste, technology and the somehow given, finite material resources of 'the system'. But as Richard Bronk points out, such a hyper-rationalist view

---

[15] John McKinney, 'Frank H. Knight on Uncertainty and Rational Action', *Southern Economic Journal* 43 (4) (April 1977): 1438–1452.
[16] Frank Knight, *Risk, Uncertainty and Profit* (Boston: Houghton Mifflin, 1921), Part III, Chapter VII.
[17] Frank Knight, *On the History and Methods of Economics* (Chicago: University of Chicago Press, 1956), quoted in McKinney, 'Frank H. Knight on Uncertainty', p. 1443.
[18] Bronk, *The Romantic Economist*, p. 197.

drains neoclassical models of the real indeterminacy of actual choices. The more complex our circumstances, the less likely a 'single' choice will present itself so clearly, and the harder it is for us to judge the possible consequences of the choices on offer.[19]

The neoclassical ambition was to search for immutable – *natural* – economic laws and regular events that would demonstrate the invariable facts of economic life. But having substituted 'utility' for 'energy', the resulting theories were not built on observations of demonstrably invariant phenomena but derived as a matter of logic from the metaphors available in mathematics. Economics in this vein would cease to study the existing dynamics of innovation and production and the contextualised inter-relationships between real social institutions – the classical tradition – and study instead the logic of choice in a closed world of given resources.[20] While it can be hard to avoid metaphors in theory-building, there is all the difference in the world between using metaphors to illustrate a theory by analogy, as classical political economists often did, and arguing from them to constitute the theory in its entirety, as happened here. The aspiration was taxonomic, to establish the formal order and hierarchy of actions; but as Veblen warned, 'it comes near being taxonomy for taxonomy's sake'.[21] Neoclassical economists nevertheless proceeded to use differential and integral calculus to 'describe' how a utility-maximising person might behave within a world of logical possibilities to which they could then ascribe the status of 'law'.[22]

The degree to which the new 'social physics' could prove effective at the level of practical application was going to depend on how far the metaphors proved 'true', that is, representative of real underlying properties,[23] but this dependence on mathematics and formal reasoning would quickly prove a fundamental flaw. This is consequently a criticism not of any specific moment in the history of neoclassical economics, nor of a particular mathematical technique,

---

[19] Ibid., p. 216.
[20] Michel Foucault, 'Lecture 9, 14 March 1979', in *The Birth of Biopolitics: Lectures at the College De France* (Basingstoke: Palgrave Macmillan, 2008), pp. 222–223.
[21] Thorstein Veblen, 'Why Is Economics Not an Evolutionary Science?', *Cambridge Journal of Economics* 22 (4) (1998): 403–414 (first published in 1898), p. 409.
[22] Mirowski, *More Heat*, p. 3, Chapter 7.
[23] M. H. Abrams, *The Mirror and the Lamp: Romantic Theory and the Critical Tradition* (Oxford: Oxford University Press, 1972).

but of the basic methodology. The mathematician and critical realist Tony Lawson argues that the use of mathematics in economics per se requires a closed-system ontology of the political economy, and the result is a fundamental category error. Thus:

> Throughout the history of mathematics in economics ... economists have concerned themselves with a form of deductivist reasoning. By this, I mean a form of reasoning that rests on the use of regularities of the form 'whenever event or state of affairs x, then event or state of affairs, y,' essentially methods involving functional analysis. Systems in which event regularities of this sort occur can be referred to as closed. These regularities, in turn, presuppose an ontology of isolated atoms. By an atom, I refer not to something that is small, but rather, to something that, if triggered, has its own separate, independent, and invariable effect, whatever the context. So my claim is that throughout the various changes in the forms and interpretations of mathematics, something has remained stable: an implicit ontology of closure, of atomism and isolationism, has been repeatedly reproduced.[24]

Neoclassical economics resides in a tautological form of reasoning. It creates conclusions and by extension – via its influence on politicians and policymakers – neoliberal strategies that are valid first and foremost by virtue of their logical form. Take the so-called marginalist revolution, in which 'value' was seen as a function of the process of exchange rather than some fixed property, such as working hours. The labour theory argued that the value of a commodity could be measured by the average number of labouring hours it took to produce it. Neoclassical economists wanted to replace this with subjective or perceived value.[25] The idea was that we make decisions 'on the margin'. We determine the value of something by how much additional utility an extra unit of a good or service will give us. But as Joan Robinson pointed out in 1962, 'utility' is 'a metaphysical concept of impregnable circularity; utility is the quality in commodities that makes individuals want to buy them, and the fact that individuals want to buy commodities shows that they have utility'.[26] No theorist since has managed to liberate this concept from this circularity and turn it into a truly independent variable, with real explanatory power – and not for want of trying.

---

[24] Lawson, 'Reorienting History', p. 457.   [25] Bockman, *Markets*, p. 19.
[26] Joan Robinson, *Economic Philosophy* (Harmondsworth: Penguin Books, 1962), p. 48.

As Peter J. Hammond explains, to make utility a more compelling concept it has variously been thought of as following some objective property, as distinct from the quality assigned to it in the model itself. Pleasure versus pain was rejected in favour of thinking of utility as 'ordinal', so that consumers maximised within subjective utility functions. What mattered was the way the 'consumer' (the agent in the model) ordered their utilities of different bundles of good – that is, the preference ordering. The trouble was that these models would then have to make suppositions about those orderings to depict the behavioural patterns supposed to follow. 'Revealed preferences' suggested you could infer the preference ordering from observable demand behaviour, so it was those preferences that supposedly created that demand. So-called cardinal utility ascribed a value of utility to given options, and so on.[27] Instead of being the object of investigation, 'preferences' are bestowed, in some form or another, by the modeller, to specify the parameters of the model.[28] The discipline consequently had little choice but to start a debate on the relative significance of utility, as Mirowski points out. Was it a central or a trivial concept? a psychological property? a merely formal notion to rationalise more complex behaviours after the fact? or simply a rule that allows for consistency?[29] So long as mathematics and functionalist reasoning remain the rule of the game, however, no conceptual innovation can violate the necessity of the system's closure.

Since what is 'rational' in a neoclassical model is supposed to be the maximisation of utility, and what is 'irrational' some failure in this regard, the concept of rationality has also had to travel around the same conceptual houses to accommodate these mutating definitions. Hence, 'rational behaviour' has included various understandings of preferences, beliefs, expectations, decision procedures and knowledge, but also, in relation to more critical work, the limits of those properties, hence 'bounded rationality' and the work in game theory that

---

[27] Peter J. Hammond, 'Rationality in Economics', *Rivista Internazionale di Science Sociale* 105 (3) (1997): 247–288, pp. 248–249.

[28] Richard Bronk and Jens Beckert, 'The Instability of Preferences: Uncertain Futures and the Incommensurable and Intersubjective Nature of Values', MPIfG Discussion Paper 22/1, p. 1.

[29] Philip Mirowski, 'Does the Victor Enjoy the Spoils? Paul Samuelson as Historian of Economics', *Journal of the History of Economic Thought* 35 (1) (March 2013): 1–17, p. 9.

considers strategies and beliefs or expectations that can be 'rationalised'.[30] Regardless of these various understandings, the atomised 'individual' in such schemes, as Lawson points out, is a caricature possessing, for example, perfect foresight, omniscience or pure greed.[31]

The neoclassical theorist must consequently struggle and ultimately fail to escape the metaphysical trap that comes from this dependence on formal axiomatic deduction. The result is an intrinsic instability in the models in their relationship with reality, an instability that becomes a social liability the moment any policymaker applies them. Whether you are talking about macro-level economic developments presumptively rooted in individual rationality or whether you focus specifically on those individual decisions, it is the mode of reasoning that must come to trouble any policy conceived in these forms. Because key motivating concepts necessarily tend towards restrictive (tautologous) statements – such as 'if extremely restrictive qualifications x, y and z apply, then the following behaviour will occur' – it follows that having simplified the world for the sake of theoretical consistency, you will find that you can tether neither the diagnosis nor the prescription to any real environment without some vital elements becoming unstuck.

To illustrate this with a well-known neoliberal policy: the notion that when states compete to lower their taxes this will lead to higher allocative efficiency. The original and most intuitively appealing argument for tax competition, by Charles Tiebout, says that other things being equal, where local authorities compete over the provision of public services the result is their optimal allocation, because perfectly informed citizens will move to the jurisdiction that satisfies their needs in a process of 'market sorting'.[32] The idea is fine, until you recognise that all other things are not equal: real local jurisdictions differ in things other than tax rates and services, and individuals have additional needs and obligations that prevent them from shopping, continuously, for their optimal tax jurisdiction. It also turns out that such 'sorting' over historical time is likely to lead to geographical

---

[30] Hammond, *Rationality*, 1997.
[31] Tony Lawson, 'The Confused State of (Equilibrium) Analysis in Modern Economics: An Explanation', *Journal of Keynesian Economics* 27 (3) (2005): 423–444, p. 429.
[32] Charles Tiebout, 'A Pure Theory of Local Expenditure', *Journal of Political Economy* 64 (5) (1956): 416–424.

concentrations of extreme wealth and poverty as the wealthy move to low tax jurisdictions and poor areas are deprived of revenue. Also, individuals are not and can never be fully informed. The approach thus constrains how economists can understand the institutional complexity of the economy, how it changes and the nature of risks in play.[33] It creates the illusion that there is such a thing as context-free economic optimality: a world of perfect efficiency, to which institutions can be made to conform.

Since it is clear that the operating assumptions within neoclassical economics can vary, it is important to highlight its most significant internal divisions, and not least because they track closely the differences in how Britain's 'New Right' Conservatives and New Labour came to absorb this way of thinking. Adapting categories from Lawson, I will refer from here on to 'Camp 1' and 'Camp 2' neoclassical economists, and also, but more rarely, to a 'Camp 3' that has continued the classical tradition of political economy, with its empiricism and more open-system reasoning. So let me explain who sits where.

1. In Camp 1 are those who adopt a taxonomic approach to economics: a group dominated in modern times by those who accept mathematical axiomatic deductivism as an orientation to science for us all and who regard any stance that questions this approach as misguided.[34] In Camp 1 the instinct is to stand by mathematical modelling as a complete method and to apply first-best reasoning and the most idealised, or perfect, conditions to the case. Camp 1 economists will tend to ignore market imperfections.[35]
2. In Camp 2 are those who accept that social reality is of a causal-processual, open-system nature and prioritise a degree of realism.[36] Despite their awareness of the limits of their methodology, however, neoclassical economists in Camp 2 continue to see value in the methods of axiomatic-deductive modelling and still deploy methods that rely on closed-system reasoning.[37] The tendency in this camp is to accept the likelihood of market imperfections and

---

[33] Lawson, 'What Is This "School"', pp. 947–983. [34] Ibid., p. 978.
[35] Dani Rodrik, 'Why Do Economists Disagree?', 5 August 2007, https://Rodrik.typepad.com.
[36] Lawson, 'What Is This "School"', p. 979.
[37] Steven Fleetwood, 'The Critical Realist Conception of Open and Closed System', *Journal of Economic Methodology* 24 (1) (2017): 41–68, Section 3.1.

market failures but to rely on the same assumptions about rational economic man as the standard economic agent. Their reasoning is that if you have a vision of the 'first-best world' and a methodology to depict it, you have a benchmark for explaining where and how markets might tend to fail and a toolkit to identify strategies for market correction in a 'second-best world'.

3. We might classify what are often called 'heterodox' economic approaches as a third camp. Camp 3 economists recognise the open-system, causal-processual nature of social reality and, in contrast to Camp 2, they fashion their methods in light of this ontological understanding. They accept the limited scope for any taxonomic social science that relies on methods of mathematical, axiomatic-deductive modelling.[38] Economics in this tradition tends towards more hypothetical deduction, more post hoc analysis in search of patterns, more interest in institutional dynamics and interdependencies, more indeterminate modelling and even psychological experimentation in behavioural economics. They are the heirs of the classical tradition, but in the neoliberal era they have been pushed to the margins in government, in mainstream politics and in academic economics. Ecological economics, which takes an altogether more holistic empiricist view, remains more marginalised still.

As we will see, the neoliberal diagnoses and prescriptions of Britain's Conservatives since 1979 have typically been founded in 'first-best-world', or 'Camp 1', models. Though New Right policies were never sold in such an abstract light, the models behind the promises assumed, inter alia, that the economic agents within them can potentially operate in a world with perfect information, perfect foresight in regard to their private calculations, complete markets and no 'externalities' – that is, no unanticipated consequences in the pricing of the good, be they positive, such as improved skills, or negative, such as pollution.[39]

The neoclassicists of Camp 2 doubt that markets can ever be made perfectly efficient, and they have used the basic ideal types of Camp 1 to explore the logic of what may go wrong at certain junctions of decision-making. By considering the possibility of imperfect information, missing markets, externalities, collusion, 'irrational' behaviour

---

[38] Lawson, 'What Is This "School"', p. 979.
[39] Nick Barr, *The Economics of the Welfare State* (Oxford: Oxford University Press, 2012), p. 42.

and so on, Camp 2 has thereby developed an often-valuable body of more critical theories that help us think about the vulnerabilities forgotten when governments choose policies inspired by Camp 1. While 'relaxing the assumptions' makes such analysis marginally more realistic and hence analytically useful, those modified assumptions nevertheless share the same underlying closed-system ontology as Camp 1. It follows that the neoclassical concept of 'market failures' presupposes that such failures can be corrected and also that if you correct them you restore the system and enhance its efficiency.[40] What 'second-best-world' neoclassicists call 'market failure' is always a failure to complete the full set of connections that allow a perfect resolution of supply and demand. The result is a narrow conception of failure as the mistargeting of given resources that would otherwise be allocated efficiently.

In reality, that is to say, in the light of epistemological uncertainty and ontological indeterminacy, you could mend as many individual points of diagnosed market failure as you like, but beyond the simplest transaction in an unchanging and isolated market system, the chance of closing a complete circle of connections is vanishingly remote. By adopting policies almost across the board based on Camp 2 neoclassical reasoning, New Labour would thus embark on a technocratic effort to resolve market failures at their microeconomic roots, only to find that, try as they might, the resulting form of capitalism bore less and less resemblance to the reconstituted market harmony of neoclassical promise. Camp 2 models are not nearly as metaphysically neutral as they first appear, as most Camp 2 economists would readily admit. Hence, their policy recommendations proved only marginally less prone to editing out the powerful relationships between the interests, institutions and operating ideas of the real economy than the policies of the New Right.

In sum, the Conservative New Right would draw its strategies overwhelmingly from Camp 1, with its faith in mathematical modelling from utopian postulates as a proxy for the real economy. New Labour would more typically develop its strategies from the neoclassical economics of Camp 2. What both camps shared is the assumption that individuals always optimise their strategies in a rational, cost–benefit

---

[40] Brian Loasby, 'Closed Models and Open Systems', *Journal of Economic Methodology* 10 (3) (2003): 285–306, p. 291.

way, and hence faith in the validity of models based on formal reasoning. Both Camp 1 and Camp 2 believe that outcomes are predictable and can be meaningfully modelled once constraints or degrees of uncertainty are ascribed values or probabilities within a model.[41] Camp 2 neoclassical economists are less convinced that market failures can be fully corrected to allow a given market to abide by the laws depicted in Camp 1, but what mattered more for policy, and its failures, was the analytical frame and its inherent determinism. New Labour would try to mend perceived market failures around information, competition and the incompleteness of rationality,[42] but the most important results would be their continuation of the transformative shift of public authority to the private sector and, with it, the elevation of highly 'imperfect' markets to the core of the British political economy. These would generate new and intensifying rounds of political conflict.

Key to understanding the unanticipated consequences of neoliberal policy is the fact that neoclassical models typically depict a logical, as distinct from a temporal, space, so that policymakers confuse the comparison of static, theoretical positions with the realistic prospect of movement between them.[43] Buried in much Camp 2 reasoning is the assumption that our economic information is imperfect only in the short run, though this is a pure artefact of closed-system reasoning. As Paul Davidson explains, they concede that economic decision-makers can make short-run errors regarding the future, but 'agents supposedly "learn" from these short-run mistakes so that subjective probabilities or decision weights tend to converge onto an accurate description of the programmed external reality'.[44] Even in the most critical neoclassical views, we are still supposed to live in a world of sufficient regularity and simplicity that we can all learn to thrive within markets, as their failures are gradually solved.

But this is a Darwinist logic, in which those who refuse to learn will fail economically and those who learn will prosper. Competition

---

[41] Richard Bronk, 'Epistemological Difficulties with Neo-classical Economics', Southern Economic Association Conference Paper, 19–21 November 2011, Washington, DC, p. 3.
[42] Herbert Simon, 'A Behavioural Model of Rational Choice', *The Quarterly Journal of Economics* 69 (1) (1955): 99–118.
[43] Joan Robinson, 'Time in Economic Theory', *KYKLOS* 33 (1980): 219–229, Abstract.
[44] Paul Davidson, 'Reality and Economic Theory', *Journal of Post-Keynesian Economics* 18 (4) (June 1996): 479–508, p. 486.

will teach us what is correct, though this requires that real choices be subordinate to an optimising logic of 'rationality'. Such an assumption is coherent only in a world without uncertainty and imagination, but this idea of information feedback loops creates an intellectual escape hatch for neoliberal failings in the short run, even as John Maynard Keynes had warned that the long run would be too late.[45] The Soviets, of course, would face the same continuous departures of reality from theory, as they sought to control the chronic losses of information and unexpected behaviours within a planning system that operated under totalitarian political control. The Beckettian default in both systems is consequently to wait for the correct consciousness, like Godot, to arrive.

Neoclassical reasoning may be instructive about the economic logics at work when applied a posteriori to markets in which transactions are notably stable, highly repetitive and relatively isolated from other influences. In practice, however, the political economies of capitalist systems vary significantly in their historical legacies, institutional architectures, organised interests and political cultures, and they evolve in ways that no one can exactly anticipate. Most remarkably of all, the neoliberal project would take hold through the 1970s, just as the Soviet planning system was demonstrating beyond a shadow of a doubt that governance systems based on closed-system reasoning were a recipe for quite staggering political and economic dysfunction.

The Soviet Path

As Bockman points out, the first models of a perfectly central planned economy per se came from the neoclassical school.[46] Following Vilfredo Pareto's lead,[47] it had become standard neoclassical practice to equate the theory of a competitive market economy with that of an idealised socialist state, with the proviso that for any perfect planning equilibrium there was an equivalent competitive equilibrium. Through the 1920s and 1930s, Western economics departments had duly debated the relative merits of planning and markets in achieving the efficient

---

[45] John Maynard Keynes, *The Tract on Monetary Reform* (Cambridge: Cambridge University Press, 1923).
[46] Bockman, *Markets*, p. 29.
[47] Vilfredo Pareto, 'The Application of Mathematics to Political Economy', *History of Economic Ideas* 17 (1) (2009): 158–179, p. 178.

maximisation of welfare, as well as the potential for mutual borrowing in between. In what became known as the 'socialist calculation debate' through this period, Ludwig Von Mises and Friedrich August von Hayek – the emerging Austrian School – would raise their prescient objection that complete socialist planning must create impossible, inescapable burdens of information and calculation,[48] objections that, as I will show, turn out to be equally relevant to neoliberalism. The Soviet path to central planning did not begin with such closed-system reasoning, however. On the contrary, it was rooted in Karl Marx's analysis of how workers trapped in a machine-like capitalism are alienated from their true potential, from their natural, human selves. How, then, had Russia's Social Democratic Labour Party made the step from Marxist social analysis to Marxism as a mode of revolutionary praxis – a project that inspired them to build that very capitalist machine, only now in socialist form?

There is a basic tension in Marx's writings between his earlier humanism versus his later materialist determinism,[49] and between his activist arguments for the necessity of revolution as the driving force in political history and his analytical conclusion that the economic conditions of the modes of production at any given time determine the political and ideological superstructure – the core principle of historical materialism.[50] Those who want to use Marxist economic analysis to support political action are consequently forced to confront the problem of epistemology. Even if you accept the thesis of *Capital*,[51] that capitalism must tend towards ever more severe crises of exploitation and social alienation, succumbing ultimately to revolution and socialism, how do you know when that revolutionary moment has arrived? And how are you to know what to do with it?

To reflect on how earnestly the Russian revolutionaries agonised over the problem of epistemology in the decades before 1917 is to notice the

---

[48] Friedrich A. Von Hayek, Ludwig von Mises, Nikolaas Gerard Pierson, George Halm and Enrico Barone, *Collectivist Economic Planning* (London: George Routledge and Sons, 1935).
[49] Michael Ellman, *Socialist Planning*, 3rd ed. (Cambridge: Cambridge University Press, 2014), p. 2.
[50] David Lane, 'Building Socialism: From "Scientific" to "Active" Marxism', *Third World Quarterly* 48 (8) (2020): 1306–1321, p. 1307.
[51] Karl Marx, *Capital*, Vol. 1 (London: Penguin Classics, 2004); *Capital*, Vols. II and III (London: Penguin Classics, 2006).

blithe complacency with which American and British political leaders embraced neoliberal economics without questioning its basic philosophical plausibility. The question of how much political economic knowledge is even possible had caused many of the most fateful schisms between the Russian revolutionary hardliners, the Bolsheviks and the more classically Marxist Menshevik minority, with their expectations that a truly proletarian revolution could only follow a period of industrialisation under a democratic government. These debates pivoted not just on the interpretations of Marx but also on Kant's philosophy of knowledge and its implications for personal morality. Alexander Bogdanov, for example, is considered the moderate alternative to Vladimir Ilyich Lenin in the paths not taken, and David Rowley shows that it was Bogdanov's loss of faith in the epistemological certainties, and hence ethical justifications for revolutionary violence, that turned him 'from an advocate of armed insurrection into a proponent of gradual cultural revolution'.[52] Lenin had reasserted his authority over the party's philosophers through 'Materialism and Empirio-Criticism' in 1909,[53] which is a deliberately dogmatic statement of the epistemological certainties that Bogdanov questioned. In 'Materialism', Lenin asserts that a material world exists that is independent of human consciousness and governed by natural laws, and knowledge consists of approximately faithful 'reflections' of that world in consciousness. The critical term is consequently 'reflections',[54] but its exact meaning is left ambiguous because its function in 'Materialism' is clearly practical. Its primary purpose is political: to oppose bourgeois 'idealists' and bestow the supposedly unique capacity to interpret history on those with the most profound understanding of 'economic science', namely on professional socialist revolutionaries as Lenin defined them.[55] The trouble with this argument is that it too was internally, logically consistent but equally impossible to

---

[52] David G. Rowley, 'Bogdanov and Lenin: Epistemology and Revolution', *Studies in East European Thought* 48 (1) (1996): 1–19, p. 2.

[53] Vladimir Ilyich Lenin, 'Materialism and Empirio-Criticism: Critical Comments on Reactionary Philosophy', in *Collected Works*, Vol. 14 (Moscow: Progress Publishers, 1972) (first published in 1909).

[54] Homer Hogan, 'The Basic Perspective of Marxism-Leninism', *Studies in Soviet Thought* 7 (4) (December 1967): 297–317, p. 297.

[55] David McLellan, *Marxism after Marx*, 2nd ed. (London: Macmillan Press, 1979), p. 106.

falsify. It was philosophically convenient rather than compelling, and the failure of such practices could only be recognised after the fact.

Lenin's unpublished 'Notebooks on Philosophy' (1914–1916)[56] reveal a more searching interest in the problems of our necessarily partial knowledge in a complex, changing world.[57] But as Rowley concludes, 'Lenin clearly saw that any retreat from realism and materialism would mean the death of revolutionary spirit ... Thus, Lenin's real philosophical insight was to know when to write bad philosophy.'[58] Lenin understood that flat-out epistemological over-confidence and revolutionary activity were mutually dependent, but as Rowley says, this would have tragic consequences for Russia, because 'Materialism' 'absolved all agents of history from moral blame, it prepared the philosophical, ethical ground for social terrorism. The long-term function of Lenin's scientific materialism was to free the builders of the new Soviet world from the burden of "subjective idealism", and individual moral responsibility'.[59]

Lenin's revolutionary idea was not to wait for the final stage of capitalism and the shift in subjective consciousness supposed by Marx and Friedrich Engels to presage the communist revolution but to instigate it 'artificially' through total 'state capitalism': to substitute the continuation of the bourgeois revolution with a socialist revolution.[60] This was a voluntarist and elitist interpretation of Marx. It framed the revolutionary party as a hierarchical organisation of heroic warriors whose mission was to inculcate the workers with that revolutionary consciousness. Their 'combat tasks' were often drawn in military terms and violence was endorsed as an indispensable means in the class struggle.[61] In the 'The State and Revolution' (1917),[62] Lenin had

---

[56] Vladimir Ilyich Lenin, 'Philosophical Notebooks 1895–1916', in *Collected Works*, Vol. 38 (Moscow: Progress Publishers, 1976): 85–400.
[57] Robert Service, *Lenin: A Political Life: Volume 2: Worlds in Collision*, 2nd ed. (London: Macmillan, 1995), pp. 90–95.
[58] Rowley, 'Bogdanov and Lenin', p. 14.   [59] Ibid., pp. 14–15.
[60] Janina Frentzel-Zagórska, *From a One-Party State to Democracy: Transition in Eastern Europe* (Leiden: Poznan Studies in the Philosophy of Sciences and the Humanities, 1993), p. 13.
[61] Veljko Vujačić, 'From Class to Nation: Left, Right, and the Ideological Roots of Post-Communist "National Socialism"', *East European Politics and Societies* 13 (3) (2003): 359–392, p. 375.
[62] Vladimir Ilyich Lenin, 'The State and Revolution: The Marxist Theory of the State and the Tasks of the Proletariat in the Revolution', in *Collected Works*, Vol. 25 (Moscow: Progress Publishers, 1964) (first published in 1917): 381–492.

followed Engels to argue it would take the socialist transformation of the material order itself for the nature of human subjectivity to take up its socialist form.[63] In the 'Principles of Communism',[64] Engels had insisted that

> industry will have to be run by society as a whole for everybody's benefit. It must be operated by all members of society in accordance with a common plan ... Private property will also have to be abolished and it must be replaced by the sharing of all products in accordance with an agreed plan.[65]

The Bolsheviks had followed the German Social Democrats in assuming that planning would pave the way to socialism. Having come to power on that commitment, however, it became apparent they had no strategy to deliver it.[66] While Nikolai Bukharin and Yevgeny Preobrazhensky could claim that '[n]o longer will one enterprise compete with another; the factories, workshops, mines and other productive institutions will all be subdivisions, as it were, of one vast people's workshop, which will embrace the entire national economy of production',[67] the more immediate challenge was that of how to build such an economy in the first place, and the theoretical debate was quickly overtaken by the practical demands of War Communism.

The new Soviet regime had started by nationalising land, banking, industry and foreign trade through 1917–1918, but the War Communism established from November 1917 to mid-1921 became a period of extreme communisation that banned private trade and seized peasant surpluses to try to master the chaos of the civil war and to commence the revolution in full. Alec Nove describes it as 'a siege economy with a communist ideology. A partly organised chaos.

---

[63] Zhivka Valiavicharska, 'Socialist Modes of Governance and the Withering Away of the State: Revisiting Lenin's State and Revolution', *Theory and Event* 13 (2) (2010): 1–21, p. 11.

[64] Friedrich Engels, 'Principles of Communism', in Jeffrey C. Isaac, *The Communist Manifesto* (New Haven: Yale University Press, 2012) (first published in 1847): 52–70.

[65] William O Henderson, *Engels, Selected Writings* (Harmondsworth: Penguin, 1967), pp. 369–370.

[66] Ellman, *Socialist Planning*, Chapter 1, p. 2.

[67] Nikolai Bukharin and Yevgeny Preobrazhensky, *The ABC of Communism (1920)* (Harmondsworth: Penguin Books, 1969), Chapter 3.

Sleepless, leather jacketed commissars working round the clock in a vain effort to replace the free market'.[68] And it proved untenable in the face of growing peasant reaction.

By 1920, Lenin had written 'Left-Wing Communism: An Infantile-Disorder', to argue it would take time to construct an industrial economy equal to Germany's but that it could be achieved by a rational, revolutionary socialist state, with flexibility as the only strategy. He claimed, 'We in Russia (in the third year since the overthrow of the bourgeoisie) are making the first steps in the transition from capitalism to socialism or the lower stage of communism. Classes still remain and will remain everywhere for years after the proletariat's conquest of power.'[69]

In 1921, the Soviet government developed the New Economic Policy (NEP) as a strategic retreat, but a retreat needed for how long? And how could they know? The NEP reverted to mixed economic methods and temporary concessions to capitalist practices, for the peasantry in particular, and it was supposed to bring a shift from the militarised planning of the war to the first stages of building socialism, only this time with popular support.[70] Through 1925–1926, however, the party would again confront the fundamental question posed by its own revolutionary promises, which was how to transform the entire socio-economic system by deliberate action from above without misreading history.[71] The planning agency, Gosplan, had been established in 1921 with a small technical staff, with its main function being to advise on economic policy. Its main experience, according to Michael Ellman, was that of struggling to reconcile the conflicts between ongoing market forces and other bureaucratic organisations, not least the People's Commissariat for Finance.[72]

Part of the challenge confronting the party was that Marxist economics was developmental. It was supposed to be a theory of dynamic socio-economic change, the very opposite of the neoclassical practice

---

[68] Alec Nove, *An Economic History of the U.S.S.R.* (London: Penguin Economics, 1992), p. 74.
[69] Vladimir Ilyich Lenin, 'Left-Wing Communism: An Infantile Disorder', in *Collected Works*, Vol. 31 (Moscow: Progress Publishers, 1964) (first published in 1920), pp. 117–118.
[70] Leonard Shapiro, *1917: The Russian Revolutions and the Origins of Present-Day Communism* (Harmondsworth: Penguin Books, 1985), Chapter 13.
[71] Nove, *An Economic History*, p. 121.   [72] Ellman, *Socialist Planning*, p. 8.

of deduction within static models. And since Marxist political economy was supposed to be a revolutionary science, the Soviet debate had to be couched in terms of the inter-relationships, not of moving economic quantities but of moving socio-economic systems as embodied by the different social classes. But such broad theorising invited competing interpretations and, hence, factionalism.[73] In the 'right opposition' by the late 1920s, for example, Bukharin had argued for a political coalition between urban workers and peasants and for the incentivisation of richer peasants via markets, so that grain exports could help pay for industrial imports. In the 'left opposition', Leon Trotsky and Preobrazhensky had opposed this coalition and instead sought the forcible collection of agricultural surpluses through a variety of more economically coercive means.[74]

Joseph Stalin's solution was to subordinate everything, including the international dimension of Bolshevism and the Communist Party's structure, to the heavy industrialisation of the country and the violent collectivisation of agriculture, all coordinated through a system of near total command planning.[75] These policies initiated a period of mass deportations and famine, most notably in Ukraine, where millions died in the 'Holodomor' as a consequence of the emerging strategy of 'revolution from above'. At the Sixteenth Party Congress in 1930, Stalin would declare 'the higher development of state power in order to prepare for the withering away of state-power – this is the Marxist Formula'.[76] It may seem grotesque to consider Stalin's views on epistemology given this violence and his suppression of debate through the party purges of the late 1930s, but it is important to notice the form of justification used, namely the copy theory of knowledge set out in Lenin's 'Materialism',[77] along with the powers of interpretation this had vested in the party, in all their brutal potential. In his 'Economic Problems of Socialism' (1951), Stalin had insisted that in socialism as in capitalism:

---

[73] E. M. Chossudowsky, 'The Soviet Conception of Economic Equilibrium', *The Review of Economic Studies* 6 (2) (February 1939): 127–146, p. 130.
[74] Marie Lavigne, *The Economics of Transition* (London: Palgrave, 1995), p. 21.
[75] McLellan, *Marxism*, p. 131.
[76] Joseph Stalin, *Collected Works*, Vol. 13 (1951), pp. 369–370. Quoted in R. W. Davies, 'Economic Aspects of Stalinism', in Alec Nove, *The Stalin Phenomenon* (London: Weidenfeld and Nicolson, 1993), p. 40.
[77] McLellan, *Marxism*, p. 135.

The Soviet Path

[The] laws of economic development, as in the case of natural science, are objective laws, reflecting processes of economic development which take place independently of the will of man. Man may discover these laws, get to know them and, relying upon then, utilise them in the interests of society, impart a different direction to the destructive action of some of the laws, restrict their sphere of action, and allow fuller scope to other laws that are forcing their way to the forefront; but he cannot destroy them or create new economic laws.[78]

While this is ostensibly an interpretation of historical materialism, as the Polish philosopher Leszek Kołakowski pointed out, the implication was that the party knew both the will and the interests of society better than society itself. Moreover, once the spirit of the party was incarnated in the will of one man, Marxism–Leninism no longer meant the transitional dictatorship of the proletariat 'but the dictatorship of one man over the proletariat. Thus, Marx's hypothesis that the working class has a privileged knowledge of the final purpose of history culminates in the assertion that Comrade Stalin is always right'.[79] It followed that whatever the scientific debate, the party's self-understanding and its self-designated role in society meant that a correct line would have to be chosen and this line in turn had to be presented as the logical outcome of high ideological principles and social forces, whatever the intraparty politics and practical necessities that had driven the actual conclusion.[80]

It was under Stalin that Soviet political economy became what Adam Leeds describes as an 'elaborate apologetics' that equated Soviet reality with Soviet ideals, as justified through studies in the methodology of the Marxist–Leninist canon.[81] The rejection of doubt in Leninism now took on its fully institutionalised, totalitarian potential. There is a long-standing debate among Soviet historians as to whether Lenin had always been more intellectually tactical than either sincere or consistent as a theoretician, but as Anthony Polan argues, what mattered for

---

[78] Joseph Stalin, 'The Character of Economic Laws under Socialism', in *The Economic Problems of Socialism in the USSR (1951)* (Peking: Foreign Language Press, 1972), Chapter 1, pp. 3–4.
[79] Leszek Kołakowski and George Urban, 'The Devil in History: A Conversation', *Encounter* (January 1981): 9–26, p. 11.
[80] Alexei Kojevnikov, 'Rituals of Stalinist Culture at Work: Science and the Games of Intraparty Democracy Circa 1948', *Russian Review* 57 (1) (1988): 25–52, p. 51.
[81] Adam Leeds, 'Dreams in Cybernetic Fugue', *Historical Studies in the Natural Sciences* 46 (5) (2016): 633–668, p. 658.

the Soviet system was the deterministic view of reality and the claims for the party's revolutionary omniscience laid down in the founding texts. What mattered was less the numerous inconsistencies within 'The State and Revolution', for example, than the fact it became venerated as a sacred work. Lenin would be idolised as the prophet through which the Truth had expressed itself, albeit the Truth that had yet to be fully realised.[82] Such controversy and debate as survived could then be made more completely subject to the political forces of social control but always in the name of scientific socialism.

The challenges to the theory were immediate. The First Five-Year Plan supposed to cover 1928–1933 was derailed by late adoption, the brutal struggle with the peasantry and an economic crisis partly generated by the plan itself but exacerbated by bad harvests and the state's repressions. The result was a devastating famine from 1931 to 1933 and no stabilisation of the economic system until 1934.[83] In what subsequently became known as the 'classic' or 'traditional' method of Soviet planning, perspective plans covering at least fifteen years ahead and five-year plans were highly aggregated and related to investment plans. At the operational level, annual plans disaggregated these goals in more detail, and these plans were then unpacked into yet more detailed plans for directorates, who each took charge of major enterprises within a given sector. Those plans and targets would then be disaggregated further with instructions for individual enterprises themselves.[84] The planning process was an almighty exercise in top-down bureaucratic coordination, with the annual plan the most important operational planning document. Within this system, information would flow not just downwards but constantly upwards through these same structures in an attempt to make planning not just distributive but dynamic and to manage what turned out to be the chronic need for adjustments.

This new architecture was supposed to provide an effective instrument of 'scientific' party control over optimised economic processes.[85]

---

[82] Anthony Polan, *Lenin and the End of Politics* (London: Methuen Ltd, 1984), p. 52.
[83] Ellman, *Socialist Planning*, p. 11.
[84] Ian Jeffries, *Socialist Economies and the Transition to the Market* (Abingdon: Routledge, 1993), p. 11.
[85] Janos Kornai, *The Socialist System* (Princeton: Princeton University Press, 1992), Part 2.

Despite the Leninist assumption that subjectivity would only change with the material order, each person who operated within the plans was supposed to be so motivated by the achievement of that condition they would complete their tasks to the best of their ability.[86] The system depended on imperative output planning, and this in turn relied on quantification and calculation in physical terms. Money became a passive, administrative form.[87] The practical result was a system of 'nested dictatorship in which each organisation duplicated the administrative and control functions of its superiors in the vertical chain of command', and each layer was forced to manage the reality of incomplete and usually inaccurate information that ran in both directions – right up and down the planning system.[88]

The economic achievements of the Soviet system were remarkable. They included the introduction of mass production, an armaments programme that enabled Soviet victory in the Second World War, full employment and the earliest successes in the space race, as well as unprecedented increases in literacy and numeracy.[89] To imagine this was a system of seamless modernising rationality was to confuse the theory for the reality, however, and the pathologies of command planning would only get worse as the party sought to move the system from extensive to more intensive forms of growth from the 1960s. While planning proved effective for the production of simple goods and war materials, and even for highly targeted areas of innovation, such as space technology, into which resources and expertise were poured, the more complex the generality of goods and services became, and the more dynamic the needs of the economy, the more the Soviet economy would fail.

Ellman tracks how critical scholarship identified the faults that undermined the claims for socialist rationality at both the individual and system-level: thus Colin Clark,[90] as well as Abram Bergson,[91]

---

[86] Michael Ellman, 'The Fundamental Problem of Socialist Planning', *Oxford Economic Papers* 30 (2) (July 1978): 249–262, p. 259.
[87] Włodzimierz Brus, *The Economics and Politics of Socialism: Collected Essays* (1973) (London: Routledge, 2003), p. 8.
[88] Paul Gregory and Andrei Markevich, 'Creating Soviet Industry: The House That Stalin Built', *Slavic Review* 61 (4) (Winter 2002): 787–814, p. 792.
[89] Ellman, *Socialist Planning*, p. 13.
[90] Colin Clark, *A Critique of Russian Statistics* (London: Macmillan, 1939).
[91] Abram Bergson, *Soviet National Income and Product in 1937* (New York: Columbia University Press, 1953); *The Real National Income of Soviet Russia Since 1928* (Cambridge, MA: Harvard University Press, 1961).

show how real and published growth rates were out of step as the use of base-rate prices in a period of massive structural change biased the measures. Joseph Berliner shows how the rational risk aversion of Soviet managers meant that, far from fulfilling the plan in a selfless manner, hoarding and the use of middlemen were commonplace, as was under-reporting capacity to avoid increased output targets and over-reporting the results.[92] Eugene Zaleski's comparative work demonstrates huge discrepancies between plans and outcomes.[93] Richard Nelson and Sidney Winter show how 'rules of thumb' or informal 'routines' were extensive,[94] and often dominated the planning process.[95]

In his synoptic work, *The Socialist System* (1992), Janos Kornai explains how bargaining prevailed over efficient calculation, storming cycles over steady production, paternalism over solidarity, and how budgets were 'softened', with pricing becoming unanchored from value: a development with terrible implications for the wisdom of investment decisions. Kornai concludes that far from a worker's paradise, the classic Soviet model was an 'economy of shortage' characterised by forced and unbalanced development, labour hoarding and chronic overemployment. Bottlenecks in any area of production cascaded through the system and disrupted the already highly imperfect and distorted information flows of the plan in its continuous operation.[96]

Despite the transformation of the material order, decades of indoctrination, terror, combat tasks and the complete politicisation of education, the Soviet system would never succeed in breeding the universal *homo Sovieticus* foretold: the materially formed and perpetually optimising socialist subject. Instead, the regime had developed distinctly traditional features of autocratic rule as early as the 1930s, as those social cohorts that failed to conform were designated 'backward' and the Communist Party consolidated its position as a super-empowered political elite. As the historian Sheila Fitzpatrick described the spirit of the time:

---

[92] Joseph Berliner, *Factory and Manager in the U.S.S.R.* (Cambridge, MA: Harvard University Press, 1957).
[93] Eugene Zaleski, *Stalinist Planning for Economic Growth, 1933–1952* (Chapel Hill: University of North Carolina Press, 1980).
[94] Richard Nelson and Sidney Winter, *An Evolutionary Theory of Economic Change* (Cambridge, MA: Belknap Press, 1982).
[95] Ellman, *Socialist Planning*, p. 13.
[96] Kornai, *The Socialist System*, Chapter 12.

To outsiders, the boiled down Marxism of Soviet political literacy courses might look simplistic, almost catechismic. To insiders it was a 'scientific' worldview that enabled its possessors to rid themselves and others of all kinds of prejudice and superstition – and incidentally master an aggressive debating style characterised by generous use of sarcasm about the motives and putative 'class essence' of opponents. Smugness and tautology, along with polemical vigour, were among the most notable characteristics of Soviet Marxism.[97]

The more completely the Stalinist system was institutionalised in the USSR and imposed on the satellite states of post-war Central Europe, the more severe the rigidities in these systems. The more all-encompassing the plan, the more the planning process suffered from informational lags, fictions and omissions, and the greater the shortages and over-allocations became. After forty years of Polish communism, you could buy armfuls of exquisitely produced classical music records, but the queues for basic foodstuffs went around the block. The 'gaming' of planning targets became routine, as did the resolution of component and consumer shortages via informal networks. Post-war studies revealed a massive second economy that not only existed in parallel to the first but often operated as the oil in the machine.[98] The weak incentives for innovation in a system that struggled to manage its existing requirements meant the socialist economies had started to fall behind those of Western capitalism in the face of the technological boom of the 1970s. As the last vestiges of belief in the harmonious communist future drained away, individuals throughout the controlling administrative hierarchies sought to maximise their private advantages within a system in which the worst abuses of power were reinforced by the ideology's basic principles.

Conclusion

To dream of realising Pareto's idealised conditions either in market or state form is to wish away the problems of information, coordination,

---

[97] Sheila Fitzpatrick, *Everyday Stalinism: Ordinary Life in Extraordinary Times: Soviet Russia in the 1930s* (Oxford: Oxford University Press, 1999), p. 16.
[98] Gregory Grossman, 'The Second Economy of the USSR', *Problems of Communism* 26 (September–October 1977): 25–40.

conflict, evolution and uncertainty in a world that remains stubbornly open-ended and three dimensional. Both the market and planning utopias place fatal constraints on empirical representation and interpretation, and, in doing so, they curtail the scope for adaptive learning and correction following trial, error and review: the scientific method. The fundamental cause of Soviet planning failure was theoretical.[99] What emerged at the level of the Soviet individual was a terrorised mirror image of neoclassical rationality and atomism. In Soviet, as in neoclassical theory, the individual was transformed into an abstract, inhuman entity that when stimulated by the material forces around it was supposed to respond with the correct, preordained behaviour. Indeed, these economic systems conceived in theory depended for their success on consistent forms of universal motivation that do not and cannot exist in practice.

Where neoclassical economics simply assumes a perfect rationality, or learning, so that the market reliably converges on the correct price, the Communist Party would try to teach everyone their role and remind them of it from birth to death to mend the constantly broken connections of a system whose efficiencies were predicated on the completeness of its closure. The result was an elaborate series of rituals and ceremonies to express the values of Soviet socialism and to educate the worker in a right understanding of their function in this scheme. As late as 1979, between the initiation rituals into the Pioneers, the Army, the working class and the Festive Registration of the Newborn Child, a young person between birth and marriage might take part in as many as nine major ceremonies of initiation.[100]

Beginning with the penetrating observations of Michel Foucault in that same year, a critical social science literature developed in the West on the making of the neoliberal subject. As Foucault said, it is the nature of *homo economicus* that 'man' becomes 'an entrepreneur of himself, being for himself his own capital, being for himself his own producer, being for himself the source of his earnings'.[101] Here Foucault captures the automaton qualities of not just neoclassical but also Soviet man, since it is in both systems that the internal will of the

---

[99] Ellman, 'The Fundamental Problem', p. 249.
[100] Christel Lane, 'Ritual and Ceremony in Soviet Society', *The Sociological Review* 27 (2) (May 1979): 251–278, pp. 253–254.
[101] Foucault, 'Lecture 9, 14 March, 1979', p. 226.

individual must operate as a pure function of the 'objective' conditions of the idealised, but rigidly two-dimensional, economistic regime.

As soon as you admit that society is constantly evolving, and with it human subjectivity, the prospects for a permanent form of universal economic rationality must collapse, however. For the Soviets, once you conceded that the saintly consciousness supposed to accompany the new material order would never arrive, the prospect of an efficient central plan was doomed. Introduce radical uncertainty into neoclassical thinking and you must equally undermine the theoretical microfoundations around information, the possibilities of a well-founded individual rationality and hence any prospect of perfect competition, calculable risk, achievable market balance and thus the predestined economic stability of a market system. Neoclassical economic man is supposed to be 'free', but unpack any Camp 1 neoclassical model and you find characters in a clockwork scheme no more capable of an unexpected thought than their Soviet counterparts. As in Leninism, it is here, in the basic determinism and epistemological conceits, that the inherent authoritarianism of neoliberalism lies in wait.

Stalin's transformation of the Soviet economy into a reality of closed-system economic governance condemned all future generations of Soviet economists to prop up the system against the accumulating weight of its motivational, informational, logistical and political contradictions. Following Stalin's death, the Soviets embarked on a 'treadmill of reforms' that only confirmed the impossibility of the basic project.[102] Central planning of the 'commanding heights' was meant to provide an efficient instrument for enabling 'conscious' party control over economic processes. When central planning was combined with Lenin's principle of 'democratic centralism', in which policy was decided centrally and binding on party members, it was supposed to create a rational system that would eclipse the 'anarchy' of the capitalist marketplace.[103] It was in the political nature of the Soviet and later the neoliberal revolution, however, that once the revolutionary transformation of the

---

[102] Gertrude Schroeder, *The Soviet Economy on a Treadmill of Reforms, Soviet Economy in a Time of Change: A Compendium of Papers Submitted to the Joint Economic Committee, Congress of the United States*, Vol. 1 (Washington, DC: Government Printing Office, 1979): 312–336.

[103] Martin Myant, *Transforming Socialist Economies: The Case of Poland and Czechoslovakia* (Aldershot: Edward Elgar, 1993), p. 13.

state was under way, the failures that immediately arose could only be explained as a lack of education among the citizenry or a residual lack of consistency in the new architectures, all to be remedied by holding course. Indeed, the revealed prophecy of Soviet and neoclassical, and hence later neoliberal, ideologies is that all propositions will become manifest through systemic completion. The most important promise in both doctrines is that economic welfare will be maximised when the conditions that create efficiency are achieved, so that no resources are wasted. Chapter 2 explores why this promise in theory can only be broken in practice.

2 | General Equilibrium and the Balanced Plan

The formative generations of both neoclassical and Soviet economists had argued about the most efficient mechanism of economic allocation: the market versus the state, or some mixture of the two. If we explore their respective concepts of perfect systemic efficiency – general equilibrium and the balanced plan – we can see why the political victories of neoliberalism and Stalinism would doom the generations of economists that followed to fixate on the problem of why efficiency was lost when information was lost, and why it must prove impossible for them to 'restore' it.

In neoclassical economics, equilibrium is the mechanical concept that a market is in balance. Supply and demand are matched and hence welfare is maximised. According to the standard, 'ordinal' reading of utility, equilibrium point is reached when the ratio of prices at which goods are exchanged is equal to the ratio of the respective marginal utilities that the agents concerned expect to derive from each good.[1] What this assumes is that economic agents can rank the benefit – the utility – they gain from different goods and hence order their preferences, and they will optimise their trading options to maximise that utility within the constraints of a theoretically given (hence 'known') set of initial conditions. It is the prospect of perfect market balance that encourages economists to imagine they can predict in a deterministic manner the outcomes of changes in the framework of initial endowments.[2] A 'general equilibrium' is when a set of prices exists such that *all* markets throughout an entire economy clear. The centrality of this argument to Camp 1 neoclassical thought, and later to neoliberal argument, was encouraged by the Cold War.[3] A perfectly efficient

---

[1] Richard Bronk, *The Romantic Economist: Imagination in Economics* (Cambridge: Cambridge University Press, 2009), pp. 263–264, p. 68.
[2] Ibid.
[3] Philip Mirowski, *Machine Dreams: Economics Becomes a Cyborg Science* (New York: Cambridge University Press, 2002).

market would demonstrate the superiority of the free market over any economy that was socially planned.[4]

As Tony Lawson notes, in practice the term 'equilibrium' has been used to cover two very different concepts in economic analysis. In the first, the economist is trying to describe and understand a feature of model-independent reality: some condition of *observable* balance in a real economy. In the second, the theoretic notion of equilibrium expresses a property of a formal, mathematical model, or system of equations, or formal logical argument, with the intention of explaining or representing social reality. The first describes a feature of reality, the second expresses the property of a model or doctrine. What Lawson points out is that not only are these approaches analytically distinct, they can never meet. Systemic completeness or closure and the reliable atomism required for any prospect of balance are so at odds with the open-ended, dynamic and interconnected nature of social reality 'that the chances of equilibrium modelling providing insight on any aspect of social reality are slim'.[5] Should model and reality converge it would be by accident, momentary, and we could not know if, let alone how, it had happened.

By contrast, the early Soviet conceptions of balanced supply and demand had aspired to be dynamic and based on an evolving social reality. The Stalinist shift to synoptic planning had nevertheless radically foreshortened the historical determinism of the Leninist view into the vision of a closed, industrialising machine of modernisation, the organisation of which would send Soviet economists trudging up the same analytical Escher staircase as their neoclassical colleagues. First Soviet, and eventually neoliberal, doctrine would claim that given a correct understanding of the necessary mechanisms, a system of consistent allocative efficiency was more than a theoretical possibility: it could be achieved through policy. If we unpack both the Soviet and neoclassical notions, we can see how they converge and why the Soviet experience should have warned us that the attempt to embody utopian doctrine must result in both economic dysfunction and social oppression.

---

[4] Ivan Boldyrev and Olessia Kirtchik, 'General Equilibrium Theory behind the Iron Curtain: The Case of Victor Polterovich', *History of Political Economy* 46 (3) (2014): 435–461, p. 435.
[5] Tony Lawson, 'Reorienting History (of Economics)', *Journal of Post-Keynesian Economics* 27 (3) (Spring 2005): 455–470, p. 455, www.tandfonline.com/doi/abs/10.1080/01603477.2005.11051445.

Neoclassical Equilibrium

General equilibrium is the essential foundation to the neoliberal claim that the more the state is withdrawn, the more the 'natural' allocative efficiencies of the marketplace will play out. What lies buried in the small print of this grand claim is a timeless, moneyless utopia in which superhumanly informed individuals activate their preferences via an exchange economy that constantly tends towards the complete and frictionless resolution of supply and demand. In the 1870s Leon Walras had taken up the debate about whether a market system would self-regulate and how it might reach this point of balance: a general equilibrium. The challenge was to set out how this might occur not just in one market but in all, simultaneously.[6] Walras argued:

> Value in exchange, when left to itself, arises spontaneously in the market as a result of competition. As buyers, traders make their *demands* by *outbidding* each other. As sellers, traders make their *offers* by *underbidding* each other. The coming together of buyers and sellers then results in giving commodities certain values in exchange, sometimes rising, sometimes falling, sometimes stationary... The markets which are best organised from the competitive standpoint are those in which purchase and sales are made by auction, through the instrumentality of stockbrokers, commercial brokers or criers acting as agents who centralise transactions in such a way that the terms of every exchange are openly announced and an opportunity is given to sellers to lower their prices, and to buyers to raise their bids.[7]

In this process of *tâtonnement*, or 'groping' towards a price, it is the acts of buying and selling that create the final price. As Benjamin Mitra-Kahn argues, this is a story of the constant clearing of one set of exchanges for a new set: a description of multiple equilibria,[8] and the result is an ostensibly dynamic theory. As Walras argued: '[S]uch is the continuous market which is perpetually tending

---

[6] Alan Kirman, 'Walras or Pareto: Who Is to Blame for the State of Modern Economic Theory?', *Review of Political Economy* 33 (2) (2021): 280–302, p. 281.
[7] Leon Walras, *Elements of Pure Economics or the Theory of Social Wealth*, 1926 edition of a text first issued in two parts (1874 and 1877), translated by W. Jaffe (London: George Allen and Unwin Ltd, 1954, emphasis in original), pp. 84–85.
[8] Benjamin Mitra-Kahn, 'Debunking the Myths of Computational General Equilibrium Models', Schwartz Center for Economic Policy Analysis, The New School, Working Paper 1-2008, pp. 46–47.

towards equilibrium without ever actually attaining it, because the market has no other way of approaching equilibrium except by groping, and, before the goal is reached, it has to renew its efforts and start all over again.'[9]

If you think about how this story might apply to social reality, however, some serious questions immediately arise. Firstly, why should it be that the prices that prevail are such that the total demand is exactly equal to the total supply? Secondly, how do buyers know when to buy, and sellers when to sell, at the point where this perfect matching occurs?[10] Though subsequent authors argued that some kind of organising authority, later known as the 'Walrasian auctioneer', must logically be at work, those deeper questions remained unanswered.[11] It is also worth noting that production as a challenge disappears from this debate on exchange value, and so all questions around where any of these products come from – about technology, investment, transport, labour and skills – are simply set aside. The result is an attempt to theorise the trading process within an already whole, ideal economy in a theory that is notably empty of empirical content.[12]

Oskar Lange and Abba Lerner drew on the socialist calculation debate from the 1920s to argue in neoclassical terms for how a Central Planning Board could set prices via trial and error in a process that amounted to the Walrasian auction made real. They were arguably encouraged by the fact the idealised Walrasian process was clearly centralised and bore no resemblance to competition as one would commonly understand it.[13] Their argument was nevertheless rejected by the Austrian critics Friedrich August Von Hayek and Ludwig Von Mises.[14] Indeed, it was the problem of general equilibrium that led Hayek to conclude that neoclassical ideas were so dependent on otherworldly a priori assumptions about the distribution of necessary

---

[9] Walras, *Elements*, p. 380.
[10] Alan Kirman, 'Walras's Unfortunate Legacy', in Bridel Pascal, *General Equilibrium Analysis: A Century after Walras* (Florence: Taylor and Francis Group, 2011), pp. 120–122.
[11] Michel De Vroey, 'Marshall and Walras: Incompatible Bedfellows?', *The European Journal of the History of Economic Thought* 19 (5) (2012): 765–783.
[12] Kirman, 'Walras or Pareto?', p. 283.   [13] Ibid., p. 287.
[14] Johanna Bockman and Gil Eyal, 'Eastern Europe as a Laboratory for Economic Knowledge: The Transnational Roots of Neoliberalism', *American Journal of Sociology* 108 (2) (September 2002): 310–352, p. 320.

information that any resulting formulations would prove impossible to reattach to social reality.[15]

As Alan Kirman points out, where Walras had assumed marginal utility based on 'cardinal' utility functions where the satisfaction derived could, in principle, be expressed numerically, Vilfredo Pareto had changed the theoretical track by assuming that people operated according to which option they would rank higher than another: their 'ordinal' preferences.[16] What became known as 'Pareto efficiency' or the 'Pareto optimal' condition was the idea that in a perfectly competitive economy in static general equilibrium the welfare of the population is maximised insofar as it is impossible to make an individual better off without making someone else worse off. It follows that a 'Pareto improvement' is when at least one person is better off, and no one is worse off after a single trade. Although this approach was illuminating about the logic of mutually beneficial transactions, it left us none the wiser about real distributions, since this approach is a formal matter of noticing relative positions rather than saying anything about the magnitudes of the gains made by anyone concerned. The Paretian turn was nevertheless hugely important. It shifted neoclassical economics to the pure logic of rational choice and thus opened it more decisively to mathematisation, although Pareto himself would later reject such reasoning in favour of sociology.[17]

Neoclassical economics would go on to 'solve' a set of equations for general equilibrium in a whole market economy by taking on Frank Knight's criticism about the need for 'practical omniscience' and factoring that in, assuming that all agents in the model are possessed of that entirely perfect information. It is acts of impractical magic such as this that inspired the venerable academic joke in which a physicist, a chemist and a neoclassical economist are stranded on a desert island, with nothing but a can of soup washed ashore with them. 'Focus the power of the sun onto a single point and burn it open', says the physicist. 'Let the salt water corrode the lid', says the chemist. 'Assume a can-opener!' exclaims the economist, triumphant. In 1954 Kenneth Arrow and Gerard Debreu thus succeeded in 'showing' mathematically

---

[15] Tony Lawson, 'The Confused State of (Equilibrium) Analysis in Modern Economics: An Explanation', *Journal of Keynesian Economics* 27 (3) (2005): 423–444, p. 439.
[16] Ibid., pp. 291–295.   [17] Ibid., p. 299.

the conditions under which the whole economy might achieve a set of prices that 'cleared' all markets simultaneously: 'general equilibrium'.[18] They proposed a formal mathematical proof of existence for a centralised system with a price setter – an auctioneer – who determines prices a priori to any trades, and at the given price all trade is exhausted.

As both Mitra-Kahn and Kirman point out, Walrasian and Arrow–Debreu's equilibrium are not the same. The first is a story of multiple and dynamic equilibria that never end, although by implication the process is continuously efficient. Arrow and Debreu equilibrium implies a centralised system with a price setter as an all-seeing and benign utility broker in which a state of general equilibrium is achieved. It was a crucial advance in pure theory because it appeared to connect Pareto's microeconomic model of decision by ordinal preferences to a macroeconomic unifying theory, and as such it laid the basis of what became 'modern macro' economics.[19]

The purpose of competition in this view is not just that firms compete to give customers what they want but that it guarantees the efficient use of scarce resources. Competition will force businesses to use finite resources in the most efficient possible way to cut costs and sustain profits.[20] This insistence that individual choices are open to perfect reconciliation contains a serious and oft-remarked paradox, however. Under perfect competition, companies in theory can only make 'normal profit', that is, zero gain over their costs, which begs the question of why a utility-maximising firm would ever seek to achieve it. I mention this because it illustrates Pareto's observation about the formal equivalence of the perfect social planner and the perfect free market. For the neoclassical promise of general equilibrium to hold true, the rational economic agent and, by extension, the rational firm must ultimately prove no less the whole-system-optimising functionaries under given endowments than the workers and enterprises of the idealised Soviet planning machine.

Arrow and Debreu's model left fundamental questions unresolved for anyone who wondered how this could work in practice, such as

---

[18] Kenneth J. Arrow and Gerard Debreu, 'Existence of an Equilibrium for a Competitive Economy', *Econometrica* 22 (3) (July 1954): 265–290.

[19] Kate Raworth, *Doughnut Economics: Seven Ways to Think Like a 21st Century Economist* (London: Random House, 2017), p. 134.

[20] Lindy Edwards, *How to Argue with an Economist: Reopening Political Debate in Australia* (Cambridge: Cambridge University Press, 2007), p. 41.

what the learning process could possibly be under which equilibrium could be achieved and the conditions under which it might be stable. As Hayek objected, '[T]he tautologies, of which formal equilibrium analysis in economics essentially consists, can be turned into propositions which tell us anything about causation in the real world only in so far as we are able to fill those formal propositions with definite statements about how knowledge is acquired and communicated.'[21] When we look at those propositions in Arrow and Debreu we can see why Hayek was so pessimistic, since they manage to be both out of this world and fantastically restrictive. In Arrow–Debreu equilibrium:

- All actors have complete information about the product being sold and the prices charged by each firm in the past, present and future. All actors are perfectly informed.
- These perfectly informed actors engage in perfect competition. Perfect competition implies that all markets sell an identical product; all firms are price-takers (and hence can't influence the price of their own product); market share has no influence on price; firms can enter and exit markets without cost and labour is completely mobile.
- There is no future uncertainty.
- There are complete asset markets – perfect utilitarian agents can buy today any asset they want.
- There is no trade of shares of firms and no bankruptcy.
- All trade takes place at the beginning of time: it is instantaneous.[22]

The proof for general equilibrium requires a world that is relentlessly unreal. As József Móczár points out, it omitted the most basic vectors of the real political economy including money, government, finance, cooperation, the possibility of monopoly, complex expectations and, last but hardly least, time. Arrow himself said that 'such a system could not exist'.[23] It is nevertheless from the work of Arrow and Debreu that

---

[21] Friedrich August von Hayek, 'Economics and Knowledge', *Economica* 4 (13) (February 1937): 33–54, p. 33.
[22] John Geanakoplos, 'Arrow-Debreu Model of General Equilibrium', Cowles Foundation Paper 1090, Cowles Foundation for Research in Economics, 2004, pp. 122–123.
[23] József Móczár, 'Arrow-Debreu Model versus Kornai Critique', *Athens Journal of Business and Economics* 3 (2) (2017): 143–170, p. 165.

we get the idea of the multiple idealised conditions collectively known as 'perfect competition': the supposedly inherent prospect of which forms the basis for so much neoliberal argument about the virtues of the market and the pathologies of cooperation.

Arrow and Debreu themselves were not market fundamentalists. In 1963 Arrow wrote a seminal paper on the failure of markets in medical care in the face of the uncertainty of disease, a paper often cited as the birth of the economics of the welfare state.[24] In the 1970s, Debreu helped demolish his own existence theorem in its own formal terms, on which more later. But the existence theorem had not been written in a political vacuum. The US Office of Naval Research had given Arrow and Debreu contracts to fund this research, and the US military and state had encouraged the most pro-market and narrowly mathematical forms of neoclassical economics because, as Johanna Bockman points out, they presented 'markets free of political intervention and other institutions but could by default assume the existing hierarchical institutions of American society'.[25] An existence proof of a perfectly competitive market appeared to offer scientific verification of the advantages of the free market over socialist planning.[26] The problem, as Mark Blaug points out, is that 'by the time we get to Arrow and Debreu, general equilibrium has ceased to make any descriptive claim about actual economics systems and has become a purely formal apparatus about a virtual economy'.[27]

The fate of Arrow and Debreu's model would become a barometer of what was happening to the political allegiances of the economics profession over time. While for many neoclassical economists it stayed well within its intended boundaries as a thought experiment, the existence proof was taken up as the Holy Grail by Camp 1 economists as they rose to the political and disciplinary fore in the 1970s and 1980s. As Till Duppe observed, from their perspective, the period before the 1954 paper was the era of 'historical rumination' whereas what came

---

[24] Kenneth Arrow, 'Uncertainty and the Welfare Economics of Medical Care', *The American Economic Review* 53 (5) (1963): 941–973.
[25] Johanna Bockman, *Markets in the Name of Socialism: The Left-Wing Origins of Neoliberalism* (Stanford: Stanford University Press, 2011), p. 47.
[26] Boldyrev and Kirtchik, 'General Equilibrium Theory', p. 436.
[27] Mark Blaug, 'Ugly Currents in Modern Economics', in Uskali Mäki, *Fact and Fiction in Economics: Models, Realism and Social Construction* (Cambridge: Cambridge University Press, 1998), p. 37.

after Arrow and Debreu had the potential to fulfil the taxonomist dream.[28] As we will see in the public policy chapters, committed neoliberals accepted general equilibrium as if it were a latent property of markets that would manifest itself as the state was withdrawn. The fateful result was a shift from the 'blackboard determinacy' of theoretical economics to a full-blown political determinism.[29]

For the more critical neoclassical economists of Camp 2, Arrow–Debreu came to be regarded as the benchmark that real world markets would fail to achieve, hence a starting point for analytical purchase on the nature of those failures. This too, however, is a trap, since while a notional measure of imbalance in named parameters seems intuitively informative, the formality of general equilibrium must pull the investigative focus away from all the dynamic relationships of practical import in the real economy: from the interdependent institutional and technological changes and power dynamics that define the nature of socio-economic development. When we look in Chapter 7 at how general equilibrium models were applied in UK corporate tax policy, for example, we will see how the pure exchange economy depicted in theory necessarily omitted the most powerful institutional realities that dictated corporate behaviour at the time, most notably financial markets and tax havens: the market for money itself. When we look at how the Soviets grappled with the problem of 'balanced development', we can see in more vivid detail why a fixation on perfect efficiency within a closed system must put analysis at odds with reality.

The Soviet Search for Balanced Development

In the Soviet case, the practical impossibility of squaring the Stalinist institutional reality of economy-wide planning with the Leninist circle of socialist doctrine would play out with a grinding of ideological gears over the lifetime of the regime. The Soviets' concept of equilibrium was political from the start. It was supposed to denote a particular form of planned social dynamics, in line with Marxian critiques of

---

[28] Till Duppe, 'Arrow and Debreu De-homogenized', *Journal of the History of Economic Thought* 34 (4) (December 2012): 491–514, p. 508.

[29] Peter Wiles, 'Ideology, Methodology and Neoclassical Economics', in Alfred Eichner, *Why Economics Is Not Yet a Science* (New York: Routledge: 1983), p. 164.

capitalism and the early Soviet experiences with planning.[30] The basic dogma said there was a necessary historical development from capitalism to socialism to communism, and this development took place through class struggle, led by a communist party ordained with the necessary political knowledge to see it through.[31] Even if neoclassical concepts had been better known at the time, the fact that the conceptual space of general equilibrium was stripped of social realism would have condemned it as an apology for the capitalist status quo.[32] So what could the Soviet concept of economic balance mean?

Regardless of the doctrinal disputes that had arisen before, Stalin's recourse to command planning had tied the Soviet project to a logic of predestination. As in neoclassical general equilibrium, the claims for balanced development in the Soviet system were tautological, although Stalin left some theoretical room for manoeuvre when he argued:

A socialist economy can be conducted only on the basis of the economic law of balanced development of the national economy. That means that the law of balanced development of the national economy makes it possible for our planning bodies to plan social production correctly. But possibility must not be confused with actuality. They are two different things. In order to turn the possibility into actuality, it is necessary to study this economic law, to master it, to learn to apply it with full understanding, and to complete such plans as fully reflect the requirements of this law. It cannot be said that the requirements of this economic law are fully reflected by our yearly and five-yearly plans.[33]

The problem with a doctrine of continuous political economic revelation was that the party was bound to suffer continuous surprises when it tried to put this into practice. As V. E. Motylev had set out in 'The Tempo of Development of the USSR' in 1929, 'the planning organs must decide upon the proper rate of development by assessing the real or "factual" possibilities which exist in the country at that time (*i.e.* the relative scarcity of factors of production, including the labour force),

---

[30] E. M. Chossudowsky, 'The Soviet Conception of Economic Equilibrium', *The Review of Economic Studies* 6 (2) (February 1939): 127–146, pp. 128–129.

[31] Joseph M. Bocheński, 'The Three Components of Communist Ideology', *Studies in Soviet Thought* 2 (1) (1962): 7–11.

[32] Chossudowsky, 'The Soviet Conception', pp. 128–129.

[33] Joseph Stalin, *The Economic Problems of the USSR* (Peking: Foreign Language Press, 1972), Chapter 1 (first published in 1951).

How Do You Turn Utopian Dogma into a Procedure? 61

and taking into consideration the latest achievements of technical sciences'.[34] In effect, the Soviet state should take every single investment, production and coordination problem conveniently 'disappeared' behind the initial endowments and mathematics of neoclassical general equilibrium, lay them out the planning table and solve them.

Since the party had asserted that under Soviet socialism there were no longer elemental, objective economic processes independent of the will of the working class and its state, the implication was that the planning authorities were a pure emanation of that will. As E. M. Chossudowsky noted in 1939, 'The most difficult task of the planning authorities consists, therefore, in creating, mobilising, and coordinating the forces and will of the working classes and applying them to *whatever is technically possible* in a given situation. "Objective" and "subjective" conditions were thus merged in the concept of the "socio-economic optimum".'[35] Vladimir Ilyich Lenin's theory of knowledge would be quite thoroughly put to the test.

Where neoliberals would later insist that the problems of efficient allocation within society would be solved within the marketplace, once the distorting interventions of the state were retracted, Stalin had used the language of historical materialism to create a totalitarian system of political economic control to achieve the same thing. Though their interpretation of how efficiency would be achieved was opposed, their ambition had the same ontological shape. It was circular, and the imposition of these visions of harmonious efficiency onto society would succeed only if their underlying assertions were true. Knight had objected that pure deduction could prove useful only if theorists were at constant pains to use descriptions that could be reattached to a 'literal truth',[36] and this was going to be a problem in both systems.

How Do You Turn Utopian Dogma into a Procedure?

The traditional method for achieving internal consistency in the Soviet plan was that of 'material balances'. Planners constructed tables that

---

[34] V. E. Motylev, 'The Tempo of Development in the USSR, Moscow, 1929', in Russian, quoted in Chossudowsky, 'The Soviet Conception', p. 134.
[35] Ibid., p. 134.
[36] Frank Knight, *Risk, Uncertainty and Profit* (Boston: Houghton Mifflin, 1921), Introduction.

showed the available resources and distribution of commodities within a given period. Balances were set up on a commodity-by-commodity basis and varied depending on whether they were producer or consumer goods. It was impractical to include every single item even in a relatively basic industrial economy, and some items were subsumed within other commodity tables or simply unacknowledged owing to information gaps and lags. Every time the planned output of any given product was changed, the outputs of all other related commodities had to be adjusted. Even though processes for continuous adjustment were built in, this was still a prohibitively difficult task, and the only practical solution was to focus on the most important direct relationships.[37] Material balances were thus mainly concerned with gross production and gross consumption of commodities and focused on supply bottlenecks.[38] For this process to be representative of the production regime continuously created out of it, all the coordination tasks would have to be achieved in an essentially frictionless space. The real world of planning, in other words, would have to create the same timeless and telepathic domain as utilitarian man in commodity space, and Soviet planners were immediately aware that this wasn't happening.

The traditional methods could manage large-scale decisions, particularly around investment projects, and the planned expansion of basic industries and fuels was in line with nationalisation practices common in the post-war West. By the 1960s, however, the Soviet system was struggling to manage the diversification of production that Nikita Khrushchev had hoped would re-legitimise socialism in the aftermath of the punishing Stalinist years. The need to produce higher standards, greater choice of commodities and improved technology had put the planning system under increasing strain.[39] Vassily Nemchinov, the head of the Soviet Academy of Science's Science Laboratory for the Application of Mathematical Methods in Economics, had warned in 1962 that '[s]hould the old planning methods be preserved, and given our present rate of growth, in

---

[37] Michael J. Swann, 'On the Theory of Optimal Planning in the Soviet Union', *Australian Economic Papers* 14 (24) (June 1975): 41–56, p. 45.
[38] Ibid., p. 47.
[39] Michael Ellman, *Socialist Planning*, 3rd ed. (Cambridge: Cambridge University Press, 2014), p. 52.

How Do You Turn Utopian Dogma into a Procedure? 63

1980 practically the entire adult population of our country would have to be engaged in the administration and planning spheres'.[40] A 1962 article in *Pravda* by Evsei Liberman labelled 'Plans, Profits and Bonuses' proposed that most of the existing planning indicators be abandoned in favour of an all-encompassing index based on profit.[41]

To escape the system's bureaucratic rigidities and information failures, Liberman's idea was that if enterprise directors could be incentivised via a profit motive, they could be left to produce what society needed and wanted. Directors would become honest about productive capacity, stop hoarding and innovate. In the 1962 plenary session of the Party Central Committee, Khrushchev conveniently recalled 'Lenin's directive that we be able, if necessary, to learn from the capitalist, to adopt whatever they have that is sensible and advantageous'.[42] After further debate and experimentation, and though Khrushchev himself was deposed in 1964, succeeded by Leonid Brezhnev as the general secretary and Alexei Kosygin as the premier, Liberman's proposals were adopted by Kosygin as the basis of reforms from 1965.

There had been designs along similar lines in the distinctive model of (non-aligned) workers' self-management in Yugoslavia from 1950 and some imitation in crisis-ridden Poland and Hungary from the 1950s onwards and in the more concerted 'New Economic Mechanism' in Hungary from the late 1960s. As in these other socialist states, however, Kosygin's goal was not to redistribute authority between market and state actors but to use the presumed informational, incentive and feedback functions of markets efficiently to help achieve the goals of the socialist plan.[43] The functionalist logic of the system would be kept intact, and so the search was on for a technical, dynamic solution to the systemic problem of information-loss within a closed, and yet ideally ever more productive, system.

Although the dogmas of the system remained, mathematical logic, cybernetics and information theory had been 'politically neutralised'

---

[40] Quoted in Harry G. Shaffer, 'Economic Growth and the Growth of Soviet Economic Rationality', *The Antioch Review* 26 (2) (Summer 1966): 187–203, p. 192.
[41] Evsei Liberman, 'Plans, Profits, Bonuses', *Pravda*, 9 September 1962; also available in *Problems of Economics* 8 (3) 1965: 3–8.
[42] Shaffer, 'Economic Growth', pp. 195–196.
[43] Ellman, *Socialist Planning*, p. 53.

after 1956 and hence freed from the doctrinal constraints of the Marxist–Leninist 'classics'.[44] This declassification allowed for renewed dialogue with mathematically inclined colleagues in the West:[45] the only other people engaged in a closed-system approach to the economic world. Having found the process of mechanical balances wanting, the death of Stalin had allowed the Soviets to turn to their last best hope: that mathematics could solve the so far unrelenting incompatibility between doctrine and reality. Those mathematical methods were now applied to the problem of how to allow for decentralisation and innovation at the enterprise level while improving the efficiency of the overall plan.[46]

'Economic cybernetics' had duly emerged as a Soviet discipline during the 1960s and sought to distinguish Soviet mathematical economics from the bourgeois interests of the neoclassicists, but as Ivan Boldyrev and Olessia Kirtchik note, it had strong affinities with Western developments in systems analysis, operations research, mathematical programming and control theory. Its task was to develop systems of control for economic systems based on cybernetic ideas of the flow and exchange of information. The economic system was increasingly depicted as an object of (technical) control, with inputs, outputs and feedback loops: the language of machines.[47] As Adam Leeds has argued, it was the transposition of cybernetics from its roots in engineering and the military, via analogy, to the problems of planning that transformed Soviet economics into a mathematical discipline, as engineers and mathematicians now worked up a radical vision of cybernetic communism.[48] In moving from narratives of conscious socialism to an increasingly pervasive language of machines, however, the concerted Soviet turn to mathematics could only reveal more explicitly the prerequisite of an inhuman inflexibility in the basic system, and it would fail both technically and politically.

---

[44] Bocheński, 'The Three Components', pp. 7–11.
[45] Ivan Boldyrev and Olessia Kirtchik, 'The Cultures of Mathematical Economics in the Postwar Soviet Union: More than a Method, Less than a Discipline', *Studies in History and Philosophy of Science* 63 (2017): 1–10, p. 2.
[46] Ibid.   [47] Ibid., p. 3.
[48] Adam Leeds, 'Dreams in Cybernetic Fugue', *Historical Studies in the Natural Sciences* 46 (5) (2016): 633–668.

Stalemate

Soviet cyberneticians would retain the language of 'balance' but the majority would move their focus to solving practical problems around input–output tables, linear optimisation problems for single enterprises and transport. The more ambitious attempts to create a comprehensive theory of optimal planning would prove disappointing, however.[49] This is because neither input–output planning nor linear programming could escape the ontological snare in which they operated. The challenge of 'optimal planning' was that of achieving static efficiency within a given system. It was consequently no more able to accommodate change or innovation than the traditional system of material balances.

Material balances had focused on gross outputs and suffered chronic coordination problems, so input–output analyses were tried through the 1960s to shift the focus in national accounts to inter-industry productive relations. The hope was that given a change in demand a more detailed statistical picture might be manipulated to show both the direct requirements and the inter-industry adjustments needed to keep the plan in order.[50] As the Harvard-educated Russian economist Wassily Leontief had argued, by assuming fixed technical coefficients, planners could calculate different vectors of total output as they corresponded to different final demand vectors, and this was supposed to ease the adjustment for bottlenecks.[51] In practice however, apt statistics were missing,[52] and the assumption of fixed technical coefficients and constant returns to scale would form new stumbling blocks, as both precluded real innovations in technology and ignored the actual variations between sectors. A still greater problem was a failure to account for the distribution of a large amount of gross output, and the upshot was that input–output techniques could still not rescue planners from the problems of internal consistency and change.[53]

A parallel ambition of cybernetics was to create a decentralised, self-regulating control and information system for the plan in

---

[49] Boldyrev and Kirtchik, 'The Cultures', pp. 2–5.
[50] Swann, 'On the Theory', p. 46.
[51] Wassily Leontief, *Input-Output Economics* (Oxford: Oxford University Press, 1966), p. 13.
[52] Albina Tretyakova and Igor Birman, 'Input-Output Analysis in the USSR', *Soviet Studies* 28 (2) (1976): 157–186, p. 170.
[53] Swann, 'On the Theory', pp. 46–47.

supposedly politically neutral, algorithmic terms,[54] with linear programming the most promising technical tool of the time. This was a mathematical technique developed from operations research to achieve the best outcomes from processes that could be depicted as linear relationship, applied to things like network flow problems. Leonid Kantorovich had already considered it in the Stalinist era, only for his work to be neglected: indeed, it survived political censorship only because of its uses for the military and the emergent field of atomic energy.[55] But by the 1960s it was unarguable the Soviets needed to move towards more intensive, efficient production, and cybernetics looked promising.[56]

As Michael Swann explains, to treat national economic planning as a problem amenable to linear programming you would need to formulate a national economic objective function and the arguments for it had to be well defined. 'Maximum output' needed to be specified in terms of type, quantity, quality, size and so on. A core proposition was that given a theory of the optimally functioning economic system you would discover the optimal price system. If you couldn't figure out what the social optimum was however, then nor could you compute what the optimal pricing system could be.[57] As an idea, optimal planning made explicit the problem that had existed from the system's inception, which is that it required a Godlike foreknowledge of supply and demand. It is a restatement of the problem of general equilibrium as expressed for an actual economy.

We can see the optimal planning debate in all its occult glory in Soviet theories of perfectly efficient decentralisation. An optimal plan would transform the existing system because you could deduce from the plan what the optimal system of relationships would be between enterprises, the optimal level of hierarchy for key decisions, the optimal share of accumulation and investment from the national income and so on.[58] As Swann explains:

---

[54] Benjamin Peters, 'Normalizing Cybernetics', *Information and Culture* 47 (2) (2012): 145–175, p. 147.
[55] Bockman, *Markets in the Name of Socialism*, p. 40.
[56] Leonid Kantorovich, *The Best Use of Economic Resources* (London: Pergamon Press, 1965), pp. 274–275.
[57] Swann, 'On the Theory', pp. 43–44.
[58] Michael Ellman, 'Optimal Planning: A Review Article', *Soviet Studies* 20 (1) (July 1968): 112–136, p. 113.

In essence, the pure theory of optimal planning may be defined as the realization of an economic system in which all economic decisions are made by the economic units. However, these decisions are exactly those that would have been made by the central authorities because the authorities have determined the criteria, such as profit or output maximization, and the parameters, such as optimal plan prices and an optimal investment norm, which all enterprises use. This state is referred to by the optimal planners as one of 'perfect indirect centralization'.[59]

In effect, the 'cycle' of the entire economy must be expressed mathematically so that the disaggregated behaviour of all economic agents operates as a perfect expression of what the centre would do if it were an omniscient planner, just without the central planning hierarchy having to manage all the information. One of the most influential books at the time, Viktor Volkonsky's *A Model of Optimal Planning and the Interconnections of Economic Indices*, deployed Arrow and Debreu's general equilibrium at its core, but as Michael Ellman concluded at the time, 'The author of the book is… a candidate of physical-mathematical sciences, and economists may find the book rather abstract.'[60] Barely twenty years later, however, general equilibrium would form the foundation of multiple neoliberal policies and modelling by Western governments, central banks and independent financial institutions.

Like Arrow and Debreu's equilibrium, optimal planning could not begin to accommodate technological change, let alone behavioural 'anomalies', and the social fact of ontological indeterminacy, quite apart from political dogma, made it impossible. The theory of optimal planning was logically coherent but stuck fast on the same drawing board as material balances and input–output planning when it came to coping with the reality of an open-ended and unpredictable economic system operated by less than perfectly rational people. You could take up mathematical methods to describe an economic system in theory, but it was folly to think that the economic system in practice would track the model you had just imagined. Linear programming could and did improve results at the level of those specific production challenges that could be coherently isolated from other interdependent factors, such as transportation, and this was how it tended to be used at the time in the West as part of the new science of 'management'.[61]

---

[59] Swann, 'On the Theory', p. 44.   [60] Ellman, 'Optimal Planning', p. 114.
[61] Ibid., p. 123.

Meanwhile, on the basic question of how to render the whole plan efficient, reality continued to bite.

The political upshot of the optimal planning experiment was to bring the idea of markets back into Soviet socialism and to emphasise that efficiency improvements were going to require some decentralisation and more dynamic systems of feedback to the enterprise level, as argued by Liberman. It introduced into Soviet practice the idea that the concept of price should be extended to include charges for the use of investment capital to prevent it being squandered in purely extensive uses and that land too should be seen as subject to scarcity.[62] The parallel experiments with economic decentralisation in the Prague Spring from 1967 to 1968 proved tragically temporary, however, as the Soviet leadership under Brezhnev concluded that economic reform could trigger a domino effect of uncontrolled political escape from Soviet strictures across the 'defensive glacis' of Central Europe. Czechoslovakia's reformers had insisted they had no intention of leaving the Warsaw Pact, but the flowering of Czechoslovak civil society in the Prague Spring had demonstrated that to open up the conversation about reform was to invite a dangerous debate about the merits of the entire system.

Though Soviet economic reforms had only begun in earnest in 1965 they were cut short by 1969. Gosplan continued with the traditional philosophy of central control, vertical flows of information, the specification of a supposedly exhaustive set of indicators to the enterprise level and the method of material balance. Input–output planning could help with inter-industry flows, and linear programming with efficiency in short-term plans,[63] but if you wanted to control planning, there was no escape from hierarchy and command and their distinctly ungodly failings. Optimal planning had never progressed beyond a highly abstract proof-of-principle and good intentions. It was not until the rise to power of Mikhail Gorbachev in 1985 that serious reform efforts began again, and this time their conclusion was the collapse of Soviet communism and of the Soviet Union itself in 1991.

To understand why the Soviets found it impossible to identify a unique optimality criterion that would allow for optimal planning,[64] it is instructive to turn back to the West and the fate of general equilibrium theory, since both doctrines were confronting the problem of

[62] Swann, 'On the Theory', p. 52.   [63] Ibid., p. 53.   [64] Ibid., p. 55.

aggregation. Volkonsky had objected that '[t]he dogmatism of Soviet economics is epitomised in the case of the rejection of Walrasian analysis',[65] but if we look at the fate of that analysis it suggests that the Soviet hardliners had been right, albeit for the wrong reasons, when they concluded that 'perfect indirect centralisation' would never be possible in states or markets.

Hugo Sonnenschein, Rolf Mantel and Gérard Debreu had written a series of papers through the 1970s that demonstrated that as soon as any degree of complexity was introduced into general equilibrium models the prospects for the stability of any equilibrium evaporated.[66] Instead, explains Frank Ackerman, 'cycles of any length, chaos, or anything else you can describe, will arise in a general equilibrium model for some set of consumer preferences and initial endowments. Not only does general equilibrium fail to be reliably stable; its dynamics can be as bad as you want them to be'.[67] Sonnenschein, Mantel and Debreu established that the prospect of a stable equilibrium tended to fall apart in formal mathematical terms with more than three variables. Beyond three variables in the model almost any continuous pattern of price movements could occur, so long as the number of consumers was at least as great as the number of commodities.[68] Ackerman's devastating point is that the idea of general equilibrium collapses as it confronts the problem of aggregation from individual to group or mass behaviour. It is not just that aggregate behaviour is not as well behaved as individual behaviour. The microeconomic model simply says too little about what individuals might want or do. There is too much scope for variation and too many degrees of freedom for

---

[65] Quoted in Ellman, 'Optimal Planning', p. 133.
[66] Gérard Debreu, 'Excess Demand Functions', *Journal of Mathematical Economics* 1 (1974): 15–23; Rolf Mantel, 'On the Characterization of Aggregate Excess Demand', *Journal of Economic Theory* 7 (1974): 348–353; 'Homothetic Preferences and Community Excess Demand Functions', *Journal of Economic Theory* 12 (1976): 197–201; 'Implications of Microeconomic Theory for Community Excess Demand Functions', in Michael Intriligator, *Frontiers of Quantitative Economics*, Vol. 3 (Amsterdam: North Holland, 1977), pp. 111–126; Hugo Sonnenschein, 'Do Walras' Identity and Continuity Characterize the Class of Community Excess Demand Functions?', *Journal of Economic Theory* 6 (1973): 345–354.
[67] Frank Ackerman, 'Still Dead after All These Years: Interpreting the Failures of General Equilibrium Theory', *Journal of Economic Methodology* 9 (2) (2002): 119–139, p. 122.
[68] Ibid., p. 128.

individual economic agents to produce results that have any useful degree of specificity.[69]

The Soviets could have attested to this: even if you planned what your population could produce and consume, they had a terrible habit of making choices of their own. Ackerman argues that both the model of behaviour and the problem of aggregation originate in the analogies from physics, which makes this a fundamental problem of the ontology that came with them. Such a form of thinking requires a dependable atomism at the micro level that is never going to play out in the behaviour of real individuals in a human system, however economically planned and politically repressive. Sonnenschein, Mantel and Debreu had demonstrated not just that the theoretic and the social realms could never meet but that the theoretic realm itself was formally incoherent. Nevertheless, by the 1980s, it was increasingly argued within neoclassical economics that for macroeconomics to have any validity it had to begin with the supposedly objective individual functions and constraints faced by individual decision-makers.

As Oddný Helgadóttir notes, for the forty years following the Second World War, the misleadingly titled 'neoclassical synthesis' in mainstream Western economics had been characterised by a marriage of convenience between a neoclassical microeconomics and a more Keynesian macroeconomics:[70] between a microeconomics that focused on the study of individual decisions and their logic and a macroeconomics framed by the empirical study of aggregates, and a willingness to stitch together macroeconomic models out of theory and empirics in a pragmatic manner.[71] Keynesians had rejected the idea that macroeconomics could be reduced to inferences from the individual level, and the post-war debates within micro- and macroeconomics had consequently tended to operate in two discrete silos. As Helgadóttir argues, the increasingly forceful assertion by the 1980s that macroeconomics had to have neoclassical microeconomic foundations was not the result of a new consensus about the superior validity of that principle. It was rather an artefact of the relative

---

[69] Ibid., p. 136.
[70] Oddný Helgadóttir, 'How to Make a Super Model: Professional Incentives and the Birth of Contemporary Macroeconomics', *Review of International Political Economy* 4 (1) (November 2021): 1–29, p. 5.
[71] Michel De Vroey, *A History of Macroeconomics from Keynes to Lucas and Beyond* (Cambridge: Cambridge University Press, 2016), Part I.

convenience of neoclassical models, their resulting attractions for theoretical construction and professional advancement and the convergence of these trends with the deepening political victory of Camp 1 neoclassical promises.[72]

From the 1980s to today it has thus become standard practice in macroeconomic modelling to use the device of the 'representative agent': an analytical sleight of hand in which all agents of the same type are presumed to be identical in their preferences, that is, the 'firm' in a model is representative of all firms and so on. This allowed for the conceptualisation of systems based on the options now faced by those agents. Rather than acknowledge the defeat of general equilibrium as even a formal mathematical possibility, this new principle was an attempt to escape the problems of aggregation by yet another convenient assumption. But, like all such acts of theoretical wizardry, the representative agent device only shuffles those problems behind a curtain, rather than making them vanish, since to test any proposition produced by a representative agent model is to implicitly test the representative agent hypothesis itself.[73] The neoclassical macroeconomic models that went on to dominate and replace the more pragmatic models of the past thus tended to reduce the macroeconomy to a black box that generated relative price shifts depending on the parameters set out in those models. In 'modern macro', the analysis sets out how individuals and firms – microeconomic agents – make decisions and then models how these choices might interact with each other to yield supposedly economy-wide outcomes. But as Mark Blyth and Mathias Matthijs point out, with its technical dependence – first on Real Business Cycle and latterly on Dynamic Stochastic General Equilibrium (DSGE) modelling, on which more later – the approach has failed to anticipate every major macroeconomic crisis thereafter, from the Global Financial and Euro crises to the failure of the Doha round of trade talks.[74] Even in the field of comparative political economy there was a shift from macrosocial models that focused on how real political and social actors tamed the market to more

---

[72] Helgadóttir, 'How to Make a Super Model', pp. 5, 7.
[73] Alan Kirman, 'Whom or What Does the Representative Individual Represent?', *Journal of Economic Perspectives* 6 (1992): 117–136, p. 125.
[74] Mark Blyth and Mathias Matthijs, 'Black Swans, Lame Ducks, and the Mystery of IPE's Missing Macroeconomy', *Review of International Political Economy* 24 (2) (2017): 203–231, pp. 203–205.

rationalist-functionalist accounts that posited the existence of stable institutional equilibria, except these equilibria were not stable, and the resulting 'supermodels' have proved every bit as analytically misleading as those in macroeconomics.[75]

This insistence on utilitarian micro-foundations for macroeconomics has effectively reproduced the Soviet belief that the subjective events of the individual level and the dynamics of the macro-level political economy can be made near pure expressions of each other, and these expressions can be reliably modelled and adapted through policy. Meanwhile, the device of the representative agent offered relief from the problem of aggregation, but it remained an assertion in logic rather than anything to do with real dynamics. The Soviet economy by the 1970s was characterised by chronic shortages, declining living standards, high corruption, the rise of a black market, environmental devastation, world-beating levels of alcoholism and declining life expectancy. It was at this point that neoclassical economics would rise to the fore in the West as the basis of neoliberal policymaking.

Conclusion

The circular nature of their economic arguments condemns Soviets and neoliberals to make assertions that depend on other assertions that prove impossible to connect to an observable social reality. It is these narrative oscillations that came to dominate the evolution of Soviet and neoclassical economic thought. The question to which the Soviets never found an answer was that of how to find a central process to rationally derive the structure of output for the entire economy before the fact: as a precise forecast.[76] It is the same problem as that posed by general equilibrium, and both proved equally impossible to solve either mathematically or practically. The principle of general equilibrium and the idea that markets, undisturbed by the state, will tend towards it nevertheless remain a touchstone of contemporary neoclassical economics and the foundation of neoliberal justification.

[75] Herman Mark Schwartz and Bent Sofus Tranøy, 'Thinking about Comparative Political Economy: From Macro to Micro and Back', *Politics and Society* 47 (1) (2019): 23–54.
[76] Paul Craig Roberts, 'The Polycentric Soviet Economy', *The Journal of Law & Economics* 12 (1) (1969): 163–179, p. 166.

Conclusion

When economics students are taught the First Fundamental Welfare Theorem,[77] they learn that any Walrasian or Arrow and Debreu equilibrium achieves a 'Pareto-optimum'. That is to say, a perfectly competitive economy in static general equilibrium achieves a situation in which the welfare of the population is maximised, in the sense that it is impossible to make an individual better off without making someone else worse off. In this light it is given that state intervention must alter the necessary conditions for a perfectly functioning competitive economy and prevent the attainment of the Pareto Optimum. It follows that once the government enters the economy, even the best possible equilibrium achievable is a suboptimal 'second-best'. It thus becomes axiomatic for Camp 1 economists and, by extension, for neoliberal politicians that when you remove state intervention you improve the competitiveness of an economy and hasten it towards balance.

Since perfect allocative efficiency is a fiction in any economy more complicated than, say, the food market on a small, fertile island, or similarly bucolic cases, however, what reasons do we have to expect that a national economy unimproved by mediating institutions will be anything better than a chaotic and unequal struggle over resources: a struggle that enables the accumulation of overweening power by the economically strong? I see none, analytically, as confirmed by the real economic history of both laissez-faire and neoliberalism. It might reasonably be concluded at this point that all schools have their fanatics. But even Camp 2 neoclassical economists operate with a scarcely modified optimism about the calculable nature of uncertainty and the essentially unchanging nature of economic reality. So for them too, general equilibrium has remained the 'magnetic north' against which the misadventures of real markets should be reviewed. Neoliberals consequently signed up to a theory of the political economy that could not imagine how state institutions, corporations, the financial sector and above all the natural environment could develop distinctive dynamics and crises of their own: dynamics that could not even be described in neoclassical terms, let alone be solved.

The story of general equilibrium shared a common political fate to that of balanced development in the Soviet system: one in which a

---

[77] Allan M. Feldmann, 'Welfare Economics', in Steven N. Durlauf and Lawrence E. Blume, *The New Palgrave Dictionary of Economics*, 2nd ed. (London: Palgrave Macmillan, 2008).

closed-system imaginary of the economy was assigned the status of the real by politicians. But as the Hayekian critic of neoclassical methods Deidre McCloskey has objected, this is a form of argument that formalises steps in an argument about whether, when or why something happens but doesn't calibrate or check itself with observable reality either in its working assumptions or in its motivating axioms, in its formal logic or in the maths that 'proves it'. For questions about how actual markets work, let alone about how states govern or a public policy operates, this level of abstraction is a fatal flaw. Such forms of reasoning cannot be wrong any more than the Pythagorean Theorem can be, as McCloskey notes: 'Under such-and-such a set of assumptions, A, the conclusion, C, must be that people are made better off… Philosophers call this sort of thing "valid" reasoning, by which they do not mean "true", but following from the axioms – if you believe the axioms, such as A, then C also must be true.'[78] The standard of proof becomes the formal, internal consistency of the model.

While McCloskey concedes that axiomatic deduction is productive for the methodological sciences such as logic, mathematics and statistics, she insists that to use nothing but theoretical reasoning to define a problem and to draw analytical conclusions from *that* for policy is a recipe for trouble.[79] Even the neoclassical and cybernetic models that apply real data points are still determined through their underlying assumptions. Indeed, with the increase in the complexity of models only comes an increase in the number of subjective modelling decisions. These typically include how you want to draw the structural parameters of the economy, which equations you want to use to define the relationships and behaviours supposedly at work and how to 'close' the model, that is, how to define how each variable within your model will 'react' to whatever exterior causal event or impulse you are choosing to motivate the story that your model is trying to tell. Newtonian physics was built on the principle of internal consistency within systems, with energy within that system always preserved. Those systems were subject to disturbances that could cause them to oscillate dynamically.[80] It follows in determinate equilibrium models that you need to make

---

[78] Deidre McCloskey, 'The Trouble with Mathematics and Statistics in Economics', *History of Economic Ideas* 13 (3) (2005): 85–202, p. 90.
[79] Raworth, *Doughnut Economics*, p. 136.
[80] Andrew Haldane, 'The Dappled World', *GLS Shackle Biennial Memorial Lecture*, Bank of England, London, 10 November 2016.

Conclusion

decisions about how the variables in your model will react to the disturbance at hand. In the absence of an objectively true model of how any, let alone all, economies work, however, this is an exercise in normative political philosophy masquerading as science. While clearly such 'reasoning through' of logical possibilities can produce a valuable thought experiment, to then drive a real political economy to conform to the terms of such experiments is to embark on social engineering in its most totalising, if not totalitarian, form. Furthermore, it requires that political speech takes on the oscillating justifications that follow from the circular arguments at their base.

Axiomatic-deductive reasoning can certainly be illuminating 'after the fact'. If analysts start with an empirical story, discover some apparent regularities and consider whether some distinctive rationale is at work, then some instructive patterns may emerge: an approach that tends to be the foundation of modern 'institutional' economics. But if we accept that political economic reality is human, historical and formed of open and irregular systems dependent on a biosphere, then we are bound to prefer the methods of Camp 3, political economy and ecological economics for public policy, as set out in Chapter 1. Their rejection of mathematical modelling and the preference for hypothetical, rather than axiomatic, deduction necessarily makes the resulting analyses less immaculate but more useful at the level of evolving practical knowledge. Such approaches are also likely to have superior, albeit necessarily limited, powers of prediction, since just because you cannot predict something does not mean you cannot comprehend it.[81]

I have suggested that when you apply neoclassical economics to the real political economy, you have little choice but to assume away most of the relationships and challenges it contains. This was nevertheless the leap the 'public choice' school took when it applied neoclassical economic reasoning to diagnose the political pathologies of liberal democracy and recommended Camp 1 prescriptions as their cure. Camp 1 economists' conclusions would go on to form the basis of neoliberal argument and policy. Over the decades that followed, these economists and their followers would prove notably more reluctant to admit the flaws in their approach than their Soviet

---

[81] Ernest Gellner, *Plough, Sword and Book: The Structure of Human History* (Chicago: Chicago University Press, 1989), p. 15.

counterparts, which is remarkable given the personal risks attending such critiques within the Soviet system. The reason for this is obvious, however. Soviet economists were forced to focus on the realities of state implementation and failure from the start.[82] The neoliberals of Camp 1, meanwhile, are still waiting for the day of spontaneous allocative efficiency to dawn, atop the mountain of abstraction, as the planet burns.

[82] D. Wade Hands, 'Crossing in the Night of the Cold War: Alternative Visions and Related Tensions in Western and Soviet General Equilibrium Theory', *History of Economic Ideas* 24 (2) (2016): 51–74, p. 67.

3 | On Bureaucracy

The political economic orthodoxies that dominated Western Europe and North America after the Second World War had argued that the economy must serve the social order, rather than the other way around. The horrors of the preceding decade had made that all too obvious. In Britain, Keynesianism applied fiscal and monetary policy to smooth out the cyclical booms and busts of the capitalist economy. French 'dirigisme' empowered the state to direct investments strategically. German ordoliberalism used the legal framework to sustain competition and stop markets degenerating towards monopoly and exploitation. The trade unionists Gösta Rehn and Rudolf Meidner focused Swedish government attention on active labour market policies and negotiation between labour and business to sustain overall demand and to help workers stay resilient in the face of an always changing economy.

Though their priorities varied, these strategies shared a conception of the political economy as an open-ended system. To be 'rational' after the war was consequently a process of complex reasoning – an inescapably contingent affair, defined strongly by context. Rejecting the totalitarian certainties of the far right and far left, policymakers accepted these limitations as they grappled with the immediate social and political conflicts that shaped the specific forms their policies could take. The result was a common international impulse in the post-war West to redistribute strategic authority across both public and private institutions. The nature of this distribution was shaped by culture, institutional inheritance, the political ideologies and the political economic coalitions of the time. Political priorities were defined by their explicit social purposes.

It followed that the post-war states in these countries were built to manage complexity and to guard it against capture by the politically extremist, paramilitary and corporate forces seen in the fascist takeovers of the pre-war years. The governing executive and civil service in these post-war systems would interact with private businesses to consult on strategic questions. They would act in co-determination with businesses and trade unions, but they were supposed to do so in a disinterested way, and state agencies remained distinctive entities. Even in France, with its planning and extensive industrial policies, the goal was to accelerate business investment and create an infrastructure of meritocratic recruitment. There was no Soviet-scale ambition to create a state–industrial complex that was the economy itself.[1] The complexity in each system was organised, and each emerging variety of capitalism would develop its own developmental logic.

The response in post-war political science was to ask, 'so how are these post-war states *really* run?' 'Who pays and who gains?' The spectrum of interpretation in the British and American literature ran from Marxist analysis and pessimism about the state's continuing de facto structural dominance by the owners of capital to a centre ground rooted in classical liberalism and a strong empiricism.[2] These liberal 'pluralists' examined the democratic state as a continuously evolving and complex system of institutions and processes that seemed increasingly capable of managing inclusive, adaptive change.[3] Commentary from the British Conservative right had tended to oppose the growth of the post-war state, but it did so in the traditionalist, practice-over-theory spirit of the Conservative political philosopher Michael Oakeshott, who preferred 'the familiar to the unknown...the tried to the untried, fact to mystery, the actual to the possible, the limited to the unbounded, the near to the distant, the sufficient to the super-abundant, the convenient to the perfect, present laughter to utopian bliss', and lamented those analytical stances he saw as 'ideological'.[4]

In what follows I explore how, from the 1960s onwards, neoclassical economic theorising was applied to politics as a new field of political science and how a diagnosis of state failure was constructed through

---

[1] Jonah Levy, 'From the Dirigiste State to the Social Anaesthesia State: French Economic Policy in the Longue Durée', *Modern and Contemporary France* 16 (4) (2008): 417–435.

[2] For example, Ralph Miliband, *The State and Capitalist Society* (London: Weidenfeld and Nicolson, 1969), and Robert Jessop, *The Capitalist State* (Oxford: Martin Robertson, 1982).

[3] Key texts include Robert Dahl, *Who Governs? Democracy and Power in an American City* (New Haven: Yale University Press, 1961), and Charles Lindblom, *The Intelligence of Democracy* (New York: Free Press, 1965).

[4] Michael Oakeshott, *Rationalism in Politics and Other Essays* (London and New York: Methuen, 1962).

axiomatic reasoning and adopted as an empirical, social fact by the emerging New 'neoliberal' Right. The resulting 'public choice' analysis of bureaucracy and the ideal constitution would provide the New Right with an exact counterpart to the Leninist account of the capitalist state and the need for its revolutionary transformation. The British Conservative Party's adoption of these ideas would go on to eviscerate its ideological traditions rooted in the anti-revolutionary concerns of Edmund Burke and to undermine the radical, cooperative traditions of the Labour Party.[5]

Public Choice and the Theory of State Failure

In the 1950s, the decade that brought the existence proof for general equilibrium, a new generation of Camp 2 neoclassical economists had also tried to set out the limits of free markets and to explore their observable pathologies, such as monopoly and the undesirable 'externalities' from market transactions. This new generation were particularly interested in the accumulations of excessive *private* power.[6] By this stage, critical thinking in Camp 2 about the limits of rationality, the imperfections of competition and the necessity of state intervention had encouraged a conceptual distinction between 'private' and 'public' goods. Paul Samuelson formalised this in his 1954 paper 'The Pure Theory of Public Expenditure', in which he distinguished between 'ordinary *private* consumption goods which can be parcelled out among different individuals... and *collective* consumption goods... which [we] all enjoy in common in the sense that each individual's consumption of such a goods lead to no subtraction of any other individual's consumption of that good'.[7]

The widespread adoption of this language of private and public goods in economics was a rationalisation of the public policies already put in place after the war. The neoclassical explanation for these new trends in state spending – a conversion of a contingent political change

---

[5] Edmund Burke, *Reflections on the Revolution in France* (Harmondsworth: Penguin Books, 1982) (first published in 1790).
[6] Andrew Hindmoor, 'Public Choice', in Colin Hay, Michael Lister and David Marsh, *The State: Theories and Issues* (Basingstoke: Palgrave Macmillan, 2006), p. 85.
[7] Paul Samuelson, 'The Pure Theory of Public Expenditure', *The Review of Economics and Statistics* 36 (4) (November 1954): 387–389.

into a universal axiom – was that where consumers preferred public goods a market would fail because individuals had few incentives to contribute to the cost of any good they could not be excluded from using. This made for a logical argument that the state should provide public goods that were either essential or popular or both.[8] Strictly speaking, much of what the democratic state had already been mandated to provide had fallen under the category of 'impure' public goods, such as education, where you could, in fact, exclude those who didn't pay. However, since societies so clearly benefitted from a universally educated population it was widely accepted by the 1950s that those costs should also be shared.

However, in the context of a deepening Cold War against communism, and provoked by the expansion of the state in the West, neoclassical economists at the University of Chicago and their colleagues at the University of Virginia now shifted their attention to the question of how collective *political* decision-making compared to that of individual decision-making by consumers in markets. The focus moved beyond the logic of private, to that of public choice. Neoclassical reasoning was now applied to the limitations of the state, and the result was a new analytical field of 'public choice theory' whose findings would amount to a deterministic prophecy of state failure within liberal democracy.

At this stage of theory-building through the 1960s, the application of an axiomatic-deductive, economistic logic to the procedures, structures and policies of liberal democracy was a purely academic endeavour. It involved economists of varied political affiliations, and given their methodological individualism, they could be joined by liberal political scientists and theorists of pluralism such as Robert Dahl and Charles Lindblom.[9] Public choice theory thus offered a fresh approach to debates hitherto dominated by political scientists and philosophers, sociologists, historians and public policy experts.

It is easy to see why theory-building using neoclassical reasoning was so intellectually tempting. One could take any complicated, multi-dimensional political or social institution and reimagine it as a two-dimensional sorting machine in which rational agents, with

---

[8] Hindmoor, 'Public Choice', pp. 84–85.
[9] Jean Baptiste Fleury and Alain Marciano, 'The Sound of Silence: A Review Essay of Nancy MacLean's *Democracy in Chains: The Deep History of the Radical Right's Stealth Plan for America*', Journal of Economic Literature 56 (4) (2018): 1492–1537, p. 1496.

pre-specified preferences, would navigate a series of supposedly representative, 'stylised', opportunities and constraints. The method was clean and quick, and it could produce conclusions that seemed impressively precise. Anthony Downs could thus assert that politicians and voters were rational, self-interested individuals,[10] who traded votes on a political market, where voters made purely instrumental decisions about how policy outcomes would benefit them.[11] James Buchanan and Gordon Tullock could make radical statements on the ideal decision-rules for the constitution of a society under a purely contractarian logic.[12] While conceding that altruism might exist as a political phenomenon on the margins,[13] the latter nevertheless insisted that politicians and bureaucrats, no less than economic agents in markets, were predominantly self-interested, which meant the substance of their policymaking must be restrained with constitutional force.[14] Gary Becker enlarged on the pathologies of political competition,[15] and he objected that market failures would not be solved as a matter of course by the state if the state too would fail.[16] But this was not all. Neoclassical methods were applied to the organisation of the state itself – to bureaucracy and budgets – not least by Downs and William Niskanen.[17] William Riker worked on rent-seeking via the political system,[18] and, in a testament to its roots in physics,[19] the field

---

[10] Ibid.
[11] Anthony Downs, *An Economic Theory of Democracy* (New York: Harper and Row, 1957).
[12] James Buchanan and Gordon Tullock, *The Calculus of Consent* (Ann Arbor: University of Michigan Press, 1962).
[13] James Buchanan, 'Ethical Rules, Expected Values and Large Numbers', *Ethics* 76 (1) (1965): 2–13.
[14] Buchanan and Tullock, *The Calculus of Consent*, p. 30.
[15] Gary Becker, 'Competition and Democracy', *Journal of Law and Economics* 1 (1958): 105–109.
[16] Fleury and Marciano, 'The Sound of Silence', p. 1496.
[17] Anthony Downs, *Inside Bureaucracy* (Boston: Little, Brown, 1967); William A. Niskanen, *Bureaucracy and Representative Government* (New York: Aldine-Atherton, 1971); *Bureaucracy: Servant or Master* (London: Institute of Economic Affairs, 1973).
[18] William Riker, 'The Paradox of Voting and Congressional Rules for Voting on Amendments', *American Political Science Review* 52 (2) (1958): 349–366; *The Theory of Political Coalitions* (New Haven and London: Yale University Press, 1961).
[19] Philip Mirowski, *More Heat than Light: Economics as Social Physics, Physics as Nature's Economics* (Cambridge: Cambridge University Press, 1989), pp. 61–66.

also dabbled in the problems of institutional stagnation, now recast as 'institutional entropy'.

This first generation of 'public choice' theorists objected that their Keynesian and Camp 2 neoclassical colleagues had assumed, rather than demonstrated, the capacity of the state to correct market failures. Keynesians, in allowing for state intervention, so the arguments ran, had unreasonably compared the reality of imperfect markets to a fiction of a perfect state. And it was a fiction, they argued, because whatever the rhetoric public servants might use about themselves, state actors were monopolists who presided over a political marketplace dangerously rigged against liberty, with liberty now rewritten as economic freedom.

Public choice theorists based their understanding of government and state on the neoclassical assumptions about rationality and utility maximisation that had hitherto been applied only to decision-making in markets. They claimed that axiomatic deduction from utilitarian micro-foundations would be equally scientific for the political realm, and hence a vast improvement on centuries of erudite philosophical debates about the nature of the 'common good' and historical, comparative analyses of actual systems. What public choice failed to acknowledge was the tautological nature of their own methodology: that if you insisted on these micro-foundations and the metaphor of a monopoly firm to describe the historical state, then the devastating conclusions simply followed from that assertion. The intellectual brute force was immense, and not least because John Maynard Keynes had never believed in the possibility of market completion in the neoclassical sense; his views on uncertainty made it inconceivable.

The deeper problem with this method is that to study non-economic decision-making as if it were *only*, essentially, economic decision-making is to take an almightily value-laden, analytical leap.[20] Public choice theory did not just ignore the real complexity of human economic behaviour. It asserted rather than demonstrated the equivalence of the historical state to a firm conceived as a bundle of contracts between rational agents: between a publicly oriented person in a socio-political institution and a privately oriented person in a marketplace. *Homo economicus* is a constant in all political and social settings.

[20] Dennis Mueller, *Public Choice* (Cambridge: Cambridge University Press, 1989), pp. 1–2.

To answer their questions about why the state had grown in the post-war era and about why government decisions were often imperfect, public choice theorists drew on Camp 2 concepts of market failure. Having depicted the state as a monopoly firm, they could now recount the logical ways in which agents in a monopoly might exploit that advantage for purely private gain, not least through state expansion. They could also offer a related argument against the electorate, with their claim that voters would rationally accept to be bribed with privileges and benefits from the state via the 'market for votes', namely, the electoral system. It follows as a matter of logic, however, that the market for votes will eventually drive the state towards totalitarianism. The result is a narrative in which democracy, as a system, is doomed to crowd itself out.

The prescription that followed this diagnosis was that politicians should retain the state's authority to safeguard property rights, the rule of law and sovereign defence, but no more. An enlightened government would respond to the prognosis by transferring the powers of the state 'back' to the marketplace, as the only reliable guarantor of individual liberty. This being an essentially Camp 1 neoclassical imaginary, however, said markets are presumed to work efficiently through voluntary exchanges between free individuals, with each pursuing their private self-interest. It is to the Camp 1 conception of a self-regulating economy that the authority of the state will be relinquished.[21] In its mutation from academic thought experiment to the political ideology of neoliberalism, these theories and conclusions were then assigned the status of the real.

Clearly, if you adopt this metaphor, if you accept as the basis for your new political economic orthodoxy the contrast between a theoretical monopoly and a theoretical and perfectly efficient competitive market, then it becomes *axiomatic* that the state is a Leviathan of nightmarish proportions – a behemoth destined to operate with all the worst tendencies that a theoretical monopoly might have, such as exploitative price-setting, parasitic rent-seeking and general budgetary greed and complacency. The complex motives behind the expansion of post-war welfare states could be defamed as mercenary and rejected as misguided. It is through this lens that the European Union could also

[21] Peter Self, *Government by the Market?* (Basingstoke: Macmillan Press, 1993), pp. 59–64.

be understood many years later by Britain's most extreme neoliberals as no better than a cartel of self-seeking monopoly enterprises. But if you conceive of the state in this way then the only rational solution is to break it. You must shatter the state's monopoly power and subject it to market forces wherever you can.

Looked at through the lens of cost–benefit maximising choices, government agencies were driven by budget-maximising bureaucrats who dominated their political sponsors. Political parties were no longer democratic agents of representation but brokerage agencies for the authority and revenues of the state. Interest groups, such as charities and trade unions, would only maintain the pressure on politicians in their own bids for an ever larger slice of taxpayer-funded pie.[22] It was no longer a new post-war social consensus that had increased the size of the state, but an unholy alliance between state actors rationally bent on enlarging their fiefdoms and voters who could bid for competing packages of taxes and services, all at the expense of market liberties, and of the taxpaying public as a whole. The resulting story was of a monopolist market for the supply of public goods and an infinite demand, as in any neoclassical marketplace, that sooner rather than later must crowd out the freedoms of the private sector and of the individuals within it. The implications were profoundly pessimistic: the contemporary democratic state was a purely transactional arrangement and geared towards a creeping totalitarianism. The conclusion was as incendiary as it was theoretical, a pure object of logical reasoning from entirely questionable metaphors.

It was in this vein that Tullock and Perlman argued that officials sought to maximise the size of their agency,[23] and Niskanen assumed that bureaucrats were like managers and firm owners who, in the absence of a corporate profit to chase, sought to maximise their budgets for reasons of 'salary, perquisites of the office, public reputation, power, patronage, output of bureau'.[24] But as Patrick Dunleavy explains, Niskanen's view *required* 'concentration on a narrow and economistic conception of what people want, and a strong view of

---

[22] Self, *Government*, p. 3.
[23] Gordon Tullock and Morris Perlman, *The Vote Motive: An Essay in the Economics of Politics, with Application to the British Economy* (London: Institute of Economic Affairs, 1976).
[24] Niskanen, *Bureaucracy and Representative*, p. 38.

individuals as inherent maximisers'.[25] Methodologically it had to – in carrying over neoclassical assumptions into the study of politics, public choice theory carried over the same closed-system reasoning and its inherent tautologies.

According to James Buchanan and Richard Wagner, Keynes had been deluded to think that well-informed politicians would 'do the right thing' regardless of the electoral incentives to do otherwise.[26] That governments over time might neglect the Keynesian imperative to restore the state's revenues in an economic upturn was certainly a possibility, even likely. There nevertheless remained a huge distance between that possibility and the assertion of limitless demand for ever-increasing expansion of tax and state control by an infinitely 'profit-seeking' bureaucratic elite and an electorate as witless as it was rapacious. To accept this thesis was to assume that voters could see no difference between a humane, developmental welfare state and Soviet communism and say 'stop' at some intervening point. It was to believe that no electorate would discipline a profligate government. It was to accept, without demur, the analogy between the state and a monopoly firm, as if the failure of the democratic state – the historical source of social integration in a capitalist society – was no more consequential than the bankruptcy of the only fish and chip shop in town.

Just as public choice theorists accused Keynesians of an 'antidote' fallacy, that is, of presuming that if markets fail then states must be an improvement, they now repeated the fallacy in various forms of reverse. A devotee of theorising from assumptions of perfect competition, George Stigler pitched a diagnosis of regulatory capture and democratic politics as an exponential growth market for taxpayer-funded privileges, as set against his prescription of perfectly functioning markets for private, impure and even public goods.[27] Buchanan counselled a more Hayekian acceptance of our insurmountable ignorance and imperfect markets and argued these could be mediated by the development of 'club goods', that is to

---

[25] Patrick Dunleavy, *Democracy, Bureaucracy and Public Choice: Economic Explanations in Political Science* (Hemel Hempstead: Harvester Wheatsheaf, 1991), pp. 154–156.
[26] James Buchanan and Richard Wagner, *Democracy in Deficit: The Political Legacy of Lord Keynes* (New York: Academic Press, 1977), Part I.
[27] George J. Stigler, 'Why Have the Socialists Been Winning?', *Ordo: Jahrbuch für die Ordnung von Wirtschaft und Gesellschaft* 30 (1979): 61–68.

say, 'non-rivalrous but excludable goods' provided by (barely specified) 'social groups'. In doing so he supposed that those groups could somehow, and for the first time in history, combine effectively and continuously to organise mutually beneficial goods and services to solve the historical problem of completely inadequate public goods provision by private markets.[28]

In these alternative, but equally utopian, futures, the fully informed utilitarian citizenry of the Camp 1 neoclassical imaginary would cheerfully engage in voluntary, and yet never-to-be-institutionalised, exchanges to maximise their self-interest in a stable manner, presumably until the end of time, liberated as they were from the distortionary effects of a self-aggrandising state. The result for Stigler would be stable forms of pure markets for all goods. For Buchanan it would be voluntaristic mutuality in a context of minimal state intervention. In the Austrian tradition, as we shall see, the modern democratic state should be replaced by an unfettered price mechanism and a highly selective, market-compatible range of 'social traditions' that under a self-limiting constitution would never encroach on that market. As public choice was taken up by the New Right in the English-speaking world, those politicians would presume the perfectly functioning closed-system economy of Camp 1 as the revealed economy. In Austrian narratives the ideal future demos would become a commodity space in which even an inescapably ignorant economic mankind could still navigate by the providential light of the price mechanism.

The assertion implicit within the First Welfare Theorem, that state intervention must distort an otherwise perfectly functioning market, was increasingly taken up as a social fact and rationalised through the 'diagnoses' of public choice. The resulting political script said the market should be understood as inherently superior to the state as a method for satisfying human needs, indeed, as the only 'honest' mechanism in a rationally selfish world. Politicians who understood this would rid society of the state's responsibilities for anything susceptible to upward bidding. Social democracy or, for that matter,

---

[28] James Buchanan, 'An Economic Theory of Clubs', *Economica* 32 (125) (1965): 1–14. See also Paul Lewis and Malte Dold, 'James Buchanan on the Nature of Choice, Artefactual Man and the Constitutional Moment in Political Economy', *Cambridge Journal of Economics* 44 (2020): 1159–1179.

One-Nation Conservatism could be dismissed as a sanctimonious veneer for raw self-interest. Public services should be privatised wherever possible. Government should reform whatever state operations remained in accordance with market-based conceptions of efficiency and competition.[29]

Public choice theory ignored complexity, change and uncertainty, though these were the realities that had driven the post-war democracies to significantly deepen their welfare states and their financial and environmental regulations, as elected governments tried to build social resilience and mitigate the gross injustices of an otherwise capricious capitalist system. As the midwives of social reconciliation and industrial modernisation, post-war democratic states had managed complicated tasks that shared few, if any, affinities to the simple goods and product markets of neoclassical storytelling. They were, and continued to be, run by people who typically spent their working lives trying to reconcile a frequently conflicting and ever-shifting set of political, cultural, social and economic needs and interests, in the pursuit of necessarily incomplete solutions.

In sum, the micro-foundations behind the public choice arguments for state failure were not only tendentious in philosophical term, they also ignored the history of actual states. Both the diagnoses of state failure and the laissez-faire prescriptions that followed assumed that individuals were superhumanly rational around their immediate economic interests but clueless about anything else – careless about sociopolitical or constitutional considerations and unmoved by ethics as distinct from private material gain, Buchanan's interest in how group size might affect the logic of such calculations notwithstanding.[30] The conclusions followed from the form of reasoning, rather than from empirical evidence, but to understand how such reasoning might drive a real liberal democracy like Britain towards a full-blown crisis of system, it is instructive to see how these claims are the exact counterpart to the early Bolshevik arguments for revolution. Both doctrines promised to dispel our romantic illusions about democracy and the state and to enlighten us with science, albeit normative political philosophy dressed up as science. If we set the Leninist and public choice analyses of bureaucracy and the ideal constitution side by side, we can see how precisely this mirroring plays out.

[29] Self, *Government*, p. ix.   [30] Buchanan, 'Ethical Rules', p. 1.

The Bureaucracy as the 'Real' Seat of Power

In his 1917 work 'The State and Revolution',[31] Vladimir Ilyich Lenin saw the bourgeois capitalist state as operating in a purely instrumental form, driven by the class interests of the bourgeoisie against those of the working classes. While Lenin's critique of the democratic state is based on class, and Niskanen's on a utilitarian logic, both impose a purely materialist form of closed-system reasoning onto the bureaucratic reality, and both remake it in that image.

For Lenin, a democratic parliament was merely a talking shop, and the real power lay with the bureaucracy – a bureaucracy controlled by, and operating in the interests of, the capitalist class. The positional advantages of these actors must separate the governing institutions from the people; bureaucrats and parliamentarians alike would strive only to benefit from their own positions at the service of the bourgeoisie,[32] and the role of parliament was to mystify this reality.[33] In Leninism, as in public choice, therefore, bureaucrats are but functionaries of the deeper material order.

For Niskanen, the 'democratic' bureaucracy is likewise the master and not the servant of the political elite and it serves its own interests, and again this follows from what is supposed to be the only salient form of subjectivity.[34] In his view this subjectivity is formed through self-interest and not class interest, but it is a subjectivity formed entirely by the prevailing material order just the same. Neither the Leninist nor the public choice argument can conceive of people who break free of their material bonds; who find motivation in the job itself, for example, whether in some high vocational sense of public service or through the simpler, professional satisfaction of solving a consequential social problem with a degree of success. Neither theory can conceive of morality or craftsmanship, as distinct from a materialist calculus. As the heroine of Tom Stoppard's play *Darkside*

---

[31] Vladimir Ilyich Lenin, 'The State and Revolution: The Marxist Theory of the State and the Tasks of the Proletariat in the Revolution', in *Collected Works*, Vol. 25 (Moscow: Progress Publishers, 1964) (first published in 1917), pp. 381–492.

[32] Lenin, 'The State and Revolution', pp. 423–424.

[33] Erik Olin Wright, 'To Control or to Smash Bureaucracy: Weber and Lenin on Politics, the State and Bureaucracy', *Berkeley Journal of Sociology* 19 (1974–1975): 69–108, p. 82.

[34] Niskanen, *Bureaucracy: Servant or Master*, pp. 22–23.

complains of utilitarian rationalisations, 'If kindness is only selfishness in disguise... the question "what is the good?" wouldn't be about anything except what's best for you, and what's moral about *that*?'[35]

In his 1971 *Bureaucracy and Representative Government,* Niskanen had argued that beyond the ease of managing his own bureau, every possible goal of a bureaucratic chief is positively and invariably related to the size of his budget, as it would be for the executive of a profit-seeking firm.[36] For both Lenin and Niskanen, it is the predetermined materialist order in an uncomprehending society that makes the bureaucracy the 'real' centre of power and continuously reinforces it, that is, until the 'correct' action is taken to release the people from its grip. For Lenin, this rupture meant the takeover of the state by revolutionary socialists who would harness its power in the construction of the socialist path to communism. For Niskanen, liberation required the state's deconstruction through market forces: its decomposition into competing units, wage incentives for cost-cutting agency managers and competition between public and private providers in service provision.

Such is the Cold War legacy of the Soviet era that a reader from 'the West' could be forgiven for thinking the Communist Party had always gloried in its centralised bureaucratic forms. But to believe that is to collapse the real history of the idea of 'democracy' in the Soviet system. In practice, the idea was a living albeit repeatedly harassed, resurrected, and defeated concept throughout the lifetime of the regime. In 'The State and Revolution', Lenin had looked to the Paris Commune of 1871 and raised the prospect of a direct democracy in which workers would represent themselves throughout new structures. Since so much of the capitalist state was taken up with the oppression of the working classes, such a bureaucratic machine should be smashed and replaced with the self-organising mechanism of a socialist economy.[37] For Karl Marx and Lenin alike, bourgeois democracy was a sham because it limited popular participation to elections alone and left real power to the bureaucracy, which was a constant.[38] In his projections

---

[35] Tom Stoppard, *Darkside*, BBC Radio 2, first broadcast on 26 August 2013.
[36] Niskanen, *Bureaucracy and Representative Government*, p. 38.
[37] Anthony Polan, *Lenin and the End of Politics* (London: Methuen Ltd, 1984), p. 58.
[38] David Priestland, 'Soviet Democracy 1917–1991', *European History Quarterly* 32 (1) (2002): 111–130.

of the communism to come, Lenin had evoked government by popular mass meetings and the election of bureaucrats. Among 'The Immediate Tasks of the Soviet Government', in 1918, he had called for 'the fight against the bureaucratic distortion of the Soviet form of organisation' and the need for varied forms and methods of control 'from below'.[39] According to Lenin, however, this distortion was no longer that of the capitalist state but the product of economic backwardness.[40]

At the start of the Soviet revolution, in other words, we can find an exact socialist reflection of the radically decentralising solutions to bureaucracy that Niskanen would embrace as long-time chairman of the economically libertarian Cato Institute. From Niskanen's perspective, choices would be made best through the frictionless marketplace of equal economic agents envisioned in the Camp 1 neoclassical imaginary. For the Soviet left, the pathologies of bureaucracy should be democratised by workers' representation and accountability at every level. To escape the instrumentalist state that exploits the predetermined laws of accumulation in a parliamentary democracy, the utopian right and left necessarily agree that the revolutionary effort should aim at maximal decentralisation in a form consistent with the essential rationality of the no longer deceived citizen. Both tell a story of radical liberation in a world of universally rational economic agents, and both anticipate a completely transformed terrain that thereafter will be free of exploitation and rentier impulses of any kind.

Leninists and neoliberals held diametrically opposed beliefs about the nature of the rationality in question, but as we shall see in Chapter 4, their shared beliefs would lead both to create parodies of that rationality through their utopia-building states as they embarked along their respective revolutionary roads. It was also in the closed-system nature of their reasoning that both doctrines possessed a ready explanation for any persistent failures. Where increasing bureaucracy within the Soviet system would be read as proof of a resilient bourgeois corruption and 'backwardness' by the Soviet left, the neoliberal right would decry their own policy failures as caused by the lingering resistance of a still self-interested, if not tactically socialist, bureaucratic 'elite'.

---

[39] Vladimir Ilyich Lenin, 'The Immediate Tasks of the Soviet Government', in *Collected Works*, Vol. 27 (Moscow: Progress Publishers, 1972) (first published in 1918), Section 8.
[40] Lenin, 'The State and Revolution', p. 383.

The only logical solution in both cases is to double down on the strategies of revolutionary change.

If we accept that Leninism offers a reductionist caricature of bureaucracy in a modern capitalist democracy, we must recognise that the caricature in public choice analyses is necessarily identical in both scale and form. Downs and Niskanen alike assume that a bureaucracy is a uniformly hierarchical organisation and the behaviour (utility function) of bureaucrats is translated into analogies for profit-seeking only. Through the standard neoclassical practice of aggregation from the particular case, any given bureau is axiomatically taken to be a 'representative agent' of all bureaus, so that every bureau is interchangeable.[41] Niskanen lifts standard concepts and behavioural axioms from neoclassical economics and essentially plays around with the possible behaviours of 'a bureaucrat' who is ascribed a utility function as an economic agent with monopoly powers. Said bureaucrat is made to dance the steps produced by logical opportunities for self-seeking within a predetermined set of parameters. Instead of dealing with the realities of administrative culture, social complexity, uncertainty, political conflict, cooperation, expertise or interdependence in actual democratic bureaucracies, these are airbrushed from the picture, but essentially because neoclassical methods leave Niskanen no other option, as Dunleavy pointed out.

Niskanen's thesis, that the self-interested behaviour of bureaucrats will lead to the chronic oversupply of public goods, is built on the idea that the combination of bureaucratic monopoly power, budget-maximising bureaucrats and fragmented political sponsors means 'the bureau' will tend to overproduce beyond some deductively derived 'equilibrium' level for social welfare. He simply assumes that a government agency has a bilateral monopoly with its political sponsor and can impose their preferences because of their monopoly power.[42] Consistent with utilitarian economic man, the desires of the bureaucratic agent are assumed to be infinite. The 'CEO' of any given bureau will seek infinite profit. Never mind that any actual permanent secretary who behaved this way would be gently encouraged to go home and lie down.

Dunleavy concluded that the resulting theoretical pathologies indicated 'the retreat into a formalised political "world"; the fragmenting

---

[41] Dunleavy, *Democracy*, p. 162.
[42] Niskanen, *Bureaucracy and Representative Government*, pp. 30, 64.

of "messy" political experience into tightly circumscribed and non-interacting technical problems; the general non-testing (indeed bolt-on proofing) of theorems against empirical evidence'.[43] What happens, in other words, is that the mechanics of the model and the depiction of key agents as human atoms, unvarying in their response to context-free triggers, make for a closed-system fiction. The story achieved the ring of political plausibility, however, not just because of existing problems within contemporary state agencies but because in the 1970s – the era of a fragile détente – Niskanen's all-consuming bureaucracy evoked a Leviathan of Soviet proportions.

The most striking thing about these arguments overall is their empirical weakness. In their work on institutional entropy, for example, Richard Auster and Morris Silver considered the liabilities of voters akin to those of dispersed shareholders as they sought, and failed, to hold the state to account. What passed unnoticed was that by seeing the state as the functional equivalent of a single monopoly firm that distorted the competitive market,[44] these authors placed themselves in the same metaphorical woods as the Soviets. The latter had often used the image of a single factory to describe the national economy in state hands – a conception of planning rejected by Leon Trotsky for requiring the capacity of a 'Universal Mind', as conceived by Pierre-Simon Laplace.[45]

As Dunleavy notes, these budget-maximising models typically justified themselves by alluding to the extent of post-war government growth, but they offered no evidence to establish any causal link from bureaucratic behaviour to expansion, and there were many alternative, and more demonstrable, explanations.[46] Among them was the fact that in the aftermath of the economic devastation of the 1930s and the collective tragedy of the war, political parties and their voters had concluded that an inclusive welfare state was not simply socially just and more economically efficient but an essential foundation for peace. The development of welfare states had offered imperfect progress in a manifestly imperfect world. Moreover, if all bureaucratic

---

[43] Dunleavy, *Democracy*, p. 259.
[44] Richard Auster and Morris Silver, *The State as a Firm: Economic Forces in Political Development* (The Hague: Marinus Nijhoff, 1979), pp. 73–74.
[45] Paul Craig Roberts, 'The Polycentric Soviet Economy', *The Journal of Law & Economics* 12 (1) (1969): 163–179, pp. 168–169, p. 173.
[46] Dunleavy, *Democracy*, p. 247.

motivations were identical, we could hardly account for the significant international variations in the post-war forms of government and in the organisation of those states, nor for the diverse forms of political economy over which they governed.[47]

Lenin on 'the Withering Away of the State'

It is one of the most remarkable achievements of the democratic state that it allows an inescapably imperfect society to adapt, continuously. A democratic state is supposed to allow universal representation and accountability, as well as to make that meaningful in practical terms through an open-ended system of policymaking and administration. The emphasis in a liberal democracy is on constitutional checks and balances on power and on divisions between the political executive, legislature and judiciary. These are built on an evolving foundation of laws to protect civil, political and, by the twentieth century, social rights.[48] It is through these institutions that an open society is, ideally, able to learn from its successes and mistakes, insofar as this is possible.

The ideal constitution of the materialist utopians is completely different, and since public choice theory and Leninism agree that the bureaucratic state in a liberal democracy stands between the people and their liberty, we should not be surprised to find their solutions are essentially the same. Both argue that the state should be transformed with a view to its ultimate 'withering away', so that the self-regulating freedoms of their 'true' economy may abide. Because of the presumed rational egotism of law makers, public choice theory prescribed a self-limiting 'neutral state'. The vision of that perfectly neutral state varied by author and school, but what they held in common is the principle that the political system should be constrained from intervening in markets by constitutional limits on the size and scope of government. Instead of procedural rules of democratic decision, and the sovereign right of the citizenry to change their minds about the substance

---

[47] See, for example, Gøsta Esping Andersen, *The Three Worlds of Welfare Capitalism* (Princeton: Princeton University Press, 1990), and Peter Hall and David Soskice, *Varieties of Capitalism: The Institutional Foundations of Comparative Advantage* (Oxford: Oxford University Press, 2001).

[48] Thomas Marshall, *Citizenship and Social Class: And Other Essays* (Cambridge: Cambridge University Press, 1950).

of policy, public choice theory dictated specific political economic content, and this vision has its analogue in the Soviet canon.

In contrast to the revolutionary guidance of his 1902 'What Is to Be Done?',[49] Lenin's 'The State and Revolution' is a largely theoretical work, and it is here that he looked into the future and set out his prophecies for the new socialist order.[50] In Chapter 5 of this work, 'On the Economic Basis of the Withering Away of the State', Lenin had argued the revolution would bring about a shift in the mode of production that would slowly enable the withering away of the administrative, judicial and executive institutions of the state and with it the apparatus of class domination. That the state be left to wither gradually rather than be abolished was a rebuke to the anarchists, but it was also a function of Lenin's assumption that it was only through the creation of a new material order that the nature of human subjectivity would change. It followed that to simply collapse the state would be to lose the directing instrument of that transformation.[51]

Though Lenin was careful not to set a date, the promise of a stateless Eden was nevertheless made. With deft use of the circular reasoning that would go on to cripple the actually existing Soviet economy, Lenin declared in Chapter 5:

It will become possible for the state to wither away completely when society adopts the [Marxist] rule: 'From each according to his ability, to each according to his needs,' *i.e.*, when people have become so accustomed to observing the fundamental rules of social intercourse and when their labour becomes so productive that they will voluntarily work according to their ability.[52]

Lenin had echoed Friedrich Engels to argue that as socialist subjectivity began to replace subjection to the old regime, so the state would cease to govern persons but would administer only things. Thus he argued in Chapter 3,

---

[49] Vladimir Ilyich Lenin, 'What Is to Be Done?', in *Collected Works*, Vol. 5 (Moscow: Foreign Languages Publishing House, 1961) (first published in 1902), pp. 347–530.
[50] Rodney Barfield, 'Lenin's Utopianism: State and Revolution', *Slavic Review* 30 (1) (March 1971): 45–56, p. 46.
[51] Zhivka Valiavicharska, 'Socialist Modes of Governance and the Withering Away of the State: Revisiting Lenin's State and Revolution', *Theory and Event* 13 (2) (2010): 1–21.
[52] Lenin, 'The State and Revolution', p. 469.

Such a beginning, on the basis of large scale production, will of itself lead to a gradual 'withering away' of all bureaucracy, to the gradual creation of an order... an order under which under the function of control and accounting, becoming more and more simple, will be performed by each in turn, will then become a habit and will finally die out as the special function of a special section of the population.[53]

In 1961, at the Twenty-Second Congress of the Communist Part of the Soviet Union, Nikita Khrushchev promised that communism would be built 'in the main' by 1980.[54]

For the theorists who would go on to furnish the New Right with the neoliberal agenda, the idealised future was a return, not to the native realm of our primitive collectivism but to an asserted natural harmony in which liberty would be best assured by a maximal market freedom and a parliament bound by a self-limiting constitution. Before we turn in more detail to the various public choice positions on the ideal economic constitution, however, it is worth pausing to reflect on the Austrian contribution to this debate. It is important, and not least because Friedrich August von Hayek's attention to the limits of knowledge expose not just the fatal flaws in Soviet expectations but, ceteris paribus, those in the neoclassical design.

The Austrian Road

For Hayek, the basis of future social harmony is to be found in a spontaneous order comprised of the invisible hand of the market, our knowledge gained from experience and, via a convenient metaphor from Darwin, the natural selection of cultural traditions.[55] As discussed in Chapter 1, Hayek had increasingly doubted that markets tended towards any kind of self-achieving equilibrium or that 'how the economy really worked' could be captured mathematically. He came instead to see competition primarily as a 'discovery mechanism' for new methods and goods.[56] Unable to explain how such workings

---

[53] Lenin, 'The State and Revolution', p. 431.
[54] William Tompson, *Khrushchev: A Political Life* (New York: St. Martin's Press, 1997), p. 238.
[55] John Gray, *Hayek: On Liberty* (London: Routledge, 1984), pp. 32, 106, 147.
[56] Richard Bronk, *The Romantic Economist: Imagination in Economics* (Cambridge: Cambridge University Press, 2009), pp. 263–264, p. 210.

could be observed, however,[57] his argument could only be rendered as an interesting intuition as distinct from a well-specified theory.

The central problem of economics for Hayek was not the neoclassical preoccupation with the efficient use of scarce resources but with the generation and use of dispersed knowledge. It followed for Hayek that the only realistic economics is microeconomics.[58] Any attempts to aggregate to the macro level, to simply scale up from individual behaviour to group or system dynamics, would be foolhardy – a warning as consequential for his neoclassical colleagues as it was for his socialist opponents. It was this pessimism around information that led Hayek to reject the modern uses of the state,[59] as well as to argue that aside from the rule of law, the most benign public institutions would be those deposited by evolving social 'tradition': from human action but not from human design.[60]

Hayek's belief that spontaneous social selection over time would preserve only the more benevolent traditional values is as implausible as it is ahistorical, however. The implication is that whatever is thrown up by the combination of social traditions and free markets within a law-abiding society must be better because it conforms best to Hayek's principles of limited knowledge and non-encroachment on individual choice, regardless of its actual social or moral shape. He appears uninterested in the possibility that traditions and interests may thrive because they are backed by higher material resources or embedded cultural power – because they have might on their side, as distinct from being in any way more economically productive or ethically superior. Speaking as a woman I find this claim so staggeringly complacent it is almost charming.

Hayek's choices are remarkably selective even within their own terms. The trade union movement in Britain was a highly spontaneous emanation of evolving social values. It had emerged to protect the liberty of individual choice to resist the oppression of exploitative and thus involuntary economic relationships. Such organic actions against economic coercion are nevertheless ruled out of court insofar as they constrain the market. Hayek's analysis also fails to acknowledge that, left unregulated, business corporations might potentially wield as

---

[57] Jeremy Shearmur, *Hayek and After: Hayekian Liberalism as a Research Program* (London: Routledge, 1996), pp. 50–53.
[58] Gray, *Hayek*, p. 83.   [59] Ibid., p. 89.   [60] Ibid., p. 32.

much socio-economic power as, if not more than, the public authorities that so alarmed him. This was no small omission. As we can see all too vividly today, if you disintegrate the state in conditions characterised by intensifying corporate monopoly and financial extraction, you find yourself in a capitalist order scarcely less coercive for many than the overbearing state of Hayek's nightmares.

Hayek's contribution to the philosophy of knowledge is immense, but it is pure dogmatism to insist that because we can know only a little, we should pretend that we know nothing at all about the tendencies of markets and states in institutional terms. The result is an impossibility theorem about the limits of rational government as constrained by limits on information, and as John Gray concluded, it amounts to 'a scientific defence of tradition against rational reform'.[61] The impulse in Hayek is to abandon the democratic institutions of the modern world in favour of a return to the laissez-faire economics that had proved so catastrophic less than a decade before he wrote *The Road to Serfdom*,[62] and it is a strange conclusion for a man who believed in the wisdom born of experience. *The Road to Serfdom* is a critique of totalitarianism written in the ardent hope of a spontaneous system of order, but as Gray points out, if history tells us anything, it is that the freer the market, the more it will actively subvert those traditions on which Hayek's superior social order is supposed to be based.[63]

Though more realistic about informational limits and more sceptical of the power of maths to capture an economy, Hayek's ideal constitution is no less wilfully selective than its neoclassical rivals. The thesis of *The Road to Serfdom*, arguably Hayek's most influential work, was that socialism inevitably leads to despotism if not totalitarianism. The book was published in 1944 and asserted that the Nazis could succeed in Germany because the socialists had completed the intellectual work of weakening the desire for liberty. He warned that Britain had set itself on this same road when its leading parties engaged in wartime and post-war planning. And yet by 1944 it was, amongst other factors, this planning capacity that had allowed Britain to defend itself, and happily Hayek too, then teaching at the London School of Economics

---

[61] Ibid., pp. 145–147.
[62] Friedrich August von Hayek, *The Road to Serfdom* (Chicago: University of Chicago Press, 2007) (first published in 1944).
[63] Gray, Hayek, p. 149.

and Political Science. For such a brilliant thinker, Hayek was capable of obviously false dichotomies. To claim that total planning must fail, therefore any planning is dangerous was to insist that because you can drown in water, you shouldn't drink.

If we return to the public choice quarter, Buchanan had objected that Hayek's insistence on evolutionary order, limited government and judicial process was too weak a defence of liberty, though he shared Hayek's scepticism about the capacity of individuals to anticipate the consequences of their actions beyond their private spaces. By assuming that the pursuit of material self-interest was a universal fact not just of economic but of political life, Buchanan and Tullock would nevertheless agree with Hayek that the dynamics of modern democratic society would enable totalitarianism. The value of democratic political exchange via the democratic state would be vitiated by the pursuit of material self-interest.[64] Rather than build legal safeguards against an authoritarian concentration of private and public power, however, they preferred to see constitutional limits on taxation and state spending. Using axiomatic-deductive reasoning, they objected that state expansions must operate as a tyranny of the majority over the minority. 'Rational individuals' under 'generational uncertainty' that prevented them from knowing how their constitutional choice might play out would choose a constitutional design that protected individual liberties and secured private capital from taxation.[65]

Buchanan was at least logically consistent. He acknowledged that agreement to such a self-limiting constitution required a unanimous support that was unlikely in a democracy given the electoral pathologies identified in public choice.[66] However, it is not at all clear, for example, why rational individuals unable to foretell the collective consequences of their private choices would not choose constitutional rules that were the exact opposite of Buchanan's.[67] Under a 'veil of ignorance', why would we not guarantee social justice and limit inequality, as argued by John Rawls in *A Theory of Social Justice*?[68]

---

[64] Self, *Government*, p. 52.
[65] Buchanan and Tullock, *The Calculus of Consent*, p. ix.
[66] James Buchanan, *Liberty, Market and State* (Brighton: Wheatsheaf, 1986), pp. 55–69.
[67] Self, *Government*, p. 53.
[68] John Rawls, *A Theory of Social Justice* (Cambridge, MA: Harvard University Press, 1971).

Buchanan's later work with Geoffrey Brennan nevertheless repeats the argument that the state will always try to exploit its citizens and that citizens should adopt constitutional rules to limit the governments' tax base.[69] Given Buchanan's earlier critical emphasis on the non-teleological elements of individual choice, however, it is unclear how he could have reached so clear a solution without the normative bias afforded him by a convenient return to Camp 1 assumptions.[70]

Though these economics philosophers offered a variety of supposedly neutral and liberty-protecting constitutional ideals, they all shared a peculiarly plutocratic vision of Eden: one review of Hayek's *The Constitution of Liberty* called it 'The Constitution of Perpetual Privilege'.[71] Their ahistorical presumptions about the socially benign character of unregulated markets expose how, though different, the Austrian and public choice schools are equally partial in their reasoning and hostile to basic liberal democratic norms. As Stigler put it openly,

The alternative [to radically shrinking the state] is to abandon total acceptance of present-day democratic institutions. I must hasten to say that this is not to argue for totalitarianism in any form. Indeed, some alternative political systems that would ensure a substantial reduction in the government role could be even more democratic in the sense that public policies could be closer to the desires of individual citizens.[72]

Not totalitarian then, so long as you shared Stigler's political beliefs, and never changed your mind. As Peter Self concluded, the aims of public choice were fundamentally hostile to a plurality of political economic preferences in free societies, and a democracy that is acceptable only when politicians with the 'right goals' are in power is no meaningful democracy at all.[73] As we will see in Chapter 9, however, precisely this logic would play out in the United Kingdom with a shift to openly authoritarian governmental practices in the aftermath of Brexit.

---

[69] Geoffrey Brennan and James Buchanan, *The Power to Tax: Analytical Foundations of the Fiscal Constitution* (Cambridge: Cambridge University Press, 1980).
[70] Lewis and Dold, 'James Buchanan', p. 1170.
[71] Christian Bay, 'Hayek's Liberalism: The Constitution of Perpetual Privilege', *Political Science Review* 1 (Fall 1971): 93–124.
[72] Stigler, 'Why Have the Socialists Been Winning', p. 67.
[73] Self, *Government*, p. 193.

The public choice arguments for the withering state are, if anything, more completely circular than their Leninist counterpart, as befits the more completely de-historicised basis of their case-making. To paraphrase Lenin, in the preferred economic constitutions of the New Right's leading intellectuals, it will become possible for the state to wither away to the 'nightwatchman' protection of property rights, the legal order and systems of defence when society adopts the rule 'From each according to his utility, to each according to his utility'. Both Hayek and Buchanan may have rejected the methodologies of aggregation in neoclassical economics, but that 'things would turn out better' in their constitutional schemes would depend entirely on the existence of a stable general equilibrium in the economy – a prospect that Hayek entirely doubted and that Buchanan was forced to rationalise in an essentially Walrasian way.[74] To Buchanan's credit he had tried to convert his neoclassical colleagues back from their purely atomistic, computational depictions of 'choice' towards individual choices within a three-dimensional social-institutional context. He had also understood this discussion as an essentially normative debate, but his selectively 'rationalist' economic constitutionalism was no less influential on the New Right for that. Where Lenin had viewed capitalist democracy as a deflection from the path of reason,[75] the market fundamentalists of the Chicago and Virginia schools had likewise determined that to as near as damn it dissolve the modern state was to clear an equally straight road to the place of everlasting peace, albeit one with a far greater choice of shoes.

Because the application of economic methods to political and social decisions is ultimately a method of reasoning, it is worth remembering that the method can operate in principle with varied assumptions about the decision-making environment and about the actor making the decision. There consequently developed a fierce debate among later generations of public choice theorists as to the value of the state's role in enhancing, rather than damaging, individual liberty. It should not surprise us, however, that this subsequent debate bears a close

---

[74] James M. Buchanan, 'What Should Economists Do?', *Southern Economic Journal* 30 (3) (1964): 213–222. p. 218.
[75] Zygmunt Bauman, 'A Post-modern Revolution?', in Janina Frentzel-Zagórska, *From a One-Party State to Democracy: Transition in Eastern Europe* (Leiden: Poznan Studies in the Philosophy of Sciences and the Humanities, 1993), pp. 3–21, p. 13.

resemblance to that between Camp 1 and Camp 2 neoclassical economists about the relative intensity of informational and other market failures in any given situation. Such a theoretical development would have to take this path because it is the highly circumscribed method, rather than empirical observation of an open-ended reality, that dictates the range of possible permutations.

The Weberian Alternative

For analytical perspective it is worth contrasting these purely materialist accounts of the state, bureaucracy and politics with the sociological account of Max Weber, written in the same year as Lenin's 'The State and Revolution'. In his 1917 'Parliament and Government'[76] and his posthumously published 1921 essay 'Bureaucracy',[77] Weber wrestled with many of the same questions about how the state could be controlled by the people and rendered accountable.[78] His argument, built from sociological observation of multiple systems, was that control over bureaucracy is a constant balancing act and only achieved through vital democratic political institutions. He had also concluded that bureaucracies were an essential and inescapable feature of modernity and of the rising sophistication and expanded applications of technology. Far from Lenin's sweeping optimism about the organisational simplicity of the socialism to come, and Niskanen's later confidence in the market, Weber saw the increase in bureaucratic capacity as arising from the disappearance of small-scale production, from increases in education, from the new technologies of communication and from the growing interdependence of economic sectors in a developed economy.[79] It was consequently clear to Weber that bureaucracy, at least in some form, could not be eliminated. How could it be, when it was the 'means of carrying "community action" over into rationally ordered "societal action"'? It followed that the

---

[76] Max Weber, 'Parliament and Government in Germany Under a New Political Order' (1917), in Peter Lassman and Ronald Spiers, *Weber: Political Writings* (Cambridge: Cambridge University Press, 1994), pp. 130–272.
[77] Max Weber, 'Bureaucracy' (1921), in Hans Gerth and Charles Wright Mills, *From Max Weber: Essays in Sociology* (Abingdon: Routledge, 1991), pp. 196–240.
[78] Olin Wright, 'To Control or to Smash Bureaucracy', p. 69.
[79] Polan, *Lenin*, p. 61.

real challenge was to guarantee its continuous flexibility and accountability to the population.

Weber had also regarded control of the bureaucratic apparatus as a 'power instrument of the first order',[80] and so society needed effective supervisory institutions and a responsible and competent political leadership to direct them. In this view it is the vitality of democratic politics that offers the best defence against excessive bureaucratic or executive autonomy. Only when a democratic parliament could meaningfully engage with the work of government would it be possible to create responsible and competent leadership, and it is this leadership in turn that will keep the bureaucracy well directed, even as their work continues to be scrutinised by a capable parliament.[81]

In keeping with the open-system ontology of liberal democracies, the actual post-war bureaucracies had developed along notably Weberian lines. Weber had famously defined the rule-bound state as enshrining 'rational-legal authority' – a mode of reasoning and rule-bound governance that distinguished the modern state from the patrimonial and feudal power struggles that had gone before.[82] Post-war bureaucracies in the advanced capitalist states had typically carried the following features:

- Fixed spheres of competence.
- A defined hierarchy of offices.
- A clear distinction between the public and private roles (and property) of officials.
- Specialisation, expertise and professionalism as the basis of action.
- Full-time career appointments for officials and public actors.
- Management by the application of a slowly evolving set of rules and professional skills.
- Indicative/input planning.[83]

In Britain, the public administration had been subject to significant modernising reforms since the aftermath of the Napoleonic wars. William Pitt the Younger had been intent on more professional government and limiting the political patronage, corruption, nepotism and

---

[80] Weber, '*Bureaucracy*', pp. 228–230.
[81] Olin Wright, 'To Control or to Smash Bureaucracy', p. 92.
[82] Weber, 'Bureaucracy', p. 196.
[83] Christopher Politt and Geert Bouckaert, *Public Management Reform: A Comparative Analysis: New Public Management, Governance, and the Neo-Weberian State* (Oxford: Oxford University Press, 2011), pp. 71–72.

incompetence that threatened a revolt, if not a revolution, unless it was pre-emptively reformed from inside.[84] Later, Victorian administrations had moved to consolidate these efforts by developing a permanent, and politically neutral, service. The 1854 Northcote–Trevelyan report on the organisation of the permanent civil service had set out the core values of integrity, honesty, objectivity and political impartiality and introduced appointments based on merit through open competition.

In 1918, the Haldane Report, highly Weberian in spirit, had set out the principles that should direct the government's research, use of evidence and formation of policy. It recommended that as government had become more complex, departments should be organised around functions; coordination should be improved but so should accountability to parliament and the evidence-based partnerships of ministers and officials.[85] Richard Haldane had argued that government required investigation and reflexive thought in all departments to do its job well, indeed, 'continuous acquisition of knowledge and the prosecution of research' were needed 'to furnish a proper basis for policy'. The report concluded that the tacit knowledge of civil servants and politicians, supported by departments invested with deep expertise in their field, would allow the state to cope with the challenges of modernity.[86] This was, in essence, a statement about the importance of the scientific method in government. Again, there were many national variations on these Weberian themes in the West European context, but in specific service sectors such as health or education, for example, professional expertise was seen as a central form of coordination, in which teachers and clinicians played a prominent role not just at the service interface but in the development, organisation and management of these services.[87] The essential principles were nevertheless those of a standing cadre of public servants who were subject

---

[84] Michael Duffy, *The Younger Pitt* (New York: Longman, 2000), Chapter 4.
[85] Hugh Pemberton, *The UK's Public Admin Failures: Round Up the Unusual Suspects*, Personal Blog, 9 October 2020; Rodney Lowe and Hugh Pemberton, *The Official History of the Civil Service. Reforming the Civil Service, Volume II: The Thatcher and Major Revolutions, 1982–1997* (Abingdon: Routledge, 2020).
[86] Ministry of Reconstruction, *Report of the Machinery of Government Committee* (London: HMSO, 1918).
[87] Janet Newman and John Clark, *The Managerial State: Power, Politics, and Ideology in the Remaking of the Modern Welfare State* (London: SAGE, 1997), Chapter 1.

to codes of political control and accountability and who operated in clearly demarcated institutions. At their best they aspired to a scientific development of policy based on hypothetical deduction, where those policies were designed to achieve the social purposes defined in the political realm.

The public choice account of an essentially wasteful, corrupt and abusive monopoly state consequently constituted no less of a threat to the liberal democratic order than Lenin's, the absence of revolutionary violence notwithstanding. Both were predicated on a materialist utopia asserted as a complete and scientific representation of reality. To make an actual system conform to the neoclassical imaginary in its first-best world form, however, would require a revolutionary shift in the institutions of state and, as with Leninism, a re-engineering of the human soul.

4 | On 'Organised Forgetting' in the Governing Science

When does the lack of realism in a 'model' matter? The London Tube map is an abstraction and useful shorthand for the real terrain. But for any heuristic device, such as a schematic model, there are degrees of simplification available, and this can become absurd, particularly when the foundational metaphors are suspect to begin with. As Steven Fleetwood explains, the process of abstraction is necessary in any kind of theoretical model, but 'it involves focusing upon certain causal mechanisms without assuming the non-existence, or non-influence of other mechanisms *not* in focus at this stage of the analysis'. In any model or theory that aspires to capture something of the social world as we experience it, the influential causal mechanisms from which we abstracted at one stage must be brought in at later stages. His point is that 'abstracting' is not just 'conveniently forgetting'. There is a critical distinction between idealising a causal mechanism and turning it into fiction, and as Fleetwood warns, when this fictionalisation occurs, 'then claims, concepts, ideas, theories, or conclusions drawn at an early stage might become null and void at a later stage'.[1]

The more complex the real environment, the more problematic the dependence on axiomatic-deductive neoclassical modelling becomes, whether in the public choice diagnoses or the prescriptions that became the bases of neoliberal policy. The London Tube map is a functionally accurate representation of a system of actual tunnels. It realistically shows you how to reach every station by an actual train. By contrast, the teleological Arrow-Debreu model of general equilibrium is completely unreal. You can travel the world looking for anything that resembles their terrain and never find it, let alone verify the putative moment of balance, as Kenneth Arrow and Gerard Debreu themselves acknowledged.

---

[1] Steven Fleetwood, 'The Critical Realist Conception of Open and Closed System', *Journal of Economic Methodology* 24 (1) (2017): 41–68, p. 45.

Economists influenced by Alfred Marshall would argue that elaborate mathematical models for general equilibrium that try to map every interdependent part of the economy are impractical. Simpler supply and demand models for individual markets or a particular subset of the economy known as 'partial equilibrium' models would give you more useable information.[2] But depending on the complexity and inter-relatedness of the market in question, the analytical value of these models would still be undermined by the reality of radical uncertainty, the complexity of intervening variables and the stubborn problems of aggregation.[3] Such models in complex environments might find coincidental points of accuracy but in the way that a stopped clock is right twice a day. The more dynamic the actual conditions, the more these models are guaranteed to be at best uninformative and at worst actively misleading about the social and institutional forces at hand. The policies of the British neoliberal state would be based on models that were remarkably pure fictions.

So long as neoclassical models remained confined to the academic economists who understood them as thought experiments they could do comparatively little harm. From the 1970s onwards, however, the claims derived from Camp 1 models, and Camp 2 for New Labour, were promoted via think tanks, political associations and business lobbies as robust statements about social reality. When translated into strategies they would prove profoundly disruptive and sometimes completely destructive of existing institutions and their functionality. To implement policy derived from neoclassical reasoning into real public institutions would undermine the existing institutional architecture, even as it failed to manifest the virtues promised in theory. With so many relationships within the institutional matrix of the actual state, the disruption of one sector would have serious consequences for others, whether already 'reformed' or not.

Whether it is through the neoclassical fictions of public choice theory or the blatant selection biases of the Austrian School, the intellectual fathers of the neoliberal revolution asserted that the idealised conditions of theory could be replicated in practice, regardless of our

---

[2] Richard Bronk, *The Romantic Economist: Imagination in Economics* (Cambridge: Cambridge University Press, 2009), pp. 263–264, p. 69
[3] Philip Mirowski, 'A Revisionist's View of the History of Economic Thought', *Challenge* 48 (5) (September–October 2005): 79–94, p. 86.

ample experience to the contrary. To offer a single but important illustration of the things we know that a Camp 1 government would prefer us to forget: if you think about how hard it is for you to foresee your future health and income, you will immediately see why individuals in private health care systems tend to systematically under-insure themselves. So, what should you do? As a neoliberal you should forget that you know this as you observe untreated illness and intensifying poverty among the poorer cohorts of your population in old age. As a neoclassical economist of Camp 1 you must interpret this hostage to fortune as a fully informed and free choice, though that is precisely what it cannot be.

What I hope is apparent by now is that the closed-system reasoning behind both Leninism and neoliberalism imposes a practice of 'organised forgetting': the consistent removal and rejection of salient information or ideas that do not fall into line with the presumed ontology. In adopting the language of science, both Soviet and neoliberal ideologies attacked their political opponents as primitives, unschooled in their singular methods of reasoning. The ethical pluralism of the post-war period was abandoned in favour of a discursive battle framed in terms of scientific knowledge versus ignorance and, ironically, 'ideology' (i.e., non-science). The reputation of the scientific method, understood as discovery, empirical justification, inductive review and theoretical refinement, could only suffer from this association.

Neoliberalism is more accurately understood as working *against* the norms of the scientific method. In a scientific paradigm shift, the replacement paradigm is more normally supposed to have solved not just the puzzles that challenged the previous paradigm but also the anomalies that had undermined it. When Thomas Kuhn demonstrated that science was not straightforwardly cumulative, he was not a relativist, arguing against the possibility of scientific progress as such, only that 'normal' (non-revolutionary) scientific progress should be understood as a growing capacity to solve problems, not as an increase in some essentialist verisimilitude.[4] Instead, Camp 1 neoclassical economics constructed a fiction through metaphor, and under neoliberalism, society was expected to conform to it – a fiction that would claim to explain all economic dynamics while proving highly misleading about most of them. In social science terms, this is just poor theory-building.

---

[4] Alexander Bird, *Thomas Kuhn* (London: Routledge, 2000), p. 209.

It strips out inconvenient factors that mess up the neatness of the theory despite their obvious relevance to the question in practice. Their ongoing reliance on axiomatic-deductive reasoning then leaves such governments marooned in circular reasoning.

The neoliberal revolution was clearly based on the opposite model of human motivation to that held by communists. Since few of us are either calculating sociopaths or selfless saints, however, both the neoliberal and Leninist schemes would rather testify to our human impulse to prefer a stress-relieving intellectual panacea in the face of a relentlessly uncertain world. As the sociologist Richard Lowenthal said of communism: 'The vision of a society without conflict has been the core of every utopia ever invented by philosophers and prophets in search of release from the unbearable personal and social conflicts of their time, and it is utopian also in the strict sense of being inherently impossible.'[5]

Selective amnesia is a common tool of ideological myth-making, but organised forgetting is an essential feature of closed-system materialist ontologies that are secular theologies to all intents and purposes. It followed that the knowledge attached to the previous paradigm might be lost, including that which explained trends that could not even be described by the new approach. This idea of the questions and answers lost to us via a paradigm shift became known in the philosophy of science as 'Kuhn-losses'.[6] After forty years of neoliberal reforms, the scale of Kuhn-loss in the art of government proved devastating to the basic functionality of the British state.

Neoclassical economics would form the bases of UK neoliberal policy strategies for the simple reason that positive scenarios for state withdrawal were so easy to generate within this form of reasoning. Friedrich August von Hayek, by contrast, offered neither scientific models nor policies and was consequently far harder to apply directly,[7] a fact that left him revered by the New Right as a philosopher of

---

[5] Richard Lowenthal, 'Development vs. Utopia in Communist Policy', in Chalmers Johnson, *Change in Communist Systems* (Stanford: Stanford University press, 1971), pp. 33–117, p. 40.

[6] Heinz R. Post, 'Correspondence, Invariance and Heuristics', *Studies in History and Philosophy of Science* 2 (1971): 213–255.

[7] Robert Skidelsky, 'Interpreting the Great Depression: Hayek versus Keynes', Institute for New Economic Thinking Working Paper, prepared for the INET Conference, Cambridge University, 8–11 April 2010, End Section III.

freedom even as he became marginalised as an economist. If we close this section by examining the crises that carried the public choice diagnosis into mainstream British politics, we can see how its closed-system reasoning would lead the New, neoliberal, Right to converge on the same governmental toolkit as Soviet socialism: on output-planning, targets, forecasting and the presumption that a welfare-optimising rationality would prevail in the governance of firms.

Political Economic Crisis and Paradigm Shift

From the late 1960s, the high economic growth of Western Europe's post-war reconstruction and industrial modernisation began to slow, and technological change and competition from emerging markets placed the region under new economic pressures. Through the 1970s its governments tried to sustain the post-war commitment to full employment by buying the peace with a permissive inflation.[8] By the 1980s, the persistence of post-industrial decline had prompted a clear set of recommendations from empiricist Camp 3 political economists. Their evidence-based diagnosis was that these economies had reached the end of the standardised mass production that had characterised their post-war growth and they needed to recalibrate themselves through stronger public investment in education, vocational training, research and development, and industrial finance. To take the high road to higher value-added economies that could remain at the technological frontier, these countries needed more relational, constructive systems of coordination between business and unions, and more flexible industrial specialisations and supportive industrial policies.[9]

Instead, their governments, albeit to varying degrees, again postponed, rather than resolved, the newly emerging social conflicts, and this ersatz adaptation lent credibility to the public choice narrative that politicians and bureaucracies would always spend their way out

---

[8] Wolfgang Streeck, 'The Crisis of Democratic Capitalism', *New Left Review* 71 (September/October 2011): Sections 2, 3 and 4.

[9] See, for example, Michael Piore and Charles Sabel, *The Second Industrial Divide: Possibilities for Prosperity* (New York: Basic Books, 1984); Michael L. Dertouzos, Richard K. Lester and Robert M. Solow, *Made in America: Regaining the Productive Edge* (Cambridge, MA: MIT Press, 1989); Lester C. Thurow, *Head to Head: The Coming Economic Battle among Japan, Europe, and America* (New York: Warner Books, 1992).

of hard decisions. As oil shocks drove inflation higher, governments increased public borrowing and public debt began to rise through the 1980s. This also occurred in the newly Thatcherite United Kingdom, where her monetary stabilisation strategies and sharp withdrawal of state support from manufacturing induced mass unemployment on a scale not seen since the inter-war period, so that the resulting income transfers acted as a widening drain on public spending.[10] It was nevertheless in this context that Margaret Thatcher argued for a neoliberal revolution in the production regime for public and private goods – the 'supply side' – with the promise that by rolling back the state a bright new day of fiscal responsibility and economic enterprise would dawn.

The developmental and distributional challenges created by radical technological change and de-industrialisation were now reframed as a fight for the future between individual endeavour and collectivist sloth. Just as Soviet propaganda had invoked the tireless Stakhanovite worker and the Young Pioneers as the embodiment of the new socialism, Britain's neoliberal revolution called forth the 'pioneering spirit' of the entrepreneur.[11] 'Business' became the neoliberal equivalent of the proletarian 'leading class': the cohort who best understood the metaphysics of the ideal material order. Trained against them in the neoliberal imaginary are the lotus-eating, Leviathan-building civil servants and non-neoliberal politicians intent on exploiting their monopoly, and the misguided citizenry, drained of their vigour by the easy prospect of government handouts. This is a narrative of muscular individualism set to liberate us from stultifying bureaucracy and the fog of communitarian lies.

As multiple authors have demonstrated, the paradigm shift in the Anglophone economies occurred through diverse channels that included right-wing think tanks and associations, sponsored television programmes and editorialising. In the United States, the Mont Pèlerin Society, the American Enterprise Institute, the Heritage Foundation, the Manhattan Institute of Policy Research and the Hoover Institute had emerged as among the most important conduits. In Britain, the initially more Hayekian Institute of Economics Affairs, which was founded in 1955, had gone on to embrace many of the narratives that

---

[10] Streeck, 'The Crisis', p. 14.
[11] Margaret Thatcher, 'Speech to Conservative Party Conference', Brighton, 20 October 1967, www.margaretthatcher.org/document/101586.

emanated from Chicago and Virginia. The Centre for Policy Studies was founded in 1974 by Thatcher, Alfred Sherman and Keith Joseph specifically to challenge the post-war Keynesian consensus and convert the Conservative Party to economic liberalism.[12] The libertarian-turned-neoliberal Adam Smith Institute was founded thereafter in 1977,[13] only to display scant interest in Smith's actual writings, least of all *On the Theory of Moral Sentiments*, in which he underscored the importance of empathy in a civilised society.[14] These organisations would become a vital source of arguments and policies for Britain's neoliberal Conservative governments from 1979 onwards,[15] to be joined, among others, by Policy Exchange from 2002. A fusion of theories from within neoclassical economics were now marshalled in support of the neoliberal turn: the monetarism of Milton Friedman; the rational expectations thesis of Robert Lucas; the public choice theories of William Niskanen, James Buchanan and Gordon Tullock; and the tax arguments of Arthur Laffer.[16] What they held in common, however, was the neoclassical basis of thought, along with the closed-system reasoning on which it depended.

The neoliberal critique of the post-war order had gained currency in Britain in the context of a destabilising combination of financial crash, price inflation, a humiliating International Monetary Fund (IMF) bail-out and intense industrial unrest in the face of rising prices. In the late 1970s, the New Right under Thatcher's leadership had asserted that the country was in crisis because, as she had insisted since the early 1960s, there was just too much government. Thatcher argued that the British state had expanded through the upward bidding mechanisms set out in public choice and this had led to the bureaucratic authoritarianism that

---

[12] Andrew Denham and Mark Garnett, 'Influence without Responsibility? Think Tanks in Britain', *Parliamentary Affairs* 51 (1) (January 1999): 46–57, p. 49.
[13] See Richard Cockett, *Thinking the Unthinkable: Think-Tanks and the Economic Counter-Revolution, 1931–1983* (London: Harper Collins, 1995); Philip Mirowski and Dieter Plehwe, *The Road from Mont Pelerin: The Making of the Neoliberal Thought Collective* (Cambridge, MA: Harvard University Press, 2009).
[14] Adam Smith, *The Theory of Moral Sentiments* (London: Penguin Classics, 2010) (first published in 1759).
[15] Denham and Garnett, 'Influence without Responsibility?', pp. 48–53.
[16] Mark Blyth, *Great Transformations: Economic Ideas and Institutional Change in the Twentieth Century* (Cambridge: Cambridge University Press, 2002), p. 155.

Hayek and public choice theory foretold.[17] By declaring that all public officials should be understood as governed by rational self-interest, the New Right could reinvent Conservativism as the force to rescue liberty and enterprise from the purely expansionist ambitions of the 'socialist' state. If you understood the state as an overbearing monopoly, and general equilibrium as the natural condition to which the market would always return as the state was withdrawn, it followed that the crisis would be solved if you shrank the state through privatisation, outsourced the government's tasks where possible and instilled the culture of 'enterprise' throughout the public offices that remained.

From this perspective it wasn't technological change or de-industrialisation, nor was it competition from emerging markets, that had driven this crisis. It wasn't the Nixon shock, as the United States withdrew from the Gold Standard, nor was it the subsequent end of the Bretton Woods system of monetary management, nor rising exchange rate instability. As for the oil crises of 1973 and 1979, these were not, apparently, a sensible part of any analysis as to what had confronted capitalist states with the need to renew their political economic regimes and the social contracts they had paid for. In this diagnosis, the crisis of development in advanced capitalism was caused by the very existence of the modern state. To be more precise, it was caused by the rise of the democratic state.

The incompatibility of this approach with liberal democracy is fundamental: it says that insofar as democracy fails to deliver laissez-faire, democracy is flawed. Moreover, it is a remarkably short step in logic to move from this to the more fundamentalist presumption that neoliberals alone, as the champions of the 'correct' materialist analysis, should be allowed to govern. This belief has only hardened over time on the political right of US and UK politics, as we explore in Part III. For now, however, let me only observe that to argue that liberal democracy is imperfect was entirely fair enough – it is a man-made institution after all. The utopian leap made under the neoliberal turn was to assume that by dismantling the precautionary, strategic and developmental modern state, it would become less so.

The structural crises of the 1970s had compounded one another with devastating effect, but no Camp 3 diagnoses offered so tempting

---

[17] Margaret Thatcher, 'What's Wrong with Politics?', Conservative Political Centre Lecture, Blackpool, 11 October 1968, www.margaretthatcher.org.

a solution to those who held capital as the arguments of Camp 1. The actual causes of political and economic stagnation were disturbing to those who held significant private wealth or aspired to, since their treatment required a renewed commitment to both public and private investments for the medium to longer term. Lowenthal had noted that, historically, both revolutionary communist and nationalist movements had emerged in underdeveloped countries as 'a response of frustrated intellectual elites to the phenomenon of partial stagnation in the midst of disruptive social change, and to the continued rule of traditional elites whose legitimate function had perished and whose values were no longer generally credible, but for whom no effective "bourgeois" successors had arisen'.[18] Thatcherism now emerged in an advanced capitalist economy that had stalled. The cross-class coalition of political, intellectual, business and financial interests and disillusioned lower-income voters that championed it would now openly reject the traditional Conservative deference to the evolving establishment, its support for 'the professions' and, though often more grudging, to the wider cultural institutions of the post-war order – institutions already strongly disrupted through the 1960s. Here again, therefore, was a utopia of reaction, as the Thatcherites decried both the solidaristic ethics of the post-war era and the social liberalism of the next generation.

Thatcher explicitly rejected the post-war order as infected by socialism and she called for its replacement by 'a man's right to work as he will, to spend what he earns, to own property, to have the State as servant not as master: these are the British inheritance. They are the essence of a free country and on that freedom all our other freedoms depend'.[19] I can only assume she had no idea that Friedrich Engels too had railed '[a]gainst this transformation of the state and the organs of the state from servants of society into masters of society', which is why Lenin had used the very same phrase in 'The State and Revolution'.[20] Forty years on, and every economy in the world's historical economic

---

[18] Lowenthal, 'Development vs. Utopia', p. 35.
[19] Margaret Thatcher, 'Speech to Conservative Party Conference', Brighton, 10 October 1975, www.margaretthatcher.org/document/102777.
[20] Vladimir Ilyich Lenin, 'The State and Revolution: The Marxist Theory of the State and the Tasks of the Proletariat in the Revolution', in *Collected Works*, Vol. 25 (Moscow: Progress Publishers, 1964) (first published in 1917), pp. 381–492, p. 451.

'core' has, to varying degrees, broken with the post-war architecture of an institutionally distinct and well-bounded state and opened it to the practices and logic of the theoretical marketplace. This holds not only for the Anglophone economies at the movement's leading edge but also for the post-war champions of corporatism and social democracy such as the Netherlands and Sweden.

What would become known as the 'New Public Management' (NPM) adopted by the British New Right, but also, eventually, by New Labour, prioritised three strategies, namely the disaggregation of public hierarchies into smaller, leaner, supposedly more firm-like units; competition between these units and with outside contractors; and incentivisation – the substitution of a no longer trusted public service professionalism with corporate management systems such as targets, budgeting by results, performance pay and high salaries for top managers, with assets to follow those who drove the most effective conformity to the new rules,[21] essentially Niskanen's remedies. NPM reforms at their broadest would go on to draw from multiple schools, including management theory, classical public administration, neoclassical public administration, policy analysis, principal–agent theory, property rights theory, the neo-Austrian School and transaction economics,[22] but its dominant 'pro-market' elements were overwhelmingly justified by neoclassical analysis and developed from the neoclassical ideas mediated through these sources.

At the level of government management, much would be drawn in the first instance from large business management practices associated with the 'scientific administration' school. The businesses in question typically operated in relatively simple product markets and deployed resource planning techniques developed in the 1960s and 1970s. Scientific administration emphasised clear objectives and divisions of function and a strict hierarchy of control, and it had driven large businesses from input to output planning and a switch from professional administrative culture to enterprise 'management'. Management was now understood as a portable skill from the marketplace that could be divorced from specialised knowledge and experience and applied

---

[21] Patrick Dunleavy, Helen Margetts, Simon Bastow and Jane Tinkler, 'New Public Management Is Dead – Long Live Digital Era Governance!', *Journal of Public Administration Research and Theory* 16 (3) (2006): 467–494, p. 470.

[22] Gernod Gruening, 'Origins and Theoretical Basis of New Public Management', *International Public Management Journal* 4 (2001): 1–25.

equally to any production system, regardless of its complexities.[23] From the Efficiency Unit of 1979–1984, and the Next Steps Report in 1987 established under Thatcher,[24] and from New Labour's 2001 Delivery Unit onwards, management was to be primarily concerned with the use of metrics to organise the efficient use of resources, with efficiency understood as low costs relative to immediate benefits, as in a neoclassical marketplace.

To swing so dramatically from the state's tendency to neglect outputs in the 1970s to a fixation on their delivery with the greatest short-term cost efficiency was only a coherent solution within a closed-system world, however. In a further affinity with the Leninist project, it was also assumed that once the forms and practices of bureaucratic agencies were made to conform to the respective theoretical models, then only productive practices would follow. In an evolving society inescapably subject to uncertainty, however, the state's capacity for policy expertise, experience and coordinating capacity, along with budgetary margins for innovation, unexpected events and error would all remain functionally necessary. Under the NPM, they would simply become less and less available.

When neoliberals abandoned input planning and the post-war conventions around vocation and professionalism in favour of departmental output planning, command hierarchy and a rage for quantification, they failed to realise that they were ushering in the enterprise management methodologies of the Soviet system, a system primarily intent on the reproduction of the nineteenth century Prussian industrial economy. The initial NPM goal was to release politicians from 'bureaucratic oversight' so they could focus on policy. But absent the divinely efficient interventions of the price mechanism in a world of perfectly informed competitors, they were about to radically expand the overall planning load of the British state within an architecture embarked on informational disintegration into 'competitive units'. This dispersal would happen in the first instance through 'agencification' and latterly through a massive shift to public sector outsourcing, and with no

---

[23] Peter Self, *Government by the Market?* (Basingstoke: Macmillan International, 1993), pp. 168–169.

[24] Catherine Haddon, 'Reforming the Civil Service: The Efficiency Unit in the Early 1980s and the 1987 Next Steps Report', The Institute for Government, www.instituteforgovernment.org/publication/report/reform-civil-service-efficiency-unit.

actively coordinating planning agency at its centre. The British state's planning requirements and liabilities would thus grow to encompass not just central ministries but all the new structures of delegated governance, from 'firm-like' government agencies to the activities of private businesses and financial agents via what would become thousands of outsourcing contracts.

Perhaps the most astonishing aspect of this revolution was the failure to acknowledge that for these changes to work as they were supposed to, the continuing existence of democracy was going to cause a fundamental problem. For this radical disintegration of state power to work as Niskanen had promised, the mechanisms of democracy, elections, mandates, taxation and accountability requirements would need to have been 'turned off' first. You would need a democratic mandate to end democracy as we know it to transform a state directed by a government into a market directed by nothing but its own spontaneous evolution under competition, and what kind of market was this supposed to be? Its theoretical foundations presumed the spreading logic of the perfectly functioning market analogue to the omniscient social planner.

In stark contrast to the hypothesised free market agent, however, the actual government would retain authority over, and hence responsibility for, the public money to be spent throughout these evolving institutional structures. Indeed, over the next forty years of neoliberal reform, the UK state would remain responsible not just for buying in these services and goods but for their quality, even as it became a giant of enterprise management. The introduction of NPM promised an increasingly spontaneous set of cost- and quality-improving market games, but as we will see in Part II, the disciplines of the theoretical neoclassical marketplace were almost never to be had. It followed that efficiency gains were less evident than rapidly rising transaction costs, rigidification of the bureaucracy as discretion was curtailed, chronic planning and coordination failures in the light of uncertainty and change, and a gradual decline in the legitimacy of the democratic state itself. The history of the Soviet Union quickly became the relevant analogue in systems terms, not the neoclassical theory of markets.

In sum, to understand why, under the neoliberal revolution, you might end up with the *worst* of both state and market, it is helpful to register the full implications of the tautological character of the neoclassical doctrine behind it. This says that if multiple utopian conditions hold, including the universal existence of fully informed, utility-maximising individuals operating in pure competitive markets under the auspices of a neutral, 'nightwatchman' state, *then* you will achieve efficiency. At the same time, the implicit promise is that by implementing supply-side strategies, the political bureaucratic state will be freed to wither away. Like its Soviet counterpart, the neoliberal revolution could never be completed because the absence of the prior state and the pervasion of perfect doctrinal rationality were *preconditions* for its reforms to work as anticipated. The unintended consequences were nevertheless all too real.

Why We Hate Politics

Metaphors can be powerful. The exponents of the neoliberal revolution argued that there was a disease in the body politic to be cured – the disease of monopoly. But what if the metaphor was just wrong? What if it was always a normative assertion by academic economists who worked from purely logical reasoning, rather than from any historically informed investigation into actual states? The colonising power of public choice theory in the social sciences and the spread of its assumptions into everyday political speech would go on to normalise attitudes and behaviours that British society would have viewed as shockingly amoral only a few years before. Here was a thesis that undermined real democratic institutions but offered only a materialist imaginary as their substitute. Apply the rule of self-interested calculation to the democratic state and you would nevertheless do violence to its integrity. As Andrew Hindmoor points out, liberal democratic institutions depend on the values of 'public service' and this ethos is a long way from strategic calculation.[25] As Colin Hay also noted in *Why We Hate Politics*, if you insist long enough and loud enough that elected politicians and the public servants who support them are in it only for themselves, then sooner or later voters might start to believe you.[26] Over time, politicians may also start to behave that way, on the basis that you may as well be hung for a sheep as for a lamb.

---

[25] Andrew Hindmoor, 'Public Choice', in Colin Hay, Michael Lister and David Marsh, *The State: Theories and Issues* (Basingstoke: Palgrave Macmillan, 2006), pp. 93–97.
[26] Colin Hay, *Why We Hate Politics* (Cambridge: Polity Press, 2007).

In the collapsed circular reasoning of Stalinism, the ideologically conscious worker was both the necessary condition for central planning to work and the hoped-for outcome so that socialism would become communism. In the neoliberal transformation, the individual operating under market disciplines would erase the inefficiencies imposed by 'too much government' and be themselves liberated by their acts – a rebirth of 'true consciousness' under the new material order. Neoliberalism thus shares the failure of Leninism to anticipate the likely interactions when its assumptions around hyper-rationality within closed-system theories were uploaded into real, interdependent institutions in evolving systems run by actual people in historical time. The neoliberal revolution was a seductive idea, but it turns out to be a practical agenda for government in the way that Baron Von-Munchhausen pulling himself out of the swamp by his own hair is a practical form of travel.

As William Davies observed, by extending neoclassical thinking not just into the narratives of state but into all domains of social and individual life through categories such as 'human capital', neoliberalism would seek to construct both a new philosophy of government and economy and a new subjectivity, one in which we would witness 'the disenchantment of politics by economics'.[27] This was a political discourse in which the complexity of human needs and wants and the pluralistic political representation of often conflicting interests were rejected in the name of a higher science. And, as Richard Bronk noted, the most frequently repeated metaphors 'tend to harden into elements of the unconscious structuring of our vision and understanding of the world'.[28] As in Leninism, the transformation of the material order was supposed to bring the citizen back to their 'true' rationality. Tragically, the far greater likelihood was that this neoliberal turn would undermine our trust both in one another and in our public sphere, even as it failed to flower within its own terms.

Thatcher's attacks on the self-serving Leviathan state had appealed to individual aspiration. She had invoked Britain's historical dominance as an enterprising and trading nation, while editing out the imperialist violence and naval supremacy that had enabled it – an appeal that would reappear in even more fanciful terms in the Brexit debate

---

[27] William Davies, *The Limits of Neoliberalism: Economics, Sovereignty and the Logic of Competition* (London: SAGE, 2014), Chapter 1.
[28] Bronk, *The Romantic Economist*, p. 275.

of 2016. She had suggested that the only real limits Britons could face in the new system would be those of self-understanding. Policies rooted in neoclassical models could now be wedded to a Hayekian narrative of tradition, family and, inevitably, the nation, all of which could be deployed to finesse what was a truly revolutionary break in the ideological traditions of the Conservative Party. The implication was that any lingering attraction we might hold towards more empathetic or solidaristic ideas was feeble-minded, whether rooted in social democratic, liberal or One-Nation conservative traditions. To reject Thatcherism was to fail tests of ingenuity and personal responsibility.

The more obvious likelihood was that in defining the social world as a marketplace, our political and social imaginations about what was either possible or moral would narrow accordingly. The danger was that we would start to understand ourselves and each other in the calculating terms of rational economic man, only without the capacities for Godlike omniscience, telepathy and time travel we would need to thrive. It was easy to obscure the totalising logic of neoliberal thought in an open society. But given that, like Stalinism, neoliberalism was built upon the functionalist individual in a closed material space, the potential for social alienation, moral nihilism, corruption and ultimately authoritarian political attitudes was scarcely less.

The circular, utopian character of utilitarian logic has been obscured because neoliberalism appeals to the very real virtues of individual freedom and entrepreneurialism and to Britain's deep reservoirs of aspiration. Another reason the neoliberal revolution goes unrecognised as the hedonistic twin of Soviet socialism, however, is because the isomorphism is so effectively obscured by neoliberalism's academic origins. The formally reasoned diagnoses of public choice and the typically mathematics-dependent prescriptions of Camp 1 neoclassical economics are about as inaccessible to non-specialist scrutiny as the founding texts of a revolutionary political argument could possibly be, short of their encryption. Thatcher had famously read the economic philosophy of Hayek, but how many ministers of mainstream political parties who subsequently implemented neoclassical strategies had delved deep into the economic theories that justified them, let alone examined the magic carpet of abstraction by which they had arrived?

The Soviet nomenklatura and wider bureaucracy by the 1980s were the closest the real world has ever come to the mercenary caste that roams the founding scripts of public choice theory, and that likeness was no coincidence. From the 1920s to its collapse, Camp 1 neoclassical economists had looked to Soviet failures to inspire their arguments about why state intervention in the economy must also fail.[29] By proceeding with the neoliberal revolution without comprehending its utopian radicalism, however, first the New Right and then New Labour were about to become re-enactment societies for the most bureaucratic state in history, only now in capitalist form.

Conclusion

The contemporary field of academic economics explores everything from behavioural psychology to systemic complexity. This diversity is nevertheless overshadowed by the continuing dominance of neoclassical approaches in universities, in the world's top-ranked economic journals and also, consequently, throughout the treasury departments of the global north and, in many cases, south. In the United Kingdom, the case that we are about to explore in depth, it was a condition of the 1976 IMF loan rules that the Treasury be given greater powers over all government department budgets. From the Thatcher government onwards, but scarcely less under New Labour, the Treasury gained significant powers throughout Whitehall via new hierarchical structures, annual reviews and accounting systems, all designed to rein in government spending.[30] The Treasury's views had always more traditionally aligned with the city and finance than with domestic industry, and now successive neoliberal governments chose Treasury ministers who tended to champion Camp 1 neoclassical beliefs and, at their most critical, those of Camp 2. In 1981 the Treasury was put in charge of civil service pay and promotion, as well as permanent secretary appointments across Whitehall, and this would prove a powerful device to spread neoclassical orthodoxy and its methods.[31]

---

[29] Johanna Bockman and Gil Eyal, 'Eastern Europe as a Laboratory for Economic Knowledge: The Transnational Roots of Neoliberalism', *American Journal of Sociology* 108 (2) (September 2002): 310–352, p. 320.

[30] Aeron Davis and Catherine Walsh, 'The Role of the State in the Financialization of the UK Economy', *Political Studies* 64 (3) (2016): 666–682, p. 671.

[31] Ibid. See also Peter Hall, 'Policy Paradigms, Social Learning and the State: The Case of Economic Policymaking in Britain', *Comparative Politics* 25 (3) (1993): 275–296.

When we review the analytical seriousness and empiricism of the post-war strategies of the democratic left, right and centre, we can see more clearly the intellectual conceit of the materialist utopias. The post-war governments of advanced capitalist states had dealt in precaution, conscious social purpose and practical improvement. They combined empirical analysis with hard-fought intellectual compromises between the social democratic insistence on relief from the vicissitudes of the market and the liberal and centre-right's concerns for the protection of society's freedoms and traditions from the state, concerns quite justified when repressive communist regimes sat behind the ironclad borders of Central Europe.

The neoliberal revolution would assert the primacy of 'economic man' far beyond its origins as a 'discrete analytical species dominating economic discourse',[32] into the presumed agent of all political, bureaucratic and interest-group activity. Like Leninism, it depended on a form of closed-system reasoning that was ontologically two-dimensional and essentially mystical. Axiomatic-deductive methods based on dubious metaphors dragged huge descriptive distortions into both the original public choice diagnosis of state failure and the solutions. As Robert Solow, the Nobel Prize-winning father of neoclassical growth theory turned critic, noted:

There has always been a purist streak in economics that wants everything to follow neatly from greed, rationality and equilibrium, with no ifs, ands, or buts… The theory is neat, learnable, not terribly difficult, but just technical enough to feel like 'science'. Moreover, it is practically guaranteed to give *laissez-faire* type advice, which happens to fit nicely with the general turn to the political right that began in the 1970s and may or may not be coming to an end.[33]

The post-war era in the advanced capitalist democracies was a relatively consensual period of state evolution in an era of high economic growth, but public choice transformed these evolving states into a self-aggrandising Leviathan as a stylised fact. Decades of unprecedented social integration in the aftermath of war were rewritten as an inevitable exercise in the private exploitation of public revenues. Unable to go directly to the minimal state of ideological preference, the New

[32] Bronk, *The Romantic Economist*, p. 225.
[33] Robert Solow, 'The State of Macroeconomics', *Journal of Economic Perspectives* 22 (1) (2008): 243–249, p. 245.

Right aimed to withdraw the state's interventions from the private sector and import the presumed efficiency gains of business practice into the state that remained.

The new spectrum of exchange-relations ranged from internal performance targets intended to imitate a firm's production output at one end – implicitly generated to satisfy consumer demand – to the direct outsourcing of state functions to private actors, if not complete privatisation, at the other. The neoliberal state in practice would thus become a laboratory for managed pseudo-markets within its own public offices and, where goods were contracted out, an institutional giant of public procurement and enterprise-planning. Like the withering away of the state under Leninism, the gains of supply-side reforms were predicated on a fantasy of completion, in which all moves that abided by doctrine were assumed to be a priori beneficial. Both doctrines were consequently silent about what could go wrong when doctrine turned out to be false. For the ideologically convinced, however, the misgivings of experienced public officials could now be dismissed as the self-serving complaints of an altogether suspect civil service class – of the 'bureaucrats' as guilty of a 'left deviationism' as the Soviets had deplored their deviationists 'of the right'.

Since Thomas More wrote *Utopia* in 1516 the term has been used to depict an ideal society or, if the ideas are being disparaged, an impossible one. As thought experiments, utopian projects – the literal translation of utopia means 'no place' or 'nowhere' – have offered a radical and fresh critique of the present rather than a too-cautious reformism.[34] The stubborn fact remains, however, that any benefits from attempting them depend on an underlying realism in their vision. Unfortunately, the wildest assumptions in neoclassical economics are built into its foundations.[35] The idea that we are all self-interested, isolated, calculating, fixed in our tastes and dominant over nature proves untrue.[36] Dependent on assertion and formal logic

---

[34] Barbara Goodwin, 'Utopianism', in *The Blackwell Encyclopaedia of Political Thought* (Oxford: Blackwell Publishing, 1987), pp. 533–538, p. 533.

[35] Frank Ackerman, 'Still Dead after All These Years: Interpreting the Failures of General Equilibrium Theory', *Journal of Economic Methodology* 9 (2) (2002): 119–139.

[36] Kate Raworth, *Doughnut Economics: Seven Ways to Think Like a 21st Century Economist* (London: Random House, 2017), p. 28.

Conclusion

at every level, the neoclassical models at the root of Britain's neoliberal revolution would describe a terrain that is, literally, nowhere. If we turn our attention to both the specific theories and their practice, we can see how the seeds of today's chronic institutional and political failures were sown in these methods.

PART II

Britain's Neoliberal Revolution

5 | *The New Public Management, or Enterprise Planning in Capitalist Form*

Outsourcing, privatisation and delegated governance to firms or firm-like agencies are core neoliberal strategies rooted in neoclassical theory. By re-engineering the state, they were supposed to drive the political economy closer towards the Camp 1, efficient-market, horizon. The analytical challenge here is to understand why these strategies produced the opposite of what voters were led to expect in terms of improved efficiency, cost and accountability. As we will see, these policies engendered severe microeconomic failures, many of which could have been anticipated had even the concerns of Camp 2 been applied. At the systems level they left vital public services at the mercy of enterprises and pseudo-enterprises that operated neither within competitive markets nor with the productive rationality ascribed to them.

Britain's post-war state had evolved through, as well as was designed to operate according to, specialist and cooperative norms, and its ministries were mindful of developmental ideas that embraced the short to the long term. Though imperfect, those methods and ideas were appropriate to their tasks because governmental systems and markets alike are made from, and develop through, the making of selective connections. It is, in fact, the very incompleteness of those connections that allows democratic governments and firms to refine and adapt their strategies over time and innovate.[1] Whatever they may think they are doing, decision-making agents within institutions have no choice but to find continuous 'trade-offs' within constantly changing and interdependent systems. Neat, complete and good-for-all-time solutions for governments are consequently not only illusory but bound to introduce unanticipated consequences.[2]

When Britain's neoliberal governments and their officials applied closed models to open systems, they either forgot, were innocent of

---

[1] Brian Loasby, 'Closed Models and Open Systems', *Journal of Economic Methodology* 10 (3) (2003): 285–306, p. 285.
[2] Christopher Hood, *The Limits of Administration* (London: John Wiley, 1976).

or chose to ignore the utopian assumptions on which those models were based. They consequently 'wrote out' key features of the terrain over which they governed. The most consequential misrepresentation in the theories behind these reforms concern the state itself. The models on which privatisation, outsourcing and delegated governance were founded tended to assume that the central state would set the rules of a new market game between buyers and sellers and then step away to allow the automatic functioning of that market to play out. While this is a neat conceit in a neoclassical model, it makes no sense in the real world of democratic government, where the central state does not wither away to reveal an efficient, sealed market machine but remains financially, legally and politically liable for the new production regime. The state also retains responsibilities for privatised goods and services where they are socially and strategically important, such as water. Since the British state had no choice but to stay in the picture, we need to understand why power imbalances emerged between the executive state and the enterprises and pseudo-enterprises to which it now delegated power.

A Camp 2 neoclassical economist will tend to interpret unfolding problems as points of microeconomic market failure, and I will use insights from that approach to identify the different junctions within outsourcing, privatisation and agencification where Camp 1 assumptions have, indeed, failed. The scope of the Camp 2 neoclassical critique remains limited by its own axiomatic-deductive reasoning, however. By its nature it cannot tell us about political conflicts of interest or about the forms of behaviour and economic-turned-political power that pre-empt and override both market and planning disciplines. It has nothing to say about the downstream institutional, social or environmental consequences of the new production regime and its feedback effects, but the history of Soviet planning can be illuminating here. The New Public Management (NPM) reforms began with a wave of privatisations under the Thatcher government, but I am going to start this analysis with outsourcing, as it best illuminates their systemic myopia.

Outsourcing

Modern democratic states have long relied on private procurement to buy the standardised goods they need, from paper to magnetic resonance imaging scanners. But since the introduction of the NPM, neoliberal governments moved to the system-wide outsourcing of complex public goods and services. British developments began with the introduction of Compulsory Competitive Tendering in local governments in the late 1980s. The Local Government Acts of 1988 and 1992 launched a government strategy that expanded in stages to become the dominant mechanism of public service delivery. From the 1990s, outsourcing progressed through a variety of modes that included partnership (particularly in the uses of private finance initiatives or 'PFIs'), strategic-commissioning and prime-contracting.[3] I focus here on the contracting out of public services. A brief history of its results reveals that outsourcing has singularly failed to live up to its promises.

Following its spread in local government, central government outsourcing accelerated from the late 1990s. Since the 'legitimate use of force in a given territory' is the classical Weberian definition of what distinguishes state authority, the post-2010 rise of outsourcing in justice and defence, as well as welfare, shows the radical scope of these changes.[4] In 2016–2017, total commercial spending amounted to 32 per cent of total central government spending, where total staff costs represented an additional 24 per cent and social transfers/benefits a further 28 per cent. In that financial year the National Audit Office estimated government spent £255 billion on commercial relationships. This included £118 billion spent by central government and the National Health Service on goods and services and £59.8 billion on capital expenditure, with £8.3 billion of that going to service the interest on ongoing PFI contracts and 'intangibles'. By 2017–2018 the central departmental spending of the seventeen largest departments on commercial relationships stood at £143.3 billion.[5]

The social purposes of outsourcing have varied. The New Labour governments of Tony Blair and Gordon Brown stayed with NPM but

---

[3] Tony Bovaird, 'The Ins and Outs of Insourcing and Outsourcing: What Have We Learnt from the Last Thirty Years?', *Public Money and Management* 36 (1) (2016): 67–74, pp. 67–68.
[4] Gill Plimmer, 'Public Service Outsourcing Jumps under Coalition', *Financial Times*, 30 April 2015.
[5] National Audit Office, 'Commercial and Contracting', Departmental Overview, December 2018, www.nao.org.uk/wp-content/uploads/2018/12/Departmental-Overview-Commercial-and-Contracting-2017-18.pdf.

moved away from the Conservative's rhetorical emphasis on market superiority to the more socially inclusive claim that the state should be made responsive to consumer choice. New Labour prioritised four mechanisms, namely top-down pressure from government through performance management, not least via output targets and inspection, and 'capability and capacity building' for public servants through leadership and strategy. The remaining two centred on outsourcing, specifically, citizen pressure through consumer 'choice and voice' and competitive pressure through markets.[6] Markets would provide the technical means to drive up standards and remove inefficiencies, and if there were no market actors willing to engage in a particular sector, government would provide incentives to bring them in.[7] In keeping with the circular reasoning that underpinned it, the new system was promoted as 'self-improving'. A systematic shift was consequently well underway when the new prime minister of the Conservative–Liberal Coalition, David Cameron, declared in 2011: 'From now on diversity is the default in our public services...instead of having to justify why it makes sense to introduce competition...the state will have to justify why it makes sense to run a monopoly.'[8] Cameron promised to 'release the grip of state control' on public services, and government spending on outsourcing between 2010 and 2015 nearly doubled from £64 billion to £120 billion.[9] Broken down by sector, the value of central government contracts had risen from £37 billion to £67 billion. In healthcare they had increased from £9 billion to £16.5 billion; in education from £1.8 billion to £3.7 billion and in local authorities from £16 billion to £32.5 billion.[10]

Parliamentary committee reports were damning of outsourcing throughout this period, and the Coalition's strategy showed its willingness to double down on the policy even as the growing body of empirical evidence spoke against it. The Coalition also eased the process in

---

[6] Cabinet Office, 'The UK Government's Approach to Public Service Reform, a Discussion Paper', The Prime Minister's Strategy Unit, London, June 2006, quoted in Steve Davies, 'Outsourcing, Public Sector Reform and the Changed Character of the UK State-Voluntary Sector Relationship', *International Journal of Public Sector Management* 24 (7) (October 2011): 641–649.
[7] Davies, 'Outsourcing', p. 642.
[8] David Cameron, 'Prime Minister's Speech on Modern Public Services', 17 January 2011, Cabinet Office, www.gov.uk/government/speeches/prime-ministers-speech-on-modern-public-service.
[9] Plimmer, 'Public Service Outsourcing Jumps'.
[10] Plimmer, 'Public Service Outsourcing Jumps'.

Outsourcing

the round. After 2010, private sector companies who took over public sector staff were no longer contractually required to hire them on the same terms. In October 2013 it was made easier for public servants to carry their pensions over to the private sector. In the 2015 budget, Chancellor George Osborne removed value-added tax charges for companies that bid for government work. Tens of thousands of staff were transferred to private sector management. These changes drove a 125 per cent increase in contracts, from 536 under the previous Labour government to 1,185 under the Coalition, which made the United Kingdom the second largest outsourcing market in the world after the United States.[11] By 2014, the UK's public service industry accounted for 6 per cent of GDP and 1.6 million staff, over three times the number of civil servants employed by Whitehall.[12] This 'second wave' had been called for by the Confederation of British Industry's Public Services Strategy Board, whose 2011 'Open Public Services' White Paper exhorted the Coalition to open as many public services as possible to private provision with the promise of 11 per cent 'efficiency' savings from a projection of £280 billion of services.[13]

In practice, Christopher Hood and Ruth Dixon establish that over the first thirty years of NPM reforms, UK administration costs *increased* by 40 per cent in constant prices, despite a third of civil service numbers being cut over the same period. Total public spending doubled, while the indicators for quality and fairness in service delivery all deteriorated. Complaints and judicial challenges soared, and contrary to the Confederation of British Industry's promises, running costs were driven up in outsourced sectors in particular.[14] By 2014, the Public Accounts Committee inquiry into outsourcing concluded that '[g]overnment is clearly failing to manage performance across the board, and to achieve the best for citizens out of the contracts into which they have entered'. It also warned that 'so far, the contracting out of services has led to the evolution of privately-owned public

---

[11] Ibid.
[12] Stephen Wilks, 'The Public Services Industry: A Constitutional Blasphemy and a Democratic Perversion', *LSE British Politics and Policy at LSE*, 8 August 2013, https://blogs.lse.ac.uk/politicsandpolicy/the-alternative-civil-service-a-constitutional-heresy/.
[13] Ibid.
[14] Ruth Dixon and Christopher Hood, *A Government That Worked Better and Cost Less?* (Oxford: Oxford University Press, 2015), Chapters 4 and 5.

monopolies, who largely, or in some cases wholly, rely on taxpayers' money for their income. The state is then constrained in finding alternatives where a big private company fails'.[15] Competition was meant to drive up quality, but 73 per cent of procurement spending had been awarded to large public service industry multinationals,[16] a tendency that has only worsened. The proportion of public sector contracts awarded to a sole bidder, so without any competitive tender at all, went up from 15 per cent in 2016 to 23 per cent by 2018,[17] and it is worth bearing in mind that lack of competitive tendering is used internationally as a measure of corruption.

By 2013 more than £4 billion of taxpayers' money was spent on four companies alone: Serco, Capita, Atos and G4S. This raised concerns in the National Audit Office that such firms were 'too big to fail'. In the meantime, outsourcing undermined democratic accountability, as widening outflows of public money were hidden behind walls of commercial confidentiality that even parliamentary committees could not breach. The National Audit Office concluded in 2018 that despite 'a clear legal and policy expectation that all contracts are made publicly available, we find that many are not published or are significantly redacted'.[18] These trends, moreover, are not unique to Britain. Outsourcing has grown across advanced capitalist economies, but an assessment across fifteen EU states found no causal link to reduced public spending or employment.[19] To the contrary, outsourcing was encouraged in the European Union's new member states, for example, only for it to replace post-communist privatisation as the main vehicle for political corruption.[20]

---

[15] House of Commons Committee of Public Accounts, 'Contracting Out Public Services to the Private Sector', 14 March 2014 (HC 777), p. 3, www.publications.parliament.uk/pa/cm201314/cmselect/cmpubacc/777/777.pdf.

[16] Report by the Comptroller and Auditor General, 'Government's Spending with Small and Medium Sized Enterprises', 9 March 2016 (HC 884), p. 4, www.nao.org.uk/wp-content/uploads/2016/03/Governments-spending-with-small-and-medium-sizes-enterprises.pdf.

[17] Gill Plimmer and Max Harlow, 'Sole Outsource Bidders Win More Contracts', *Financial Times*, 14 January 2019.

[18] National Audit Office, 'Commercial and Contracting', p. 9.

[19] José M. Alonso, Judith Clifton and Daniel Díaz-Fuentes, 'Did New Public Management Matter? An Empirical Analysis of the Outsourcing and Decentralisation Effects on Public Sector Size', *Public Management Review* 17 (5) (2013): 643–660, p. 656.

[20] Abby Innes, 'Corporate State Capture in Open Societies', *East European Politics and Societies and Cultures* 30 (3) (August 2016): 594–620.

The trend of rising financial abuse and taxpayer losses is a consequence of a basic architectural flaw. The flaw is that outsourcing in practice contravenes all the Camp 1 assumptions used to justify its adoption. Instead, it not just fulfils the baleful predictions of Camp 2 but it actually reinvents the pathologies of Soviet enterprise planning. Public sector outsourcing requires the government planning of private enterprises. It follows that both Camp 2 and Soviet economics can help us account for its chronic failures, the unanticipated path-dependencies that play out once the policy is implemented and the creation of monopolistic public sector industry firms that consistently violate the promise of higher quality services that cost less.

The Analytical Sins of Omission

Where does outsourcing go wrong? The contention here is 'at the start' – in the acts of 'organised forgetting' in the theory. The original case for outsourcing assumes that an efficient public services market can be achieved through competition between informed actors and multiple producers, but what does that really mean? In the theory of perfect competition, all firms sell an identical product, all firms become price-takers as competition flattens the profit margin (i.e., they cannot influence the market price of their given product) and all players have complete information about the product being sold and the prices of other firms; resources are perfectly mobile, and firms can enter or exit the market without cost. Even looked at through the lens of Camp 2, the implication is still that market failures can be resolved to complete a full set of connections, so that a public services market is ultimately bound to work more effectively than the non-market system that went before.

As in Leninism, the dependence on axiomatic deduction is total, except that the requirement for perfect informational capacity rests here with the individual economic agents – and by extension the firm – rather than at the planning system level, as the price mechanism is expected to coordinate an efficient allocation of resources between buyers and sellers. To sustain the machine-like efficiency of the market projected in this view, however, the firm as an organisation, as an institution, must be impotent, a perfect cipher for the theory. The nearest real-world approximation would be a market stall or, as Lazonick pointed out, a sweatshop. And yet, at the same time, the idea of competitive public service markets presupposes the existence of multiple, competing, firms with the capacity to produce products and services of a quality that people want, at a price people (or, more accurately, state agencies) are willing and able to pay. It simply presupposes a competent production regime: the existence of firms with all the necessary suppliers, skills, experience and investment in technology and facilities and an entire legal and logistical infrastructure that permits legal transactions and trade.[21] Such fictional firms are the market analogue to the Soviet enterprise – the agent that will fulfil their part in the otherwise fully functioning coordinating mechanism and with no distinctive institutional or behavioural features or constraints of its own.

The fictionalised nature of the firm is not the only reason that such faith in the price mechanism is misplaced. Practical difficulties become apparent as soon as you consider the real market for collective goods. In most commercial transactions in simple goods and services it is passably realistic to assume a functional market and customers who can find the product that suits them, though there are challenges around production, management and scale economies even here. Nevertheless, in a half-decent market for a simple private good the consumer can move on if the product is bad: if the coffee you just bought is bitter and expensive you can probably find an alternative. But in 'public service markets' there may be the following difficulties, and only the first two of these lend themselves to Camp 2-type discussions about missing markets or information problems. The rest reflect the complexity of public services that caused them to be uploaded to the state in the first place.

- Few (or no) providers with a track record in supplying that service, and barriers to entry may be high (e.g., training costs, lack of experience).
- If performance is poor, a lack of alternative suppliers makes it difficult to switch provider.
- Lack of clarity about who the customer is – there may be a range of parties with conflicting, incommensurable preferences (consider the probation service; is its 'customer' the offender, the victim, the government, the courts, the society?). This is not a problem you can solve in neoclassical terms.

[21] William Lazonick, 'Innovative Enterprise and Sustainable Prosperity', Paper presented to the Institute for New Economic Thinking, Edinburgh, 23 October 2017, pp. 4–5.

The Analytical Sins of Omission

- No established way of determining a fair price (what's the outcome to be priced? Reoffending rates, inspection ratings, feedback from users?).
- No easy way to measure performance (the causes of reoffending rates, e.g., are complex, so what does the 'rate' show?).
- All markets have to contend with competition and company law, but public service markets need additional regulation to reflect the public interest and often complex statutory obligations.[22]

When governments talk up price competition in a public service market, they assume an existing market full of apt providers, but outsourced work is frequently to run complex public assets or to provide and manage large teams of essential personnel, that is, to provide services on a large scale, just as the state has done. In these situations, only large businesses will tend to be eligible for this scale of production and credible as project managers, so the new market will immediately tend towards monopoly or oligopoly. The only meaningful competition is further downstream, when those large service industry firms recruit multiple smaller firms to provide what is sometimes a significant proportion of the specific tasks the large firm will manage. Since government must tend to contract with large, monopoly or oligopoly, providers, however, their smaller, downstream suppliers typically find themselves subject to a monopoly buyer who can exploit that position to impose punitive deals and engage in late payments, and late downstream payment to small and medium-sized enterprises (SMEs) have become a chronic feature of UK government outsourcing.[23] This is the scenario of 'monopsony' or 'sole buyer' identified by Joan Robinson back in the 1930s, in which a dominant power in the buying relationship can set prices to maximise profits free from less exploitative competitors.[24] In effect, then, government often contracts itself to a dominant if not monopoly firm that can then leverage its power to exploit smaller firms for its own profit, which further limits market deepening.

---

[22] Institute for Government, 'Private versus Public Markets'. This page was accessed on the www.instituteforgovernment.org.uk website in 2016 but has since been removed.
[23] Gill Plimmer, 'UK Warns Government Contractors to Pay Suppliers or Risk Ban', *Financial Times*, 4 April 2019.
[24] Joan Robinson, *The Economics of Imperfect Competition* (London: Macmillan, 1933).

These dynamics are a far cry from the competitive market ideal, but SMEs are also unlikely to move up into the market for direct government contracting over time. This is not just because of their barely sustainable profit margins as downstream suppliers and their comparative lack of experience with government procurement but because of the punitive costs of low-chance competitive tenders for SMEs or social enterprises. Large public sector industry firms employ entire back offices of personnel that work exclusively on competitive tendering, whereas for a small firm that process demands valuable time, often from their whole team, and if they fail that cost is never recouped. SMEs literally cannot afford to play against the multinationals even if they could, in theory, grow to manage a larger scale of work, and that's before we talk about political lobbying and party donations.

While the supply side of this marketplace is hardly healthy in competitive terms and glosses over numerous dimensions of production, such as skills, the real 'buyer's market' bears even less resemblance to the theory. When governments asked the question 'who is the real customer?' this encouraged theoretic analyses and commissioning models to focus on choice versus non-choice environments for the end-users of services. The models and the political narratives focused on customer choice as opposed to straightforward allocation. This is because that was the only interface in public services that could resemble a marketplace – the only part of this story a neoclassical model could describe. Insofar as the state exists in these models it is depicted in the abstract terms of a sovereign, single event 'setter' of a market game in which the dynamics of choice and competition would subsequently play out, somehow autonomously. In reality, the only actual *market* relationship in public sector outsourcing is for procurement, in which the state or state agency is the only customer in any financial and economic sense.[25] And the state is not a standard neoclassical economic agent (in this case, as the customer) because it remains ultimately liable for service delivery, failures and their costs.

The marketplace for public service provision is fraught with pitfalls for the government as a buyer because the state will still have to manage the values of the service, its pricing and performance, the arising issues of company law and the difficulties of switching providers, all now

---

[25] Colin Crouch, 'The Paradoxes of Privatization and Public Service Outsourcing', *Political Quarterly* 86 (December 2015): 156–171, p. 161.

supposed to be resolved through the outsourcing contract and its oversight. For outsourcing to work, this agreement between the state and the public sector industry firm needs to operate as an effective junction of instruction, control and reward. Problems of contract, essentially the problem of whether a contract is watertight, is an area where Camp 2 insights about information asymmetries are instructive. But when you unpack the likely contractual failures – the asymmetries in the bargaining and monitoring positions between these 'players' – it becomes clear why even an application of second-best-world neoclassical reasoning leaves none of the promises of the first-best-world view intact.

Complexity and Incomplete Contracts

Within neoclassical economics both 'transaction cost economics' and 'contract theory' take Camp 1 ideas about market transactions and contracts and think critically about how problems might arise. These fields are dominated by Camp 2 economists who explore the conditions under which market failures are likely to occur. Both approaches tend to agree that all contracts for complex and dynamic goods or services are unavoidably 'incomplete': contracts will cause problems when they cannot specify what is to be done in every important circumstance the contract is supposed to cover.[26] The higher the complexity and contingency of tasks the contract is supposed to supervise, the higher the risk the contractor will only satisfy what's written in the contract, and this will be insufficient to protect the buyer. We could consequently expect 'satisficing' behaviour in contracts for complex services, when the contracting agent offers the minimum written requirement to save effort or cost.[27]

Transaction cost and contract theorists tend to agree that complex contracts are incomplete by reason of 'bounded rationality'; that is, each actor wants to act rationally – where each agent makes a fully informed cost–benefit analyses of their options to maximise their utility – but they will be constrained by incomplete information due to the

---

[26] Oliver Williamson, 'The Theory of the Firm as Governance Structure: From Choice to Contract', *Journal of Economic Perspective* 16 (3) (2002): 171–195, pp. 174, 188.

[27] Herbert Simon, 'Rational Choice and the Structure of the Environment', *Psychological Review* 63 (2) (1956): 129–138.

uncertain, contingent, complex or unquantifiable character of the task at hand.[28] In contrast to government procurement for standardised goods or physical structures, most public goods and service tasks are frequently marked by all these characteristics. Both transaction cost and contract theory would consequently stress that 'promises to behave' by providers signed up to incomplete contracts are unreliable because it would be rational for providers to behave opportunistically in these conditions. Nor could the courts be relied on as a last resort to sanction poor service providers because a court cannot transcend the lack of information about real behaviour any more than the government can. The contract is incomplete, and that's the problem.[29]

When unforeseen problems in an incomplete contract arise, the government will have to approach the contractor to renegotiate, but this provides profit-seeking companies with the opportunity to raise their prices.[30] It is in the nature of government services that the financial, organisational and political costs of trying to switch from one provider to another are prohibitive, and alternative providers are often unavailable.[31] The same risks attend cost overruns. In theory, a government could have a penalty clause that allows for a switch to another provider in the case of rising costs, but that is rarely an attractive option given the disruption of service it causes. As a result, the state's threats to walk out of a contract lack credibility, and it will find itself over a barrel in the face of contractors who rationally operate according to a satisficing 'plain text' reading of the contract. As Oliver Williamson warned in the 1970s, the leverage firms have in incomplete contracts means the much-publicised financial savings a government might make at the beginning of the contract disappear over time, to be replaced by significantly higher costs.[32] Governments can often claim a cost saving in the first year, but the real evidence comes later.

---

[28] Herbert Simon, *Models of Man, Social and Rational: Mathematical Essays on Rational Human Behavior in a Social Setting* (New York: John Wiley and Sons, 1957).

[29] Oliver Williamson, 'Opportunism and Its Critics', *Managerial and Decision Economics* 14 (2) (1993): 97–107.

[30] Oliver Williamson, 'Franchise Bidding for Natural Monopolies in General and with Respect to CATV', *Bell Journal of Economics* 7 (1) (1976): 73–104, p. 83.

[31] Paul Jensen and Robin Stonecash, 'Incentives and the Efficiency of Public Sector Outsourcing Contracts', *Journal of Economic Surveys* 19 (5) (2005): 767–787, p. 775.

[32] Williamson, 'Franchise Bidding'.

Looking through the analytical lens of Camp 2 it is clear that 'market failures' are rife in this context and likely to prove insurmountable. Public service markets are dominated by monopoly or oligopoly firms that are relatively immune from the disciplines of competition. Once the government is signed up, chronic information problems arise in the contract because the provider gains far more operating information than the buyer: the state. So-called hold-up problems will also develop where the government makes investments specific to that contractual relationship, since those investments – the state's 'sunk costs' – encourage the contractor to exploit the state's loss of bargaining power. The negative spillovers can be exceptionally socially damaging. Hard to codify tasks are often inherent in the public service in question and cannot be written into the contract in a binding form, but when vague requirements for service integrity are 'rationally' dropped by private providers it is families, volunteers, charities and other public services that are left to pick up the pieces. When interdependent services become subject to satisficing corporate performance, more systemic failures in provision become inevitable.

Camp 2 approaches assume that if you mend any points of market failure then the allocative system is en route to a cure. But that is to mistake the closed system of neoclassical economics for the open-system terrain. The promise of efficiency gain is a promise 'by theoretical definition', not an empirical likelihood. Such an approach can tell us little to nothing about how authority and resources are going to be redistributed by these policies and what kinds of feedback loops might be created by such a redistribution of institutional and financial powers. The picture that emerges resembles Soviet enterprise planning because the relationship between state and enterprise is similar, and as a result, so are the developing pathologies. This isomorphism between the two systems is rooted, firstly, in the establishment of an asymmetric power relationship between the state and the enterprises managed by it and, secondly, in the shared hegemony of a closed-system economic ideology. What both Soviet and neoliberal output planning for enterprises created was a constellation of vested, and co-dependent, institutional interests and firms too essential to production to fail. In both systems this proved a recipe for poor service, rising costs and straight-up exploitation of labour and resources at the public's expense.

The Reinvention of Soviet Enterprise Planning by Other Means

Advocates for outsourcing argued it would reduce costs and improve performance because high-powered incentives for efficiency are created by market competition and by the discipline of the capital market, because (shareholder) owners will supposedly require transparency and high performance from their own companies and because private firms are free of political interference.[33] But these ideas are all dependent offspring of the First Fundamental Welfare Theorem. In practice, public service industry firms (PSIFs) bear a marked resemblance to Soviet state-owned enterprises (SOEs). Like Soviet SOEs they operate in a doom loop of low incentives for high performance, high incentives for satisficing performance and immunity to government discipline, whose hands are tied by contractual incompleteness, the oligopolistic or monopolistic characteristics of the provision and the state's appropriate anxieties about breaks in production. These combine to give firms leverage over the government as the procurement agent. The arrow of political interference can fly the other way.

The isomorphism is not exact: Soviet planning hit some of its most serious failings around often simple private consumption goods, whereas outsourcing concerns mostly pure and impure public goods and services, often of real complexity. There are nevertheless extensive similarities between PSIFs and Soviet SOEs, specifically in the co-dependent relationship that plays out between the managerial state and the enterprise. As soon as the contract or plan begins there are information asymmetries in both systems between the state and the enterprise in year 't'. The state is then dragged into bargaining games it cannot win in years t+1, t+2, ad infinitum because the bargaining advantages only accrue to the enterprise. Although good news for neoliberals in theory, those enterprises then fail to display any of the virtues of productive wealth-building ascribed to them. Governments that outsource complex work are duly beset by what the critical economics of communism called 'soft budget constraint', where the state is locked into dysfunctional relations with firms. As Janos Kornai explained in *The Socialist System*, 'The concept of "budget constraint" is familiar

---

[33] David Osborne and Ted Gaebler, *Reinventing Government: How the Entrepreneurial Spirit Is Transforming the Public Sector* (New York: Addison-Wesley, 1992).

from the microeconomic theory of the household: the sum available to a decision-maker places a constraint on the consumer's spending that he or she can choose to incur.'[34] So, what happens, asks Kornai, if a state-owned firm's spending exceeds its budget constraint? And what happens if this is a regular occurrence? Kornai identified four forms of regular assistance in the 'classic' Soviet system, for which we can identify the functional equivalents in public sector outsourcing.

1. *'Soft subsidy*. The adjective 'soft' implies that this is not a case of a state subsidy at a level expressly laid down for a longer period. The amount of the subsidy is the subject of bargaining…Negotiations are made either in advance, before the amount of subsidy has been laid down, or during and after the period covered by the subsidy, to improve on the sum promised in advance.'[35]

In outsourcing too, the state is fated to engage in permissive bargaining when needs arise that it couldn't codify in a contract, and when PSIFs overspend. In their extensive studies of UK outsourcing, Bowman et al. identify multiple instances of significant direct and indirect subsidy in major contracts.[36]

2. *Soft taxation*. 'Soft' does not imply that the amount of net income the firm is obliged to pay in (the 'tax') is low. It means the amount is subject to prior and/or subsequent bargaining. The more possible it is to 'beat down' the firm's taxation by pressure or pleading, the softer it is.[37]

When it comes to outsourcing, tax-avoidant 'tax planning' is the likely primary route for large companies to soften their liabilities. In 2012, for example, the PSI conglomerates Atos and G4S were judged to have paid no corporation tax at all, owing to 'tax planning'.[38] However, tax bargaining is also undoubtedly part of this picture. Under neoliberal tax competition policies, the United Kingdom introduced selective discretion

---

[34] Janos Kornai, *The Socialist System* (Princeton: Princeton University Press, 1992), p. 140.
[35] Ibid., p. 141.
[36] Andrew Bowman, Ismail Ertürk, Julie Froud et al., *What a Waste: Outsourcing and Why It Goes Wrong* (Manchester: Manchester University Press, 2015), Chapters 3 and 4.
[37] Kornai, *The Socialist System*, p. 142.
[38] Simon Bowers, 'Public Sector Paid Big Outsourcing Firms 4 Billion Pounds NAO Report Reveals', *The Guardian*, 12 November 2013.

into the tax authority, Her Majesty's Revenue and Customs (HMRC). This shift from the convention of strict law enforcement to one of 'partnership' with large corporations increased the discretionary power of the regulator, but only in one direction. This situation was further intensified by simultaneous cuts in enforcement capacity (see Chapter 7). For the Soviets, these soft taxes were a particular feature of the demoralised 'bargained socialism' of the Brezhnev years, when Soviet governments all but abandoned the possibility of an efficient planning system. For neoliberals this discretionary tax lowering was an active ideological choice. At the same time, UK PSIFs have made massive use of debt financing for corporate expansions through mergers and acquisitions enabled by highly permissive tax write-offs against borrowing. Soft taxation is also matched by a capitalist version of Soviet 'soft credit' practices.

3. *Soft credit.* Under the Soviet system, 'soft' refers to the situation where the credit contract with the bank does not follow general, uniform principles, but a firm in trouble can 'whine' for credit that actually includes a veiled grant.[39]

The functional equivalent for large PSIFs in private financial markets is credit that is secured without any innovation or productive development but to facilitate new incomes streams via mergers and acquisitions. This occurs even though the increased gearing ratio for the company (the ratio of debt to shareholder equity) makes it more vulnerable to changes in discount rates, growth rates and cash flow forecasts. In addition, the tendency of the stock market to cheerlead for corporate growth and market concentration through mergers and acquisitions has tended to drive conglomerates to enter new service sectors where they lack any competence or knowledge.[40]

In a world of elastic accounting rules, as Adam Leaver has pointed out, Britain's large PSIFs have also increasingly borrowed against the future either by securitising their future income streams, using special dividends to holding companies in tax havens, or by over-optimistically booking profits based on forecasts and estimates. This last strategy was particularly available to outsourcing companies involved in long-term government contracts because they could book current profits based on total forecast profits, adjusted for whichever stage they could

---

[39] Kornai, *The Socialist System*, p. 142.
[40] Bowman et al., *What a Waste*, p. 58.

demonstrate they were at in the contract cycle. As Leaver explains, this accounting strategy 'pulls income from the future', which may not reflect the actual cash flows paid in the contract. Should firms get these forecasts wrong and book a large impairment that destabilises their business, the government is demonstrably likely to bail them out or adjust the contract to the benefit of the company.[41] There is an additional opportunity for creative accounting in large infrastructural projects, such as hospital trusts. As Mark Hellowell and Veronica Vecchi have shown, payments to the private operator are likely to be indexed in the contract to the Retail Price Index, which is typically higher than other measures such as the GDP deflator. This means that the indexing charges in most years will result in a real-term increase in the unitary charge.[42] This reliance on forecasting is itself an artefact of the closed-system economic ontology and the embedded concept that the future is a statistical shadow of the past.[43] As such it repeats the forecasting and business planning failures long suffered in the Soviet enterprise system but now with strong financial incentives and discrete creative accounting opportunities to game the methodology.

Finally, Soviet firms could benefit from what Kornai called 'soft administrative pricing'.

4. *Soft administrative pricing*. A significant proportion of prices in a classical socialist economy are set administratively. These appear to be prices dictated bureaucratically to the firm, but, in fact, they can be 'softened' by bargaining with the price authorities. There is advance bargaining in which the goal of the firm, branch directorate or ministry is to make the pricing authority 'acknowledge' the costs in the price, however low the efficiency of production. In subsequent bargaining a price increase is sought if extra costs have been incurred. In some other cases a disguised price rise is made in which the quality assumed when the price was set is lowered, a

---

[41] Adam Leaver, 'Outsourcing Firms and the Paradox of Time Travel', *SPERI Political Economy Blog*, 12 February 2018, www.speri.dept.shef.ac.uk.

[42] Mark Hellowell and Veronica Vecchi, 'The Non-incremental Road to Disaster? A Comparative Policy Analysis of Agency Problems in the Commissioning of Infrastructure Projects in the UK and Italy', *Journal of Comparative Policy Analysis: Research and Practice* 17 (5) (2015): 519–532, p. 529.

[43] Paul Davidson, 'Reality and Economic Theory', *Journal of Post-Keynesian Economics* 18 (4) (June 1996): 479–508, p. 479.

good material is substituted by an inferior material or certain finishing processes are omitted.[44]

This scenario plays out within public service industry outsourcing where prices and processes are set by the valuation of complex target indicators priced 'administratively'. The risk of price softening to the corporate advantage is high when the state has heavily invested in the contract or where high costs are attached to any disruption of the service or supplier substitution (given the new opportunity for hold-up) – that is to say, under the typical conditions.

Clearly, between their initial operating conditions and the lack of available disciplinary measures over time, large PSIFs and Soviet SOEs have far more in common with each other than with the firms in the competitive markets of the neoclassical imaginary. In practice, the outsourcing contract operates as a form of imperative planning instruction and not as a forecast or 'indicative plan' to be considered; prices are predominantly administrative and soft; contracts are usually long, incomplete and exit is punitively expensive financially, organisationally and politically; and the continuation of production is essential, so government operates under chronic soft-budget constraints. Demand for the good or service is often guaranteed. Under doctrinaire neoliberal governments PSIFs likewise benefit from an ever-increasing list of products to be produced.

The relationship between government and enterprise is also intrinsically politicised. In fact, in the light of chronic contractual failures, the Cabinet Office in 2011 was forced to create a body of 'Crown Representatives' to explicitly coordinate the 'Strategic Suppliers' of important goods and services. In the 2020–2021 financial year alone, these Strategic Suppliers earned £15.7 billion in government contracts. As the market analyst Tussell reported, this 'close proximity to the heart of government [offers] unrivalled liaison opportunities with key procurement stakeholders'[45] – in effect, a conduit for non-market relationships, if not outright corruption. Crown Representatives nevertheless have few meaningful powers under the favoured risk management tool, a Memorandum of Understanding. Beyond their contractual commitments the only corporate obligation under the Memorandum

---

[44] Kornai, *The Socialist System*, pp. 142–144.
[45] James Piggott, '2021 Analysis of UK Government Strategic Suppliers', 16 September 2021, www.tussell.com/insights/uk-government-strategic-suppliers.

(and therefore the only leverage available to Crown Representatives) is to report anything that 'may present a risk' to the government.[46]

From the UK taxpayers' perspective, this outsourcing architecture is *more* dysfunctional in how it sets up corporate incentives than the Soviet system. Soviet SOEs had poor incentives to fulfil targets because wages were flat and political motivation was far weaker than required and further undermined by corruption. It didn't help that the new period target was typically set on the previous year's performance – the 'ratchet principle' – so that if you fulfilled your target, you were guaranteed a tougher target for the following year with no further reward. Under outsourcing, PSIFs are incentivised to sweat their contracts for profit by their stock-holding executive pay structures and by the incompleteness of contractual specifications, since beyond creative accounting measures corporate profit margins reside in fulfilling their contracts on the plain-text reading. The dominant principle for corporate governance under neoliberalism is that firms should 'maximise shareholder value' (see Chapter 7). Firms consequently operate under powerful financial market pressures to maximise shareholder dividends, even at the expense of productive reinvestment in the firm's productive capacity, a process referred to as 'financialisation' in economic sociology.[47]

The important distinction with Soviet enterprise planning is that money is clearly anything but passive within the public services outsourcing regime, and not in a positive way for the taxpayer or for the citizens who depend on these services. Exceptionally sheltered from competition as they are, PSIFs have proved even more prone to financialisation than those in sectors more exposed to competition.[48] In addition, the tougher any government tries to be in its contract pricing, the more damaging the persistent margin-seeking by firms is likely to prove. The 2018 collapse of the PSI multinational, Carillion, was not a freakish case but typical of firms under the prevailing incentive

---

[46] Cabinet Office, 'Crown Representatives and Strategic Suppliers', 7 November 2012, www.gov.uk/government/publications/strategic-suppliers.

[47] Natascha Van der Zwan, 'Making Sense of Financialization', *Socio-Economic Review* 12 (1) (2014): 99–129.

[48] Colin Haslam and Nick Tsitsianis, Written Evidence to the Public Administration and Constitutional Affairs Committee, 'After Carillion: Public Sector Outsourcing and Contracting', 3 July 2018 (HC 748), p. 29, www.publications.parliament.uk/pa/cm201719/cmselect/cmpubadm/748/748.pdf.

structure. Carillion's management misjudged when the capital market would call 'time', but as Gill Plimmer, Adam Leaver, Colin Haslam and Nikolaos Tsitianis have all shown, the entire sector has long tended towards deepening debt, self-cannibalising dividend pay-out ratios, poor service provision and late payments to suppliers. Another conglomerate, Interserve, went into administration in March 2019. This chronic tendency to gear companies to high debt and high pay-outs to shareholders makes a mockery of government calls on PSIFs to end late payment to suppliers – so long as their balance sheets are gamed in this way the government's enforcement of timely payments could be fatal, as the government well knows. When Carillion went bust it owed over £2 billion to 30,000 suppliers, subcontractors and short-term creditors.[49]

The neoclassical defence of monopoly is that reputational effects discipline dominant firms against satisficing behaviour, and their profit motive remains high,[50] but this presumes that financially extractive, 'rentier' behaviour would not be enabled by state actors. Context matters, clearly. As doctrinaire British governments became dependent on the survival of dominant firms, the reputational damage to poor providers was evidently nil, and the pressures only grew for government collusion in extractive corporate governance. A Public Accounts Committee investigation found that Serco and G4S were awarded fourteen new contracts by five departments worth £350 million even as they were being investigated by the Serious Fraud Office for defrauding the Ministry of Justice (MoJ). This happened even though the justice minister, Chris Grayling, had committed to make no awards until the case was resolved. The MoJ was among the five.[51] Interserve put out profit warnings in May 2016, October 2017 and November 2018 but was still awarded £665 million in public contracts through 2017–2018.[52]

---

[49] Gill Plimmer, 'UK Warns Government Contractors to Pay Suppliers Promptly or Risk Ban', *Financial Times*, 4 April 2019.
[50] Michael C. Jensen and William H. Meckling, 'Theory of the Firm: Managerial Behaviour, Agency Costs and Ownership Structure', *Journal of Financial Economics* 3 (4) (October 1976): 305–360.
[51] Gill Plimmer and Sarah Neville, 'G4S and Serco Won Whitehall Work despite Being "on Probation"', *Financial Times*, 10 December 2014.
[52] GMB Union 2019, 'Interserve Handed £660 Million Taxpayer Contracts Months before Facing Collapse', March 2019, www.gmb.org.uk.

The trouble with insisting that a policy has a scientific basis when it does not is that when it fails, its advocates can insist the fault lies in the execution of the policy, not its conception. The result in British outsourcing was a series of Camp 2 efforts towards the resolution of the microeconomic market failures. If we run through these analytical 'sins of commission', we can see why they would prove so inadequate. Following its highly critical 2014 inquiry, the cross-party Public Accounts Committee concluded that '[g]overnment needs a far more professional and skilled approach to managing contracts and contractors, and contractors need to demonstrate the high standards of ethics expected in the conduct of public business and be more transparent about their performance and costs'.[53] The failures are conceived here as the Camp 2 problems of excess costs arising from failures of understanding and information. The proposed remedy was to tighten the negotiation and cost component of contracts and improve the commercial and corporate expertise of the *state*. In the meantime, PSIFs were politely requested to, in effect, 'behave more like Camp 1 theory says you will', a request they promptly ignored.

What would it take to create competitive service markets and sustain them against their historical tendency to fail around complex goods? Or to somehow build a bureaucratic imitation of a functioning market? The Camp 2 answer implies an administrative effort that would have made the Soviet planners blush. The Institute for Government is a UK think tank that works closely with Whitehall on administrative reforms. To tackle the higher complexity of public service markets the Institute designed a 'market stewardship framework', which is worth reviewing because it sets out precisely what Camp 2 neoclassical economics would advise to improve the situation. The Institute notes that whereas '[c]ommissioning models often focus on understanding user needs and choosing the right providers, market stewardship takes a broader perspective, considering how to set the rules of the market so that competition between those providers works effectively' (i.e., thus completing the circle of market connections). Their framework required the following:

- Determine the outcomes you are looking for, balancing the needs of all those affected by the service.

[53] Public Accounts Committee, 'Contracting Out Public Services to the Private Sector', p. 3.

- Ensure there is enough money to pay for the services required.
- Ensure users have good information on which to base their decisions.
- Decide how to encourage new entrants into the market.
- Decide the criteria to use for selecting providers.
- Decide how to monitor performance, reward high performers and punish poor performers.
- Decide the process for switching providers if performance is not acceptable, while maintaining service continuity and standards.[54]

While the remedies are consistent in theory – market failures are to be mended at their individual junctions of failure – they are extraordinary in their practical implications. In the first place, the requirement to 'determine the outcomes you are looking for' in an uncertain and synergistic world invites government to try to anticipate and quantify outcomes. This is a recipe for extensive bureaucratic rigidification, and in the absence of Godlike foresight it is bound to fail. Even without attempts to build 'complete' outcome indicators, contract theory has long warned that where an agent must perform many different tasks their effort will be allocated to the task most easily measured and hence rewarded. Increased 'productivity' will duly come at the expense of output quality.[55] To examine this measurement problem the contract theorists Oliver Hart, Andrei Shleifer and Robert Vishny modelled how, in a world of incomplete contracts, a private firm has stronger incentives to reduce costs and improve quality than the public sector but the incentive to reduce costs may overwhelm the incentive to improve quality if quality is difficult to measure (i.e., it is non-contractible).[56]

Soviet experience is again instructive here. The combination of cash limits and targets under communist planning had created incentives against innovation or performance optimisation. So long as the objective was to fulfil the agreed plan target there was no incentive to reach

---

[54] Institute for Government, 'The Market Stewardship Framework', www.instituteforgovernment.org.uk. Accessed in 2016, this work is no longer available on the website.

[55] Bengt Holmstrom and Paul Milgrom, 'Multitask Principal-Agent Analyses: Incentive Contracts, Asset Ownership, and Job Design', *Journal of Law, Economics and Organization* 7 (1991): 24–52.

[56] Oliver Hart, Andrei Shleifer and Robert Vishny, 'The Proper Scope of Government: Theory and an Application to Prisons', *Quarterly Journal of Economics* 112 (1997): 1127–1161.

The Reinvention of Soviet Enterprise Planning by Other Means 149

any level of output, sales or profit defined outside the sphere of bargaining.[57] When the state responded with more complex targets the result was simply more rigid bureaucracy in the face of changing needs and technologies, and often incompatible targets that the producers would sort by ease of fulfilment over functional importance. The greater the clarity of the performance outcome, the lower the incentives for adaptation, initiative or innovation.[58] The accurate planning of outcomes had also depended on forecasts, which in turn depended on precise information about the status quo and on the past being representative of the future. It follows that if you apply pseudo-synoptic outcome targets and intensify payment-by-results incentives for PSIFs around those targets, the most likely outcome is that you will provoke the same misreporting and widening discrepancies between production and allocation that had characterised Soviet planning. The only difference, and it is not a good one, is that PSIFs will also prioritise cost and quality reductions to boost profits.

As Kornai also noted of the Soviet system, if the regulatory net was not dense enough to cope, its holes had to be plugged with a succession of new regulations and an expansion of bureaucracy. Similarly, in the United Kingdom, the more comprehensive imperative planning became, the more government agencies had to develop synoptic oversight capacity not just over, but *between*, all interdependent contracts. As noted in Chapter 2, the distorting effects of extensively determined target outcomes in the Soviet system had been quickly understood, but criticism was impolitic until Joseph Stalin's death. As soon as he achieved power, Nikita Khrushchev tried to reduce the indicators in national plans and Alexei Kosygin's reforms sought to reduce targets and increase enterprise management flexibility.[59] In short, the Soviets abandoned synoptic enterprise targets by the 1960s, but here they are, at the methodological frontier of neoliberalism.

To stay with the Institute for Government's list of requirements for good stewardship, ensuring sufficient funds for services is difficult around outsourcing given the informational asymmetries between

---

[57] Martin Myant, *Transforming Socialist Economies: The Case of Poland and Czechoslovakia* (Basingstoke: Edward Elgar, 1993), p. 17.
[58] Kornai, *The Socialist System*, p. 130.
[59] T. Laverty, 'The Soviet Central Planning Process: New Methods and Continuing Problems', *The Journal of Social, Political, and Economic Studies* 7 (3) (Fall 1982): 207–240, p. 211.

supplier and buyer. As the Public Accounts Committee concluded, cost overruns are a chronic feature of outsourcing and by no small amount. In 2014, the National Audit Office concluded that the Aspire IT contract with HMRC had cost double the original contracting price, along with double the profit for the contractors.[60] Without practical solutions to these contractual asymmetries this cost inflation must continue as it did under Leninism, and Leninism operated without financial market pressures for rising dividends. The third stewardship rule, that users must operate with good information, is more difficult than it sounds. For the market metaphor to work, the end-user 'customers' must be able to make an informed choice, and a choice has to exist, but this picture is just a bad description of the majority of outsourced service conditions. To take just one example, people with disabilities who need to reliably access their financial support are not out shopping for a t-shirt.

Moreover, to encourage higher public service industry competition (the fourth point in the Institute's list) the state is supposed to encourage not just new large firms but also SME and third-sector providers. For central departments and government agencies to employ smaller contractors directly would at least protect those firms from the abuses of private monopsonists. But consider the ideological contortion involved in this idea. Here the state is no longer the self-seeking Leviathan that justified these reforms but an agent that should think not just about its own immediate financial interest but also about how to build a better future market for itself, as the customer, regardless of the increased logistical complexity for tendering and the increased transaction costs from that effort. The more obvious solution is to think undogmatically about economies of scale and to understand the perils of contracting out for complex, contingent services, particularly from 'the centre'. Do this and the debate would immediately reopen about the devolution of resources and authority to local and regional governments and about how to build their capacity to sustain public service provision where close monitoring, complete contracting and competitive markets aren't possible.

Regarding the last three requirements for 'market stewardship', the 2014 Public Accounts Committee followed the NPM line and called

---

[60] John Stokdyk, 'HMRC Aspire Contract Will End in 2017', *Accounting Web*, 30 March 2016, www.accountingweb.co.uk/tax/business-tax/hmrc-aspire-it-contract-will-end-in-2017.

on government to increase business expertise within the state, as if the private sector's delinquency in this story was purely a function of government failure. But the more state capacity is outsourced to private companies and consultancies, the more in-house policy expertise and institutional memory are further degraded, and those corporate actors will themselves advise on procurement strategies in which their own firms might well carry a financial interest. This is an environment in which critical, disinterested civil servants and Members of Parliament will lose influence, and this too is an affinity with the Soviet system. Specialist knowledge was often screened out under Stalin on the basis that experts were politically unreliable. Real authority was given instead to those who lacked competence but supported orthodoxy, and in the neoliberal context this means political and business actors alike.[61] Successive British governments have endowed large business corporations and major accountancy firms, which have already proved incompetent (c.f. Carillion), with enhanced policymaking influence and new contracts, and the result is a significant increase in avoidable ignorance and systemic risk, as in the Soviet system.

When the architecture of the state becomes this porous to business, all it takes to translate these networks of informal ties into corrupt networks is for ministers to become opportunistic, a step that the second Johnson cabinet clearly took during the Covid pandemic of 2020–2021. Of the 1,200 government contracts made public, worth around £18 billion, a staggering £9 billion went via a designated 'VIP track' to companies run by friends, party donors and associations of that cabinet and to companies with a record that included poor credit ratings, declared assets of less than £5, no trading history at all or a history of fraud, tax evasion or even human rights abuses. Many companies with the right experience and capacity but no political contacts got nowhere.[62] With informality came more complete policy failure. The National Audit Office likewise found that 70 per cent of early contracts for the test and trace system so critical to manage the pandemic had been awarded without competition and that, despite spending £22 billion, there were systematic failure to reach targets

---

[61] Michael Ellman, *Socialist Planning*, 3rd ed. (Cambridge: Cambridge University Press, 2014), p. 43.
[62] Jane Bradley, Selam Gebrekidan and Allison McCann, 'Inside Britain's Pandemic Spending', *New York Times*, 17 December 2020.

and integrate the work of the private companies involved with the more experienced and informed local public health teams.[63] By May 2021 the Public Accounts Committee found that the same 'track and trace' system had failed to make a 'measurable difference' against the pandemic, and it identified a 'staggering' deployment of around 2,500 private consultants who had failed to make it work.[64]

British public sector outsourcing in practice refutes not just the promises of Camp 1 neoliberals but also the more inclusive promises of New Labour that had hoped for 'a plural state, where multiple interdependent actors contribute to the delivery of public services, and a pluralist state, where multiple processes inform the policymaking system'.[65] To the contrary, outsourcing demonstrates the most dysfunctional potentialities of states and markets. Large swathes of the state are dominated by highly financialised public service industry multinationals and the large, networked fields of business around those firms, not least in law and accountancy. The market power of this constellation has been reinforced by rights-to-tender under domestic and EU competition rules, strengthening a powerful lobby for yet further 'market' expansion, though it hardly deserves the name. This market in practice is characterised by concentration, poor-to-atrocious performance and increasingly elaborate but inescapably lagging bureaucratic oversight, as well as increasingly open political corruption. Given parallel cuts in civil service capacity and the drive towards disaggregated administrative function (as discussed later), the paths were laid for multi-level institutional asymmetries in resources, information and political economic power.

More than any reversion to either unified public ownership or towards the recommended methods for an improved market stewardship, the government solution under post-Global Financial Crisis 'austerity' after 2010 was to drive a harder bargain around pricing and costs in outsourcing, with government agencies accepting only

---

[63] Report by the Comptroller and Auditor General, 'The Government's Approach to Test and Trace in England – Interim Report', 11 December 2020 (HC 1070), p. 5, www.nao.org.uk/wp-content/uploads/2020/12/The-governments-approach-to-test-and-trace-in-England-interim-report.pdf.
[64] Sarah Neville, 'England's £23 Billion Test and Trace System Condemned by MPs', *Financial Times*, 10 March 2021.
[65] Stephen Osborne, ed., *The New Public Governance: Emerging Perspectives on the Theory and Practice of Public Governance* (London: Routledge, 2010), p. 9.

the lowest cost tender as a matter of course, at least until the Covid pandemic. The strict recourse to cost efficiency as 'the correct line' created a serious adverse selection problem. Given the objective difficulty of knowing what accurate pricing in complex or uncertain contracts would be, only companies with least regard for service quality and most determined to deploy a strategy of subsequent 'hold up' could rationally underbid for contracts with no guarantee they could stay within those margins. Carillion was just such a repeat 'winner' in competitive tendering, and its bankruptcy and liquidation alone cost UK taxpayers £148 million.[66]

The United Kingdom's central government outsourcing resolved the always-hypothetical bureaucratic rent-seeking behaviours of public servants by creating still–expanding opportunities for real rent-seeking by highly financialised large private business actors, while the taxpayer continued to foot the bill. Moreover, these policies now operated in conditions less covered by ethics codes and informational transparency than the public systems that preceded them. The result, as in the Soviet Union, is epic scope for moral hazard. Deteriorating service quality, rising costs and the demoralisation of de-professionalised public servants are baked into the prevailing incentive system around outsourcing, as they were under Soviet central planning. When institutional architectures are misconceived but enforced as 'scientific' doctrine, then rational people are incentivised to do damaging things, and conscientious people are forced to spend huge additional effort to limit the harm inflicted by the systems within which they work. When that effort becomes too exhausting, as it must, the most vocational, conscientious and experienced people leave. The most devastating unanticipated aspect of public sector outsourcing is consequently that it hollows out the public sector but leaves a super-corruptible, capitalist version of Soviet enterprise management in its stead.

Privatisation

On the face of it, privatisation looks more ideologically coherent. It implies a straight sale of all or part of a public asset to private ownership. But privatisation has rarely produced the market efficiencies

---

[66] 'Carillion Collapse to Cost Taxpayers £148 million', BBC News, 7 June 2018.

envisaged in neoclassical theory.[67] This is because the state has had to step in to compensate for failures in what remain strategically important sectors, only now it has to do so via the arm's-length direction and control that is 'regulation'. It is in the nature of the majority of public assets being privatised, however, that regulation is incomplete for the same reasons we see in the outsourcing of complex goods. It follows that this too will engender bargaining games that the state cannot win so long as the prevailing orthodoxy holds.

The public choice critique of public ownership in general is that incentives for efficiency are low and vote-seeking governments will maximise consumer surplus and workers' wages and skew pricing at the expense of profitability, with underinvestment the result.[68] However, when it comes to natural monopolies and industries where a network becomes more valuable the more people use it (a 'positive network externality'), such as a mobile phone network, the privatisation of a public monopoly will most likely result in a private monopoly. The risk with utility privatisation is that government and society are left with a private monopoly now free to exploit networks of both high strategic and social importance for purely private advantage. A private firm might use its monopoly power to extract the maximum price for meeting consumer demand with a purely profit-based – satisficing – consideration of social needs and strategic interests[69] – no trivial matter in the era of climate change.

The extent to which a traded corporation will act opportunistically depends strongly on the dominant culture of corporate governance. The neoliberal principle of maximising shareholder value has led to the systematic downgrading of investment as a managerial priority. The financialisation of traded businesses in neoliberal economies has led to profit-taking that is excessive, extractive and damaging to the sustainability of the firm. As a matter of Camp 1 neoclassical logic, however, the idea that firms will be less than highly functional cogs in the market machine is excised from its closed-system reasoning no less than it was from its Soviet counterpart.

---

[67] Crouch, 'The Paradoxes', p. 157.
[68] David Parker, 'Editorial: Lessons from Privatization', *Economic Affairs* 24 (3) (2004): 2–82, p. 4.
[69] Cento Veljanovski, 'Monopoly Manacles the Capital Market', *Economic Affairs* 7 (3) (1987): 20–22.

Contrary to the fantasy of the state withering away, privatisation changed but could not abolish the necessary role of the state.[70] In principle, ownership is not the decisive factor in determining whether a firm is well managed and will tend to reinvest in its long-term survival; opportunistic behaviour is as possible in private as it is in public ownership, particularly under conditions of monopoly. From the Camp 2 perspective, what matters is consequently the capacity of the state to constrain this more opportunistic behaviour. However, having handed away direct responsibility for the performance of a major public utility such as gas, electricity or water and, with it, the extensive information about the needs and risks that attend their supply, the state has to establish a system of regulation to prevent the private abuse of monopoly powers.[71] The problem is that the regulator will now have less information and far less control than the state once had as owner. British governments thus chose to establish industry regulators and in the first instance retained so-called golden shares – a significant, if not 51 per cent, stake of shares to retain voting rights, although typically only for a limited period.

Technological changes and improvements in economic regulation through the 1970s and 1980s had made it more plausible that at least some formerly natural monopolies such as telecommunications might operate more competitively. In practice, however, the incentives for any government to break up natural monopolies for sale were poor since the pricing of the firm on financial markets (and hence the expected government receipts) reflected expected future profits. A future monopoly had better prospects than a smaller number of firms.[72] It was also unclear in many cases how best to divide the monopoly in functional terms. The result was ironic. A theory built on the premise that governments are self-interested never anticipated that privatisation would create the Hobson's choice that governments could either be fiscally prudent and privatise a monopoly or be market-makers and break it up (assuming that was functionally possible). They couldn't do both.

---

[70] Peter Self, *Government by the Market?* (Basingstoke: Macmillan International, 1993), pp. 98–101.
[71] Ibid.
[72] Stephen King, 'A Privatized Monopoly Is Still a Monopoly, and Consumers Pay the Price', *The Conversation*, 24 June 2014, https://theconversation.com/a-privatised-monopoly-is-still-a-monopoly-and-consumers-pay-the-price-28384.

The UK telecommunications, energy and water sectors have all seen the continuation of dominant firms precisely because of the strong positive 'network externalities' intrinsic to their services. Regulators have consequently had to consider how to influence prices to benefit those networks. It soon became apparent that the best operating set-up might have to include subsidy or an equivalent funding mechanism to encourage network-building, as well as that the best way to encourage this was to keep at least some prices below cost.[73] The resulting competition has been oligopolistic at best,[74] and effective regulation extremely difficult. As a highly competitive market failed to materialise naturally, and the market that existed failed to add long-term value to these firms, the new regulators found themselves operating under the same informational constraints as the outsourcing departments of the previous section.

As Colin Crouch points out, rather than the original expectation that the regulator would only have to concern itself with price behaviour in a newly diversified market, UK regulators confronted private monopolies and immediately had to act on additional policy concerns such as whether to ensure political balance or to restrict pornography in broadcast media. Around pricing, the regulator faced major problems such as how to persuade energy suppliers to offer lower prices when demand failed to rise or fall with price, contra the price-competition assumptions of privatisation.[75] Such 'inelastic' demand is a gift for monopoly suppliers since it tempts them to raise prices in the certain knowledge that their indispensable product will still be consumed. It also turned out that consumers had better things to do than monitor electricity prices, contrary to the rational actor assumptions of neoclassical theory. In the absence of competition in their sector, Britain's Office of Water Supply had attempted 'yardstick competition', wherein rates charged in different regions plus cost differentials were compared to assess relative cost performance. Water prices nevertheless rose considerably faster than inflation.[76] According to the National Audit Office household

---

[73] 'Network Externalities in Telecommunications: Theory and Application', *Frontier Economics*, 29 June 2005.
[74] Crouch, 'The Paradoxes', pp. 158–159.   [75] Ibid., p. 159.
[76] Steven Vogel, *Freer Markets, More Rules: Regulatory Reform in Advanced Industrial Countries* (Ithaca: Cornell University Press, 1996), pp. 126–127.

water bills by 2014–2015 had risen by 40 per cent in real terms since privatisation in 1989.[77]

As for the firms themselves, these large public service industry firms are again associated less with the competitive dynamism of neoliberal promise than with financialisation. Future profitability and investment have been leveraged for present extraction.[78] Between 2010 and 2017 privatised water companies paid out £13.5 billion in dividends,[79] and the drought of 2022 brought home how consequential the lack of investment in infrastructure could prove for future food security. As the business became primarily a financial vehicle, its assets had become resources to be sweated rather than enhanced.

As Dieter Helm and Tom Tindall have shown, the ownership characteristics of infrastructure and utilities have tended to progress through remarkably consistent stages. Once privatised, the state's policy was to focus on achieving dispersed share ownership of those assets since, in keeping with doctrine, more flexible and dynamic shareholding was supposed to discipline the company to retain its profit margins through efficient operation. In practice, the concentration of share ownership in these utilities began almost immediately, and the companies became high prizes for mergers and acquisitions given their large cash balances, low debt levels and high revenues from initially poor price control by inexperienced regulators. The first wave of concentration was mostly conducted by UK companies to create vertically integrated multi-utility companies and there were genuine regional economies of scale available in IT, billing and operational planning. However, given Britain's open market for 'corporate control' – British governments are willing to allow takeovers of even strategically important companies – the next wave of takeovers came from US and European corporations less equipped to monitor the managers of their distant investments. The dominant EU energy companies duly began what the authors call 'an extraordinary period of consolidation'. While theoretical arguments could be made about economies of scale and vertical integration (all virtues that a state-owned firm could, and indeed typically had, exercised

---

[77] Report by the Comptroller and Auditor General, 'The Economic Regulation of the Water Sector', 14 October 2015 (HC 487), p. 4, www.nao.org.uk/wp-content/uploads/2014/07/The-economic-regulation-of-the-water-sector.pdf.
[78] Leaver, 'Outsourcing Firms and the Paradox'.
[79] Toby Helm, 'Private Water Pay-Outs Are a Public Scandal Says Labour', *The Guardian*, 11 February 2018.

in the public interest) the practical upshot was an immense accumulation of market power on the part of a few multinational corporations creating new, unanticipated risks around the security of supply and long-term investment.[80] The governing Camp 1 assumption that profits would be produced by higher quality and lower cost performance in a competitive marketplace turned out to be completely naive.

It is the most recent changes in ownership that have proved the most socially and environmentally damaging, however, and these follow the arrival of the truly dedicated financial engineers, namely private equity and infrastructure funds. As Helm and Tindall explain, following acquisitions, equity (shares) have been substantially replaced by debt and asset sales, not least to other private equity firms, often after only a four- to five-year timeframe. These seriously misnamed 'investment' funds have no obvious interest in the long-term quality or sustainability of their assets, which they effectively strip for value in whatever way is compatible with regulatory conditions. The problem is that those conditions are inescapably permissive for the same reasons of asymmetrical information and structural dependence that afflict outsourcing. The neoclassical analytical monoculture also means that the regulator has tended to underestimate how willing corporations would be to take on high risk debt over more prudent long-term corporate governance. The result has been increased gearing of balance sheets to the point of exhaustion, where debt is unsustainable. The upshot is that share and bond holders in private equity funds have gained at the cost of investment, service quality, pay and conditions in companies that are a critical dimension of UK infrastructure.[81] The social and environmental consequences can be grotesque: in 2019 it was found that water companies in England had discharged raw sewage into rivers on more than 200,000 occasions, in a context where dividends of over £57 billion had been paid out since 1991.[82] In 2021, Southern Water was fined £90 million for deliberately dumping billions of litres of raw sewage into the sea.[83]

---

[80] Dieter Helm and Tom Tindall, 'The Evolution of Infrastructure and Utility Ownership and Its Implications', *Oxford Review of Economic Policy* 25 (3) (2009): 411–434, pp. 420–425.
[81] Ibid.
[82] Sandra Laville and Niamh McIntyre, 'Water Firms Discharged Raw Sewage into English Rivers 200,000 Times in 2019', *The Guardian*, 1 July 2020.
[83] 'Southern Water Fined Record £90 m for Dumping Raw Sewage', BBC News, 9 July 2021.

Counter-intuitive though it may be, there are established neoclassical corporate finance arguments for the potential 'disciplinary gains' of debt, since in theory, debt holders might be 'rationally' motivated to constrain future risk-taking by the company to ensure that they get repaid.[84] In the reality of modern financial markets, the 'securitisation' of debt in which debt can be re-parcelled and sold on within the financial system means that it is far less straightforward to track corporate debt, and hence corporate risk, than it used to be. Helm and Tindall concluded that by 2009 all privatised utilities of the United Kingdom had become far more highly geared, but borrowing had not been used to fund investment, which was simply neglected. In separate research Helm estimates the total capital expenditure required in UK utilities and infrastructure at close to £500 billion from 2009 to 2020.[85]

In the absence of renationalisation or any shift away from financialisation, any actions by the state to restore the fundamentals of these firms would simply enable the same financially extractive game to be played all over again at the consumers' and taxpayers' expense.[86] In the meantime, none of this takes into account the fact that a resilient and sustainable national infrastructure is of ever greater importance in the era of climate change. The current regime has the virtues of neither the historical public regime nor the private regime of the neoclassical imaginary, since neither the high information, strategic oversight and policy-directedness of the mandated public sphere nor the theoretical allocative efficiency of the market sphere is predominantly in play.

Though the focus here is on institutional dynamics, we should register the social as well as environmental consequences of this uncritical faith in the superiority of markets to govern all forms of activity. To take just one example, the Cameron Coalition government privatised Britain's world-class Forensic Science Service (FSS) in 2012 and argued that private and police laboratories could do the same work at lower cost. In a survey taken by *New Scientist*, 75 per cent of the 365 forensic scientists questioned believed the closure of the FSS would lead to

---

[84] Matthias Dewatripont and Jean Tirole, 'A Theory of Debt and Equity: Diversity of Securities and Manager-Shareholder Congruence', *The Quarterly Journal of Economics* 109 (4) (November 1994): 1027–1054.

[85] Dieter Helm, 'Infrastructure Investment and the Economic Crisis', in Dieter Helm, James Wardlaw and Ben Caldecott, *Delivering a 21st Century Infrastructure for Britain* (London: Policy Exchange, 2009), p. 6.

[86] Helm and Tindall, 'The Evolution of Infrastructure', p. 433.

more miscarriages of justice.[87] The FSS itself warned that both expertise and the impartiality of forensic evidence would be lost and that the private market lacked the capacity to deal with demand. Following five years of continuous warnings the UK police were forced to review 10,000 cases in forensics in 2017 after they discovered data manipulation and disclosure failures by private companies, a recall that had dire implications for public trust in the justice system as a whole.[88]

If we count only the major privatisations from 1970 to 2014, the United Kingdom sold off £71.6 billion in public assets – a major loss in terms of future government revenues given the long-term profitability of a very large proportion of these assets, most notably in those sectors prone to natural monopoly such as energy, utilities and transport.[89] These income losses helped to pull the bearing floor out from under UK public finances as liabilities failed to shrink even as revenues were handed away. A single generation of doctrinaire neoliberal governments sold off public assets created over decades and even centuries, all paid for by the taxpayer for the common good, only to create a utility infrastructure that is less and less fit for purpose.

Agencification

Camp 1 logic assumes that delegating governance to market actors will automatically be more efficient than the vertically integrated bureaucracy or any other more relational, cooperative forms of organisational solution. This error followed directly from the implicit public choice assertion that the state's tasks are no different from those of simple markets, and hence all tasks are equally well-governed through market transactions. In addition to outsourcing and privatisation, Britain's neoliberal governments have insisted on transforming what remained of state structures into 'firm-like' units wherever possible. They assumed that this would mean an increasingly cost-effective production system and that 'cost-effectiveness' was always open to meaningful measurement. The logic was that politicians should focus on

---

[87] Robin McKie, 'Axing of Forensic Science Service May Lead to Miscarriages of Justice Scientists Warn', *The Guardian*, 12 February 2012.
[88] Hannah Devlin and Vikram Dodd, 'Police Review 10,000 Cases in Data Manipulation Inquiry', *The Guardian*, 21 November 2017.
[89] Chris Rhodes, David Hough and Louis Butcher, 'Privatisations', *House of Commons Library Research Paper* 14/61, 20 November 2014, p. 14.

their core brief – policy development – while implementation would be improved via more market-like production regimes, as if form and function were never connected. Politicians would be liberated to 'steer, not row'.

This promise of market-like efficiency tended to wish away the continuous need for high-quality feedback to decision-makers, not just about how a policy was working but about how needs were changing. It tended to sidestep the problem that such informational fragmentation would reduce the executive's understanding of the sector itself and its relationships and interdependencies with other sectors. As in outsourcing and privatisation, therefore, the policy of agencification assumed that the virtues present within the theoretical archetype of a rational firm operating within a competitive market would come to bear, even though that idea was a utopian fiction and this was an environment that offered none of the necessary conditions for competition to apply. Public choice theorists had argued against the existence of virtues in the post-war Weberian state such as the flexibility that came with input planning, devolved authority and discretion; the state's distinctive boundaries and accountability; the development of a public service ethos; political disinterest, neutrality and hence the effort towards objectivity; clear attention to and respect for the law; and institutional continuity and significant tacit knowledge and expertise.[90] Convinced governments could now assume that the virtues of markets would obtain and there was little of value to lose.

As Matthew Flinders points out, the modern state could hardly function without some delegation as its responsibilities grew. But rather than empower democratically accountable local or regional authorities with higher responsibilities and the resources to match, the neoliberal revolution opted to create agencies, arm's length bodies and public–private partnerships of various forms. The result according to Flinders was a blurring of the boundaries of the state by 'nature, role and direction'.[91] The idea of agencification in the United Kingdom originated in the *Improving Management in Government: Next Steps*

[90] Christopher Politt and Geert Bouckaert, *Public Management Reform: A Comparative Analysis: New Public Management, Governance, and the Neo-Weberian State* (Oxford: Oxford University Press, 2011), Section 1.8.
[91] Matthew Flinders, 'Public/Private: The Boundaries of the State', in Colin Hay, Michael Lister and David Marsh, *The State: Theories and Issues* (London: Palgrave Macmillan, 2006), p. 224.

review of 1988 under Margaret Thatcher's first administration.[92] *Next Steps* had argued that agencies and other delegated bodies should become the new vehicle for the delivery of public services and civil servants should transfer into them. Conceived along public choice lines these measures were supposed to break up the monolithic civil service with its centrally set rules and improve them through an idealised corporate-style dynamism.[93]

Agencies were designed to imitate firms. Emphasis was laid on production outputs, as if the outputs of central state departments were the social equivalent of nuts and bolts and could be made to conform to processes designed for material production. In practice this meant that the outputs of public agencies were determined not by the perfectly informed consumer demand in a neoclassical marketplace but by operational and financial performance targets – output targets – set by the parent department. The agency became accountable for meeting those targets, and the chief executive had strong personal accountability written into their employment contract.[94] According to the new logic, agencies would be 'semi-detached' from Whitehall departments with the chief executive in the role of corporate CEO. To a remarkable extent this strategy translated the formerly Weberian units of coordinated public administration into the market-imitating enterprises of the Soviet system.

Cabinet Office guidance now recommended that executive agencies should be carved out of the administrative hierarchies where (1) functions or services to be delivered are not likely to be subject to perpetual parliamentary or public scrutiny; (2) it is neither appropriate nor realistic for ministers to take personal responsibility for day-to-day functions; (3) the function is predominantly concerned with the delivery of services to the public; (4) the number of staff is large enough to justify a separate organisation and (5) the function can be independently

---

[92] Efficiency Unit (Karen Caines, Andrew Jackson, Kate Jenkins and Sir Robin Ibbs), *Improving Management in Government: Next Steps* (London: HMSO, 1988).
[93] Oliver James, Alice Moseley, Nikolai Petrovsky and George Boyne, 'Agencification in the UK', in Koen Verhoest, Sandra van Thiel, Geert Bouckaert and Per Laegreid, *Government Agencies in Europe and Beyond: Practices and Lessons from 30 Countries* (Hampshire: Palgrave Macmillan, 2012).
[94] Oliver James, *The Executive Agency Revolution in Whitehall* (Basingstoke: Palgrave Macmillan, 2003), p. 52.

accountable within the sponsoring department.[95] Such agencies were usually funded by their own departments and could generate their own income streams. They varied in size from specialist units such as the Government Decontamination Service to Jobs Centre Plus, Her Majesty's Courts Service and Her Majesty's Prisons. They lacked legal independence but carried differing degrees of managerial autonomy.[96]

Rather than upgrade the civil service through investment in new skills and new technologies, the logic of radical institutional fragmentation followed the assembly line Taylorism or 'scientific management' of the early to mid-twentieth century. In search of efficiencies in industrial engineering, Taylorism had recommended the maximum fragmentation of jobs to minimise skill requirements and time learning the job. It had also encouraged the separate execution of planning work and the work itself and the separation of direct from indirect labour. Enamoured of the new science of production processes, Stalin had claimed in his 1924 lecture on 'Style in Work' that the 'combination of the Russian revolution's sweep and American efficiency is the essence of Leninism'.[97] Thanks to the supply-side revolution it was also about to become a foundation of the neoliberal state.

In the same speech, however, Stalin had warned of 'unprincipled practicalism'.[98] Earlier, in 1920, the wonderfully named Moscow Group of Communists Actively Interested in Scientific Management had criticised Taylorism as having the 'aim of transforming the living person into an unreasoning and stupid instrument without any general qualifications or sufficient all-round development'.[99] They had a point. Despite the lack of coherent physical product or profit tests, Britain's new bureaucratic Taylorism would call for the replacement of rule-of-thumb productivity estimates with precise measurements, output planning and metrics for optimum job performance, cost accounting and payment by results. The logic of such design failed to admit the

---

[95] Cited in Matthew Flinders, *Delegated Governance and the British State: Walking without Order* (Oxford: Oxford University Press, 2008), p. 113.

[96] Oliver James and Sandra van Thiel, 'Structural Devolution to Agencies', in Tom Christensen and Per Laegreid, *The Ashgate Companion to New Public Management* (Farnham: Ashgate, 2010), pp. 209–222.

[97] Joseph Stalin, 'Style in Work', in *The Foundations of Leninism* (Peking: Foreign Languages Press, 1970) (first published in 1924): 101–103, p. 101.

[98] Ibid., p. 102.

[99] Michael Ellman, *Socialist Planning* (Cambridge: Cambridge University Press, 2014), p. 252.

difficulty of choosing functional measures and ignored the limits of codifiability already discussed. In effect, it left less and less room for experience, professional judgement and creativity. Leadership effort would now be diverted to the creation and fulfilment of plans.

Bureaucratic Taylorism assumes that bureaucracies are directly analogous to a production regime for simple manufacturing goods rather than tasked with solving multi-dimensional challenges with complex ethical, practical, fiscal and political dimensions. What may have been efficiency-enhancing measures in low complexity manufacturing now risked crowding-out the analytical capacity of public administration and public services. Agencies were meant to articulate their new core missions, but this wholesale shift to the quantification of effort directly reproduced various methods of Soviet enterprise planning, and agencies consequently operated under the same highly problematic incentives.

Agency directors were expected to satisfy numerous goals set from above, with the fulfilment of targets now chief among them. Just as Soviet enterprise directors were given bonuses for plan fulfilment, so the new 'CEOs' operated via payment by results. As Evsei Liberman had pointed out in the Soviet Union in 1962, the rational director would bargain for low, easily achievable goals so that his enterprise would normally operate under-capacity. They would rationally over-purchase goods to be assured of their availability when required by a target. They would rationally avoid innovation and the introduction of new products because the success goals didn't require them. It was even rational to produce the wrong goods if they could be passed off as target completion.[100]

Under agencification, a rationally self-interested agency CEO who followed the pure logic of incentives was likely to do dysfunctional things. In the meantime, a conscientious and experienced director in this new system would have to figure out how to retain public service values despite rigid and often perverse systems of incentives, since the culture of output targets would cripple the corporate intelligence rooted in hard-won professionalism. Over time the incentive systems were liable to re-engineer the agency to think of itself as a passive delivery system, with a weakened ethical sense of its own powers and responsibilities, a situation unlikely to be helped by sharpening pay differentials.

---

[100] Bertrand Horwitz, 'Profit Responsibility in Soviet Enterprise', *The Journal of Business* 41 (1) (1968): 47–55, p. 48.

This is not to say that the earlier, vertically integrated departments and distinctive government organisations could not, and did not, decay into complacency. Only that this is a classic example of the antidote fallacy that says 'the opposite of what you have must solve your current problems'. In practice, if you reject input planning and professionalism in favour of output planning, then more, rather than less, bureaucratic rigidity is bound to occur, and once again the outcomes could not be further from the supposed disciplines of the price mechanism under competition.

As Sandra van Thiel and Frans Leeuw note, the move to delegated governance meant the system-wide adoption of what were supposed to be exciting new private sector techniques to measure and improve performance and to make those measured improvements the basis of future targets (the Soviet ratchet principle). Within central government, however, the number of audit agencies increased, as did the spending. As in the early decades of the Soviet system the consistent response to inadequate results within NPM regimes was to double down on the strategies of quantification.[101] The result was the recreation of the 'local orders of importance' and rigidities endemic under Soviet planning. Already by 1991, Geert Bouckaert and Walter Balk noted thirteen diseases of public productivity measurement that stemmed from faulty assumptions in underlying measures, measurement errors and problems around the content, position and quantity of measures.[102] Peter Smith likewise identified eight unintended consequences of auditing, including the inhibition of innovation and ossification, tunnel vision around the quantified targets and 'narrow objectives' by local managers.[103]

In their discussion of the 'performance paradoxes' that result, van Thiel and Leeuw confirm that performance measurement takes on a life of its own under quantification, and one that can strongly distort

---

[101] Sandra Van Thiel and Frans Leeuw, 'The Performance Paradox in the Private Sector', *Public Performance and Management Review* 25 (3) (2002): 267–281.

[102] Geert Bouckaert and Walter Balk, 'Public Productivity Measurement: Diseases and Cures', *Public Productivity & Management Review* 15 (2) (1991): 229–235.

[103] Peter Smith, 'On the Unintended Consequences of Publishing Performance Data in the Public Sector', *International Journal of Public Administration* 18 (2–3) (1995): 277–310.

behaviour and misrepresent performance.[104] Soviet economists had grappled with these problems from the 1920s, and the more complex and interdependent the tasks, the more dysfunction was bound to emerge from a similar 'materialisation' of planning. The human consequences of bureaucratic rigidity in the United Kingdom have been grave. To take just one example, the target-driven immigration system by 2018 produced a situation in which lifelong British citizens with roots in the Commonwealth 'Windrush' generation – a generation invited by post-war governments to move to the United Kingdom to work and abide – were wrongfully detained, threatened with deportation, denied legal rights and healthcare, and in many cases wrenched from their lives and families and deported to countries of which they knew nothing. British citizens of colour died after being actively persecuted by their own government either for their own decision or that of their parents, to fulfil the request of a previous administration. In April 2018, *The Guardian* published a leaked Home Office memo copied to the secretary of state's office. The memo said that the department had set 'a target of achieving 12,800 enforced returns in 2017–18' and 'we have exceeded our target of assisted returns'.[105] Historically, bureaucracies have shown the potential to operate at a responsive, constructive and well-informed best and at an unyielding, faceless and dehumanising worst. The Windrush tragedy illustrates all too clearly how neoliberal reforms had institutionalised the bitter end of that scale.

By the mid-1990s, the agency model had become the principal organisational type for UK central government public service delivery, with the organisational separation of policy from delivery as a key principle. The number of executive agencies grew from none in 1988 to 139 in 1998, when they employed over three quarters of the UK civil service. This was reduced to some 50 per cent by 2011 as governments started to comprehend how poorly these structures worked.[106] The Office of Public Service Reform within the Treasury noted by 2002 that there was a 'silo mentality' in some agencies and a lack of joint working between other agencies and organisations to deliver

---

[104] Van Thiel and Leeuw, 'The Performance Paradox'.
[105] Nick Hopkins and Heather Stewart, 'Amber Rudd Was Sent Targets for Migrant Removals, Leak Reveals', *The Guardian*, 28 April 2018.
[106] James et al., 'Agencification in the UK', p. 62.

outcomes. As James et al. summarise: 'It identified poor information sharing and communication between agencies and departments, insufficient thought about implementation at the policy design phase, inaccurate customer information sharing between agencies and local authorities, and missed opportunities for developing shared services such as IT infrastructure among the wider systemic performance problems' reported.[107] Another feature that repeated the Soviet experience is that executive agencies proved more attentive to the political executive than to service users despite the explicit policy goal of a more customer-focused approach.

The logic within *Next Steps* had made an appealing sense-by-analogy if viewed from within the neoclassical paradigm. Smaller, leaner and supposedly more firm-like units would develop the customer-oriented virtues of idealised firms in competitive markets. But to create a theatre of such a marketplace by calling your director a CEO and citizens your customers was not to make an agency a firm in any meaningful sense. Agencification and the wider dissemination of NPM terminology called on public servants to engage in a kind of performance art of business, which could only work to the extent that employees bought into the language, regardless of the perverse incentives they faced in practice.

Flinders achieved an insider's account of delegated governance through a UK Cabinet Office fellowship, and he found that the implications of agencification for systemic efficiency to be threefold and negative. The first was the loss of strategic oversight and capacity. The second concerned failures to create parallel structures of accountability that could match the new complexity. This problem became most acute around private sector players who operated with none of the codes of ethics and conflicts of interest rules applied to civil services and whose behaviour could be hidden under commercial confidentiality rules. The final problem came from de-politicisation, that is, the tendency to put issues of public and hence political importance at arm's length from ministerial responsibility. Technocrats and politicians might see this as positive, but in the inescapable absence of perfect technical fixes it undermined open and informed political debate in the context of persistent policy failures.[108]

---

[107] Ibid., p. 66.   [108] Ibid., pp. 235–238.

To these unanticipated consequences we can add a fourth, which is cost: the very significant increase in 'transaction costs' incurred for every aspect of policy implementation that had to travel around the ever-expanding network of players and processes. As Hood and Dixon note, for a reform built on efficiency justifications it is all but impossible to compare the cost or performance of agencies with those of core ministerial departments over time because of data churn, statistical discontinuities and because Public Expenditure Statistical Analyses made no distinction between agencies and their parent ministries. Their own solution was to compare running costs between departments with high agencification and those with little, between 1980–1981 and 2002–2003. They found that running costs in agency-heavy departments rose faster.[109] In a 2001 study Oliver James likewise found that agencies were associated with lower improvements in economy than central government as a whole.[110] The proliferation of delegated forms of governance both complicated and extended the lines of command from centre to periphery, and these lines were stretched yet further when those agencies engaged in further delegation and contracting out.[111] The result was that government cost, size and complexity all increased under a revolutionary agenda to shrink the state.

Neoliberals had assumed that functionality would follow form, but the upshot was a runaway bureaucracy.[112] The NPM had proved a hostage to reality. As the head of the British Civil Service in 1999, Sir Richard Wilson, concluded: 'I would not claim that the manner in which we implemented all these reforms over the years was a model to emulate. There was not enough overall vision or strategic planning.'[113] Had governments tried to understand the nature of the vision from which these policies arose, they might have noticed the Soviet flavour of their endeavour. The strategy depended not just on the assumption that the neoclassical world was real but that the bureaucratic environment of the stubbornly non-withering state could be turned into its functional equivalent. The Organisation for Economic Co-operation and Development's 2002 analysis of distributed public governance in

---

[109] Dixon and Hood, *A Government*, pp. 135–126.
[110] Oliver James, 'Evaluating Executive Agencies in UK Government', *Public Policy and Management* 16 (3) (2001): 24–52, p. 30.
[111] Flinders, *Delegated Governance*, Chapter 5.   [112] Ibid., p. 314.
[113] Flinders, 'Public/Private', p. 234.

Agencification

nine countries found that the strong trend towards delegated governance was unmatched by any systematic reflection or analysis of the consequences for control and coordination.[114]

Even before the intensifying neoliberalism of the 2010 Conservative–Liberal Coalition and subsequent Conservative governments, the British state had developed an extremely elaborate topography. Beyond the 20 or so departments of state, by 2006 there were 26 non-ministerial departments, 11 public corporations, 127 executive agencies, 17 national special health authorities, 439 advisory non-departmental public bodies (NDPBs), 36 tribunal NDPBs, over 200 executive NDPBs and 147 monitoring boards. There were in addition more than 550 private finance initiatives with hospitals, schools, transform projects, police and fire stations, prison, waste and water installations and so on, which excludes contractual outsourcing.[115] This list constituted an expanding web of delegated governance structures by increasing degree of relative autonomy from elected politicians.

A discrete but important aspect of this changing topography was that it became a major source of nominally private employment. Calculations made by Buchanan et al. counted state employees but also estimated the 'para-state' employees created by outsourcing and delegated governance and found that more than half of all job growth in the United Kingdom between 1998 and 2007 (so under New Labour administrations) was sourced in public funding. The ratio was higher for the ex-industrial regions.[116] Far from the promise of a retreating state in a new enterprise economy, these figures suggest a taxpayer-funded stimulus programme that compensated for the steeply declining, unsupported manufacturing sector, a finance sector that recruited on a far smaller scale and the investment famine that came with financialisation, as discussed in Chapter 7. Vital though this was, it was pulled away after 2010 under the Coalition policy of austerity, with devastating social consequences.

What these histories of delegated governance tell us is that the further down the doctrinal road a government travels, the higher the

---

[114] Ibid., p. 234. [115] Ibid., p. 227.
[116] John Buchanan, Julie Froud, Sukhdev Johal, Adam Leaver and Karel Williams, 'Undisclosed and Unsustainable: Problems of the UK National Business Model', Centre for Research on Socio-cultural Change Working Paper Series Number 75, December 2009.

bureaucratic burden is bound to become, and in this light, we should only expect the state's costs to go up. Over time the failures of agencification encouraged later neoliberal governments to move towards ever greater outsourcing. However, far from curing the problems of delegation, as we know, outsourcing simply floated them away from the relatively direct public accountability of public offices. Under post-2010 austerity, successive Conservative-led governments would also choose to deal with the ballooning complexity and cost of government with across-the-board spending cuts, so that organisational failures only intensified as every service was now expected to deliver more for less. The result was fewer civil servants to manage increasingly elaborate and opaque structures. At the time of writing there is not a single British public service – whether that is health, education or justice, social care, policing or the prison service, from the Serious Fraud Office to HMRC – that doesn't report demoralisation and a staff retention and recruitment crisis. It was this set of structures that was expected to cope with the onslaught of the coronavirus in 2020 – a tragedy that exposed like nothing else the stresses experienced by vocational public servants forced to operate in a system no longer adequately funded, equipped or structured for purpose.

Conclusion

In the name of market efficiency, neoliberal governments vastly increased the planning and budgetary units of the British state under new systems of imperative output planning, and all within intrinsically non-competitive conditions. The reforms resulted in systemic failures of function and accountability. Far from withering away, the neoliberal state became a giant of enterprise coordination and procurement and hence closer to its Soviet counterpart than its Weberian predecessor ever was.

When we strip away the rhetoric of markets around these reforms and compare the actual, ongoing mechanisms of instruction and control it becomes clearer why they reproduce the failures of the Soviet system so closely, from bureaucratic rigidity to rising costs, and from the exhaustion of the state's personnel in the face of administrative overload to systemic crisis. What governments created was an explosion of control requirements across an increasingly disintegrated institutional framework. They built a new state–corporate production regime more complicated than Soviet central planning but no less driven by closed-system reasoning to operate within a logic of quantification. As in Leninism, the gains of the neoliberal revolution were predicated on a fantasy of completion in which all doctrinally motivated actions are assumed to offer a systematic improvement.

In Britain the result is less a totalitarian state than its chaotic fragmentation and the accelerating extraction of public authority and revenues by large business, law and accountancy firms, while governments act as their brokers. These are the dynamics of rentier-capitalism, in which a growing number of UK firms seek their profits not through the disciplined endeavours of the competitive marketplace but through the pursuit of asymmetric contracts with the state – contracts that allow them to control or run public assets in an extortive manner at the public expense,[117] with wholly negative consequences for the quality of public services, investment and the terms of employment. It is a system that actively invites political corruption.

Public choice theory did not anticipate that reforms would upend the state's former capacity for impartiality, tacit knowledge, informational transparency and institutional coherence, built as it was on the assertion that none of these qualities existed. But the ironies run deeper. A resilient insight of classical Marxist, as distinct from Leninist, analysis concerns the impulse of 'capital' to continuously breach the boundaries of non-commodified human activity in search of additional profit so that it can reproduce itself. Capital will always seek out circumstances where costs are reduced to the minimum and profits are maximised.[118] Given the ever-expanding sources of public revenues transferred with ever less transparency into private hands through outsourcing and privatisation and the ever faster revolving door of business recruitment into the state administration, the analytical promises fulfilled in these reforms are far more obviously those of Karl Marx than those of William Niskanen.

Just as Leninism proved impossible to reform without contradicting the principles on which it was built, it is likewise in the nature of

---

[117] Brett Christophers, *Rentier Capitalism: Who Owns the Economy and Who Pays for It?* (London: Verso, 2020).

[118] Andrew Gamble, 'Marxism after Communism: Beyond Realism and Historicism', *Review of International Studies* 25 (1999): 127–144, pp. 140–141.

neoliberalism as a tautological doctrine that it is hard to recant. Accept the realities of radical uncertainty and the micro-foundations of neoclassical economics fall apart, and a practical and problem-solving empiricism must roar back into view as the necessary approach, along with the need for 'directionality' in government.[119] The neoclassical imaginary leads us to forget what post-war political governments had understood, which was that 'purpose is independently causative in the world'.[120] Once we accept that we are vulnerable to threats inconceivable in the predetermined two-dimensional neoclassical world, the importance of the precautionary principle, institutional capacity and resilience-building necessarily return as leading principles of good government. In a world that is not a timeless materialist utopia, governments should also remember the distinction between investment and expense. Once we reject the belief that markets will tend towards general equilibrium if the state withdraws, our recognition of the inequality and arbitrariness of economic power within an unbridled capitalism must return, with all that this implies for the potential value of interventions by a democratic state. In neoliberalism as in Leninism, the misapplied language of science demonstrably stops government from applying the scientific *method* and the recalibration of theory based on evidence. We can consequently observe in both cases how the misappropriated language of science forestalled a substantial critique because the political stakes were almost immediately too high. The basic orthodoxy could simply not survive it.

---

[119] Mariana Mazzucato and Douglas Robinson, 'Directing versus Facilitating the Economic Development of Low Earth Orbit', in Patrick Besha and Alexander MacDonald, *Economic Development of Low Earth Orbit* (Washington, DC: National Aeronautics and Space Administration, 2016), pp. 122–123.

[120] Herman Daly, 'The Illth of Nations and the Fecklessness of Policy: An Ecological Economist's Perspective', *Post-Autistic Economics Review* 30 (1) (March 2005).

6 | *Quasi-markets in Welfare, or the Non-withering State*

Western Europe's welfare states were expanded after the Second World War to heal the scars of the Depression and of the mass slaughter that had followed on its heels. Systems based on mutual aid were built to educate all and provide care for the unpredictable but unavoidable periods of misfortune in a normal life. The political narratives from right and left were of common endeavour, belonging and reciprocity.[1] The ambitious programmes for growth, full employment and improved social welfare consolidated democracy on wider class foundations, and social rights became central to the democratic 'social contract'.[2] In Britain's case, the Soviet communist threat, but perhaps more significantly the shared hardships and endeavours of the war, had moved the pre-war political 'centre' substantially to the left. The new National Health System was designed by a Liberal in a Conservative-led Coalition, implemented by a Labour government and supported on the right.[3] All three parties agreed that without the state as an active, purposeful agent of social integration there would be unnecessary strife and suffering.

Following the neoliberal turn, however, Margaret Thatcher argued that the welfare state had suppressed the native will to enterprise – a far cannier political argument than the abstract theory that underpinned it, be that Friedrich August von Hayek's epistemological pessimism or the Camp 1 insistence that a welfare state would violate the freedoms of the perfectly calculating agents in the grand democracy of consumer choice.[4] The neoliberal revolution

---

[1] Paul Collier, *The Future of Capitalism: Facing the New Anxieties* (London: Allen Lane, 2018), pp. 48–49.
[2] Alan Milward, *The European Rescue of the Nation State*, 2nd ed. (Florence: Taylor and Francis Group, 2000), Chapter 2.
[3] Collier, *The Future*, p. 49.
[4] Lindy Edwards, *How to Argue with an Economist: Reopening Political Debate in Australia* (Cambridge: Cambridge University Press, 2007), p. 39.

thus began its deep cuts to welfare state provision even as the advent of mass unemployment under Thatcher caused a significant hike in spending on income transfers. Cuts to the welfare state were accompanied by calls for its improved efficiency via market modalities wherever it remained.

By the 1990s, the political centre had shifted dramatically to the right, and what passed for the centre-right and centre-left now turned to favour what scholars would later call a 'social investment state' – a welfare system re-conceived as a 'trampoline and net' within a liberalising marketplace.[5] The social investment state aimed to channel investment to individuals so that they could build their personal resilience within newly 'flexible', deregulated labour markets. The debate between what became New Labour and the Conservative New Right now shifted into almost purely neoclassical terms. The argument was no longer about whether, but how, market failures could best be resolved in this still ethically and electorally sensitive area.

The technological revolution and the advent of the 'knowledge economy' mean that education policy is more than ever a key determinant of development and social mobility.[6] This chapter thus focuses on secondary education not just because it is a policy of critical socio-economic importance but because it is the key vector in the theory of the social investment state. In the logic of social investment, education is the principal basis for personal resilience. The theory consequently presumes a great deal, for example, about the supportive social conditions of those children trying to learn and about the viability of the labour and housing markets into which they will emerge. Education is the key variable, in other words, in a theory that assumes an otherwise fully functioning neoclassical marketplace.

Though the narrow logic of the social investment state was increasingly the field on which education politics was fought, we should remember the deeper case for the importance of secondary education to a functioning society. We know that in the fully three-dimensional

---

[5] Anton Hemerijck, 'Social Investment as a Policy Paradigm', *Journal of European Public Policy* 25 (6) 2018: 810–827.

[6] Marius Busemeyer and Rita Nikolai, 'Education', in Francis G. Castles, Jane Lewis, Herbert Obinger, Chris Pierson and Stephan Leibfried, *The Oxford Handbook on Welfare State Policy* (Oxford: Oxford University Press, 2010), pp. 494–508.

world in which we live, education leads to higher economic productivity and prosperity, but it also expands our access to cultures. It helps us to express and to defend ourselves, and to understand each other. It can't rescue us from our human frailties, but it improves the quality of reasoning and empathy in both our public and private lives. Even if we were to focus on the economic aspect alone, it is clear that the more efficient provision of education services alone is *not* a sufficient condition for socially inclusive prosperity and accord, because a hungry child that lacks the basic securities of life must study through the roar of their distress.

The overwhelming consensus in empirical research is that what drives higher educational attainment is the recognition and reward of highly educated teachers, their professional autonomy and classes of a size that allow for mutual attention. The consistent evidence is that if you give accomplished teachers manageable class sizes and discretion to focus on character and creativity, as well as attainment, you achieve the happiest educational outcomes in every sense. But despite this well-founded body of research, Britain's neoliberal education reforms would depend instead on neoclassical, axiomatic-deductive reasoning. Education is a devolved responsibility in the United Kingdom and so the focus here is on English reforms to the school system since the Welsh, Scottish and Northern Irish governments all proved more wary of this ideological path. In this chapter's first half I set out the theoretical argument for 'quasi-markets' in welfare and examine which vital aspects of reality had to be written out of the theoretical picture for the sake of formal model consistency. We should not be surprised to find that, as in outsourcing more generally, it is the role of the state that all but evaporates in theory but fails to wither in practice. In the second half I explore how the unanticipated risks then played out in England's outsourced school system. What transpires is that this hyper-theoretical approach to 'rolling back bureaucracy' transformed what were supposed to become 'competitive firms' into far more constrained objects of planning than the state schools of before.

The Logic of Reform and Its Unanticipated Risks

As we know from Chapter 1, the conditions under which 'free market' choice and competition are the most efficient solution for managing resources are highly restricted even in neoclassical theory.

A non-exhaustive list of necessary conditions for markets to be efficient would include:

- Perfect competition: there are multiple suppliers of identical products, so all firms are price-takers and market share has no influence on price.
- Perfect information: buyers and sellers have all the relevant information on the product and the market and hence on past, present and future prices.
- Perfect mobility of resources: there are no lag times, no barriers to market entry and free flow of capital, resources and labour.
- No strong negative externalities: there are no damaging effects on third parties not reflected in the original price.
- Not a public good: It is not a good that is non-exclusive and not reduced by its consumption by another person.
- No interdependencies: There is no collusion between buyers' decisions to buy and sellers' decisions to sell.

Such utopian requirements mean there have rarely been anything like pure forms of market provision in the modern world for private, let alone for public, goods. Camp 2 economists would also acknowledge that new markets usually need more state intervention than existing ones to encourage competition where it did not exist before.[7] When economists come to the provision of welfare, however, they have to bring another value into the frame and that is the question of how to ensure equal access to a good – social equity – as well as cost efficiency. The problem here is that measures for higher efficiency understood as lower cost might actively reduce equity. For example, schools that only accept high-performing children are going to be relatively cost efficient, but that kind of selection is going to reinforce social inequality, not reduce it. The neoclassical economics of the welfare state duly sought to model the various compromises or 'equity and efficiency trade-offs' that were available in theory. More empirically minded economists have since gone on to test and calibrate those theories against the evidence.

The goal of a 'mixed market' in welfare could give you several institutional variations in principle, with public versus private options

---

[7] Nick Barr, *The Economics of the Welfare State*, 5th ed. (Oxford: Oxford University Press, 2012), p. 72.

being available in the following realms: (1) in which sector *production* takes place and (2) which sector *finances* it. But there are also options regarding the relative influence of *regulation*, in particular the regulation of (3) the degree of producer sovereignty (e.g., operating for profit or not-for profit) and (4) the degree of consumer sovereignty (e.g., whether insurance is mandatory or optional, the choices of the producer limited, etc.).[8] When economic libertarians talk about 'complete privatisation' it follows that what they mean is private sector production and finance combined with maximal producer and consumer sovereignty.[9] The Chicago economist Milton Friedman had already argued in 1955 that the most effective means for reforming American education was to completely expose schools to the competitive forces of the free market.[10]

The theory of 'quasi-markets' that emerged in Britain in the 1990s sought to combine the virtues of both the public and private forms. As such it constituted one of the very few major neoliberal policies of the last forty years to emerge from Camp 2 rather than Camp 1. The basic premise of the quasi-market strategy was that if you cared about equity then private provision alone was not going to work. It duly offered a solution to the practical political problem for neoliberals of both New Labour and the New Right, which was this: how do you introduce market principles into an education system when the electorate is not yet ready to privatise it?

At the heart of the theoretical case for quasi-markets is the argument that politicians and electorates should stop getting hung up on traditional assumptions about means and ends. The left in particular should abandon the 'Old Left' assumption that the public sector is made up of public-spirited 'knights' and the private sector of self-interested 'knaves', when what matters is the creation of the 'right incentives' to create a good service.[11] Julian Le Grand became a pioneer of hybridisation in social policy and the leading academic theorist of actual reforms under New Labour. His arguments for educational reform were an innovative but consistently Camp 2 statement about the efficiency of

---

[8] Ibid., p. 72.   [9] Ibid., p. 74.
[10] Milton Friedman, 'The Role of Government in Education', in Robert Solo, *Economics and the Public Interest* (New Brunswick: Rutgers University Press, 1955), pp. 123–144.
[11] Julian Le Grand, 'Knight and Knaves or Pawns: Human Behaviour and Social Policy', *Journal of Social Policy* 26 (2) (1997): 149–169.

competition in which the social equity desired in education could be secured while attaining the distinctive benefits of markets.[12]

Le Grand's solution – quasi-markets – had a common-sense appeal: competitive provision, user choice and equality of access as guaranteed through taxpayer funding would combine the best of markets and states. Le Grand had also made a shrewd case from New Labour's perspective by pointing out that as things stood, the middle and upper classes already had choice, and they exercised it to the detriment of the working class: they could send their child to a public school (confusingly in the United Kingdom the term 'public school' means a 'private', as distinct from 'state', school) or they could afford to move house to the areas where the schools were supposedly best. In this light, far from introducing private choice into a universal system, quasi-markets would level the playing field. A diversity of providers would be responsive to the needs of consumers, and the fact of competing providers would incentivise them to constantly improve their service to sustain and increase their 'market share'. It followed that if schools could be given the freedom to generate different approaches and parents could be given the rights to select a school based on the results, then the best approaches would be amplified via successful schools and failing schools would be unable to reproduce.

Le Grand's argument is that if the incentives are right, and market competition will make them right, then the knights and knaves of the 'old Left's' discourse will behave in the same way. Opening up education, or health, or social services to diverse providers will deepen competition, and all providers will 'feel impelled to provide a good service in a competitive market because it is in their self-interest to do so'.[13] Le Grand duly wrestled with the three main critiques of the wider case at the time: (1) that 'people' don't want choice so much as good service, (2) that choice is a middle-class obsession and (3) that choice threatens the public domain. He rejected each in turn by arguing (1) that choice as empowered through competition was the necessary condition for good service, (2) that data on social attitudes

---

[12] Julian Le Grand, *Equity and Choice: An Essay in Economics and Applied Philosophy* (London: Harper Collins, 1991), Chapter 3.

[13] Julian Le Grand, 'Knights and Knaves Return: Public Service Motivation and the Delivery of Public Services', *International Public Management Journal* 13 (1) (2010): 56–71, p. 65.

suggested otherwise and (3) that public services have always operated in mixed markets to some degree. All good answers on the face of it.

The logic of combining consumer choice and competitive provision was that user choice without producer competition would do little to improve services if providers had no incentives to attract new users. Conversely, for competition to focus on the quality of service delivery, as opposed to some other factor, users had to have a real option to reject a failing service provider for a better one.[14] Choice and competition would supposedly outperform all alternatives, which were: the professional public service of the post-war era, known as the 'trust' model; the 'targets' driven model of Thatcher's first wave of welfare reforms that experimented with managerial practices and internal competition within still entirely public institutions; and the neo-Weberian model that looked to enhance services through improved communication between users and providers and enhanced accountability. This last option, the 'voice' model, was adopted in those continental European states still unconvinced by marketisation in this period but keen to improve the accountability of their existing structures.

At first sight, the school environment has clear potential for a quasi-market given the appealing logic of parents as consumers, and this makes it a critical test case. If the logic fails here, it will certainly fail in environments where the necessary conditions for competitive supply and consumer choice look even less plausible. But Le Grand's theoretical representation of the players involved in a real choice and competition scheme is fatally incomplete. What the theory depicts are the choices and incentives on the part of end-user consumers and the choices and incentives for providers in relation to those consumers. Its outcomes are supposed to be superior to those when the end-user has no choices and providers do not compete. However, given that the taxpayer is still paying, and the state is still responsible and liable for the results, what is missing in the theory of quasi-markets is the initial and continuous market for service *procurement*.

The Wishing Away of the State

Le Grand was well-aware of the risks of competitive failures within the frame of his own theory, and his own necessary conditions for

[14] Ibid.

competition were suitably strict within the confines of Camp 2 neo-classical logic. For competition to work in his scheme – for the end-user market to be efficient – competition would have to be real. Parental choice would have to be consequential. Alternative providers would have to be available, and you would need mechanisms to allow new providers to enter the market and failing ones to exit. Le Grand insisted that 'all the incentive arguments in favour of choice are contingent on there being consequences for schools of being chosen or not'.[15] He also insisted that end-users, that is, parents, had to be informed consumers, as informed, in fact, as providers. Since perfect information was a necessary condition for rational behaviour within a competitive marketplace, schools should consequently be required to produce robust public prospectuses and accounts, like a firm, although this would still leave many vital aspects of the teaching and school environment unrecorded. On the equity front, Le Grand also warned that providers might prefer student selection to raise their reputation, and so game the competition, and he argued that such practices could be limited through regulation to enforce 'burden sharing'.[16] As for parents, they were going to have to gather all this information and to know all their options on a continuous basis for the logic of rational choice to have meaning.

To empower new consumers, Le Grand had also argued for public funding to follow parents' choice and for the 'creation' of a diverse choice of schools. And, while this made perfect sense in the abstract, as a practical matter this took no account of the likely dynamics in the intervening period in which real choices did not exist, nor of the economies of scale provided by Local Education Authorities (LEAs) that were about to be lost. Le Grand had said that to ease subsequent market entry and exit schools should be allowed to be profit-making to incentivise entry and that an independent regulatory agency should exist to oversee exit.[17] It is nevertheless hard to see how the exorbitant cost component of real school exit and replacement, or, more realistically, takeover, could be easily regulated away. Nor were the criteria for a failing school easy to define. Given the multiple aims of schools

---

[15] Julian Le Grand, 'School Education', in Julian Le Grand, David Lipsey and Alain Enthoven, *The Other Invisible Hand: Delivering Public Services through Choice and Competition* (Princeton: Princeton University Press, 2009), p. 48.
[16] Ibid., pp. 48–51.   [17] Ibid.

and their social as well as educational purposes, who should decide what failure looks like, and on what grounds? If the grounds for defining failure were relatively poor test scores, for example, then 'failing' schools could well be those with the most disadvantaged intakes, though the real internal progress of those students may have been high, and in this case providing the school with more resources rather than closing it would be the more productive solution.

The most serious piece of organised forgetting in this model, however, is the state, as it is in outsourcing models more generally, though this is a particularly wilful elision when it comes to welfare services. It is a central part of this scheme that the state still provides public funds, which means it will remain accountable for their use and not just as a regulator of information flows. What is missing, in other words, is the only actual market relationship in this whole story, which is between the state and the providing enterprises. As Steve Fleetwood warned, we move from stylisation to fictionalisation through a model.[18] When the democratic state procures the provision of school education, it is simultaneously entrusted to guarantee educational standards, value for money, social equity, social cohesion, childhood mental and physical health and safeguarding, and public investment in the physical school estate. Sooner rather than later, therefore, the theoretical sovereignty of the end-user consumer was bound to be compromised by these democratic requirements.

Among the reasons that the sovereignty of the consumer would prove hard to sustain is that the 'rational choices' of individual parents, of individual schools and of democratic government are not automatically compatible. To take just one example of how complicated the real choices are, the accelerated exclusion of 'underperforming' pupils is simultaneously a rational consumer choice by a majority of parents in a given school, a rational choice for an individual school evaluated by pupil performance, a calamity for the struggling students so excluded and for the teachers who care about them, a cost to the remaining education and social services system, and a suboptimal outcome for the national skills base, let alone for society. Inherent in education policy are issues that cannot be accurately depicted in a theory that is methodologically individualist, but

---

[18] Steven Fleetwood, 'The Critical Realist Conception of Open and Closed System', *Journal of Economic Methodology* 24 (1) (2017): 41–68, Section 1.4.

insofar as the state exists as a concept in this axiomatic-deductive argument it is again in the abstract terms of a disinterested market-maker. The inadequacy of this abstraction is immediately apparent when you assess the real challenges that the state will face in setting up and sustaining this system.

The State and Incomplete Contracts Revisited

As in outsourcing more generally, when we bring the state back in, the Camp 2 literature on contractual incompleteness remains instructive.[19] The immediate problem for the state is that contracts to procure education are necessarily at the extreme end of the spectrum of contractual 'incompleteness' – that is, contracts that suffer gaps, ambiguities and missing provisions that render the buyer vulnerable because of the complexity of the service required. In this case the state is rendered ill-informed as a buyer, and the school is rendered vulnerable as an educational entity insofar as attempts by the central state to codify what the school should do will strongly inhibit the professional discretion and knowledge of its teachers.

As soon as you consider the necessary contract between the state and a private provider the common sense appeal of outsourcing starts to fall apart.[20] Camp 2 contract theory tells us that if the commodity in question is intrinsically complex, vulnerable to change in requirement and ethos of delivery, and/or multi-consequential, and if its central element is unobserved behaviour that is hard to codify and hence monitor – education and health are prime examples – it is intrinsically impossible to write a 'complete contract', one that dependably matches the interests of the producer and the state. Moreover, if the state can't easily exit the contract, that is, if the constant delivery of

---

[19] See Sanford Grossman and Oliver Hart, 'The Costs and Benefits of Ownership: A Theory of Vertical and Lateral Integration', *Journal of Political Economy* 94 (4) (1986): 691–719; Oliver Hart and James Moore, 'Property Rights and the Nature of the Firm', *Journal of Political Economy* 98 (6) (1990): 1119–1158; Oliver Hart, *Firms, Contracts and Financial Structure* (Oxford: Oxford University Press, 1995); Oliver Hart, Andrei Shleifer and Robert Vishny, 'The Proper Scope of Government: Theory and an Application to Prisons', *Quarterly Journal of Economics* 112 (1997): 1127–1161.

[20] Amir Hefetz and Mildred Warner, 'Contracting or Public Delivery? The Importance of Service, Market and Management Characteristics', *Journal of Public Administration Research and Theory* 22 (2) (2012): 289–317.

the product is statutorily required and any new contract is liable to the same incompleteness, then the state buyer can be 'held up' by the provider and hence face rising costs as discussed in Chapter 5.

Incomplete contracts also leave the state-buyer vulnerable to negative spillovers. The practices of 'cherry-picking' via pupil selection or exclusion become just two possibilities in a long list of 'rationally' perfunctory or 'satisficing' behaviours by providers, when what theory had promised was improving, if not perfect, behaviour. Le Grand had paid great attention to the problem of how to share good information with prospective parents to make them 'rational' consumers. Incomplete contracts between the state and private providers would nevertheless leave open a wide range of hard to quantify managerial and pedagogic practices that both parents and the state would struggle to monitor and that the providers have no obvious incentives to report. To name but a few, these practices ranged from satisficing staff attention to test scores at the cost of deep educational development; from selling off playing fields, buildings or land to non-meritocratic pay decisions; and from discriminatory exclusion practices for children seen as 'challenging' in any way, including through disability and neurodiversity, to failures to support teachers in underfunded environments. In practice, incomplete contracts would open schools to perfunctory behaviour both on the equity and on the efficiency sides of the equation. From the transaction cost economics point of view there were also likely to be high costs from the increased incentives and opportunities for opportunistic behaviour.[21] In essence, the issues arising here repeat those outlined in Chapter 5, where unified, cooperative ownership (vertical integration) remained the better solution in the absence of credible contracts, that is, where the bilateral hazards of incomplete contractual relations mount up.[22]

Given the poor performance of outsourcing over time it is hardly surprising that public management scholars have become interested in the potential for so-called relational contracts, that is, in purely outline contracts where more implicit terms and conditions built on relationships of trust are developed to try to resolve the problems in more

---

[21] Oliver Williamson, 'The Theory of the Firm as Governance Structure: From Choice to Contract', *Journal of Economic Perspective* 16 (3) (2002): 171–195, pp. 174, 188.
[22] Ibid., p. 176.

formal contracting.[23] As we shall see, however, the perverse incentives established in the contracts themselves make these unpromising, as do the real financial dynamics at work.[24] Given the multiplication of diverse contracts across a disaggregated school system, the more tempting solution was for the state to resort to the universal applications of further managerial codes and output targets, which is what happened, and it would move the academy school system more completely into the realm of Soviet enterprise planning.

As Camp 2 reasoning could tell us, when the state tries to codify performance to gain purchase on the quality of its investment in education, the indicators it chooses will be inescapably partial, but the incentives around them will become powerful and potentially dominant. Tests and exams are among the few codifiable elements, but if either the parents' or the state's selection of a school provider is based on exam performance as a measure of success, then schools are actively incentivised to bias their effort towards that measure, for example, by 'teaching to the test' or cherry-picking high-quality students through selection. Such distortion operates at the expense of both equity and overall teaching quality, and this is bound to damage teacher morale.[25] As Soviet planners had discovered long before, when contracts proved incomplete and the state engaged with increasingly elaborate targets, then professional discretion and specialist knowledge were crowded out by quantification and the gaming of indicators became routine. These insights around perverse incentives had been presented by Daron Acemoglu, Michael Kremer and Milan Atif in an influential game-theoretical paper in 2007, but they had already been explained half a century earlier by Alec Nove in his study of Soviet industry.

As Nove pointed out, even if we ascribed 'ultimate wisdom' to the central planning (or procurement authority) 'there remains the problem of having these decisions implemented'.

---

[23] Anthony Bertelli and Craig Smith, 'Relational Contracting and Network Management', *Journal of Public Administration Research and Theory* 20 (1) 2009: 121–140.

[24] George Baker, Robert Gibbons and Kevin Murphy, 'Relational Contracts and the Theory of the Firm', *Quarterly Journal of Economics* 117 (1) (2002): 39–84, p. 41.

[25] Daron Acemoglu, Michael Kremer and Milan Atif, 'Incentives in Markets, Firms and Governments', *Journal of Law, Economics and Organization* 24 (2) (2007): 273–306, p. 274.

The planners then must so stimulate the behaviour of plant managers as to achieve efficiency. This can only be done by rewarding 'desirable' behaviour, either in cash or increased esteem, improved chances of promotion, the issue of Orders of Lenin, or some other form of incentive. These rewards, in their turn, must be associated with some definable achievements. Therefore, it becomes necessary to define what I have called 'success indicators' (in Russian, *pokazateli*) under various desirable heads, such as volume of output, reduction in costs, labour productivity, and so on... many of these indicators have operated in ways which cause management to deviate from the pursuit of efficiency, and have largely defeated their own ends... The basic difficulty has always been the absence of any objective criterion for price-fixing.[26]

When the state puts itself at arm's length from private producers and depends on contracts to manage that relationship, then quantification and codification will come to the fore both in the contracts themselves and in the regulatory systems used to try to compensate for their failures in those cases of incompleteness. As Nove had pointed out back in 1958, it was precisely those indicators that could be quantified that were likely to go into the plan and those that were easiest to fulfil that were most likely to be produced.[27] As a result, the real system of incentives around schools in a nominally quasi-market is unlikely to bear much resemblance to those advocated by Le Grand. In the meantime, many of the substantive practices of education most essential to making a school a vibrant place of learning – the capacity to engage openly with the unpredictable life experiences and views of the children in the classroom – must remain largely unobserved by the state as a distant buyer, and the danger is that it is these practices that are crowded out. But codify these practices too, to re-establish their status, and you can only produce formal rigidities and circumscribe how creatively teachers can respond to their students.

The implementation of the choice and competition agenda will consequently tend to introduce several systemic risks in the education system. First, incomplete contracts in which the supplier has asymmetric power over the state are likely to produce a downward bias in educational quality given the non-codifiable nature of most of the core tasks

---

[26] Alec Nove, 'The Problems of Success Indicators in Soviet Industry', *Economica* 25 (97) (1958): 1–13, p. 3.
[27] Nove, 'The Problems', pp. 8–9.

of education. Second, the scope for opportunism that arises from the incomplete contract is likely to create an upward bias in financial costs.

Third, these problems from contractual incompleteness are likely to prove impossible to solve over time. As in outsourcing more generally, the state's single moment of consumer power is the fleeting choice it makes when the original, often open-ended procurement contract is awarded.[28] When that contract is incomplete, however, it is unclear on what legal basis the state-as-consumer can insist on post hoc intervention in any issues not anticipated in the original contract. The result is that governments are doomed to plug the gaps in the contracts they signed with ever more elaborate systems of statutory regulation, inspection and audit. Instead of a dynamic free market for education provision, what you end up with is a regulatory exoskeleton that can never complete the essential contracts but whose authority must tend to drive schools away from responsive and creative forms of provision. The more regulatory tests the state introduces to 'catch up', the more rigidifying and bureaucratic the incentive systems will become.

The lessons from Soviet planning are that these dynamics are highly damaging to morale, both at the sharp end of production and at the administrative centre. The remedial regulatory output planning will tend to induce the same 'private orders of importance', gaming, performance paradoxes and disinformation that characterised Soviet enterprises. As a result, the central state will once again find itself in bargaining games that it cannot win. Le Grande had expected a failing school to be sanctioned through the departure of disappointed parents, if not ejected completely from the marketplace, but was that ever a practical solution? Such sanctions would more obviously penalise the remaining students and simply worsen the school's performance. Complete failures, and all the costs and upheavals they implied, would also damage the reputation of what remained a fundamentally political project. It always seemed far safer to assume that a government concerned about costs and education would prefer to bail out the failing provider on condition it would improve its behaviour. The persistent asymmetry of the contract would nevertheless make any such agreement unreliable, but a more thoroughgoing audit process that would gear the school to satisfy that audit would leave the school

---

[28] Colin Crouch, 'The Paradoxes of Privatization and Public Service Outsourcing', *Political Quarterly* 86 (December 2015): 156–171, p. 162.

no meaningful autonomy to speak of. What you end up with then is not the disciplinary mechanism of the marketplace but a re-enactment of the Soviet syndrome of moral hazard, soft-budget constraints and bureaucratisation faced by Soviet enterprise planning, where providers have few incentives to avoid risk because of the de facto insurance built in by the ongoing responsibilities of the state. The state – and the taxpayer – is left to pick up the pieces, continuously and ineffectively.

It is fair to object that the risk of soft budget constraints in which the state would rather pay than fail is always there, including in vertically integrated public structures, as are the costs of any crisis-led intervention. But my point is that it is a fantasy to imagine these costs go away or are less in an outsourcing state. On the contrary, the systematic incentives towards satisficing behaviour by providers and reactive, remedial regulation in outsourcing are likely to make them higher. Problems of underperformance are likely to be greater and more expensive to manage in a strongly disintegrated production regime of poorly controlled private autonomous producers governed through incomplete contracts that are paid for from the centre. In such conditions the class teacher will consequently find themselves with a thankless choice. They can attend to their students' needs and interests beyond the fixed criteria of achievement but endanger themselves and their manager colleagues in the face of intensifying inspection. Alternatively, they can obey the incentives at the expense of the idiosyncratic needs of their students and their own professional agency. In the public choice theory that motivated these changes, however, public servants have neither professionalism nor vocational commitment, so such tensions can hardly be imagined.

As we know from Chapter 5, the contracting state would be smart to think about the market in which its providers will operate. But, as we shall see, the question of market deepening would prove thorny here too, not least because Le Grand's insistence that profit-making was a necessary right for providers was cut from the policy. In practice, successive neoliberal governments would allow for two forms of workaround. The first was that of related-party payments, in which providers could buy services from profit-making firms in which they themselves shared an interest, on which more later. The second was to let providers coalesce to improve their economies of scale and so enable them to make higher profits from that related-party procurement. The risks of this concentration into multi-academy trusts (MATs) were significant. Not only would it render void the entire justification for this programme – parental choice between different providers – it would do little to solve the underlying problem of contractual incompleteness, only now these incomplete contracts could be gamed by large providers of multiple schools: effective monopolies or at best oligopolies over significant population areas. At this point the state would become structurally dependent on providers potentially too big to fail.

Finally, as these new quasi-markets would tend to become dominated by large private providers you were also going to see institutional dynamics that neoclassical theory simply cannot describe. The emergence of larger private players would significantly change the interest group dynamics around the sector in question. In education, education-business companies, large accountancy firms, large public service industry firms, charitable educational trusts, churches and parents would have very different capacities for participation in these markets, let alone for lobbying within them. Such activities constitute a pure expense for non-profit actors but an investment for business actors. These new interest-group dynamics were likely to increase the pressures on governments to expand quasi-markets without any realistic prospect of those markets becoming more competitive. The more likely outcome was a seller's market for rent-seeking firms. Taken together these risks are remarkably severe and all-encompassing. As the contract theorists Oliver Hart, Andrei Schleifer and Robert Vishny concluded: '[T]he bigger the adverse consequences of (non-contractible) cost-cutting on (non-contractible) quality the stronger is the case for in-house provision in principle.'[29]

In sum, given the introduction of quasi-markets in secondary education five unanticipated and adverse trends are likely:

1. Lower educational standards.
2. Higher costs.
3. Chronic regulatory instability and failure in a context of inescapably incomplete contracting, which is likely to lead to ever more rigidifying 'remedial action' through ever-expanding performance measurement.
4. Systemic demoralisation of the administrative centre, the teaching profession and related professionals.

[29] Hart, Schleifer and Vishny, 'The Proper Scope', p. 1130.

5. Systematic dependence on non-competitive businesses and related fields of business that may engage in satisficing behaviour, rent-seeking and political lobbying.

Secondary Education in the United Kingdom

So how have the risks embedded in the theory of quasi-markets played out in practice? First, a bit of history. The 1944 Education Act established the post-war structure of UK secondary education and enabled a universal system provided by state and religious schools. The Act instituted streaming by aptitude and split students across three school types: selective grammar schools, non-selective 'secondary moderns' and technical schools. The three pillars were meant to enjoy 'parity of esteem', but it became a mainstay of the post-war critique of UK competitiveness that this was never achieved.[30] The decentralising 1944 Act had given democratically elected LEAs responsibility for school admissions, planning, staffing and funding allocation to schools. The absence of a fixed curriculum or timetable had given teachers and heads real latitude on pedagogical and organisational issues.[31]

Labour governments came to oppose pupil selection as elitist, and from the mid-1960s they turned to create mixed ability 'comprehensive' schools. The United Kingdom saw 90 per cent of its students educated in comprehensives by the 1980s, up from only 40 per cent in the 1970s – a shift that provoked many in the Conservative Party to decry the lowering of standards.[32] In the multiple economic crises of the 1970s the media had formed a chorus of disapproval at excessively 'progressive' teaching practices, inner-city school failures and LEA policies out of touch with parental concerns.[33] The stage was set for a party political debate over 'provider capture' – the public choice argument that said public servants, as monopolists, will *inevitably* build services that suit

---

[30] Correlli Barnett, *The Audit of War: The Illusion and Reality of Britain as a Great Nation* (London: Macmillan, 1986).
[31] Denis Lawton, quoted in Jane Gingrich, *Making Markets in the Welfare State: The Politics of Varying Market Reform* (Cambridge: Cambridge University Press, 2011), p. 137.
[32] Paul Bolton, 'Education: Historical Statistics', House of Commons Library, 27 November 2012.
[33] Gingrich, *Making Markets*, pp. 137–138.

their own needs but not those of their 'consumers'. The review of teaching philosophy and resources inevitable in a time of rapid economic change was quickly translated into dogmatic attacks on the integrity of teachers and LEA staff per se.

The claim that schools were suffering from heavy state bureaucracy at the national and local levels was bogus. The traditions of the old Ministry of Education had always been of minimal interference with local authorities (excluding school building approvals post-war), and Her Majesty's Inspection regime, separated from civil servants and government, carried a high level of esteem.[34] While the question of teaching philosophy was a perfectly reasonable arena of democratic dispute, the charges of chronic bureaucratic interference and incompetence were largely confected within the terms of neoliberal argument. By the 1980s the education sector had succumbed to the narratives of systemic capture by self-interested, fiefdom-building public sector workers and their unaccountable failures, a tale rendered credible by some real, complex cases of highly dysfunctional inner-city schools. Hereon the LEAs were to gradually lose many of their powers.

Sam Sims characterises the growth of quasi-markets in UK education as progressing through four stages.[35] The first shift, from 1980 to 1996, saw the advent of internal competition within the public sector. The 1980 Education Act required schools to publish exam results and allowed parental choice for non-oversubscribed schools. Education Secretary Kenneth Baker's later reforms began the centralisation of LEA powers. The 1988 Education Act allowed schools to opt out of LEA control via a parental vote: one in six schools moved, and almost immediately began 'cream-skimming' their student intake. The Act incentivised competition between schools by allowing 80 per cent of funding to follow pupil attendance. It also introduced a National Curriculum and standardised content and examinations. In what would become the template for later reforms, Baker created City Technology Colleges (CTCs). These could be established free of LEA control and made directly accountable to the Department for Education (DfE) and sponsored by businesses. It was hoped that

---

[34] Author's written correspondence with Professor Howard Glennerster (LSE and former Treasury advisor), 2 July 2018.

[35] Sam Sims, 'The Development of Quasi-markets in Secondary Education', Institute of Government, 27 November 2012, p. 4.

CTCs would engage dynamic business governors, but the programme remained small, with only fifteen established.[36]

In the second phase, from 1997 to 2002, the first New Labour government shifted emphasis, via the White Paper 'Excellence in Schools'. The governance of education was devolved within the four nations of the United Kingdom in 1999, but thereafter, in England, Labour's focus was less on structural change and more on content, cooperation and leadership within the existing system. New Education Action Zones sought to create partnerships between schools and other social actors, notably business, to promote better practice in poorer areas. Good schools were designated 'beacons' and additionally funded based on enhanced cooperation. The incipient quasi-market was not reversed, although grant-maintained schools were abolished and all schools were obliged to comply with the centrally determined Admissions Code.[37]

In the third phase, under New Labour's second government from 2002 to 2007, experiments with quasi-markets were brought to the fore. The last CTC had been set up in 1993, some four years before the end of the Conservative government. Then, in 2000, Labour had proposed the creation of a City Academies programme.[38] Statutorily based on the Conservative's 1988 Act, City Academies were intended by the then secretary of state for education and employment, David Blunkett, to achieve the following aims:

- To drive up standards by raising achievement levels for their own pupils, their family of schools and the wider community by breaking the cycle of underachievement and low aspirations in areas of deprivation with historical low performance.
- To be part of local strategies to increase choice and diversity in education and to introduce innovative approaches to governance, curriculum, staffing structures and pay, teaching and learning, structure of the school day and year, using ICT.
- To be inclusive, mixed-ability schools.[39]

---

[36] Ibid., pp. 4–5. [37] Ibid.
[38] Andrew Curtis, Sonia Exley, Amanda Sasia, Sarah Tough and Geoff Whitty, *The Academies Programme: Progress, Problems and Possibilities* (London: The Sutton Trust, 2008), p. 13.
[39] Ibid., p. 5.

Informed by the Charter school experiment in the United States,[40] the idea was that troubled inner-city schools could be replaced with a new type of state school run outside of local authority control and managed by a private team of independent co-sponsors. For the first time since the Second World War, a Labour government now looked to the private sector to replace the state in tackling poor educational outcomes. Academy sponsors would appoint the majority of governors on a board to whom they would delegate school management. The board of governors would employ all academy staff, agree pay levels and conditions of service and decide on the policies for staffing structure, career development, discipline and performance management.[41] Sponsors would have places on the governing body and governance was not regulated beyond the minimal statement that all academies must have one elected parent and one governor appointed by the local authority. The policy was to give sponsors serious institutional autonomy.[42]

Academies exemplified New Labour's increasing adoption of the Camp 2 neoclassical perspective: its embrace of markets modified by a concern for equality of opportunity seen as contingent on the correction of microeconomic market failures. The choice and competition agenda also chimed with the 'Third Way' arguments of the influential sociologist Anthony Giddens, who insisted that by combining public and private sector virtues you would make the public sphere more innovative and dynamic – that in contrast to the neoliberal New Right and the statist Old Left, a reformed social democratic politics should be defined by the idea that social justice and wealth creation could be achieved together and should no longer be dichotomised.[43] The agenda had a powerful advocate in Andrew Adonis both as the education advisor to Tony Blair in 1998 and as the head of the Number 10 Policy Unit after 2000. Adonis brought in Le Grand as the senior

---

[40] Philip Woods, Glenys Woods and Helen Gunter, 'Academy Schools and Entrepreneurialism in Education', *Journal of Education Policy* 22 (2) (2007): 237–259, p. 239.
[41] Andrew Eyles and Stephen Machin, 'Budget 2016: Highly Questionable Whether the Academisation of All Schools Is Good Policy', British Politics and Policy at LSE, 16 March 2016, https://blogs.lse.ac.uk/politicsandpolicy/budget-2016-the-effects-of-mass-rollout-of-academies-programme-remain-uncertain/.
[42] Woods, Woods and Gunter, 'Academy Schools', p. 240.
[43] Anthony Giddens, *The Third Way: The Renewal of Social Democracy* (Cambridge: Polity Press, 1998).

policy advisor to the Policy Unit from 2003 to 2005 after which Adonis served as the minister of state for schools. From the outset he espoused a heroic vision of the enterprise and dynamism of private providers, a charismatic narrative used to sell a theory that depended completely on a strict utilitarian rationalism. Seasoned educationalists were less convinced. Professor Howard Glennerster said of the Blair response that it lacked any diagnosis of the causes of failure in laggard schools. 'It was a solution looking for a problem. The logic [of the problem] would have suggested stronger, quicker intervention with the proven mechanism of new head and senior staff and with lots of local inspectorate support.'[44]

New Labour governments saw a high turnover in its secretaries of state for education: six between May 1997 and May 2010. Education reform had become a defining ideological conflict within the Labour Party, as opposing factions sought to stake out the new boundaries between public and private provisions. Blair won this debate on the educational front in June 2004 when he proposed an ambitious expansion of academies despite opposition from Deputy Prime Minister John Prescott and Education Secretary Charles Clarke. Blair was determined to go into the election with a radical 'choice' agenda for welfare reform and wanted to follow Adonis's recommendation to create 200 academy schools by 2010, a figure raised to 400 in 2007.[45] What had begun as a cautious roll-out in 2002 was thus accelerated after the 2005 election, prior to any empirical proof of the effectiveness of the programme. Academy schools thus became part of a wider public service reform that promised to rebuild public services around consumers, as if the sovereignty ascribed to them in Le Grand's theoretical model was real. The justificatory logic was now essentially neoliberal: to diversify provision to create competition and enable consumer choice. Under the leadership of Gordon Brown (2007–2010) the more cooperative projects of the first New Labour administration were expanded, notably through the City Challenge and National Leaders of Education schemes, but the active promotion of quasi-markets in

---

[44] Author's written correspondence with Professor Howard Glennerster (Professor of Social Policy at the London School of Economics and Political Science and former Treasury advisor), 2 July 2018.

[45] Department for Education and Skills, '400 Academies: Prospectus for Sponsors and Local Authorities', DfES, London, May 2007.

secondary education remained the established New Labour policy and it was embraced with a vengeance by the Conservative government that followed.

The number of academy secondary schools increased from 3 in 2001, to 203 in 2010, to 2,474 by 2018, by which point they made up some 72 per cent of total secondary schools.[46] The transformative expansion came under the new Liberal–Conservative Coalition of 2010, under Michael Gove as the education secretary (2010–2014). A concerted effort to make all existing secondary schools academies continued during the Conservative government of David Cameron and in the post-Brexit Conservative governments of Theresa May (2016–2017, 2017–2019) and Boris Johnson (2019; 2019–2022). By October 2018, half of state-educated students were studying in an academy or a 'free school'.[47] Sims defines this post-2007 era as one of 'competition and cooperation?' and his question mark highlighted the potential for contradiction, as illustrated by the fact that after 2010 government offered incentives for cooperation and mutual learning between schools via the development of best practice 'teaching schools' even as expansion was justified in the terms of autonomy and competition.[48]

In July 2010, the new Coalition government allowed all schools to seek academy status with priority to be given to schools judged outstanding by the Office for Standards in Education, Children's Services and Skills (Ofsted). For the new secretary of state for education, Michael Gove, the public choice logic of the strategy was its central virtue. In a 2009 speech invoking a 'post-bureaucratic schools policy', he had asserted that the success of the existing academies was based on their independence. He argued:

They were established independent from local and central bureaucracy, free from central control over the curriculum, free to adopt the reading and

---

[46] Figures are drawn from DfE, Open Academies, free schools and projects awaiting approval as of September 2016; Report by the Comptroller and Auditor General, 'Converting Maintained Schools', 22 February 2018 (HC 720), www.nao.org.uk/wp-content/uploads/2018/02/Converting-maintained-schools-to-academies.pdf.

[47] Department for Education, 'The Proportion of Pupils in Academies and Free Schools in England, in October 2018: Ad hoc Notice', DfE, London, January 2019.

[48] Sims, 'The Development of Quasi-markets', p. 6.

maths policies which help the most disadvantaged, free to pay good staff more, free to have longer and more fulfilling school days, free to establish Saturday schools to help stretch and challenge pupils, free to shape and enforce more rigorous discipline policies, free to deploy resources more efficiently, free to develop excellent extra-curricular activities and free to spend the money on their own pupils which would otherwise be spent, beyond their control, by the local authority.[49]

It was certainly the case that under Gove many of the residual regulatory powers of the DfE, Ofsted and local authorities were removed in the name of cutting 'red tape', even as the DfE became significantly more prescriptive in terms of curriculum. As we shall see, however, since much of that capacity had fulfilled essential functions, the same tasks would either find their way back but in the form of unsupported planning instructions – either from the administrative centre or through the inspection process – or were simply no longer completed, which meant shifting the problems into another social account; for example, parents with excluded children with special educational needs were left to search for appropriate support elsewhere. The informational disruption here was tremendous. These cuts occurred at the point where the secretary of state was becoming the statutory officer of accountability for a rapidly growing number of schools, as primaries too were encouraged to join the scheme (with some 27 per cent having done so by January 2018).[50] Within a decade academies went from being a niche solution to failing inner city schools to a quasi-market that covered half of the English sector and rising. While 'sponsored' academies continued to open, most of the subsequent expansion up to 2015, almost 80 per cent, came from 'converter' schools.[51]

Converter academies could either remain standalone schools or join existing groups, but successive Conservative governments developed a strong preference for the development of chains or so-called multi-academy trusts, even though these significantly negated the original principles of autonomy and parental choice, but the economies of scale were unarguable. These developments added another

---

[49] Michael Gove, 'A Comprehensive Programme for State Education', Centre for Policy Studies, London, 6 November 2009.
[50] Comptroller and Auditor General, 'Converting Maintained Schools', pp. 1–13.
[51] Andrew Eyles, Stephen Machin and Olmo Silva, 'Academies 2: The New Batch', Centre for Economic Performance Discussion Paper 1370, September 2015.

layer to the burgeoning organisational complexity of the system because the organisational models of MATs could vary from loosely cooperative structures to operations under strictly hierarchical control. Meanwhile, the growing imbalance in the conversion of primary and secondary schools left local authorities still largely responsible for primary education and specialist schools but now unable to take a 'whole system' approach to education in their jurisdiction: basic practical issues such as how to keep track of school transport needs in any given community had never featured in the model. Local authorities were also left with the deficits of maintained schools that converted with a sponsor.[52]

Urged on by the right-wing think tank Policy Exchange, the 2016 (pre-Brexit) budget had announced that *all* schools would be made to convert to academy status by 2022, to free them 'from the shackles of local bureaucracy', with details quickly following in a White Paper. What the government had clearly failed to appreciate, however, was that no constituency had been built for such a move and having failed to mention it in campaigning, the proposal was met with such vocal opposition not just from Labour but also from Conservative Councils, from MPs across all parties, head-teachers and educational experts that the education secretary, Nicky Morgan, was forced to retract it. The policy thus remained that any school could choose to convert, but those deemed to be struggling or failing to improve 'sufficiently' could be compelled. The government nevertheless continued to aim for complete conversion.[53]

The result was a deeply ambiguous position for local authorities. As the National Audit Office (NAO) noted as of 2017–2018, the department withdrew the 'general funding rate' previously paid to local authorities and academies for school support services as part of the Education Services Grant. This created the risk that local authorities would be forced to reduce their support for maintained schools, and this would harm primary schools in particular. Recognising that local authorities would need alternative revenue the department allowed them to retain a proportion of their maintained schools' budgets but now with less clarity about the demands on that budget. For example,

---

[52] Comptroller and Auditor General, 'Converting Maintained Schools', p. 10.
[53] Hannah Richardson, 'Government Climbdown over Forced Academies Plan in England', BBC News, 6 May 2016.

regardless of the mix of maintained schools and academies, local authorities retained important responsibilities, including an obligation to provide enough school places, even though they had no control over the number of places in academy schools.

Did Gove's vaunted freedom to excel produce excellence? In what follows I'll explore how the risks predicted by Camp 2 contract theory and Soviet experience have played out in practice. What we will find is that the academy programme produced fragmented, nominally autonomous schools characterised by a growing trend towards concentration into MATs, all operating under an expanding shadow of bureaucratic audit and regulation that was highly dependent on synoptic target-setting. Financial management has been particularly poor and scandal-prone, and educational performance is below that of state-maintained schools and plagued by the gaming of indicators. Public accountability has been all but extinguished. What academies programme created is a system with high affinities to Soviet enterprise planning but with more informational fragmentation. These outcomes help explain why a Conservative government intent on transforming the entire English school system into a quasi-market was ultimately thwarted by its own backbenchers.

Educational Standards

Researchers into academy performance have faced the challenges of rapid institutional change, lack of pre-treatment research on factors that rose to the fore in academies and the problem that the factors being measured were typically influenced by conditions internal and external to the school itself.[54] The evidence on attainment nevertheless indicated that the first, smaller batch of sponsored schools raised overall attainment to a small degree, did little to improve conditions for the most disadvantaged students and revealed high variation between academies.[55] The second batch of mostly converter academies after 2010 showed radical heterogeneity of outcomes, if anything slightly poorer outcomes than local authority-maintained

---

[54] Stephen Machin, Claudia Huplau and Andrew Eyles, 'School Reforms and Pupil Performance', *Labour Economics* 41 (C) (2016): 9–19.
[55] Stephen Machin and Olmo Silva, 'School Structure, School Autonomy and the Tail', Centre for Economic Performance Special Paper 39, March 2013.

schools and persistent failures to lift the tail of disadvantaged students.[56]

After 2010, the wider roll-out of academies appeared to make little difference in standards overall while masking the tendencies predicted in contract theory: predominantly satisficing, non-dynamic behaviour, the 'gaming' of league tables and the higher rates of student exclusion and cream-skimming. In the first report to compare LEA schools and MATs, Jon Andrews showed that the academies group offered no systematic improvement on LEA schools. Indeed, while the top performing 5 per cent of schools showed equal participation of LEA and academy schools, schools within MATs were more highly represented in the worst performing, lowest 5 per cent of schools.[57]

The question of performance differences between single academy schools and MATs and between large and small MATs became more significant as governments intensified the shift towards conglomeration. The 2016 White Paper 'Educational Excellence Everywhere' demanded that all maintained schools join or begin planning to join a MAT by 2022, although it was unclear on what pedagogic basis this was justified. In 2014 the performance of MATs came under serious scrutiny by the educational charity the Sutton Trust.[58] Their third report found that the sponsored academy chains had lower inspection grades compared with the national figures for all secondary schools and academies. The academies in their analytical group (i.e., those sponsored for at least three years) were twice as likely as mainstream schools to be below the floor standard and twice as likely to be judged 'Inadequate' by Ofsted. Four in ten of the academies in the analysis group were not yet regarded as 'Good' by Ofsted. The Sutton Trust also found significant variation in outcomes for disadvantaged pupils, both between and within chains. Given the dynamism government attributed to the academy system, it is also worth noting that the Sutton Trust's longitudinal analysis found little change to the rankings and insofar as there were developments they were negative: additional chains moved into the significantly below average group in two years out of three. The authors concluded that 'while a handful of chains continued to achieve

---

[56] Eyles and Silva, 'Academies 2'.
[57] Jon Andrews, 'School Performance in Multi-academy Trusts and Local Authorities – 2015', Education Policy Institute, July 2016, p. 22.
[58] Merryn Hutchings, Becky Francis and Philip Kirby, *Chain Effects: The Impact of Academy Chains on Low-Income Students* (London: The Sutton Trust, 2016).

impressive outcomes for their disadvantaged students against a range of measures... the main picture is one of a lack of transformative change [and] a real danger that the programme becomes part of the problem rather than part of the solution'.[59] In the 2016 Education Committee inquiry into MATs a panel of leading researchers was asked 'is the evidence on MATS' performance and impact strong enough to justify that ambition [to expand MATs]?' and their unanimous reply was 'no'. Those same experts reminded the committee that the overwhelming international evidence remained that the quality of teaching and class sizes led to improved standards, not academy-style adjustments in system governance, and there was nothing peculiar to MATs that would guarantee enhanced quality in that respect.[60]

The evidence was also negative when it came to the gaming of performance indicators. When Terry Wrigley analysed the performance of 269 academies listed in the 2011 league tables and compared them with remaining secondary schools, he found that in all schools, 59.1 per cent of pupils gained five strong grades in both General Certificate of Secondary Education (GCSE) and equivalent vocational qualifications and this dropped to 53.2 per cent when vocational courses, widely deemed easier than GSCEs, were stripped out. These results fell from 50.1 per cent to 38.3 per cent when equivalents were removed in the case of academies. In fact, two-thirds of academies saw their results fall by more than the national average of six percentage points.[61] These findings were confirmed by research with Afroditi Kalambouka, which showed that academies relied on equivalent qualifications at twice the rate of other schools and how, in a fifth of academies, such equivalent qualifications inflated attainment figures by over 20 per cent. They also found that 'compared with other schools, 3 out of 5 academies show either a deteriorating performance, no change, or an apparent "improvement" resulting from the heavy use of "equivalents"'.[62]

---

[59] Ibid., pp. 5–6.
[60] Education Committee, Oral Evidence, 'Multi-academy Trusts', 7 September 2016 (HC 204), Questions 222–301, https://data.parliament.uk/writtenevidence/committeeevidence.svc/evidencedocument/education-committee/multiacademy-trusts/oral/37594.html.
[61] Graeme Paton, 'Academy Schools Inflate Results with Easy Qualifications', *The Daily Telegraph*, 3 February 2012.
[62] Terry Wrigley and Afroditi Kalambouka, 'Academies and Achievement: Setting the Record Straight. Research Report', Changing Schools, 2013, pp. 1–3.

Both the first and second batch of academies also operated higher rates of student exclusions. It took a Freedom of Information inquiry by the Local Schools Network to discover that, on average, non-academy state secondary schools permanently excluded 1.7 students out of every 1,000 each year but academies in the first batch excluded 3.1 out of every 1,000 (2008–2009).[63] These figures deteriorated further in the second batch of academies where the DfE's own figures released through 2015–2016 confirmed that the permanent exclusion rate in primary academies was double that of maintained primary schools, with the root of that higher rate in sponsored academies, while converters were on a par with maintained schools. Their figures also confirmed that sponsored academies excluded at nearly twice the rate of maintained secondary schools and almost triple the rate of converter academies.[64] By 2017–2018, pupils were still found to be 1.5 times more likely to be permanently excluded and twice as likely to be fixed-term excluded from a sponsored secondary academy, and twice as likely to be permanently excluded in sponsored academies at the primary level. Pupils registered for special educational needs were five times more likely to be permanently excluded than their peers with no recorded needs, and pupils eligible for free school meals were four times more likely to be excluded than their non-eligible peers.[65] This clearly discriminatory exclusion process was also occurring in the context of wider cuts to supportive social services.

Costs

Academies and their trusts are instructed to operate on a not-for-profit basis, but the DfE has moved through various 'model funding agreement' in its contracts for standalone academies and, later, for MATs, as it realised the conditionalities it should have included and pursued new ideas. The result is the accretion of extremely varied and opaque

---

[63] Marie Faulkner, 'Revealed, Academies Exclude 82 Percent More Students', 9 February 2011, www.localschoolsnetwork.org.uk (page no longer available).
[64] Department for Education, 'Permanent and Fixed Exclusions in England 2015–2016', DfE, London, 18 September 2017, www.gov.uk/government/statistics/permanent-and-fixed-period-exclusions-in-england-2015-to-2016.
[65] Laura Partridge, 'School Exclusions Are a Social Justice Issue, New Data Shows', *Royal Society for Arts, Manufactures and Commerce Blog*, 6 August 2019, www.thersa.org/blog/2019/08/exclusions.

funding agreements across the sector when it comes to initial grants, though continuing per-pupil funding is supposed to be the same, school sector-wide, and thus to follow 'choice'.[66] Before we look at their internal financial management, however, it is worth beginning with the start-up costs of the academies programme because the 'opportunity costs' – the alternatives foregone – were immediately significant.

Although funded at the same basic rate as other secondary schools, the first batch of academies under new Labour were also part of a 'Building Schools for the Future' programme – an ambitious project for architect-designed schools. Estimates issued by the Department for Education and Skills showed a total overrun of £48.5 million – or 8 per cent – on the first twenty-seven academies, related to building design.[67] These academies cost an average of £24 million each, which made them more expensive than other secondary schools.[68] There is nevertheless compelling evidence for poor achievement and morale in low quality buildings and so these costs at least constituted a long-term investment in a high-quality estate.

An altogether more ethically questionable set of costs hit the rapid roll-out from 2010. Unanticipated funding needs drove £1 billion in additional spending between April 2010 and April 2013, a deficit that forced the department to raid funds from other budgets to manage the resultant financial risks.[69] This raid included £95 million intended for improving underperforming schools, a socially regressive transfer now that academy conversions were occurring in high-performing schools.[70] Part of the unforeseen costs came from the complexity of the academy funding system that reportedly led to overpayments and errors including around £350 million paid to academies not recovered from local authorities.[71] The DfE also relied on private sector companies to enable the roll-out. From May 2010 to December 2013, the DfE spent £76.7 million on fourteen private firms for legal, accountancy,

---

[66] Anne West and David Wolfe, 'Academies, the School System in England and a Vision for the Future', Claire Market Working Papers 23, LSE, 2018, p. 13.
[67] 'Academy Cost Overruns Reach £48.5m', BBC News, 9 June 2006.
[68] Report by the Comptroller and Auditor General, 'The Academies Programme', 20 February 2007 (HC 254), The Stationery Office, London, 2007, p. 6.
[69] Report by the Comptroller and Auditor General, 'Managing the Expansion of the Academies Programme', 20 November 2012 (HC 682), www.nao.org.uk/wp-content/uploads/2012/11/1213682es.pdf.
[70] Ibid., p. 14. [71] Ibid., p. 4.

management consultancy and property service support needed either to create an entirely new school in the case of free schools a new form of academy – or to convert school governance and legal structures in the case of existing but converting schools.[72] In effect, the department spent nearly £77 million to private companies to recreate individual school capacities that already existed with more sustainable economies of scale under LEAs. By January 2018 some 6,996 schools had converted to academies at a cost of £745 million (since 2010–2011), a high price for converting schools that were predominantly already performing extremely well as maintained schools.[73]

For schools converting with a sponsor, the department gave funding to the sponsoring trust rather than to the school itself. As the programme developed, however, so the availability of sponsors began to dry up, so that since 2012–2013 the department has given out grants aimed at improving sponsor capacity but with no test of whether those grants had a positive impact. Indeed, the department does not routinely collect data on the total amounts spent on conversion by other bodies, including schools, sponsors and local authorities, so that while the formal cost of conversions in 2016–2017 alone was some £81 million, the NAO concluded that this was not the full amount spent by all bodies. The same 2018 report on conversion also noted that sponsors were particularly difficult to find 'for the most challenged schools'.[74] If we recall what the theory had forecast by way of competition, this policy could instead be characterised not so much as market-making as government rent-giving.

Not only did the roll-out prove expensive but so did the brokerage of transfers when existing academies were taken over. Market exit has proved extremely costly and a long way from the neoclassical image of a frictionless transfer of capital and labour. Some 167 existing academies changed hands between 2005 and 2016, although the cost breakdowns of these changes are available only in fragments.[75] The DfE revealed it had spent £3 million in relation to twenty-three academy transfers (2013–2014) but only after their refusal to release

---

[72] Martin Johnson and Warwick Mansell, 'Education Not for Sale: Research Report', Trades Union Council, 2014, p. 34.
[73] Comptroller and Auditor General, 'Converting Maintained Schools', pp. 1–13.
[74] Ibid., pp. 1–13.
[75] John Winstanley, 'List of All Switches between Academy Sponsors', Freedom of Information Request to the Department for Education, 26 April 2016.

the figures due to 'commercial sensitivity' was overturned in court. When a trust failed suddenly the costs were eye-watering: when the Prospects Academies Trust folded in 2014 the DfE had to pay Attwood Academies £6,450,000 when it took over Bexhill High Academy, just one of the six academies left in limbo.[76]

If we put aside these opportunity costs as the legitimate price of innovation, even if that innovation was driven by utopian politics rather than empiricism, we get to the overall spending trends relative to those in state-maintained schools. Here we hit a remarkable data problem, however. The DfE's approach to academy finance has combined inconsistency between cases with weak regulatory oversight, and it has consequently failed to put either detailed or consistent accounts into the public realm. Even under consistent NAO and Public Accounts Committee pressure the DfE only agreed to put the costs of academies relative to LEA-maintained school into the public realm by June 2017, and even then, it treated them separately when the Consolidated Annual Report and Accounts were finally published in October. In the meantime, the funding agreements are private individual agreements between the secretary of state and the academy trust, which are only made public on the opening of the school and thereafter they are typically marked with redactions justified against a potential breach of commercial interests and data protection rules.[77]

Before academies, LEAs had been in charge of commissioning, procurement and insurances, along with payroll management, human resource management and contract vetting, and this had enabled economies of scale for contract pricing. It had also given LEAs high legal and financial capacity not just in relation to UK but also EU law. The very idea of economies of scale, however, is rooted in a biological metaphor,[78] and it was forgotten in the neoclassical models behind 'choice and competition'. Withdrawn from local authority control, academy schools were immediately confronted by higher costs simply as a matter of losing expertise, economies of scale and value-added tax

---

[76] Janet Downs, 'Six Academies in Limbo as Academy Chain Folds', *Local Schools Network Blog*, 20 May 2014, www.localschoolsnetwork.org.uk (this webpage is no longer available).
[77] Johnson and Mansell, 'Education Not for Sale', p. 29.
[78] Alfred Marshall, *Principles of Economics*, 8th ed. (1890) (New York: Palgrave Macmillan, 2013), Book 4, Chapter 2.

exemptions – a reality that bit at the moment of roll-out.[79] To take just one example, 71 per cent of converters between September 2010 and June 2012 reported increases in costs for accountancy, finance staff and services.[80]

Even in those countries where it is allowed, such as Sweden and the United States, profit-making in state-funded autonomous schools is not straightforward. The dominant cost in a school is for staffing, and the quality of its staff is the basis of its performance, so margins are slim.[81] The decision to ban profit-making in academies was intended to guarantee value for money, but it contradicted Le Grand's imperative to encourage businesses into the sector as dynamic players. An extraordinary opening for financial opportunism nevertheless arose that had formed no part of the original justification for this system.

Academy trusts are granted significant discretion in how they use their funds, which are provided from central government, not the local authority; they determine their own spending profiles, and they can carry forward unspent grant. They are also given extra funds for the services that councils would otherwise provide. More remarkably, trusts are also allowed to make 'related-party' payments. In related-party transactions a trust can award a contract to a company in which a trust director or a member of their family has a direct interest. Related-party payments can also occur between affiliated companies or a parent company and its subsidiaries. Not only do such payments breach public sector norms they also contravene a necessary condition for competitive markets, namely, no collusion between buyers' decisions to buy and sellers' decisions to sell. To enable such conflicts of interest is legalised clientelism and naïve at best, corrupt at worst, and its enactment produced exactly the abuses one would expect.[82]

---

[79] Comptroller and Auditor General, 'Managing the Expansion'.
[80] Ibid., p. 35.
[81] Sam Freedman, 'Why I Changed My Mind on Not-for-Profit Schools', 27 September 2013, http://samfreedman1.blogspot.com/2013/09/why-i-changed-my-mind-on-for-profit.html.
[82] Preston Green III and Chelsea Connery, 'Charter Schools, Academy Schools, and Related Party Transactions: Same Scams, Different Countries', *Arkansas Law Review* 72 (2) (2019): 407–442.

The decision to move to MATs meant that for businesses qua businesses (as distinct from businesses as foundations for philanthropy), control of schools became increasingly attractive as a procurement vehicle. Beyond the opportunities for private gain that already existed for trust management given control over pay scales, a potentially significant profit margin could now be found if a business combined school management with the formation of companies signed up to long-term contracts for services such as management, catering, school improvements, human resources development, ICT or curriculum and teaching packages.

The consolidated accounts for academies in 2017 showed that the number of (recorded) related-party payments increased from 2,005 in 2014–2015 to 3,033 in 2015–2016. This 50 per cent increase far outstripped the 16 per cent growth in academy numbers. Related-party transactions of more than £250,000 had risen by 17 per cent, and schools paid out some £61.9 million in taxpayers' money on these 'high-value' transactions in 2015–2016, compared with £53 million the previous year.[83] Of those reported for 2014–2015, only 7 per cent were deemed to warrant government scrutiny, with twenty-four trusts found to have broken rules when paying funds to related parties.[84] However, not only were those moneys not repaid, the whole question of what counts as a breach of these rules, and hence how you trigger government scrutiny, remains unclear. The requirement that companies charge only 'the cost of their work' was put in place only after November 2013, but how was that evaluated? At the level of academies themselves, it assumed that school managers had the objectivity, time and expertise to engage in competitive tendering, as well as levels of financial knowledge akin to those of the LEAs who operated at scale and had designated, trained, financial officers. It hardly helped that senior executives of academy trusts and the chief executive officers of MATs could serve as the accounting officers, and frequently did.[85]

---

[83] Jonathan Owen, 'Boom in Controversial Payments to Related Parties by Academy Trusts', *Times Education Supplement*, 17 November 2017.
[84] John Dickens, 'A Third of Academy Trusts Paid Businesses Linked to Staff', *Schools Week*, 25 October 2016, https://schoolsweek.co.uk/a-third-of-academy-trusts-paid-businesses-linked-to-staff-and-7-other-findings-from-todays-education-committee/.
[85] Education and Skills Funding Agency, 'Academies Financial Handbook 2021', June 2021, p. 63, https://assets.publishing.service.gov.uk/media/6101908dd3bf7f045b57b677/Academy_Trust_Handbook_2021.pdf.

There is nothing in the current *Financial Handbook* that prevents trustees from contracting out to profit-making companies, and while there is a requirement that academies undertake competitive tendering, an Institute of Education survey found little evidence for it, or for it being monitored by the Education Funding Agency (EFA), the financial management and regulatory body established in April 2012 as an executive agency of the DfE. There is a *Financial Handbook* requirement that trusts report on the extent to which they provide value for money, but a survey of annual reports for the Education Select Committee suggested that 'these statements are largely meaningless'.[86] Indeed, the emerging financial scandals were hardly surprising; the incentives for them were so clear, but the systemic laxity revealed at the EFA was truly remarkable. Its CFO, Simon Parkes, admitted that even by 2014 the EFA didn't automatically look at even the related-party transactions brought to its attention. Nor did it keep a log of how many there were, so that he could not tell how many related transactions had actually been disclosed.[87]

The rise of academy chains was first encouraged to allow high-performing philanthropic sponsors such as the Harris Federation to expand their offering in the earliest days of the scheme. As the programme grew, however, the performance of MATs remained resolutely mixed, but successive governments continued to move towards them. The new public reasoning was that large chains would mitigate the risks associated with 'standalone' academies and enable the school-to-school support integral to the notion of a self-improving system,[88] never mind that the entire programme had been justified on the promise that this mechanism would be competition. The number of MATs duly increased from 391 in March 2011 to 846 in July 2015 and 1,324 by January 2018.[89] And, though MATs may tend to recreate some economies of scale, their dominance has completely undermined the parental sovereignty, school autonomy and hence competition that was the basis of Le Grand theory, particularly when a given MAT became a de facto monopoly in a given community.

---

[86] Toby Greany and Jean Scott, 'Conflicts of Interest in Academy Sponsorship Arrangements: A Report for the Education Select Committee', Institute for Education, September 2014, p. 4.

[87] Pat Sweet, 'DfE Slammed over Related Party Payments at Academies', *Accountancy Daily*, 10 March 2014.

[88] Hutchings, Francis and Kirby, *Chain Effects*, p. 11.

[89] Comptroller and Auditor General, 'Converting Maintained Schools', p. 42.

Le Grand had argued that within competitive systems there are no meaningful distinction between knights and knaves, but within state-dependent and highly incomplete markets it turns out that there are. Following a 2014 Education Select Committee report that was highly critical of the regulatory environment in which academies operated, Nick Weller, chairman of the Independent Academies Association, concluded:

> We believe that the best forms of academy sponsorship are either the original philanthropic one or one where outstanding schools have built a family of schools around them... Some of the later models of sponsorship, for example by suppliers of educational services, are often weaker in impact, are often a throw-back to the failed local authority model, and almost invite conflicts of interest. In our opinion, such models should be avoided.[90]

What his comments reflected was that in educational terms there had been a consistently strong record of the original philanthropic trusts and of those academies that had already proved outstanding under LEA maintained governance. In the meantime, those providers who had oriented themselves to the institutional incentives alone had performed poorly, because educationally and financially speaking those incentives were perverse. What had worked, and continued to work, was the committed altruism of the philanthropic agents and the best practices already established under the old state system – a clear 'disproof of principle' for quasi-markets and the efficiency gains of self-interest.

Regulatory Instability

The legal status of academies has constantly evolved but it has yet to establish a governance model that satisfies the NAO, the cross-party parliamentary Education Committee or the Public Accounts Committee. Legally, academy trusts – the companies that run academies – are charities, and the first 200 had to register with the Charity Commission. The Academies Act 2010, however, granted academy trusts 'exempt charity' status, and after 1 August 2011 this exempted them from registration and primary regulation by the

---

[90] Katherine Sellgren, 'Academy Regulation "too weak" says MPs' Report', BBC News, 14 September 2014.

Charity Commission. The secretary of state duly became the principal regulator of academies while their everyday financial oversight was handed to the EFA.

As exempt charities, academies have to publish their accounts at Companies House, but they have the financial benefits of registered charities, which include reliefs not only on income, corporation and capital gains tax but also on business and non-domestic rates. Trustees are expected to perform the same general duties as those of other charities, which include acting reasonably and prudently in all matters relating to the charity.[91] While educational quality control is regulated by Ofsted, the theory of incomplete contracts predicts chronic regulatory problems in the outsourcing of education and this has been the reality. Adonis had argued that '[i]n my experience charisma, persuasion and money, not legislation and regulation are the great drivers of reform',[92] and from the outset the programme was conceived within a 'light touch', self-regulatory paradigm to maximise school autonomy. Successive governments have consequently found themselves playing catch-up in the face of repeated financial scandals and polarising educational performance.

In relation to financial regulation, the then Comptroller and Auditor General, Sir Amyas Morse, told the Education Committee in 2016 that 'there is not necessarily an easy conclusion lying out there to be reached' because of the intrinsic tension that had now been institutionalised between autonomy and accountability. So, '[H]owever long you run the academy sector it is always going to need fine-tuning because at a particular stage you are always going to be striking a balance between not putting in too much regulation and not having too much public outcry about individual examples.'[93] The DfE's efforts to achieve this balance have caused constant institutional adjustments in financial management and oversight, including the establishment of the EFA to administer education revenue and capital funding but also to act as the designated financial regulator of schools. The self-regulating

---

[91] Andy Hillier, 'Analysis: Academies Schools – Charities, but Not as We Know Them', *Third Sector*, 5 February 2013.

[92] Andrew Sparrow, 'What Do You Want to Ask Lord Adonis?', *The Guardian*, 27 November 2012.

[93] Education Committee, Oral Evidence, 'Financial Management at the Department for Education', 25 October 2016 (HC 203), Question 98, https://committees.parliament.uk/oralevidence/6158/pdf/.

Regulatory Instability 209

EFA is consequently not the independent regulatory agency Le Grand required.

Because of New Public Management reforms across the board, the new EFA itself was also expected to absorb an exceptional degree of institutional change. It took over the responsibilities of the Young People's Learning Agency, Partnerships for Schools and the department's distribution of funding to local authorities, and its 'customers' were projected to increase by 50 per cent between 2012–2013 and 2015–2016. Even as its responsibilities grew it was expected to implement a 14.6 per cent reduction in its annual recurring administrative costs. In January 2013, only 36 per cent of the EFA's 'customers' rated the agency's services as good or excellent – a poor review in a financial year in which it distributed £51 billion to local authorities and educational institutions.[94] The NAO's 2014 report on the agency also judged that the DfE lacked sufficient high-quality data to analyse the agency's performance in matching the departmental objectives.[95] This was reinforced in the 2016 NAO report on the sustainability of schools, which concluded that 'until more progress is made, we cannot conclude that the department's approach to managing the risks to schools' financial sustainability is effective and providing value for money'.[96] Such progress looked difficult, however, where the centre was now trying to oversee a completely fragmented system of accounting agents, themselves empowered to engage in the most non-transparent form of procurement possible.

These concerns over financial probity provoked an increasingly exhortatory tone in the EFA's chief executive's letters to the academy trust accounting officers between 2013 and 2016. By 2016 these instructions included a new rule that academies adopt clear policy on whistleblowing,[97] a policy that, given the autonomy of trusts over pay,

---

[94] Report by the Comptroller and Auditor General, 'Performance and Capability of the Education Funding Agency', 23 January 2014 (HC 966), p. 4, www.nao.org.uk/wp-content/uploads/2015/01/Performance-and-capability-of-the-Education-Funding-Agency.pdf.
[95] Ibid., p. 8
[96] Report by the Comptroller and Auditor General, 'Financial Sustainability of Schools', 12 December 2016 (HC 850), p. 11, www.nao.org.uk/wp-content/uploads/2016/12/Financial-sustainability-of-schools.pdf.
[97] Peter Lauener, 'Letter to Academy Trust Accounting Officers', October 2016, www.gov.uk/government/publications/letter-to-academy-trust-accounting-officers-october-2016.

promotion and conditions, would have to be ironclad. The realisation that these new institutional arrangements constituted a systemic financial risk, as predicted, has required ever greater remedial bureaucratic intervention, but now without the comprehensive local oversight formerly provided by LEAs. What we have, in other words, is a striking parallel to the Soviet experience in which the inevitable informational holes in the Soviet enterprise planning had caused relentless bureaucratic accretion. To manage the risks to financial health, a range of information, tools and training was developed for Schools Accounting Offices that included advice on financial planning, data to support self-assessment such as benchmarking and practical advice about buying and collaborative procurement. From November 2017, a new pool of School Efficiency Advisers (SEAs) was announced to provide practical support to those trusts 'that needed it most'.[98]

Since LEAs were identified as prime culprits in the public choice narrative of provider capture, the shift in the era of academies had aimed to sharply reduce their role, and this had pulled out the 'middle tier' of oversight and one that in the previous system had enabled economies of scale, specialised expertise and institutional memory. By contrast, the institutional architecture of academies combined radical devolution of budgets, decision-making and governance to schools with exceptional centralisation in the form of direct but incomplete foundation contracts between academy schools and the secretary of state, as overseen by the EFA. Such individual funding agreements and their adjustment had been relatively manageable in the very first years of the programme, given the possibility of high communication with a small number of schools.[99] As the scheme grew, however, the new architecture created an unprecedented increase in the planning burdens of the central state.

There is not sufficient space here to trace the complex history of regulatory change in the DfE since 2002, but expectations were

---

[98] Department for Education, 'Academies School Sector England: Consolidated Annual Report and Accounts, for the Year Ended 31st August 2016' (HC 425), p. 60, https://assets.publishing.service.gov.uk/government/uploads/system/uploads/attachment_data/file/654811/Academy_Schools_Sector_in_England_Consolidated_Annual_Report_and_Account....pdf.

[99] Author Interview with Conor Ryan, senior special advisor to David Blunkett (1997–2001) and senior education advisor to Tony Blair (2005–2007), 19 December 2016, The Sutton Trust, London.

wrong-footed even in the first exploratory wave of academies under New Labour. The NAO first reported on the programme in February 2007 and found that while the first twenty-seven academies were on track to deliver good value for money, the capital overruns on the school estate apart, the number of genuinely philanthropic sponsors was in shorter supply than anticipated. Under the original scheme the sponsors were expected to provide a financial contribution, but the NAO found that of the forty-five academy schools pledged endowment contributions between 2007–2008 and 2009–2010, fully 58 per cent had not received any of these contributions by March 2010. Moreover, the proportion of endowments owed to academies that opened in 2007 and 2008 was no lower than that owed to academies opening in 2009–2010, which indicated that the DfE had failed to collect the older debts.[100] The payment of capital contributions followed a similar pattern. By March 2010, eighty-eight academies pledged capital contributions had still not received some £42 million of the £148 million owed them by their sponsors.[101] In September 2009, as several philanthropic trusts took on more schools and sponsors started to emerge from within the school system itself, the government simply scrapped the requirement for sponsors to make any financial contribution to new academies that opened in the 2010–2011 academic year.[102]

Thereafter the quality of financial data and hence of regulatory enforcement has been a constant weakness. By 2016 the DfE could publish its accounts for 2014–2015 only a full nine months after every other government department. The NAO found a level of 'misstatement and uncertainty' in the financial statement that caused the Comptroller and Auditor General to provide an 'adverse opinion' on the 'truth and fairness' of the department's financial statement – the most negative verdict an auditor can give, though it only repeated the adverse opinion given in the previous year. The NAO's 2016 'Report on the Department for Education's Financial Statements 2014–2015' warned that the rapid expansion of the academies programme had

---

[100] Report by the Comptroller and Auditor General, 'The Academies Programme', 10 September 2010 (HC 288), p. 16, www.nao.org.uk/wp-content/uploads/2010/09/1011288.pdf.
[101] Ibid.
[102] Ibid.

made it difficult to keep track not just of spending but also of the fate of the schools' physical estate, its land assets.[103] In October 2016 Morse told the Education Select Committee, 'You do not know who owns the property or whether we have title to it.' The NAO report concluded: 'The department's policy of autonomy for academies brings with it significant risks if the financial capability of the Department and academies are not strengthened.' The department's financial statements also failed to meet the accountability requirements of Parliament.[104] In an earlier report the NAO had also identified the following oversight problems: that measures of school performance were too narrowly focused on educational performance; that the DfE knew too little about school governance to identify risks; that the roles and responsibilities of the oversight bodies were unclear; and that the criteria for often costly interventions (which had increased) were inconsistent and the effectiveness of those interventions was unclear, as were the reasons why some sponsors were apparently more successful than others.[105] The NAO gave its third adverse opinion in a row for the 2015–2016 accounts, issued in 2017.[106]

It remained impossible to evaluate whether the academies programme has achieved value for money in terms of impact on educational performance relative to spending. As the EFA's then CFO, Peter Lauener, wrote to academy trust accounting officers, 'Many of the findings by trusts external auditors in 2014/2015 were about basic weaknesses in internal controls such as procurement and financial reporting.'[107] The DfE consequently lacks adequate accounts on

---

[103] Report by the Comptroller and Auditor General, 'Report on the Department for Education's Financial Statements 2014–2015', 20 April 2016 (HC 46), Paragraphs 19–14, www.nao.org.uk/wp-content/uploads/2016/04/The-Report-of-the-Comptroller-and-Auditor-General-on-the-Department-for-Educations-2014-15-financial-statement.pdf.

[104] 'DfE's Accounts Contain Pervasive Errors Warns Spending Watchdog', *Times Education Supplement*, 20 December 2016.

[105] Report by the Comptroller and Auditor General, 'Academies and Maintained Schools: Oversight and Intervention', 30 October 2014 (HC 721), pp. 8–10, www.nao.org.uk/wp-content/uploads/2014/10/Academies-and-maintained-schools-Oversight-and-intervention-summary.pdf.

[106] Comptroller and Auditor General, 'Report of the Comptroller and Auditor General to the House of Commons', 24 October 2017, www.nao.org.uk/wp-content/uploads/2017/10/Report-of-the-Comptroller-and-Auditor-General.pdf.

[107] Lauener, 'Letter to Academy Trust'.

expenditure. Moreover MATs, that is, those institutions arguably most vulnerable to large-scale opportunism and moral hazard in financial terms, do not have to provide school-level expenditure accounts at all. Trusts do not have to include per-pupil costs and the data are not comparable with that available for maintained schools. The result is unprecedented opportunity for clientelism, profit-taking and misspending in the English school system – a shocking predicament for a programme justified by claims that it would greatly improve cost efficiency, transparency, responsiveness and quality.

In September 2014, the department established eight Regional Schools Commissioners to create a middle administrative tier tasked with deciding the creation of new academies within a remit to encourage ongoing conversion. By 2016, Richard Ward, Clerk of the Education Committee,[108] cited the continuing development of these Commissioners and the expansion of their governance powers as an example of how the DfE was seeking to swiftly 'scale-up' oversight of schools, a major intervention for a policy that had never anticipated the need. In its report on the role of Regional Schools Commissioners, the cross-party Education Committee concluded that 'the introduction of RSCs is a pragmatic approach to managing the growing task of overseeing academies. Once the mix of school structures becomes more stable a fundamental reassessment will be required'.[109] After the vast public expense and disruption of academisation, the apparent direction of travel is thus towards the reinvention of the mid-tier institutions so despised by Michael Gove, where the obvious economies of scale sit, only now in an altogether less accountable form.

Under the 2015 Conservative government's policy of more radical austerity, schools were expected to make savings of £1.1 billion (equivalent to 3.1 per cent of the total schools budget) in 2016–2017, rising to £3 billion (8.0 per cent) by 2019–2020, with the expressed hope that much of this could be done through more efficient procurement, although schools had already failed to achieve the department's

---

[108] Author Interview with Richard Ward, 19 December 2016, Tothill Street, London.
[109] Education Committee, 'The Role of Regional Schools Commissioners', 13 January 2016 (HC 401), p. 7, paragraph 10, www.publications.parliament.uk/pa/cm201516/cmselect/cmeduc/401/401.pdf.

aspiration to save £1 billion during the previous government and the DfE had offered no detailed advice on how such savings could be made.[110] The problem of underfunding was consequently added to the pathologies already outlined. By 2022 the Conservative government found it necessary to issue regulatory guidance on the elaborate and complex procedures for the closure of an academy school, and they were about as far from a simple consumer choice as could be imagined.[111]

The Policymaking Environment

As Sonia Exley has shown, policymaking in English education has become subject to 'overt politicisation and privatisation of the formulation of policy over time'. In addition to the growing scepticism regarding the civil service's neutrality, she argues, this privatisation occurred alongside the marginalisation of teacher trade unions and local government, that is, those actors judged guilty of the 'provider capture' of the 1970s.[112] Exley's research demonstrates an incremental introduction of policy advisors from multiple right-wing think tanks such as the Centre for Policy Studies and the Institute for Economic Affairs, as well as a movement towards overtly politicised advice that accelerated under New Labour from 1997 to 2010 and became firmly embedded under the Conservative tenure of Gove in the DfE. Gove notoriously referred to his own civil servants and the wider 'educational establishment' as 'the Blob' – the self-interested monopoly of public choice lore, whose asserted 'capture' of the system he was determined to break.[113]

The political advisors from the right tended to insist that only by avoiding the 'formal hierarchies of the civil service' and cutting through 'complicated loops' could the radicalism of the reform agenda be

---

[110] Comptroller and Auditor General, 'Financial Sustainability of Schools', p. 17.
[111] Department for Education, 'Closure of an Academy by Mutual Agreement: Departmental Guidance for All Kinds of Academy Trust', January 2022, https://assets.publishing.service.gov.uk/government/uploads/system/uploads/attachment_data/file/1133038/Academy_closure_by_mutual_agreement_guidance_2023.pdf.
[112] Sonia Exley, 'Think Tanks and Policy Networks in English Education', in Michael Hill, *Studying Public Policy: An International Approach* (Bristol: Policy Press, 2014), p. 180.
[113] Dennis Sewell, 'Michael Gove vs the Blob', *The Spectator*, 13 January 2010.

preserved.[114] In its stead has emerged a complex network of highly activist think tanks and education charities such as the Sutton Trust, that is to say 'do tanks' that are politically diverse and moving directly in and out of political advisory roles with direct policymaking influence. The radical expansion of the academies programme is often attributed to the influence of Policy Exchange, the free marketeer think tank founded by Gove and, more specifically, to its 2010 paper 'Blocking the Best'. Similarly, a 2009 report that supported the radical downsizing of 'bureaucracy' in education recommended abolishing eleven 'school quangos' in England, seven of which were subsequently abolished in 2012.[115]

The boundaries of policymaking and implementation are also increasingly blurred by the lobbying and consultation of charities, non-governmental organisations and educational trusts, and also by much more highly resourced commercial 'edu-business' players, as private and third-sector actors are brought into formal roles and influence.[116] Over ten years, Exley observed an increasingly direct role played by public service industry multinationals such as Serco and Capita in taking over LEAs deemed to be 'failing' by Ofsted. She also observed the rising ubiquity of the major management consultancies and accountancy firms, Price Waterhouse Coopers, McKinsey and KPMG, in conducting policy development and major evaluations for the DfE.[117] Stephen Ball also noted the assiduous lobbying by education-business companies for government to enlarge the business model around academies and to allow private finance initiatives for anything up to thirty-year contracts, not just for the management of the physical estate and service provision but directly for teaching and learning.[118] Ball and Exley thus converge on finding a new culture of 'policy by experiment, policy by increment and detailed policy formulation taking place very clearly outside the state'.[119] The results nevertheless continue to be paid for by the taxpayer.

---

[114] Sonia Exley, 'The Politics of Educational Policy Making under New Labour: An Illustration of Shifts in Public Service Governance', *Policy and Politics* 40 (2) (2012): 227–244, p. 236.
[115] Exley, 'Think Tanks', p. 183.
[116] Ibid., p. 185.
[117] Stephen Ball, cited in Exley, ibid.
[118] Stephen J. Ball, *Education Plc: Understanding Private Sector Participation in Public Sector Education* (Abingdon: Routledge, 2007), p. 55.
[119] Exley, 'Think Tanks', p. 186.

Under the 2010 Coalition it became policy to restructure Whitehall departments, consolidate departmental agencies and enact large staff cuts; these changes were headlined by the introduction of new non-executive board members (NEBMs) to join departmental boards otherwise constituted by ministers and senior civil servants. NEBMs were to be brought in largely 'from the commercial private sector, with experience of managing complex organisations'.[120] The board members were chosen via informal, non-transparent means and the first four had primarily private sector backgrounds, of which two had made donations to the Conservative Party and had ties to the New Schools Network and Policy Exchange. Under the next Conservative government, the NEBMs were either participants in the academies programme or engaged in industries with a clear commercial interest in education outsourcing. In contrast to the neutral civil service, they provided an ideological echo chamber. In a staff survey regarding the reforms in 2011, only 21 per cent of DfE staff believed 'that changes made in the Department are usually for the better'.[121]

Massive cuts in staffing were made at the DfE even as it failed to manage its existing statutory duties. In 2012 the secretary of state commissioned a further review of the DfE by the management consultancy Bain and Company. Among its headline goals were a 50 per cent cut in the department's administrative budget by 2015, the introduction of flexible working and the reduction of its estate by half. It thereby initiated a further transformation of the department's capacity even as it presided, already chaotically, over one of the biggest institutional changes in the school system since the war.

In the theoretical section I argued that the promise that parents would be fully informed and powerful agents would be voided by the reality of the private contract between the state and the provider. In practice there has been a loss of public accountability across the board. The shift from Acts of Parliament to private contracts as the legal basis of the state–school relationship collapsed the former legal accountability for parents, Parliament or LEAs. As a specialist on education law, the barrister David Wolfe, put it: '[A]cademies are set

[120] HM Government, 'Corporate Governance in Central Government Departments: Code of Good Practice', HM Treasury, July 2011, p. 17.
[121] Education Committee, 'Governance and Leadership of the Department for Education', 5 November 2012 (HC 700), pp. 8, 20, www.publications.parliament.uk/pa/cm201213/cmselect/cmeduc/700/700.pdf.

up by a legal contract between two parties [the academy trust and the secretary of state]. They both have rights. No-one else does.'[122] The reason for this is that academies and free schools weren't created through statute law, but Parliament gave powers to the education secretary to enter into agreements with people who undertook to provide schools in exchange for state funding. Statute law was thus overtaken by contract law as the legal basis for providing educational institutions, despite the reality that those contracts are chronically and necessarily 'incomplete' and hence provide only poor protections to children, parents and taxpayers.

The upshot is a profound loss of democratic and financial accountability and for an educational gain that is anything but clear.[123] A 2019 report by the parliamentary Public Accounts Committee concluded that MATs were not sufficiently transparent to parents or communities, even as a succession of trust failures proved damaging to children and the taxpayer. The committee's Members of Parliament found that most parents had to fight to obtain even basic information about their children's schools.[124] Meanwhile, the entire sector proceeds towards concentration into MATs of an ever larger size: the average number of schools within a MAT had increased from 3.3 in 2016 to 5.5 by 2020, and the financial health of the sector remained volatile in the light of continuing real-term cuts in public funding.[125]

Conclusion

In a *Spectator* article called 'Michael Gove vs the Blob', Dennis Sewell concluded that Gove's 'reforms will represent a massive and permanent shift of power away from bureaucrats and the quangocracy towards parents and ordinary class teachers'.[126] But this organised

---

[122] Johnson and Mansell, 'Education Not for Sale', p. 29.
[123] Graham Clayton, 'The Alarming Democratic Void at the Heart of Our Schools System', *The Guardian*, 26 April 2012.
[124] The Committee of Public Accounts, 'Academy Accounts and Performance: Seventy Third Report of Session 2017–2019', 23 January 2019 (HC 1597), p. 3, www.publications.parliament.uk/pa/cm201719/cmselect/cmpubacc/1597/1597.pdf.
[125] Jonathan Ford and Andrew Jack, 'Number of Academies Reporting Deficits Still Rising', *Financial Times*, 30 January 2020.
[126] Sewell, 'Michael Gove'.

forgetting of the state, first in neoclassical theory and then in policy justification, created an academy and free school regime that is neither fish nor fowl: neither an efficient market nor a well-organised public system but a capitalist parody of Soviet planning – a system of barely accountable private enterprises managed by central, no longer local, government, via an elaborate exoskeleton of intrusive and rigid bureaucratic oversight, which is the exact opposite of what was promised.

As for empowering parents, over a decade into this experiment, 'choice' as the determinant of competition has been centralised as the prerogative of the DfE now assisted by its regional commissioners, who operate according to private contract law in relation to which parents have no rights. In fact, parents usually receive notification of their schools joining or forming MATs after a trust directly seeks that option from the DfE or is requested to do so by the DfE. As of July 2020, some 84 per cent of academies were in a MAT.[127] Indeed, to understand the value the Conservatives afforded parental oversight, their ill-fated 2016 White Paper had tried to remove the requirement to have *any* elected parent governor on the board of a trust.

Far from liberating class teachers from bureaucracy, a 2015 survey by the National Union of Teachers and YouGov found that over half had considered leaving the profession in the next two years, with 61 per cent citing the volume of workload.[128] By May 2016, English schools had spent £800 million in supply teaching costs because of the ongoing recruitment crisis.[129] In 2018, excessive workload had driven the number of teachers considering exit to 80 per cent.[130] In that same year the *Ofsted Inspection Handbook* as of April 2018 – supposedly a less onerous process after years of protest – came in at seventy-eight pages, and thirty-three pages of its second half were devoted to 'the

---

[127] Department for Education, 'Academy Schools Sector in England: Consolidated Annual Report and Accounts for the Year Ending 31 August 2020' (HC 851), p. 11, https://assets.publishing.service.gov.uk/government/uploads/system/uploads/attachment_data/file/1041568/Academy_schools_sector_in_England_consolidated_annual_report_and_accounts_.pdf.

[128] Daniel Boffey, 'Half of All Teachers in England Threaten to Quit as Morale Crashes', *The Guardian*, 4 October 2015.

[129] Rachael Pells, 'Schools Spent £800m on Supply Teachers Last Year amid Recruitment Crisis', *The Independent*, 17 May 2016.

[130] Richard Adams, 'Vast Majority of Teachers Consider Quitting in Past Year – Poll', *The Guardian*, 1 April 2018.

evaluation schedule and grade descriptors' listed under some seventy-nine distinct sub-categories.[131]

As for attainment, the academies programme has performed as well as LEA schools at the top of the performance range, but most academies cluster at the average and have higher tendencies than LEA schools towards intensified gaming of exam indicators, high exclusion rates, more stagnant performance and poorer performance regarding disadvantaged children. Academies have nevertheless proved extremely costly, enabling huge losses and forms of misspending from inflated 'executive' pay, corrupt related-party payments, costs of transfer as schools go under and the massive opportunity costs of creating an entire system of school governance no better than the one it replaced but more inequitable and altogether less accountable. According to repeated Public Accounts Committee and NAO reports, the DfE has yet to achieve the informational and administrative capacity for effective meta-governance across the system as a whole.

Most school practitioners now consider themselves constrained by central government targets to an extent unheard of in the 1970s: the vaunted high point of the socialist Leviathan. 'Autonomy' has come largely in the form of far greater responsibilities in terms of delegated financial, human resources and site-management duties. Professional autonomy has been reduced via subjection to increasingly intense forms of central government oversight, target-setting and intervention,[132] while the increased autonomy over admissions, curriculum and the hiring of teachers without educational qualifications has produced highly variable outcomes, given the prevailing incentives, and the rise of MATs reduced autonomy still further.[133] Far from encouraging leadership that is visionary, creative and entrepreneurial, the incentives within academies are towards leadership that is reactive, compliant and managerial,[134] as it was in the Soviet system. Trust

---

[131] Ofsted, *School Inspection Handbook: Handbook for Inspecting Schools in England under Section 5 of the Education Act 2005* (April 2018, Reference Number 150066).

[132] Rob Higham and Peter Earley, 'State Autonomy and Government Control: School Leaders Views on a Changing Policy Landscape in England', *Educational Management Administration and Leadership* 41 (6) (2013): 701–717.

[133] West and Wolfe, 'Academies, the School System', p. 23.

[134] Dean Fink, *Building and Sustaining Leadership, the Succession Challenge* (London: SAGE, 2010).

leadership is nevertheless far better remunerated than Soviet managers ever were. In 2017–2018 some 32 per cent of trusts paid salaries of £100,000–£150,000 to at least one person and 5 per cent salaries of over £150,000. By 2018–2019 that figure had risen to 47.5 per cent and 11.1 per cent of trusts respectively (including employer pension contributions) – that is to say, a rise to six-figure 'executive' salaries in well over half the sector.[135]

Academisation exemplified the high hopes of the neoliberal revolution in its most socially inclusive, Camp 2 mode. But quasi-markets in practice are characterised by continuous enterprise planning from the centre, and where services are complex and amenable to neither effective contracting nor market competition, they tend instead to reproduce many of the pathologies of Soviet enterprise planning: informational failures, incentive-distorting reliance on success indicators, increasingly Kafkaesque efforts towards regulatory completion and the financial abuse of clientelistic relationships between non-competing producers, all shielded from public scrutiny. The results are higher cost and lower quality education, particularly for those students who were least advantaged to begin with.

[135] Department for Education, 'Academy Schools Sector in England: Consolidated Annual Report and Accounts for the Year Ending 31 August 2019', (HC 486), p. 21, https://assets.publishing.service.gov.uk/government/uploads/system/uploads/attachment_data/file/968362/SARA_Academies_Sector_Annual_Report_and_Accounts_201819_-_accessible.pdf.

7 | Tax Competition, or *the Return of Regulatory Bargaining*

For over forty years British chancellors have argued that to keep Britain competitive corporate tax rates must be lowered and regulations removed, reduced or remade in favour of capital. What they have failed to mention is that the models on which these policies are based are so stylised as to guarantee a profound mismatch between theory and practice. It is only through such models, however, that neoliberal governments could keep alive the conceit that reduced corporate tax rates would increase overall investment, that we could estimate by how much and that deregulation too would only improve economic performance. It is no coincidence that the main macroeconomic models used in this realm either have direct roots in the closed-system input–output exchange models developed for the Soviet economy or depend on the unrealistic assumptions behind general equilibrium theory. The history of tax and regulatory competition confirms that Soviet and neoclassical statecraft will tend to converge, and it shows again how serious the unanticipated consequences from closed-system reasoning can be for the real political economy.

Following the Second World War, democratic governments in advanced capitalist states had used their systems of tax and regulation to help direct firms towards productive investment. A key purpose of the 1944 Bretton Woods Agreement on monetary and exchange rate management was to create an international financial regime that would allow for interventionist economic policies at home. The cross-border mobility of capital was restricted by high tariffs, strict capital controls, limited currency convertibility and tough visa and immigration laws, all intended to prevent any repeat of the disastrous capital movement volatility of the 1930s. They also limited international tax avoidance and evasion.[1] A 'politics of productivity' was the basis

---

[1] Philipp Genschel and Peter Schwartz, 'State of the Art: Tax Competition, a Literature Review', *Socio-Economic Review* (9) (2011): 339–370, p. 340.

of America's post-war foreign economic policy and, as the historian Charles Maier put it, this sought 'to adjourn class conflict for a consensus on growth'.[2] In this same spirit, the international coordination of regulatory powers became a defining feature of the first decades of European cooperation in the European Steel and Coal Community and the European Economic Community (EEC).

But, for neoliberals, both taxation and regulation distort the otherwise efficient markets promised by general equilibrium, and a 'competitive' state should reduce both. Milton Friedman famously insisted that businesses, as 'artificial persons', should face no obligations beyond profit-making and that to act otherwise was to impose a coercive political power onto the universal liberties of the free market.[3] In neoliberalism, such arguments were joined to the public choice assertion that governments bent on budget maximisation should be forced to tighten their belts. Over the last forty years not only the United Kingdom but the majority of advanced capitalist states and emerging markets have embarked on tax and regulatory competition based on this vein of reasoning.

In the 1990s it was argued that technological improvements had made capital investments less expensive in multiple sectors, and this had made the competitiveness of goods increasingly sensitive to price changes. It then followed as a matter of neoclassical logic that the competitiveness of goods would become more vulnerable to the 'distortion' of their prices imposed by taxes and regulation.[4] Competition in practice was neither one-dimensional nor static in any sector, however. Costs in some assembly lines had come down and some goods had indeed become more price sensitive, but this was hardly the whole picture. Competition was typically intra-regional – as within Europe – rather than global. It was also increasingly multi-dimensional. As John Zysman, Eileen Doherty and Andrew Schwartz showed in the electronics sector of the 1990s, competition was about a lot of things – 'architectures, standards, high value-added components and subsystems

---

[2] Charles S. Maier, *Between Power and Plenty: Foreign Economic Policies of Advanced Industrial States* (Madison: University of Wisconsin Press, 1978), Chapter 2, p. 23.

[3] Milton Friedman, 'A Friedman Doctrine – The Social Responsibility of Business Is to Increase Its Profits', *The New York Times*, 13 September 1970.

[4] Steven Vogel, *Freer Markets, More Rules: Regulatory Reform in Advanced Industrial Countries* (Ithaca: Cornell University Press, 1996), pp. 10–11.

that are defended with intellectual property, and an outsourcing of the commodity assembly and commodity components'.[5]

That improved competition actually required state intervention was taken as a given in the design of the Single European Market – the SEM, prepared for through the Single European Act of 1987 and launched in January 1993. Though Margaret Thatcher had been a driving force behind its creation, the logic of the SEM operated in Camp 2 terms. The SEM enshrined four of the standard and comparatively intuitive neoclassical conditions for a perfectly efficient market in a single economy: the free movement of capital, persons, goods and services. But from the perspective of Camp 2 it was clear that such a market had to be positively constructed and actively sustained, not left to emanate from the deregulatory voiding of national structures. The SEM was thus created by banning restrictive practices on the one hand while positively harmonising standards and regulations on the other across agreed terrains – in effect, by anticipating market failures around competition and information and pre-emptively guaranteeing the rules of the game. The European Union thus put its institutional weight behind the acceleration of global financial and factor mobility and economic liberalisation while adopting strong Camp 2 reasoning on microeconomic market failures.

When it came to developing an economy that would thrive in such a single market, however, the Camp 3 message for any government wanting to improve competitiveness in anything beyond simple commodities or services was that they should engage in more, not less, strategic intervention. The increase of price sensitivity in some areas could not change the fact that if you wanted your economy to reach, let alone stay at, the technological frontier, the state would still have to sustain the intellectual, technological, educational and infrastructural capacity of the national economy and, indeed, improve it. To do this it was going to need tax revenues. Companies too were going to have to sustain if not increase their investment in their own productive capacity, and so a logic of cost-cutting would clearly have its limits.[6]

---

[5] John Zysman, Eileen Doherty and Andrew Schwartz, 'Tales from the "Global Economy": Cross-National Production Networks and the Reorganization of the European Economy', *Structural Change and Economic Dynamics* (8) (1997): 45–85, p. 82.

[6] See Michael Piore and Charles Sabel, *The Second Industrial Divide: Possibilities for Prosperity* (New York: Basic Books, 1984); Michael L. Dertouzos, Richard K. Lester and Robert Solow. *Made in America: Regaining the Productive*

In effect, the impulse towards Camp 1 reasoning stopped economists from asking 'what supports innovation and development?' and sidestepped the scholarship on that question from Joseph Schumpeter, Alfred Marshall, Edith Penrose, Alfred Chandler onwards.[7] Neoliberal governments opted instead for the simpler fictions of the price mechanism as the mystical source of allocative efficiency in a world of somehow pre-existing products, and a radically oversimplified narrative around globalisation was consolidated. The world became a single marketplace and cost the only location factor, though this could be true only in a frictionless marketplace en route to general equilibrium. In this narrative, our real political economic choices and developmental challenges are voided by the supposedly predetermined laws of economic motion. Rational corporations in such a world have no choice but to engage in tax and regulatory arbitrage: the gaming of different rates and standards. Rational governments have no choice but to get out of the way to render business free to engage in a process of increasingly 'pure' competition.

In reality, governments had at least three strategic options depending on which analytical narrative they believed.

1. If a government accepts the neoclassical logic of Camp 1, it accepts the primacy of cost competition and can legislate accordingly, believing that lower corporate tax rates and their lax regulation will get it onto the right side of corporate arbitrage and market dynamics, as well as supporting the wider aim to shrink the state.
2. If a government accepts the neoclassical logic of 'globalisation' but continues to be concerned by market failures in line with Camp 2 reasoning, then an option within the European Union is to harmonise tax regimes. Tax harmonisation would allow EU member states to set minimum rates and standards to protect national economies from corporate arbitrage, the calculated risk being that multinational corporations were not about to pull out of so rich a trading bloc.

Edge (Cambridge, MA: MIT Press, 1989); Lester Thurow, *Head to Head: The Coming Economic Battle among Japan, Europe, and America* (New York: Warner Books, 1992).

[7] William Lazonick, 'The Theory of Innovative Enterprise: Foundations of Economic Analysis', The Academy-Industry Research Network, AIR Working Paper #13-0201, August 2015.

3. The third logic follows if the economy is understood to be institutionally and technologically complex and dynamic, that is, in Camp 3 terms. If it is recognised that minimising short-term costs quickly turns into a false economy for the production of complex goods and services, then governments should embark on a 'race to the top', maintaining tax revenues to foster long-term investment and social inclusion.[8] This is also the only option that can enable the rapid transition to a sustainable economy in the light of the climate emergency (Chapter 8).

Neoliberal states adopted the first strategy. For higher income economies, the median corporate tax rate stood at 50 per cent as late as the 1980s. By 2020, the average top corporate rate among EU countries was 21 per cent (though in practice reductions in some of the less neoliberal states had been balanced by the closure of loopholes for tax evasion to increase the effective corporate tax rate).[9] As we shall see, however, the practical record of corporate tax cuts in the United Kingdom confirms that continuous development is not given to us by some innate property of freer markets.

Models, Maths and Dubious Metaphors

Why did neoliberals come to believe that higher corporate taxes would only blunt the incentives to work, invest and save?[10] The case for jurisdictional competition is rooted in the 'Tiebout hypothesis', which started life as a neat theory about allocative efficiency in local taxation, though Charles Tiebout's ideas had been neglected from the 1950s until the neoliberal ascendancy.[11] Tiebout argued that competition between governments promotes efficiency in much the same way as competition between firms: it allows the 'sorting' of supply and demand, so that communities are free to pay the taxes for the specific

---

[8] Justin Lin and David Rosenblatt, 'Shifting Patterns of Economic Growth and Rethinking Development', *Journal of Economic Policy Reform* 15 (3) (2012): 171–194.

[9] OECD, 'Table II.1. Statutory Corporate Income Tax Rate', https://stats.oecd.org/index.aspx?DataSetCode=Table_II1.

[10] Tony Atkinson, *Public Economics in an Age of Austerity* (Abingdon: Routledge, 2014), p. 39.

[11] John Singleton, 'Sorting Charles Tiebout', *History of Political Economy* 47 (2015): 199–200, p. 202.

goods they want and need. From here it was a short step for theorists in the 1970s to replace residents with firms as the relevant choice-makers and infrastructure as the relevant good.[12] It was another short step to model competition over regulatory 'burdens' writ large, rather than just tax rates.[13] The logic of 'Tiebout sorting' was eventually transferred to make the case for the local control of securities regulation, antitrust enforcement and environmental policy.[14]

Tiebout's idea is intuitively attractive, but as with all iterations of perfect competition it depends on the fiction of a simple, closed system. He assumes that different localities are identical apart from their tax rates and the public goods they offer and that there is only one perfectly mobile factor (residents), of which there is a fixed supply.[15] His analogies with perfect competition require agents with perfect information about public provision in each locality, as well as that this provision is priced exactly by current local tax rates. Not only is the Tiebout citizen all-knowing about tax options and what they represent by way of costs and benefits, they are financially, socially and psychologically light-footed, as they ceaselessly relocate to optimise their tax position. Tiebout sorting assumes there are no unintended consequences or 'spillovers' between jurisdictions, negative or positive. It implies that a bankrupt local government is no more problematic than a bankrupt firm.[16] It makes perfect sense but only in a neoclassical world.

Although the economic debate for and against tax and regulatory competition became more prominent from the 1960s, the move towards formal mathematical models was only made in the later 1980s. As the literature evolved, the arguments in favour of competition tended to replace the logic of Tiebout sorting with arguments that focused less on the sovereignty of individual choices and more

---

[12] Michelle White, 'Firm Location in a Zoned Metropolitan Area', in Edwin Mills and Wallace Oates, *Fiscal Zoning and Land Use Controls* (Lexington: D.C. Heath and Company, 1975), pp. 31–100.

[13] Jason Campbell Sharman, *Havens in a Storm: The Struggle for Global Tax Regulation* (Ithaca: Cornell University Press, 2011), p. 38.

[14] Richard Rosen, 'Is Three a Crowd: Competition among Regulators in Banking', *Journal of Money, Credit and Banking* 35 (6) (2003): 967–998, p. 969.

[15] Sharman, *Havens*, p. 37.

[16] Nicholas Shaxson and John Christensen, 'Tax Competitiveness – A Dangerous Obsession', in Thomas Pogge and Krishen Mehta, *Global Tax Fairness* (Oxford: Oxford University Press, 2016), pp. 265–297, p. 278.

on the opportunities for increased investment. For the neoliberal left of Camp 2, the implication emerged that a lighter tax burden would encourage more companies into their jurisdiction and expand both investment and the tax base. For the neoliberal right of Camp 1, the core argument was that with the removal of price 'distortion', firms would automatically convert their higher retained earnings into more productive investment.

The formal models in this field have classically been built via stylised facts regarding 'a household', 'a state' and a 'firm or sector' taken to represent 'the economy'. A 'stylised fact' in social science is a simple presentation of a supposedly dependable empirical finding. But to paraphrase Robert Solow, while the phenomena in neoclassical tax models are certainly stylised, they are scarcely facts. In the game-theoretical, partial equilibrium and general equilibrium models that dominated, agents and institutions were idealised to the point where they could be mathematically formalised, but this in turn made them difficult-to-impossible to connect back to a real economy. If we quickly look at how these stylisations tend to be drawn, you can see the scale of the reductionism and get a sense of what disappears from the narratives these models can tell.[17]

Consider the state as a stylised fact. When setting out his 'Ethical Limits of Taxation', James Buchanan conceded some revenues would be needed to guarantee basic property and contractual rights to enable anyone to risk being economically active at all. Beyond the 'nightwatchman' state, however, the principle of 'maximal equal liberty' from taxation needed to apply.[18] Following in Buchanan's footsteps, so-called Leviathan models assume that government is bent on maximising the size of the public sector regardless of the economic consequences. How the state is stylised in a model thus predetermines how damaging the resulting economic 'distortion' will be. The more Buchananite the Leviathan state in a model, the greater the 'distortion'.[19]

---

[17] Thushyanthan Baskaran and Mariana Lopes da Fonseca, 'The Economics and Empirics of Tax Competition: A Survey and Lessons for the EU', *ELR* 1 (May 2014): 3–12.

[18] James Buchanan, 'The Ethical Limits of Taxation', *Scandinavian Journal of Economics* 86 (2) 1984: 102–114, Section IV.

[19] Geoffrey Brennan and James Buchanan, *The Power to Tax: Analytical Foundations of the Fiscal Constitution* (Cambridge: Cambridge University Press, 1980).

The state is typically stylised in formal neoclassical models as an economic actor with preferences. Depending on the author's chosen value assumptions, these preferences are for expenditure that benefits state actors (in the public choice view) or 'a representative citizen' (in models from a Camp 2 perspective). The state is thereafter depicted in an equation as an 'objective function', that is as a business goal expressed in mathematical terms. It is thus turned into a symbol put into an equation that also contains the other parameters such as 'the economy' or 'the firm' and 'solved' according to the accompanying behavioural assumptions. How sophisticated can the depiction of the state be in these models? The respected 'synthetic' model of Jeremy Edwards and Michael Keen from the mid-1990s supposed that policymakers are neither wholly benevolent nor wholly self-serving, represented mathematically as 'quasi concave preferences'.[20] Though this model might be relatively refined, it reduces policymaking around taxation to a decision point over a *single* item of expenditure – a limit dictated by the method.

Now consider 'the economy' as a stylised fact. In the 1990s, general equilibrium models of tax competition typically depicted the economy as producing *one* good under constant returns to scale with the help of labour and homogenous capital. It follows that neither complexity nor economies, or diseconomies, of scale are present.[21] Such an economy 'operates' with no internal variation or internal institutional complexities, power imbalances or interdependencies. There are no challenges of coordination, and the same is assumed of the competing economy into which the theoretical firm might move.

By contrast, several political economic studies have long demonstrated that real-world firms in different sectors need profoundly different skills, forms of finance, infrastructure and regulatory intervention. Even the dominant institutional political economy theory that uses the neoclassical micro-foundation of the 'rational actor', the so-called varieties of capitalism theory, makes a compelling case that the institutional arrangements that firms need vary depending on

---

[20] Jeremy Edwards, 'Tax Competition and Leviathan', *European Economic Review* 40 (1) (1996): 113–134, p. 118.
[21] Karl-Josef Koch and Gunther Schulze, 'Equilibria in Tax Competition Models', in Karl-Josef Koch and Karl Jaeger, *Trade, Growth and Economic Policy in Open Economies* (Heidelberg: Springer Verlag, 1998), pp. 281–311, p. 281.

the product markets in which they operate.[22] Firms of any sophistication need a nurturing economic environment on everything from skills to infrastructure to technology, and that requires state capacity, and hence tax revenue, but such issues are too complicated for neoclassical models to consider. Even when game-theoretic models tried to set out the kind of strategic decisions a firm might take between competing jurisdictions, it was still a rarity by the late 1990s for the diversity of firms to be taken into account, and even then, it tended to be on one dimension, such as the 'high' or 'low' cost of their production. As soon as some realism was added by assuming, for example, that not all capital is arbitrarily divisible and not all investment is mobile to the same degree, then no meaningful equilibria could be found.[23]

Finally, the realism of formal neoclassical models finds no improvement with the stylisation of 'the firm'. In standard neoclassical equilibrium models, economic transactions take place between consumers and producers – households and firms – who create supply and demand for goods and labour via somehow pre-existing markets. They are conceived either as individual agents in microeconomic models or as radically simplified 'representative agents' in macroeconomic models. 'Firms' are reduced to black boxes that turn inputs into outputs minus costs, with tax conceived as a cost. As Brian Loasby explains, 'Demand curves [are] conceived to be directly derived from individual preferences, which are subjective but well-ordered, and supply curves from costs, which are determined by technology and resources; and preferences, technology and resources are all presumed to be objective data.'[24] If they have any institutional life at all, firms are understood as organisationally frictionless bundles of contracts between rational, informed and utility-maximising individuals. As Joseph Schumpeter pointed out,[25] this is an imaginary that has no conception of the entrepreneurial effort, the coordination challenges or the investment risk it takes to create something more complicated than a fruit stall, and even that takes some horticultural skill.

---

[22] Peter Hall and David Soskice, *Varieties of Capitalism: The Institutional Foundations of Comparative Advantage* (Oxford: Oxford University Press, 2001), p. 6.
[23] Koch and Schulze, 'Equilibria in Tax Competition', p. 282.
[24] Brian Loasby, 'Ronald Coase's Theory of the Firm and the Scope of Economics', *Journal of Institutional Economics* 11 (2) (2015): 245–264, p. 247.
[25] Joseph Schumpeter, *The Theory of Economic Development* (New Brunswick: Transaction Publishers, 1934), Chapter 6.

As John Kay points out, the corporation in the eyes of the Chicago School is 'an empty shell'.

The managers and employees are a group of individuals, who find it convenient to do business with each other, and with customers and suppliers. There is no collective interest (and, of course, no collective responsibility) only a coincidence of individual interests. The internal organisation of the corporation... is reduced to a matter of command and control, to be treated as a principal–agent problem in which any information asymmetry between manager and managed (or owner and manager) is to be handled by suitable targets and incentive systems.[26]

Camp 1 authors usually assume that managers act in the best interest of the firm's owners. In this 'stewardship theory', the personal utility of managers is fully compatible with their function as wealth builders for their owners. The way both managers and shareholders sustain that wealth is presupposed to be through productive reinvestment. Why? Because they serve an intermediary function in the theoretical, closed-system machine in which a free market will continuously match supply to demand via the price mechanism, just as their Stalinist counterparts were supposed to achieve through the plan. In the wider neoclassical debates about investment, one finds that all four of the main neoclassical theories of aggregate investment suffer serious fallacies of composition – specifically, from their inability to factor in the arrival of new firms, innovations, real adjustment costs and the excessive simplifications that need to be made around the complex and evolving nature of capital and employment markets.[27]

Mathematical models do not necessarily preclude a state that responds to capital mobility with policies of cooperation or 'racing to the top', as demonstrated in the important Camp 2 arguments of George Zodrow and Peter Mieszkowski (1986),[28] as well as John Wilson (1986),[29] known as the 'ZMW' model. These authors

---

[26] John Kay, 'The Concept of the Corporation', *Business History* 61 (7) (2019): 1129–1143, p. 1132.

[27] Daniele Girardi, 'Old and New Formulations of the Neoclassical Theory of Aggregate Investment: A Critical Review', UMASS Amherst Economics Department Working Paper 2017-03, 2017.

[28] George Zodrow and Peter Mieszkowski, 'Pigou, Tiebout, Property Taxation, and the Under-Provision of Local Public Goods', *Journal of Urban Economics* 19 (1986): 356–370.

[29] John Wilson, 'A Theory of Interregional Tax Competition', *Journal of Urban Economics* 19 (1986): 296–315.

formalised the idea that a shift in taxation from mobile factors to immobile factors could leave taxes too low and induce a 'race to the bottom' among competing states. The point, however, is that whether for or against competition, these models are simply exercises in playing out the consequences of varied normative assumptions in a closed-system world. The closer to the Camp 1 neoclassical view these assumptions travel, the more frankly utopian they tend to be. Their confirmation biases are rooted in the stylisation of the pre-idealised firm and the pre-demonised state and in all the discrete behavioural axioms of how the relevant representative agents will then travel in commodity space.

The problem is not just the closed-system reasoning that comes with mathematics but what Nobel Laureate Paul Romer calls 'mathiness': the translation of words into mathematical symbols 'that leaves ample room for slippage between statements in natural versus formal language and between statements with theoretical as opposed to empirical content'. 'Perhaps', worried Romer, 'our norms will soon be like those in professional magic; it will be impolite, perhaps even an ethical breach, to reveal how someone's trick works'.[30] The more serious problem, however, was that these models and 'simulations' were far from 'merely academic'. Under neoliberalism they were treated as science and transformed into public policy, though their empirical robustness was staggeringly weak, as many modellers themselves were well aware. Friedman argued that the reductionism of a model was immaterial so long as it produced accurate predictions that could then be tested empirically.[31] What Friedman failed to mention is that by the time such models proved completely misleading, the policies they justified would have created a powerful constituency of extractive profit-takers and tax-avoiders with a vested interest in seeing this line continued.

When the attempt is made to ask how a whole economy might react to a policy intervention such as a corporate tax cut, neoclassical economists have no choice but to either borrow directly from Soviet central planning methods or to rationalise time series data via the logic of

---

[30] Paul Romer, 'Mathiness in Theories of Economic Growth', *American Economic Review: Papers & Proceedings* 105 (5) (2015): 89–89.

[31] Milton Friedman, *Essays in Positive Economics* (Chicago: University of Chicago Press, 1953), p. 14.

general equilibrium – the only toolkits that will let you hold an entire economy 'constant' and 'determine' what factors will go where following different stimuli. If we look at how these models work, we can see how the realities of who pays and who gains become mystified.

In recent decades, applied economists and policymakers have tended to rely on Computational General Equilibrium (CGE) and Dynamic Stochastic General Equilibrium (DSGE) models to explore what would happen to a given economy after a policy change in taxation or trade. But CGE models are theoretically ad hoc macro input–output models of the whole economy that owe more to the socialist calculation debate and the history of planning than to Kenneth Arrow and Gerard Debreu.[32] The purpose of a CGE model is to offer two static pictures of the economy that show the state of the world before and after the given policy change. In practice, their combination of numerical data with economic theory requires idiosyncratic manipulation via multiple, discretionary modelling decisions to make the statistical data 'work', that is, to make it conform to a closed-system conception of the economy. Modellers may use statistical data, but their models are still politics by other means. Change one parameter choice among the many, and you change the 'impact' of the policy shock when the economy supposedly self-adjusts.[33]

As Mitra-Kahn explains, the input–output analyses found in CGE models have their roots in the work of Wassily Leontief, which dates from the 1930s. Leontief had shown that input–output modelling of an economy might be equally useful to Soviet socialist and Western Keynesian planning systems, and by the late 1950s his methods were used by both.[34] He had promoted transnational discussions about how to solve the problem of efficient production and allocation, and though CGE models since the 1980s have been adapted to use standard neoclassical microeconomic behavioural equations, they are no less rooted in the basic Leontief scheme. The reference to 'general equilibrium' is rhetorical.[35]

---

[32] Benjamin Mitra-Kahn, 'Debunking the Myths of Computational General Equilibrium Models', Schwartz Center for Economic Policy Analysis, The New School, Working Paper 1–2008.

[33] Ibid., pp. 74–75.

[34] Johanna Bockman and Gil Eyal, 'Eastern Europe as a Laboratory for Economic Knowledge: The Transnational Roots of Neoliberalism', *American Journal of Sociology* 108 (2) (September 2002): 310–352, p. 330.

[35] Mitra-Kahn, 'Debunking the Myths', p. 33.

Why are CGE models problematic? Working for the American Bureau of Labour Statistics, Leontief had built an accounting system that 'encompassed all branches of industry, agriculture, [and] also the individual budgets of all private persons'.[36] Having got that system underway, however, he needed a model of the economy that would motivate the interactions between the sectors reported in his accounts. The result was a 'national account' of the economy wherein all sectors produced goods or services consumed fully by another sector, together with an analytical scheme of how this closed economy supposedly worked.[37]

An important addition came from a Norwegian economist (and communist), Leif Johansen, in the 1960s. Johansen chose a base year, a national accounts data set constructed for a specific point in time. As Mitra-Kahn explains, he then set out to simulate a dynamic change in the economy by changing an 'exogenous' independent variable, such as a tax change, to simulate a one-time change in the economy. What makes this story so touchingly human is that when it became clear that the inputs and outputs in Johansen's 'economy' didn't tally, he simply adjusted the data until they did. Once the national accounts were 'in balance', production functions were ascribed to producers and demand functions to consumers. Further assumptions were then made about the labour market and exports, and investments were reworked into the core interactions of the domestic economy. Johansen could then check the results of the theoretical model against unadulterated empirical data to see if the model matched the statistical record, and where it didn't, he could adjust the model assumptions accordingly and draw inferences from it. While those inferences were surely thought-provoking, the combination of simplifying framing assumptions, statistical brute force and adjustments for coincidences with highly aggregated data hardly made them robust.

Mitra-Kahn shows that today's CGE models are built on these very same foundations,[38] and given the rapidly evolving nature of the capitalist economy they must lead the modeller towards even more grievous failures of representation than they did for the Soviets. At

---

[36] Wassily Leontief, *The Structure of the American Economy, 1919–1939*, 2nd ed. (New York: International Arts and Sciences Press, 1951), p. 11.
[37] Mitra-Kahn, 'Debunking the Myths', pp. 7–8.
[38] Ibid.

least the Soviet 'balance method' of inching forward at repeated negotiations relied on leading planners who represented actual producers and users.[39] In the CGE process, the input–output discrepancies and relational contradictions are ironed out by design, and the resulting models and their elastic parameters can then be used by the government as a justification for the policy they prefer. CGE modelling is consequently an exercise in subjective construction, not mathematical revelation.

The conceptual starting point for a CGE model is a circular flow of commodities in a closed economy 'in equilibrium'. In models designed to figure out the impact of a given public policy, the CGE model can represent the government, but its role in the circular flow is typically passive: to collect taxes and disburse revenues to firms and households as subsidies and lump-sum transfers, subject to rules of budgetary balance.[40] We can illustrate what this looks with the actual 2013 UK Her Majesty's Revenue and Customs (HMRC)–Treasury CGE model (Figure 7.1) used to calculate the macroeconomic impact of tax changes. In an image reminiscent of Soviet cybernetic thinking, the HMRC model depicts the economy as a closed system with a circular flow.

Although relatively sophisticated, this CGE model is hopelessly weak at the level of representation. Unemployment is voluntary and all assets held by firms are equally productive – standard Camp 1 assumptions needed to sustain the double-entry book-keeping involved. The model excludes the financial sector, monetary effects and tax havens; the investment component is a conduit only. Nor can it cope with foreign trade and foreign investment. All investment is assumed to be sourced from domestic savings 'on the first order conditions from the optimising behaviour of firms and households'.[41] One might object that this was also a Keynesian assumption, but while John Maynard Keynes had argued, before the days of credit mobility, tax havens and financial derivatives, that savings and investments are by definition equal, he had stressed that this did not mean they were balanced in

---

[39] Janos Kornai, *The Socialist System* (Princeton: Princeton University Press, 1992), p. 112.
[40] Ian Sue Wing, 'Computable General Equilibrium Models and Their Use in Economy-Wide Policy Analysis', MIT Technical Note Number 6, September 2004, Section 2.
[41] Ibid., 'CGE Model Documentation', pp. 5–6, Appendix A2.

Models, Maths and Dubious Metaphors 235

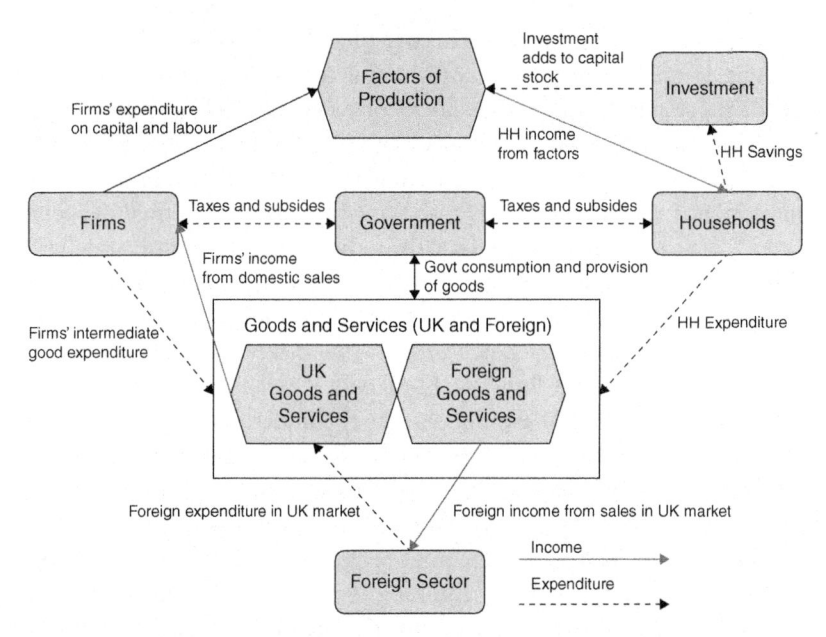

Figure 7.1 The 2013 HMRC CGE model
HM Revenue and Customs, 'HMRC's CGE Model Documentation', December 2013, Figure 2.1, p. 6, https://assets.publishing.service.gov.uk/government/uploads/system/uploads/attachment_data/file/263652/CGE_model_doc_131204_new.pdf

practice. To the contrary, they could not be unless all 'lags' between production and consumption factors were as nearly as possible eliminated, which would require a strongly progressive tax system.[42] We know that the financial behaviour of firms is critical to the real dynamics of employment, wages, pensions, investment and innovation, but it cannot be captured here at all.

In addition to CGE models, governments and central banks rely more often on DSGE models, but these macroeconomic models are also based on microeconomic foundations rather than historical analysis. DSGE models get around the complexity of real firms and households through the highly problematic device of the 'representative agent', where a theoretical firm is taken as representative of all firms,

---

[42] John Maynard Keynes, *The Collected Writings of John Maynard Keynes, Volume 7: The General Theory of Employment, Interest and Money* (Cambridge: Cambridge University Press, 1973), pp. 94–95, 372–373.

a theoretical household representative of all households and so on. But as Alan Kirman objects, it is unjustifiable to assume that the reactions of the representative agent to shocks or parameter changes must coincide with the aggregate reactions of the represented agents.[43] DSGE models are consequently no less ad hoc in their formulation than CGE models, not least because they also typically assume 'rational expectations'[44] – that is, that all agents within the model share the modeller's theoretical assumption, hence they have complete system knowledge so that all expectations are model-consistent. This contrivance allows the modeller to set out a range of probable behaviours under alternative scenarios. As the Bank of England's Chief Economist, Andrew Haldane, explains, DSGE models apply the underlying assumptions of Arrow and Debreu to depict reactions to stimuli within a whole, closed economy, in which Newtonian form 'every action has an equal and opposite reaction, every shock an equal and proportional reaction'.[45]

CGE and DSGE model outcomes are often cited with such authority you might be forgiven for thinking they can resolve statistical data via general equilibrium theory with the aid of increased computing power to give you an accurate forecast. But they can't. DSGE models would have been of tremendous interest to the Soviets, had they been prevalent in the 1960s. The shift from the original Arrow and Debreu assumption of 'all individuals as utility maximising agents' to a 'single representative optimising agent' would have let planners talk of 'collective agents' and freed them from the bourgeois individualism that made neoclassical modelling so politically sensitive.[46] But the techniques would have been no better at warning them of impending crisis than they have been in the capitalist economies.

So, do any of these models tell us anything useful? Professor of Public Finance David Wildasin admits it is 'possible to construct an

---

[43] Alan Kirman, 'Whom or What Does the Representative Individual Represent?', *Journal of Economic Perspectives* 6 (1992): 117–136, p. 118.

[44] Roman Frydman and Michael Goldberg, *Beyond Mechanical Markets: Asset Price Swings, Risk and the Role of the State* (Princeton: Princeton University Press, 2011), p. 62.

[45] Andrew Haldane, 'Uncertainty in Macroeconomic Modelling', in Jens Beckert and Richard Bronk, *Uncertain Futures* (Oxford: Oxford University Press, 2018), p. 147.

[46] D. Wade Hands, 'Crossing in the Night of the Cold War: Alternative Visions and Related Tensions in Western and Soviet General Equilibrium Theory', *History of Economic Ideas* 24 (2) (2016): 51–74.

entire series of models of fiscal competition that yield a wide range of positive and normative implications ... [Hence] it is relatively easy to see how the implications of fiscal competition can vary widely as critical assumptions are altered'.[47] Reviewing twenty years of literature for the Institute for Fiscal Studies, Rachael Griffith and Alexander Klemm agreed that 'while the view that capital mobility puts downward pressure on corporate income taxes is more widely held than the opposite view, there is little consensus on whether this is beneficial, harmful or irrelevant to economic welfare'.[48] Tax models are an ideologically moveable feast of formal speculation, but we should not mistake that for theoretical neutrality; the dependence on axiomatic-deductive, micro-founded models over observation has led to a profound failure in the analytical toolkits of governments to apprehend the most damaging trends in the real political economy. The most dysfunctional of these in the United Kingdom, as we shall see, is that large firms have increasingly switched from productive investment to financial extraction: 'financialisation'. While not about tax competition directly, it is impossible to understand the real history of corporate tax competition without understanding adjacent developments in corporate governance and their own roots in Camp 1 theory.

Financialisation

In a separate discussion to the tax debate, 'agency theory' in the neoclassical economics of corporate finance sought to problematise the potential relationships *within* firms and between firms and their financiers. In doing so it narrowed this topic to the microeconomic problems of how to align the interests of the shareholders (the owners or 'principals') and their legal 'agents' (boards of directors, managers and employees) or relationships with similar tensions, for example between investors and fund managers. Agency theory from the 1980s became increasingly dominated by the Chicago School assertion that the purpose of the firm was to *maximise* shareholder value, in other

---

[47] David Wildasin, 'Fiscal Competition', in Donald Whitman and Barry Weingast, *The Oxford Handbook of Political Economy* (Oxford: Oxford University Press, 2008), Section 2.

[48] Rachael Griffith and Alexander Klemm, 'What Has Been the Tax Competition Experience of the Last Twenty Years', Institute for Fiscal Studies Working Paper 04/05, p. 3.

words, to make the business as attractive as possible to shareholders.[49] This idea was rooted in Friedman's assertion in the early 1960s that '[f]ew trends could so thoroughly undermine the foundations of our free society as the acceptance by corporate officials of a social responsibility other than to make as much money for their stockholders as possible',[50] never mind that such responsibility had characterised the Golden Age of post-war growth, with its unprecedented social mobility. The dominant analytical question instead became that of how to prevent firm managers from operating in self-interested ways that damaged that maximisation, on the assumption that shareholders were entitled to the 'residual' profit as the only players judged to have taken a financial risk.[51]

With their particular interest in informational asymmetries at the microeconomic level, Camp 2 economists would explore how managerial agents, with their access to superior information, might abuse their powers vis-à-vis owners.[52] But as James Kirkbride, Steve Letza and Xiuping Sun noted already back in 2004, the basic approach in agency theory, whether in first-best-world or second-best-world terms, remained axiomatic-deductive and hence 'culture-free, historically separated and contextually unrelated'.[53] As Kay concluded, 'This fundamentally financially driven view of the corporation would probably have had little impact outside the academic world had its implications not been so congenial to investment bankers – and to corporate executives themselves.'[54] The result is that, while neoclassical corporate governance theory continues to work its way through all the possible logical permutations of microeconomic decision-making, UK traded firms in practice have engaged in an accelerating trend of

---

[49] Tom Clarke, 'The Impact of Financialization on International Corporate Governance: The Role of Agency Theory and Maximizing Shareholder Value', *Law and Financial Markets Review* 8 (1) (2014): 39–51, p. 46.

[50] Milton Friedman, *Capitalism and Freedom* (Chicago: University of Chicago Press, 1962), p. 133.

[51] William Lazonick, 'When Managerial Capitalism Embraced Shareholder Value Ideology', *International Journal of Political Economy* 44 (2015): 90–99, p. 97.

[52] Deborah De Lange, *Cliques and Capitalism: A Modern Networked Theory of the Firm* (Basingstoke: Palgrave Macmillan, 2011), p. 45.

[53] James Kirkbride, Steve Letza and Xiuping Sun, 'Shareholding versus Stakeholding: A Critical Review of Corporate Governance', *Corporate Governance* 12 (3) (2004): 242–262.

[54] Kay, 'The Concept of the Corporation', p. 1133.

self-cannibalisation. Shareholder value has been maximised at the expense of quality in outputs, investment in skills and technology, timely payments to suppliers, wages, pensions and, as I explore later, meaningful adaptation to the climate emergency.

In line with agency theory recommendations, managers have been paid in stock options alongside their salaries to align their interests with those of shareholders. The practical result, however, is an intensifying trend in the United Kingdom and the United States, but also increasingly across the European Union, for managers to hollow out their own firms to maximise share pay-outs from which they too now benefit. Higher share prices have been achieved not through productive investment but its opposite – through raids on retained earnings reserves, pensions, investment funding, not least in research and development (R&D), the manipulation of 'fair value accounting', downsizing in employment and the minimisation of employment security, and the active avoidance of corporate taxation. In the United States in particular, managers have also used profits to repurchase their own corporate shares ('buybacks') to inflate the price of that stock.[55]

Kay identified the ideological reframing of corporate purpose as a driving factor behind this financialisation, which has only accelerated since the 1970s.[56] Financial accountants have effectively turned firms from socially productive institutions into speculative market instruments, and their basic capital maintenance and longer term existence are threatened by the increasing impact.[57] When firms are hollowed out to maximise short-term financial gains and pay-outs consume, and even exceed, net income, then the underlying Camp 1 assumptions about productive stewardship and investment are, essentially, toast.

What you see instead are some truly alarming structural trends that run directly counter to the promises of theory. Germán Gutiérrez and Thomas Philippon examined thirty years of US private investment and asked why investment had been so weak compared to profitability and valuation, particularly since 2000. They found that the investment gap is mainly driven by large investment funds that hold shares across firms in sectors with less competitive entry and more concentration.

---

[55] Mustafa Erdem Sakinç, 'Share Repurchases in Europe: A Value Extraction Analysis', ISI Growth Working Paper, 16/2017.
[56] Kay, 'The Concept of the Corporation', p. 1133.
[57] Clarke, 'The Impact of Financialization', p. 40.

This cross-ownership then encourages firms to spend a disproportionate amount of free cash flows buying back their own shares to keep those powerful shareholders on board. This is a financing structure that reduces incentives for intra-sectoral competition and investment, even as it drives up the pressure for the sector-wide maintenance of dividends.[58] It creates, in effect, a sector-wide mechanism for financial extraction.

The asset management industry itself is also increasingly concentrated. Jan Fichtner, Eelke Heemskerk and Javier Garcia-Bernardo have documented the rising colonisation of share markets by passive index funds, by Blackrock, Vanguard and State Street in particular. Already by 2015 the 'big three' constituted the largest shareholder in 88 per cent of all S&P 500 firms.[59] The speed with which these funds are accumulating shares internationally, with their comparatively low overheads and hence fees, is breath-taking. By the close of 2020 the passive asset management firms controlled nearly 40 per cent of the £2.5 trillion value of the London Stock Market's Financial Times Stock Exchange (FTSE) 350, a doubling in twenty years.[60] These index funds are intermediaries for end investors who seek exposure to entire markets, but contrary to neoclassical assumptions, they make no investment decisions following the scrutiny of corporate fundamentals and calculations of expected return. Instead, they reject 'active' investing on the basis of one of the most utopian of all Camp 1 theories, the 'efficient markets hypothesis' (on which more in Chapter 8), which insists the capital market is perfectly efficient and converges constantly on the correct pricing of all assets. It follows that you cannot beat 'the market' through active investment: you only need to track it.

Corporate control is thus increasingly centralised in the hands of the big three American funds that are developing into what Fichtner and Heemskerk call 'Permanent Universal Owners', an institutional

---

[58] Germán Gutiérrez and Thomas Philippon 'Investment-Less Growth: An Empirical Investigation', National Bureau of Economic Research Working Paper number 22897, December 2016, p. 1.

[59] Jan Fichtner, Eelke Heemskerk and Javier Garcia-Bernardo, 'Hidden Power of the Big Three? Passive Index Funds, Reconcentration of Corporate Ownership, and New Financial Risk', *Business and Politics* 19 (2) (2017): 298–326.

[60] Adrienne Buller and Benjamin Braun, 'Under New Management: Share Ownership and the Rise of UK Asset Manager Capitalism', Asset Management Project, Common-Wealth, 1921, p. 9.

development that shreds the assumptions that justify it. The unprecedented market power of the index funds means corporate governance will be strongly determined by how these funds choose to vote, or are instructed to vote by end investors, in the annual general meetings of the investee companies.[61] As asset managers become common owners of all the major competitors in a given sector, these funds create incentives for anti-competitive, oligopolistic pricing to maximise profit.[62] It follows that the more these funds expand, the more the prices in the market will be shaped by their behaviour, rather than anything very much to do with the fundamental value of the assets they own.[63] I point this out in a chapter on tax competition because, entirely contrary to Camp 1 promise, this dynamic is likely to repurpose any tax cut that comes down the pipe into a dividend pay-out or, in the United States, as a way to pump helium into the share price via share buybacks.

In sum, a real firm, or state, or economy, is hard to spot in the neoclassical models that both support and oppose tax competition. The agency theory of the firm as dominated by Camp 1 doctrine has driven real-world firms towards non-productive financial extraction. Meanwhile, the macroeconomic CGE or DSGE models supposed to describe the macroeconomic effects of a policy change cannot integrate the financial sector at all. Even as financialisation has taken hold, neoclassical theory has instructed governments to look the other way – to withdraw claims on good corporate governance for society, employees, their consumers or the environment as 'distortions' on presumptively welfare-optimising behaviour by rationally optimising economic agents. The result is a world in which governments might embark on tax competition persuaded it must lead to increased productive investment and higher, better quality employment, only to find it builds trends that are pathological for

---

[61] Jan Fichtner and Eelke Heemskerk, 'The New Permanent Universal Owners: Index Funds, Patient Capital, and the Distinction between Feeble and Forceful Stewardship', *Economy and Society* 49 (4) (2020): 493–515, p. 498.

[62] José Azar, Martin Schmalz and Isabel Tecu, 'Anticompetitive Effects of Common Ownership', *The Journal of Finance* 73 (4) (2018): 1513–1565.

[63] Adam Leaver, Eelke Heemskerk and Jan Fichtner, 'If This Is Capitalism, Where Are the Price Signals? The Glacial Effects of Passive Investment', *Sheffield Political Economy Research Group Blog*, 3 September 2018, https://corpnet.uva.nl/speri-blog-post-if-this-is-capitalism-where-are-the-price-signals-the-glacial-effects-of-passive-investment/.

democratic capitalism: sky-high executive pay regardless of corporate performance, stagnating real wages and investment, unsustainable corporate debt, extreme wealth inequality and new and potentially spectacular systemic risks posed by the trend towards corporate concentration and oligopolistic financial actors such as index funds. If neoclassical theory were a cartoon, index funds would be the elephants that can saw off the theoretical branch on which they sit and yet stay in mid-air. But this is not a cartoon. It is the corporate and financial reality of the UK economy.

Speculative models can be interesting, but neoclassical models dominate both academic and institutional analyses, so it is a serious problem that these models of tax competition are 'not even wrong' in the strict sense that they are not remotely informative about what is actually happening in corporate governance and finance and why it is so socially, politically and environmentally dangerous. We think of the Soviet planning system as ideologically hidebound, but by the 1980s Gosplan had at least recognised that the underground economy was very large, and Soviet economists had been put to work to measure and understand its growth.[64]

Tax Havens

Though the rise of tax havens post-dates the 'classical' Camp 1 tax competition arguments of, for example, George Stigler, Buchanan and Friedman, for today's neoliberal think tanks such as the American Cato Institute and the United Kingdom's Institute of Economic Affairs, tax havens unshackle the presumptively equilibrium-consistent behaviour of the rational actor.[65] Unburdened by social obligations, the rational investor can take their money unmolested to supposedly optimal investment opportunities worldwide.

Havens, or 'financial secrecy jurisdictions', are states that rent their sovereignty to financial actors and provide them with anonymity and freedom from legal enforcement of both taxes and regulations, and they are one of the leading sources of increasing fiscal pressure on

[64] Valeriy Rutgaizer, 'The Shadow Economy in the USSR', Berkeley-Duke Occasional Papers in the Second Economy in the USSR, Paper number 34, February 1992.
[65] Daniel Mitchell, 'The Necessary and Valuable Economic Role of Tax Havens', The Cato Institute, 11 May 2016.

contemporary governments. Havens require no, or nominal, tax on income, offer no exchange of information with national fiscal authorities, lack transparency in their activities and are essentially passive in terms of productive economic activity. Their primary function is to enable private wealth to be put 'offshore', beyond the reach of the nation-states in which that wealth is made.[66] As such they represent an important ideological battlefield.

Until the global Camp 1 utopia arrives, tax havens constitute the giant sucking engines that enable multinational companies to remove profits from both host and home economies, either to consume those profits or recycle them via financial markets – markets that have themselves significantly diversified from the business of productive investment in favour of lucrative, socially harmful activity such as leveraged lending and property speculation. In today's financial markets the 'discipline of debt' presumed in neoclassical economics is diluted through its securitisation.[67] Havens also facilitate organised crime and political corruption worldwide by enabling the corrupt to hide their gains as the first stage in money laundering, which makes them more fiscal parasite than paradise.

I will talk about the practical consequences later, but the thing to note here is that if general equilibrium models are models of balance in a whole economy, then the remembrance of tax havens and real financial markets necessarily breaks that closed-system reasoning wide open at the national level, but with no hope of confirming it at the global level, a prospect no greater than the advent of a harmonious world communism. The liberalisation of capital movements gave a boost to the world's tax havens to a degree that should have placed them at the centre of any analysis of the real dynamics of tax competition, but their real effects are nigh on impossible to describe within neoclassical terms.

If governments depend on narratives and models in which financialisation and tax avoidance should not exist and cannot be explained, then how are they to register the world as it is, in which firms inflate their market value through share buybacks, asset depletion, profit-shifting,

---

[66] James Henry, 'Let's Tax Anonymous Wealth', in Thomas Pogge and Krishen Mehta, *Global Tax Fairness* (Oxford: Oxford University Press, 2015), p. 51.
[67] Willem H. Buiter, 'Central Banks and the Looming Financial Reckoning', *Project Syndicate*, 4 October 2021.

debt accrual and fuzzy accounting to increase annual dividends year on year? The neoclassical world does not feature an oligopoly of large accounting firms engaged in dubious accounting practices around when and how to book profits, how to value assets within the highly subjective rules allowed by 'fair value accounting' and hence how to enable firms to avoid taxes altogether. But in the meantime, the fixation on jurisdictional competition has diverted political debate from the questions about what enables domestic growth, innovation and foreign investment we should have been asking all along.

Even the briefest view of these discussions produces a radically different perspective. Douglas North had concluded that to understand growth without investigating how institutional architectures create the incentive systems towards it is to doom analysis to sterility.[68] In their long-range historical analysis of economic development and failure, Daron Acemoglu and James Robinson demonstrate the centrality of strategic and inclusive economic and political institutions.[69] The literature on the successful emerging markets likewise emphasises the pivotal role played by developmentally purposeful control of domestic finance.[70] When it comes to innovation, Mariana Mazzucato has shown that America's leading edge in technology originates in its exceptionally high rates of state-funded research. It was the federal state rather than private venture capital that made the high-risk early stage investments in Google and in companies such as Intel, Compaq and Apple, and the venture capitalists arrived only at the point those innovations could be monetised.[71] As Martin Wolf concluded, 'The failure to recognise the role of the government in driving innovation may well be the greatest threat to rising prosperity.'[72]

Since neoliberals often insist that tax competition will attract new investment, it is also worth asking what the scholarship on foreign investment has to say about it, and the answer is: very little. There is

---

[68] Douglass C. North, *Institutions, Institutional Change and Economic Performance* (Cambridge: Cambridge University Press, 1990), pp. 133–134.
[69] Daron Acemoglu and James Robinson, *Why Nations Fail: The Origins of Power, Prosperity and Poverty* (London: Profile Books, 2012).
[70] Rachel Epstein, *Banking on Finance: The Transformation of Bank-State Ties in Europe and Beyond* (Oxford: Oxford University Press, 2017).
[71] Mariana Mazzucato, *The Entrepreneurial State: Debunking Public versus Private Sector Myths* (London: Anthem Press, 2013).
[72] Martin Wolf, 'A Much-Maligned Engine of Innovation', *Financial Times*, 4 August 2013.

scant evidence that tax differentials make any difference to FDI rates except on the margins.[73] The most empiricist FDI scholarship confirms that what investment is done in a country is driven by what developmental factors exist in a country relative to other countries, of which tax is a relatively trivial element.[74]

The Unanticipated Risks of Competition and Their Consequences

Starting from the work of Wallace Oates in the early 1970s,[75] the critical public finance literature had argued that an inefficiently low tax rates would mean inadequate investment – a classic piece of Camp 2 reasoning that drew this inference from a hypothetical economic equilibrium that was missed. The real consequences of tax competition are far more perverse than what mechanical images of imbalance can capture, however. For example, without cuts in overall public spending, declining corporate tax revenues will mean higher taxes are shifted onto other, less mobile actors in the economy, such as small and medium-sized enterprises (SMEs), consumers via value-added tax (VAT), and social insurance contributions. These moves potentially inhibit SME development, lower aggregate demand and increase the tax wedge on labour. If employers adopt temporary or 'zero hour' contracts to avoid those costs, the economy only stores up fiscal pressures for the future in the shape of a weak skills base and underfunded pensions.

The developmental opportunities foregone are significant. We are living in an era of exceptional returns to capital. The era of tax competition has coincided with a period of exceptional corporate profits due to unprecedented technological innovation, as well as sharp practices. It follows that given a more responsible corporate culture, the last forty years could have been an era of rising corporate tax revenues

---

[73] Lael Brainard, 'An Empirical Assessment of the Proximity Concentration Tradeoff between Multinational Sales and Trade', *American Economic Review* 87 (4) (1997): 520–544.

[74] See Bruce Bloningen, 'A Review of the Empirical Literature on FDI Determinants', *Atlantic Economic Journal* 33 (2005): 383–403; James Anderson, 'The Gravity Model', *Annual Review of Economics* 3 (1) (2011): 133–160.

[75] David Bradford and Wallace Oates, 'The Analysis of Revenue Sharing in a New Approach to Collective Fiscal Decisions', *Quarterly Journal of Economics* 85 (3) (1971): 416–439.

and higher corporate investment without any rate increases, or with more moderate reductions. The increased revenues would have helped to regenerate economies from the structural crises of the 1970s, and they are certainly needed now for the transition to a sustainable production regime.

What of the political risks? The neoclassical economics literature completely ignores the damage jurisdictional competition causes to the state as a competent and democratic fiscal authority, and for the simple reason it has no way to talk about it. The public choice argument that a smaller state must be more efficient depends on the fantasy that the only efficient state is a nightwatchman, so that any moves to shrink the state are seen as a priori positive. But the debate is consequently mute on the implications for state capacity, political legitimacy and the rule of law in a state that does not and cannot wither away. And, as in Leninism, there is no narrative or remedy for the unanticipated failures of the 'interim' other than 'holding course'.

The democratic state is largely funded by taxpayers aside from revenues gained from interest and government assets. All taxpayers provide subsidies that add value to corporations, whether in terms of educational investments, infrastructure, publicly funded research, law and order, regulatory stability or trade missions. They, along with the employees who make the wealth, retain a legitimate claim on the distribution of corporate profit.[76] But the economics of Camp 1 cannot describe this process, and the result is a doctrine that has driven the profit share compared to the labour share of corporate income to an historical high.[77]

When we add regulatory laxity to tax competition, we can see the true scope of the political damage. If we think of the basic idea of fiscal consent, the willingness to contribute to our collective society requires a prior conception of who the collective is.[78] When a government says large corporations should be given lower tax rates and be largely forgiven when they fail to pay even these, it declares that corporations,

---

[76] William Lazonick, 'The Financialization of the US Corporation: What Has Been Lost and How It Can Be Regained', *Seattle University Law Review* 36 (2013): 857–909, p. 889.

[77] Loukas Karabarbounis and Brent Neiman, 'The Global Decline of the Labor Share', *The Quarterly Journal of Economics* 129 (1) (2014): 61–103.

[78] Evan Lieberman, *Race and Regionalism in the Politics of Taxation in Brazil and South Africa* (Cambridge: Cambridge University Press, 2003).

and corporations alone, are exempt from the shared responsibilities of citizenship. While Friedman might agree, this idea is only popular on the radical fringes of the economic hard right. Lower corporate tax rates have been justified to the electorate with the promise of a boost in jobs and productive investment, but the corresponding idea, let alone the practice, of deliberate laxity in enforcement has only been revealed in the United Kingdom via repeated scandals. Even neoliberals understood that 'competitive' non-enforcement of the law would damage the 'fiscal contract',[79] since, while we may disagree on what we mean exactly by 'fair and transparent' tax payments, when small businesses and those on middle and low incomes pay proportionally more than the wealthiest individuals and largest companies in the country, then our sense of natural justice must be offended.[80] When the promises of competition then fail to materialise, the risk is that governments show they are willing to use the powers of the state to let corporations actively exploit the societies in which they operate.

It is also worth recalling that the neoclassical economics has nothing to say about interest group development even as corporate tax competition creates and mobilises a constituency of exceptional power. The corporate lobby has unrivalled resources to call on governments for tax and regulatory exemptions and further rate reductions. The lobby includes tax accountants who earn profits through strategic tax planning, the legal services who facilitate it and the public relations companies who foster this uniquely wealthy client-base. It also includes tax havens and the financial sectors that launder their proceeds. With such power comes the risk that tax competition and regulatory laxity are locked in long after they have failed to produce any socially positive effects.

The final risk attached to tax competition is the pressure for other jurisdictions to follow suit in an international race to the bottom. Out of a misguided fear of 'losing out', analytical monoculture, or because of the sheer lobby power of the traded corporate and financial sectors, political elites may continue down the road of tax competition even as that policy sharpens the dilemmas they face in every other domain. The core risks of tax competition are thus, in sum:

---

[79] Margaret Levi, *Of Rule and Revenue* (Berkeley: University of California Press, 1988), p. 54.
[80] Thomas Piketty, *Capital in the Twenty-First Century* (Cambridge, MA: Harvard University Press, 2013), Foreword.

- Failure in the core task: no improvements in economic growth.
- Failure in the most useful task: no significant improvements in private investment.
- Shifting the burden of taxation onto less mobile factors, for example, SMEs, consumers, labour.
- Increases in the anti-productive financialisation of firms.
- Reduced state investment capacity in education, R&D and infrastructure.
- High opportunity cost in revenues foregone.
- The undermining of the rule of law and fiscal consent.
- The demoralisation of the tax authorities.
- The creation of powerful political lobby for the extension of socially and economically dysfunctional policy.

Tax Competition in the United Kingdom

Introduced in 1965, Corporation Tax had been charged at a set rate on all profits, and to encourage the reinvestment of those profits, additional tax was payable on shareholder dividends. A Conservative chancellor, Anthony Barber, had introduced Advanced Corporation Tax (ACT) in 1973, which further required corporations to pay tax on dividends at the basic rate of income tax before they were distributed, a charge that could then be set against their final tax bill. This created a main rate of 52 per cent with a reduced rate of 42 per cent for smaller companies, and it also constrained tax avoidance.[81]

The Chancellor of the Exchequer has exceptional autonomy around tax rates and budgets. A change in government philosophy could thus be translated directly into policy change with less risk of veto than in practically any other policy domain.[82] With the exception of the 2015 Corporate Tax (Northern Ireland) Act, which sought to make Northern Ireland more competitive with the Republic of Ireland, corporate tax remains a reserved, that is, non-devolved, policy domain, the establishment of devolved national

---

[81] Richard Brooks, *The Great Tax Robbery: How Britain Became a Tax Haven for Fat Cats and Big Business* (London: A Oneworld Book, 2014), p. 73.

[82] Jill Rutter, Bill Dodwell, Paul Johnson et al., 'Better Budgets: Making Tax Policy Better', Institute of Government, 2016, p. 6.

administrations in 1999 notwithstanding.[83] Indeed, the majority of UK taxes are still set in Westminster, and neoliberal chancellors with governing majorities could enact tax policy practically at will, and they did so with the following results.

By the time the Conservatives were returned to power in May 1979 under Thatcher, their beliefs had changed: lower income taxes and a shift from taxes on earnings to tax on spending would improve market incentives.[84] This followed the Camp 1 assumption that, left to their own devices, the wealthy would redirect their wealth into productive investment and build a deep social prosperity – the so-called trickle-down effect. Although the biggest cuts in headline rates were in personal income tax between 1979 and 1988, the small companies' rate was also cut from 42 per cent to 25 per cent, the main rate from 52 per cent to 35 per cent. Tax incentives to retain and reinvest profits were also reduced: stamp duty on the purchase of shares and bonds was gradually cut from 2 per cent to 0.5 per cent and dividend payment controls were abolished in 1982. The corporate tax cuts under Chancellor Lawson (1983–1989) were paid for by removing capital investment allowances for machinery and plants. VAT on goods and services was steadily increased even as financial and insurances services were made VAT-exempt.[85] The main corporate tax rates were stabilised under John Major's marginally more One-Nation Conservatism from 1992 to 1997, and the pace of reductions in the main and small companies' rate slowed to 33 per cent and 24 per cent respectively.[86]

More significant than the corporate tax cuts, however, was Thatcher's decision to abolish capital controls, followed by an end to credit controls and by the 'Big Bang' deregulation of the City of London. In addition to the widening international move towards abolishing controls, the latter was driven by the growing power of institutional investors and embraced by the Bank of England. The bank now

---

[83] Aron Cheung and Akash Paun, 'Tax and Devolution', Institute for Government, 25 November 2020.
[84] Peter Riddell, 'Commentary', in *Tax by Design: The Mirrlees Review* (Oxford: Oxford University Press, 2010), p. 1280.
[85] Aeron Davis and Catherine Walsh, 'The Role of the State in the Financialization of the UK Economy', *Political Studies* 64 (3) (2016): 666–682, p. 673.
[86] 'Fiscal Facts, Public Finances, Tax and Benefits', Institute for Fiscal Studies, www.ifs.org.uk/tools_and_resources/fiscal_facts.

saw high competition and less regulation as key to the renewal of the City of London as an international financial centre.[87] Together, these measures reinforced the narrative of rational investors, optimising firms, international price competition and the logic that governments had but one liberalising path for adjustment in the face of corporate arbitrage.

Under successive New Labour governments (1997–2001, 2001–2005 and 2005–2010) Chancellors Gordon Brown and Alistair Darling continued a steady reduction in the main corporate tax rate by five points (from 33 per cent to 28 per cent). Brown cut the small business rates from 24 per cent to 19 per cent by 2002, only to return them to 21 per cent by 2008. These cuts in basic rates were partially paid for in 2008 by a further decrease in the allowance for plant and machinery (from 25 per cent to 20 per cent) and a phase out of allowances for industrial buildings by 2011, with the rate reduced by 1 per cent per year.[88]

Of more lasting importance, however, was Darling's modification of the Controlled Foreign Companies (CFC) Rules and the shift from a 'worldwide' to a 'territorial' system of taxation for international companies. The CFC rules had been set up in 1984 by Nigel Lawson to tackle the problem of UK multinationals who sent their financing income to tax havens, so that any corporate profits diverted to subsidiaries would still be taxed in the United Kingdom at the home country tax rate.[89] By 2009, however, EU-15 states had moved to a 'territorial' system that exempted foreign income from large companies (who had threatened exit), and a European Court of Justice ruling cited UK CFC rules as in breach of the 'freedom of establishment' in the single market.[90] The UK government duly weakened the CFC rules in 2009 and moved to a 'territorial' system of corporate taxation, and this made the foreign profits of UK firms tax-exempt.[91] Under this new system, UK multinationals gained incentives to relocate real activities to lower tax rate jurisdictions if not tax havens. It nevertheless remained an article of faith that that money would be recycled as predominantly

---

[87] Vogel, *Freer Markets*, pp. 101, 116.
[88] Georgia Maffini, 'Corporate Tax Policy under the Labour Government 1997–2010', Oxford University Centre for Business Taxation, Working Paper 13/2, p. 4.
[89] Brooks, *The Great Tax Robbery*, p. 65.
[90] Maffini, 'Corporate Tax Policy', p. 6.   [91] Ibid., p. 5.

productive investment and return, somehow, to the United Kingdom. Given any weakening of such investment, these changes would require a compensatory increase in FDI. Short of either, the state would have to shrink or find alternative sources of revenue.

The Coalition's strategy after 2010 sought to create the most 'competitive' corporate tax regime in the G20, as attested in the 2010 Coalition Agreement and repeated in the 2010 'Corporate Tax Road Map' and thereafter.[92] In addition to radical cuts in headline rates there were plans to further reform the CFC regime and to further reduce capital allowances.[93] The main policy changes were a cut to the main corporate tax rate from 28 per cent to 20 per cent from April 2015. This was reduced further under the 2015–2016 Conservative government to a 19 per cent main rate by 2017, to be reset at 18 per cent beginning April 2020. The Coalition also introduced a preferential regime for patent income – the Patent Box – which enlarged the tax breaks already available on income derived from patents in the early 2000s. Insofar as there was any subsequent deviation from the 'Road Map' it was to cut the main rate faster.[94]

There was more: where the Labour government had moved to the 'exemption of foreign profit' system, the Coalition extended that to foreign branches in 2011, so both overseas subsidiaries of UK firms and overseas branches became tax-exempt. But in an attempt to limit the outflow of funds, the Coalition also amended the CFC regime so that the new rules from 2013 aimed to capture income shifted offshore purely for tax purposes rather than for genuine economic activities, a distinction that proved difficult to enforce. In a move that recognised this problem, the 2014 Autumn statement announced a Diverted Profits Tax (DPT), which applied a 25 per cent tax rate to profits deemed related to UK activity but diverted offshore.[95] In practice the shift to a territorial corporate tax system enabled significant tax avoidance – a process also made easier in an era that saw intellectual property rights and brand value overtake material production in

---

[92] HM Treasury, 'The Corporate Tax Roadmap', 29 November 2010, www.gov.uk/government/publications/the-corporation-tax-road-map.

[93] Paul Johnson, 'Tax without Design: Recent Developments in UK Tax Policy', Institute of Fiscal Studies, May 2014, p. 19.

[94] Helen Miller and Thomas Pope, 'Corporation Tax Changes and Challenges', IFS Briefing Note BN163, Institution for Fiscal Studies, pp. 4–6.

[95] Ibid.

importance, both difficult to police. As former tax inspector Richard Brooks noted in written evidence to the Treasury Select Committee,

Tax policy is strongly distorted in favour of the very largest corporations... Together with other recent changes (notably the 2009 exemption of overseas dividends) these [reforms] mark the most fundamental shift in the corporate tax base since residence-based taxation, under which a UK resident is taxed on worldwide income, was introduced in 1914.... Her Majesty's Treasury's proposals make the UK corporate tax system a largely territorial one under which UK income is taxed, whilst tax allowances are still given for costs, including funding costs, that might support non-taxable overseas operations. This is an extremely lenient arrangement that will see large multinationals' effective tax rates fall drastically. In adopting the most generous features of two contrasting systems of taxation (a territorial view of income, and a residence-based view for allowances) it is unique. And even without this move the UK was set to have the lightest corporate tax regime among major western economies.[96]

Before we turn to the practicalities of enforcement, however, we need to look at the wider effects of tax competition for UK economic development – investment, wages and firm behaviour – and ask to what extent the promises of Camp 1 have been fulfilled.

Has Tax Competition Produced Higher Investment?

From 1997 to 2017 not only did the United Kingdom have the lowest average non-government sector investment (as measured in Gross Fixed Capital Formation) as a proportion of GDP of the G7 economies,[97] from 1995 to 2015 it had the lowest percentage across the Organisation for Economic Co-operation and Development (OECD) countries, and this is an era of unprecedented corporate profits.[98]

---

[96] Richard Brooks, 'The Principles of Tax Policy', Written Submission to the Treasury Select Committee, 31 January 2011, www.publications.parliament.uk/pa/cm201011/cmselect/cmtreasy/memo/taxpolicy/m46.htm.

[97] Office for National Statistics, 'An International Comparison of Gross Fixed Capital Formation', 2 November 2017, www.ons.gov.uk/economy/grossdomesticproductgdp/articles/aninternationalcomparisonofgrossfixedcapitalformation/2017-11-02.

[98] Office for National Statistics, 'An Analysis of Investment Expenditure in the UK and Other OECD Countries', 3 May 2018, www.ons.gov.uk/economy/grossdomesticproductgdp/articles/ananalysisofinvestmentexpenditureintheukandotherorganisationforeconomiccooperationanddevelopmentnations/2018-05-03.

Contrary to the promises of tax competition, the United Kingdom has also seen comparatively weak productivity growth across all industrial sectors; indeed, there are large numbers of unproductive firms in ever sector in every size band.[99] Since 1979, the United Kingdom has seen the slowest increase in GDP per hour worked compared to that in the far higher corporate taxing Germany, France and Norway, and performance has essentially flatlined since the Global Financial Crisis. By 2014 the United Kingdom was categorised as an 'innovation follower' as distinct from an 'innovation leader', such as the higher taxing Germany, Sweden and Denmark.[100] Insofar as any inference can be made it is that higher, not lower, corporate tax rates are associated with higher performances, and this would be consistent with the later generations of growth theories from institutional economics that stress the importance of continuous investment from both states and businesses.

If we investigate the investment behaviour of UK traded firms, there is little evidence that tax cuts translated into increased investment and improved future wages. On the contrary, the United Kingdom has far more evidently followed the US trajectory of financialisation. As William Lazonick has demonstrated, the maximisation of shareholder value has driven US firms from the 'retain and reinvest' model of the post-war era to a 'downsize and distribute' model that has proved devastating for investment.[101] It is not the tax rate as such that causes this shift but its conjunction with the Chicago School principles of maximising shareholder value and light touch self-regulation in financial markets. Put simply, the more neoliberal the wider policy regime, the more extractive the corporate culture in which corporate tax cuts occur. This is important, as it changes the equation from 'lower tax equals higher investment' to 'lower tax equals additional resources for extraction'. To persist with corporate tax cuts when the evidence of accelerated financial extraction is clear is to endorse this culture. In December 2017, when the Trump administration slashed the 35 per cent corporate tax rate to 21 per cent, along with many other

---

[99] LSE Growth Commission, 'UK Growth: A New Chapter', Centre for Economic Performance, LSE, 2017, p. 33.
[100] Eurostat, 'Innovation Union Scoreboard, 2014', p. 4, https://op.europa.eu/en/publication-detail/-/publication/d1cb48d3-4861-41fe-a26d-09850d32487b.
[101] William Lazonick, 'When Managerial Capitalism', p. 97.

reductions, a 2019 study by the non-partisan Congressional Research Service found the cuts produced less than one-twentieth of the economic gain needed to pay for them. Real wages grew slower than GDP, but corporations launched a record-breaking surge in stock buybacks to further inflate share values – some $1 trillion announced by the end of 2018. Shareholder dividends skyrocketed in the first quarter of 2018 and were mirrored by a deep slump in reinvested earnings.[102]

Good indicators of whether large UK corporations have switched to downsize and divest are the 'pay-out ratio', namely the proportion of net earnings paid out as dividends to shareholders, and the parallel 'repurchase ratio' trend in share buybacks, which assesses the ratio of repurchase cost to capitalisation. The evidence for the changing nature of the UK pay-out ratio suggests that before the Covid pandemic it had been higher than in the United States, Europe, Japan, Latin America or wider emerging markets. Andrew Haldane had warned in 2015 that British businesses were giving excessive pay-outs to shareholders at the expense of financing new projects. UK firms, he argued, were 'eating themselves' by favouring pay-outs and buybacks over investment. He viewed this trend as central to understanding the United Kingdom's 'subpar' growth and called on UK firms to revise their practices to favour their customers and employees.[103] Haldane's comments echoed those of Kay's 2012 review of corporate governance and UK equity markets for the Coalition government. Kay had also identified endemic short-termism and recommended changing managerial pay structures and an end to quarterly reporting to encourage an engaged, long-term time investment horizon. The Coalition ignored his warnings.[104] The increase in short-termism is stark. In the 1960s the average company share was held for nearly eight years. By 2008, this had dropped to three months.[105]

---

[102] Jane Gravelle and Donald Marples, 'The Economic Effects of the 2017 Tax Revisions: Preliminary Observations', Congressional Research Service, 22 May 2019, p. 12.
[103] Ferdinando Giugliano, 'BofE's Haldane Says Corporations Putting Shareholders ahead of Wider Economy', *Financial Times*, 25 July 2015.
[104] John Kay, *The Kay Review of UK Equity Markets and Long-Term Decision Making: Final Report* (London: Crown Copyright, 2012).
[105] High Pay Commission, *The State of Play: One Year On from the High Pay Commission* (London: High Pay Commission, 2012).

The broad consensus in investment circles is that a pay-out ratio of over 55 per cent switches from healthy to high. The higher the ratio, the more it implies a drain on long-term earnings potential and raises the risk of reversals. The higher the ratio, the higher the risks. Anything over 100 per cent means a firm is paying out more than it earns. From 2009 to 2018 it is estimated that net income earned by all FTSE 100 companies was £898 billion while dividends stood at £571 billion and share buybacks at £167 billion; in other words, some four-fifths of total net income was distributed. Almost half the FTSE 100 paid out more than three quarters of their net income, and a quarter distributed more than 100 per cent.[106] Aggregate dividend pay-outs by the FTSE 350 in 2020 represented 90 per cent of aggregate pre-tax profit, a figure that followed a two-decade rise alongside stagnating real wages and the unparalleled accumulation of corporate debt.[107] In contrast to the United States, UK companies are obliged to use accumulated distributable profits to finance buybacks, as distinct from issuing debt, and so the share repurchase trend is less steep but still rising. UK repurchase rates have been higher than in France or Germany, and this confirms Haldane's observation that untenable ratios are a peculiarly neoliberal trend, a result of the more permissive regulatory environment and weaker representation of stakeholders in corporate governance.[108] These patterns are the opposite of the promised renaissance in investment, and it makes a mockery of the still pervasive Camp 1 idea that UK firms need continuous tax cuts to improve their investment picture.

A change in ownership patterns is another spur to financialisation, and this too emanates from the change of philosophy. As Aeron Davis and Catherine Walsh show, the control of UK corporations was passed to financial markets through government policy, not least through its unusually open UK market for corporate control in which governments allow mergers and acquisitions regardless of the strategic significance of any given corporation. Thus:

---

[106] Miranda Wadham, 'Pay-Out Ratio Exceeds Net Profits in FTSE 100', *UK Investor Magazine*, 10 August 2016.
[107] Buller and Braun, 'Under New Management', p. 20.
[108] Dimitris Andriosopoulos and Meziane Lasfer, 'The Market Valuation of Share Repurchases in Europe', *The Journal of Banking and Finance 55* (2015): 327–339.

In 1981 individuals held 28 percent of shares, UK-based pension and insurance funds 47 percent, and overseas investors 4 percent (Golding, 2003, p. 23). By 2012, individuals held 10.7 percent, pension and insurance funds 10.9 percent, and foreign investors 53.2 percent (ONS, 2012). Hedge funds and high frequency traders were responsible for 72 percent of market turnover (Kay, 2012)... UK companies had become increasingly owned by foreign-based and short-termist financial institutions, which treated companies as simple units to be traded on fast-moving secondary markets.[109]

The high corporate pay-out culture has also created a vicious circle of inflated market expectations so that companies that try to cut dividends to increase investment or reduce debt face more or less direct pressures from large shareholders and index providers to persist in reckless payments. As I'll show in Chapter 8, this delinquency is a systematic barrier to the climate transition. These patterns have caused widespread unease in the less rapacious quarters of the investment community because the trend is not only towards the hollowing out of UK corporate value but also towards an increase in ownership concentration as shares are taken out of the market.[110] It is worth pointing out, therefore, that the dynamics of financialisation were already entrenched when the Conservative chancellor George Osborne (2010–2015, 2015–2016) urged the civil service to make greater use of CGE modelling in its policymaking, and one can see the attraction.[111]

If we recall the Treasury's 2013 CGE tax model, the flowchart and the Social Accounting Matrix that underpinned it made no measure of corporate reinvestment but simply assumed a positive relationship. Whatever the parameter values used, however tempered the *magnitudes* of change, this model and the theory that underpinned it (Figure 7.2) predetermined that a tax cut would produce a virtuous investment result, because there was simply no option in this model for shareholders to consume their profits or place them offshore. Nor was it conceivable that shareholders could place their non-consumed funds in private equity companies whose dominant strategy was increasingly one of asset stripping. Both the standard HMRC and Treasury model

---

[109] Davis and Walsh, 'The Role of the State', p. 679.
[110] Alpha Dhanani, 'Corporate Share Repurchases in the UK: Perceptions and Practices', *Journal of Applied Accounting Research* 17 (3) (2016): 331–355.
[111] John McDermott, 'Why You Should Care about Dynamic Modelling', *Financial Times*, 15 April 2014.

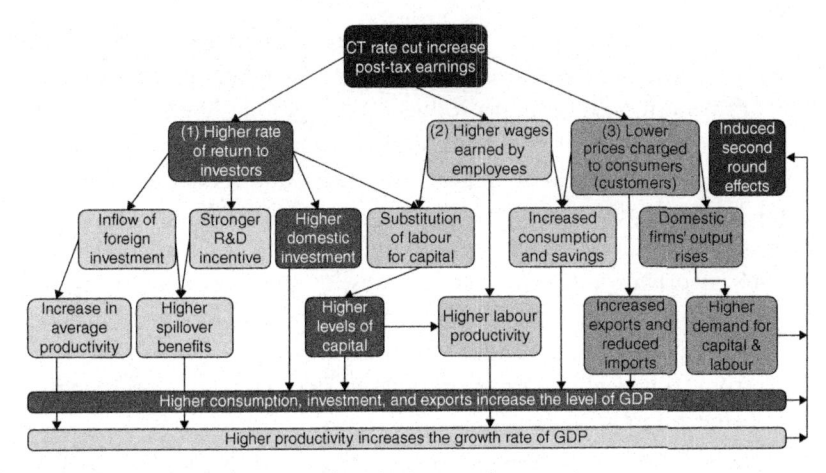

Has Tax Competition Produced Higher Investment? 257

Figure 7.2 Channels through which a reduction in corporate taxation affects GDP
HM Revenue and Customs and UK Treasury, 'Analysis of the Dynamic Effects of Reductions in Corporate Taxation', 5 December 2013, Chart 3.1, https://assets.publishing.service.gov.uk/government/uploads/system/uploads/attachment_data/file/263560/4069_CT_Dynamic_effects_paper_20130312_IW_v2.pdf

and this iteration failed the basic social science test that a model that aspires to capture the real world should include the most salient causal mechanisms you can see in practice.

In effect, the CGE methodology was used to assert that the neoliberal ship was still on course through the simple expedient of editing out all the evidence to the contrary. But how should voters know that such technical models can be used to smuggle utopian economic assumptions into the 'evidential' bases used for policy? The 'predictions' from the 2013 model were immediately cited as fact by the Conservative press to reinforce Osborne's overall policy direction. Quoting the 'results of the Treasury's study of the dynamic impacts of the cuts to corporation tax' *The Spectator* argued in a piece called 'How Corporation Tax Cuts Are Helping Wages' that the results of the cuts would be 'impressive' and any attempts by Labour to reverse them 'dreadful'.[112] *The Spectator* criticised the model only insofar as it failed to capture the new innovations that would surely arise.

---

[112] Matthew Sinclair, 'How Corporation Tax Cuts Are Helping Wages', *The Spectator*, 6 December 2013.

Did increases in FDI make up for the stagnation of domestic investment? Here again there are methodological spanners in the works, as the trans-nationalisation of production has gradually undermined the validity of balance of payments statistics and measures and concepts have failed to keep pace with practical realities.[113] As Oliver Blanchard and Julien Acalin point out, these statistics don't let us distinguish between long-term investments and the more purely speculative investments of private equity or hedge funds,[114] and the United Kingdom as a major financial sector, such as Switzerland or Luxembourg, has acted as an enabling custodian of inward investment that covers the spectrum from real investment to inflows that never touch the sides of the real economy.

As Europe's key financial centre prior to Brexit, it is hardly surprising that the United Kingdom saw high net investment inflows, as well as inflows with comparatively severe peaks and troughs in frequency, through the 1990s and up to the Global Financial Crisis. The lack of long-term investment components in those inward flows is nevertheless shown by the sudden stop in inward investment in 2009 at the peak of that crisis, whereas investments with higher sunk costs, as in complex manufacturing, were sustained elsewhere in Europe. How FDI flows are distributed by sector into the United Kingdom also tells us something about the quality of FDI. As Bruno et al. point out, a large share of FDI has gone into services since 1985 including into financial intermediation, that is, borrowing and lending money. Indeed, this percentage has risen over time to over 70 per cent of the total in 2011. By the same token, the share of investment in manufacturing has declined to less than 20 per cent more recently. Not only does this highlight the importance of the services sector in the UK economy, where wage inequality is higher than in manufacturing, it also points to the increase in systemic risk given the continuing growth of the financial sector, the high likelihood of the 'custodial' as distinct from the productive basis of much of this investment and the failure to reform many of the practices that caused the Global

---

[113] Lukas Linsi and Daniel Mügge, 'Globalization and the Growing Defects of International Economic Statistics', *Review of International Political Economy* 26 (3) (2019): 361–383.

[114] Oliver Blanchard and Julien Acalin, 'What Does Measured FDI Actually Measure?', Policy Brief, Peterson Institute for International Economics, October 2016.

Financial Crisis.[115] The fact is that the size of the financial sector is not just tenuously connected to the real economy. International Monetary Fund research shows a bell-shaped curve relationship with growth and economic stability, so that an overlarge financial sector starts to have an actively negative effect on both, as activity shifts away from productive investment and towards more purely speculative activities, a dynamic that can only be tempered by strong regulation.[116] A Sheffield University Report estimated the United Kingdom's lost growth potential from the financialisation, brain drain and distortionary pricing emanating from the excessively large financial sector at £4.5 trillion between 1995 and 2015.[117]

Who Paid for Corporate Tax Competition?

It is a standard argument of the pro-competition tax literature that higher tax rates will mean lower wages to employees or higher prices to consumers, the so-called tax incidence question. This argument is used in particular against the political left because it suggests they don't understand the interests of their natural constituents, but the evidence tells the opposite story. In the absence of the state withering away it is the reduction in corporate taxes that has shifted tax duties onto less mobile taxpayers. The proportion of UK tax revenue derived from onshore corporation tax has nearly halved since 1989, from 11 per cent to 5.7 per cent for 2018–2019. In the meantime, the shares coming from income tax, national insurance contributions and VAT have all risen.

While personal income tax revenues have increased from soaring incomes, most notably from the top 1 per cent of taxpayers, personal income tax rates have been steadily reduced since 1979. In the meantime, National Insurance Contributions have increased – most sharply

---

[115] Randolph Bruno, Nauro Campos, Saul Estrin and Meng Tian, 'Foreign Direct Investment and the Relationship between the United Kingdom and the European Union', CEP Discussion paper Number 1453, October 2016, p. 11.
[116] Ratna Sahay, Martin Čihák, Papa N'Diaye et al., 'Rethinking Financial Deepening: Stability and Growth in Emerging Markets', IMF Staff Discussion Notes, 8 May 2015, p. 5.
[117] Andrew Baker, Gerald Epstein and Juan Montecino, 'The UK's Finance Curse? Costs and Processes', Sheffield Political Economy Research Institute, September 2018.

for employees, from 5.5 per cent in 1979 to 13.25 per cent by 2022 at the main rate, but also for employers, who saw their payments rise from 10 per cent to 15.05 per cent from 1979 to 2022.[118] The upshot is an increasing effective tax rate on earned income and a rise in the cost of employment. Set this alongside a radical increase in the disparity between executive and employee pay, and polarisation is far more obvious than anything that resembles the promised 'trickling down'. Analysis of six major UK companies in 1980 found that CEOs were paid between thirteen and forty-four times their average employee. By 1998 the average FTSE 100 CEO was paid forty-seven times their average employee. By 2015 this ratio stood at 129:1.[119]

Greece aside, the United Kingdom has experienced the worst falls in real wages in the OECD since the financial crisis;[120] in fact, it stands alone among the advanced economies in seeing the expansion of the economy and the simultaneous contraction of wages.[121] Underlining all of this, however, is the deeper trend of financialisation. As Karel Williams and Adam Leaver have shown, businesses fail to invest or cross-subsidise to develop innovative firms, and they pass costs and liabilities down the production chain wherever possible. Problems and costs are passed into another social account, such as increasingly precarious wages. These in turn require massive public subsidy in the shape of in-work benefits.[122] In the light of this evidence, it is untenable to insist that tax relief has been conducive to the more sustainable management of firms, increased productive investment or improvements to long-term wages, all of which have demonstrably more complex determinants. The picture is equally damning when we review the damage tax competition has inflicted on the UK state, its tax revenues, and spending and administrative capacity as a fiscal authority.

Tax competition advocates might argue this entire debate is moot because UK corporate tax revenues have stayed consistent since 1979.

---

[118] Thomas Pope and Tom Waters, 'A Survey of the UK Tax System', IFS Briefing Note BN09, November 2016, p. 14.
[119] The High Pay Centre, 'Fat-Cat Wednesday, 2017', *High Pay Centre Blog*, 1 January 2017, www.highpaycentre.org/fat-cat-wednesday-2017/.
[120] LSE Growth Commission, 'UK Growth', p. 31.
[121] Valentina Romei, 'UK Is Alone among Advanced Countries', *Financial Times*, 2 March 2017.
[122] Karel Williams and Adam Leaver, 'After the Thirty-Year Experiment: The Future of the Foundational Economy', *Juncture* 21 (3) (2014), p. 219.

Despite their volatility over economic cycles there has indeed been no persistent downward trend in onshore tax revenues up to the Global Financial Crisis. However, though the gross has remained the same it has constituted a relatively declining source of revenues overall, even as demands have risen, and not just from the growing and aging population but from the many unanticipated costs of the neoliberal project. We can account for this consistency in revenues by both the increase in the size and profitability of the corporate sector and the partial broadening of the tax base,[123] but this confirms the costs in revenues foregone given the massive increase in corporate profits through this period combined with rate cuts. Between 1999 and 2011 British companies' profits increased by 58 per cent, while corporation tax payments went up by less than 5 per cent.[124]

Stable or less sharply reduced corporate tax rates would have given a non-utopian government far greater room for manoeuvre in its spending choices, that is, more 'fiscal space'. In terms of the revenues foregone, the Institute for Fiscal Studies estimated a government loss of £16.5 billion a year by 2016–2017 from the tax plans launched in 2010 alone. The plan to reduce the top rate further from 19 per cent to 17 per cent in 2020 was forecast to lose the exchequer some £12 billion by 2022, but the Treasury justified it on the basis that 'low corporation tax supports the economy by enabling companies to reinvest in their business, create jobs, and increase wages'.[125]

There were many services that needed greater support, but the most perverse cuts in developmental terms were in education, where the UK school performance already lagged behind its international peers. UK government spending on education in real terms fell significantly from 2009–2010 – the first fall in real terms since 1953–1954 and a stark contrast to the sustained education spending of Germany, France and Sweden. Both UK government and business spending on R&D have also been consistently low compared to similarly developed economies, and patents per person have trended below the OECD average.[126] By

---

[123] Helen Miller and Thomas Pope, 'The Changing Composition of UK Tax Revenues', IFS Briefing Note BN182, April 2016, p. 16.
[124] Richard Brooks, *The Great Tax Robbery*, pp. 24–25.
[125] Delphine Strauss, 'Corporate Tax Cut to Cost UK Government Coffers £12 Billion', *Financial Times*, 28 January 2019.
[126] LSE Growth Commission, 'UK Growth', p. 35.

2019 UK government spending on R&D was 1.74 per cent of GDP, as against 1.84 per cent in 1985.[127]

UK public sector net investment measured in Gross Fixed Capital Formation fell throughout the 1990s under the Conservatives and then rose steadily under the New Labour governments. This investment rose steeply after the Global Financial Crisis as a stimulus measure, only to fall sharply again under the Coalition's austerity policies. The Conservatives were doctrinally committed to shrink the state and used the financial sector bailout as the pretext. They proceeded to cut capital spending by nearly 50 per cent between June 2010 and 2014, so that already inadequate infrastructure spending was flat through this period.[128] As the Trades Union Council report concluded, 'If there is a British disease it is over-consuming and under-investing in the future.'[129] In a renowned piece of international political economy scholarship, Andrew Janos identified precisely this dynamic as the defining feature of the global political economic 'periphery', as distinct from its developmental 'core'.[130]

The overall picture is one of prolonged public investment shortfall in the United Kingdom and the state's weakening as a developmental actor. The United Kingdom has languished under three chronic problems since the Second World War: high educational inequality and underinvestment in education; the neglect of infrastructure; and a world-leading financial sector that has persistently failed to attend to domestic investment, a legacy of its outward-facing function in financing the British Empire.[131] Far from solving them, however, neoliberalism has made these tendencies worse. When it came to identify the key factors holding back business investment, the 2017 LSE Growth Commission cited policy uncertainty, short-termism in business and financial markets and associated problems accessing finance, especially for young, innovative firms.[132]

---

[127] Georgina Hutton, 'Research and Development Spending', House of Commons Library, 2 September 2021.

[128] Trades Union Council, 'Falling Behind: Britain's Investment Gap', ESAD/March 2014, pp. 8–9.

[129] Ibid.

[130] Andrew Janos, 'The Politics of Backwardness in Continental Europe, 1780–1945', *World Politics* 41 (3) (1989): 325–358.

[131] LSE Growth Commission, 'UK Growth', pp. 13–14.

[132] Ibid., p. 15.

Regulatory Competition, Tax Avoidance and HMRC

To close this section, I want to look at regulatory competition as it relates to corporate taxation. While tax evasion through deceit or omission is straightforwardly illegal, tax 'avoidance' is a more elastic concept. Tax avoidance is the legal reduction of tax liability through the exploitation of legal loopholes. The history of corporate tax collection is that of cat and mouse between tax authorities and large corporations who hire tax code experts to minimise their liabilities. Avoidance is against the 'spirit' of the law, but that spirit has changed with the prevailing economic orthodoxy. Today it is multinational companies that can pay the most for 'tax planning' and manage the most substantial abuse. This matters tremendously for revenues since, for example, in 2007–2008, some 1 per cent of companies accounted for fully 80 per cent of UK corporate tax revenues, which is a symptom of the unhealthy trend towards market concentration.

The combination of an information and communications technology revolution and jurisdictional competition increased avoidance options. The digital economy spurred a move away from investment in physical machinery towards 'intangible' assets such as 'intellectual property' as the source of 'value added'. In the United Kingdom, investments in intangible assets overtook investment in physical assets in the early 2000s, and this made it harder to value different activities and identify where they should be taxed.[133] To take just one example, the Coalition's 'Patent Box' policy was designed as a tax break on profits from patented products and processes on the assumption that this would encourage firms to produce more of them. What it did not anticipate was that corporations would adopt a highly elastic interpretation of patent-related activities and prefer 'tax planning' around these new rules to actual innovation.[134] It had cost the exchequer an estimated £740 million by 2016–2017, with little evidence of any uptick in R&D spend.[135]

The existence of tax havens enables these problems. Switzerland and EU states such as Luxembourg, Ireland and, both before and

---

[133] Helen Miller and Thomas Pope, 'Corporate Tax Avoidance: Tackling Base Erosion and Profit-Shifting', Institute for Fiscal Studies, February 2016, p. 173.
[134] Paul Johnson, 'Tax without Design: Recent Innovations in UK Tax Policy', Institute for Fiscal Studies, May 2014, pp. 1–2, 20–22.
[135] Miller and Pope, 'Corporate Tax Avoidance', p. 184.

after Brexit, the United Kingdom have proved highly permissive of tax havens either because they preside over havens themselves or, in the UK case, because they also run a financial service industry that thrives on the avoidance business. Neoliberal governments have duly refused to do more than offer minimal regulation of the multiple tax haven jurisdictions under UK authority. These are an imperial legacy made up of three Crown Dependencies, Guernsey, Jersey and the Isle of Man, and fourteen Overseas Territories, which include the major tax havens of Bermuda, Cayman and the British Virgin Islands.

Until recently the critical work on tax havens was by investigative journalists,[136] and non-governmental organisations such as the Tax Justice Network. Academic economics had been notably silent, and not least because neoclassical methods cannot describe, let alone diagnose, the three-dimensional problems havens cause. This made Gabriel Zucman's 2015 *The Hidden Wealth of Nations* a particularly important work.[137] In a 2017 update, Annette Alstadsæter, Niels Johannesen and Gabriel Zucman estimated that the equivalent of 10 per cent of global GDP was held in tax havens globally.[138] The United Kingdom could be said to have discouraged domestic corporate tax evasion via its havens so long as it retained a worldwide rather than a territorial system of taxation, but that constraint was abandoned in 2009. Thereafter it repeatedly diluted EU and OECD efforts to counter the most flagrant abuses, a veto power it lost with Brexit. The United Kingdom's stance ran directly against not only its own national interest but also the international interest, since in 2019 it ranked second, globally, for the loss of its own revenues and it also ranked second as the country most responsible for revenue losses worldwide, some 29 per cent of all losses, given its role in overseeing its extensive network of tax havens and the financial centre in London that systematically enabled them.[139]

---

[136] Nicholas Shaxson, *Treasure Islands: Tax Havens and the Men Who Stole the World* (London: Penguin Books, 2011).
[137] Gabriel Zucman, *The Hidden Wealth of Nations* (Chicago: Chicago University Press, 2015).
[138] Annette Alstadsæter, Niels Johannsen and Gabriel Zucman, 'Who Owns the Wealth in Tax Havens? Macro Evidence and Implications for Global Inequality', *Journal of Public Economics* 162 (2018): 89–100, p. 92.
[139] Multi-Agency Report, 'The State of Tax Justice: Tax Justice in the Time of Covid 19', Tax Justice Network, 2020, p. 12.

The neoliberal principle of regulatory laxity and the 'partnership' between government and business not only legitimised tax avoidance, it also enabled the significant corporate capture of policymaking and enforcement capacity. In corruption research, the conventional definition of 'corporate state capture' is the subversion of legitimate channels of political influence for private gain, classically, through payment to officials.[140] This form of capture is often presumed to be a feature only of developing economies with weak institutions, but this is clearly not the case. Neoliberal narratives effectively invite corporate state capture on the basis that corporate actors are deemed to understand markets best – the neoliberal equivalent to the industrial proletarian vanguard in terms of correct consciousness. The players in this case are not just multinational corporations but also the big four international accountancy firms whose main source of income, after auditing, is from their advisory role in 'tax planning'. Hence, they alone among stakeholders are brought in as the expert partners in government. Step outside of that analytical frame, however, and the assumption looks naïve at best, corrupt at worst. As Richard Brooks noted to the Treasury Select Committee in 2011, when it came to changes in the CFC rules, for example, 'policymakers are writing the rules in conjunction with the very vested interests that stand to gain most from their decisions. The result is policy development reduced to not much more than giving the largest corporations the tax breaks they want in the name of "competitiveness" (with the words "whilst protecting the UK tax base" usually tacked on for form's sake)'.[141]

As the Public Accounts Committee noted in 2013, multinational companies and the big four accountancy firms have not just been regularly consulted on legislation but given senior appointments and placed on powerful HMRC advisory panels that exclude other stakeholders.[142] This occurred as the neutral civil service capacity within the tax inspectorate was cut, which raises serious issues of accountability

---

[140] Joel Hellman, Geraint Jones and Daniel Kaufmann, 'Seize the State, Seize the Day: State Capture, Corruption and Influence in Transition', World Bank Policy Research Working Paper 2444, 2000.
[141] Brooks, 'The Principles of Tax Policy'.
[142] House of Commons Public Accounts Committee, 'Tax Avoidance: The Role of Large Accountancy Firms', 26 April 2013 (HC 870), pp. 9–10, www.publications.parliament.uk/pa/cm201213/cmselect/cmpubacc/870/870.pdf.

in the tax system.[143] Electorates get to choose their governments and reject those with tax policies they oppose, but they have no information, let alone power, over the selection processes and discrete technical choices of the regulator. It would be over-simplifying to think of this institutional capture as an historical constant, however. The relationships between the Treasury, the City of London and the Bank of England have shown significant variation over time depending on the orthodoxy of the day. The more Keynesian Conservative governments from the post-war era to the 1970s pushed back far more often against City preferences than they have ever done under neoliberalism.[144]

As for the evolution of HMRC itself, since the late nineteenth century, the Board of Inland Revenue had been in charge of direct taxes – on income, capital gains, inheritance and corporation income – while the Board of Customs & Excise was responsible for indirect taxes on goods and transactions such as import duties and sales taxes – VAT – and excise duties on alcohol and tobacco.[145] Thus, while tax policy was set by the Treasury and the chancellor, the tax boards were autonomous bodies of civil servants on the principle that ministers should be put at one remove from individual casework decisions (they would later be used as models for the 'agency' reforms discussed in Chapter 3).[146]

After a 2004 review, the Labour government decided to merge the two tax offices to 'improve compliance with taxation, reduce businesses' compliance costs and reduce the Government's revenue collection costs'.[147] HMRC was duly created in 2005. The review recommended a cut of 16,000 posts out of 98,000 within three years and 'efficiency saving' of £500 million over the same period.[148] The

---

[143] Prem Sikka, Michele Christensen, John Christensen and Christine Cooper, 'Reforming HMRC: Making It Fit for the Twenty-First Century', Report Commissioned by the Shadow Chancellor, John McDonnell MP, September 2016, pp. 26–27.
[144] Ranald Michie, 'The City of London and the Government: The Changing Relationship', in Ranald Michie and Philip Williamson, *The British Government and the City of London in the Twentieth Century* (Cambridge: Cambridge University Press, 2009), pp. 39–49.
[145] Christopher Hood and Ruth Dixon, *A Government That Worked Better and Cost Less?* (Oxford: Oxford University Press, 2015), pp. 88–89.
[146] Ibid.
[147] Treasury Select Committee, 'The Merger of Customs and Excise and the Inland Revenue', 11 November 2004 (HC 556), p. 10, quoted in Hood and Dixon.
[148] Hood and Dixon, *Better Government*, p. 89.

subsequent 'Change' programme meant further cuts of 58,000 staff by 2015, a reduction of 42 per cent from the point of the merger. This meant that in the aftermath of the Global Financial Crisis, between 2008 and 2012, the United Kingdom cut more revenue collectors than any other European tax authority. The only country that cut more as a proportion of their total headcount was Greece.[149]

In the decade that followed, HMRC saw year on year funding cuts in real terms. The 2010 Coalition spending review cut the HMRC budget by 25 per cent, so that the resources available to HMRC were 30 per cent lower in cash terms in 2015–2016 than in 2005–2006. The Departmental Transformation Programme from 2006 to 2011 was followed by the Change Programme from 2011 to 2015, and both were based on the New Public Management norms that preferred competitive, transactional and cost-cutting attitudes over those of cooperation.[150] These were notably doctrinaire strategies for an agency whose work depended on deep professional expertise, experience and information-sharing, and by May 2009, staff morale in HMRC was the lowest of the eleven government departments surveyed.[151] The programmes themselves were expensive. The Transformation Programme was planned to cost £2.7 billion over its lifetime, the Change Programme some £2.2 billion,[152] and yet by the time of the 2015 Civil Service People Survey, only 2 per cent of respondents agreed strongly with the statement 'I feel that change is managed well in HMRC'.[153] In a clear parallel with the Department for Education reforms outlined in Chapter 6, huge cuts in institutional capacity coincided with dramatic policy changes that increased the workload to be managed, making the institution unfit for purpose.

By 2015–2016, HMRC interacted with 45 million individuals and more than 5.4 million businesses and paid tax credits to 4.4 million families and child benefit to 7.4 million families.[154] The challenges of corporate tax collection were constantly evolving as multinational

---

[149] European Public Service Union, 'The Impact of Austerity on Tax Collection: One Year On and Still Going Backwards', October 2014.
[150] Brooks, *The Great Tax Robbery*, p. 174.
[151] Richard Brooks, 'Morale among HMRC Workers Falls to a New Low', *Accountancy Age*, 9 July 2009.
[152] Public Services and Commercial Union and the Tax Justice Network, 'HMRC. Building an Uncertain Future: The Cuts Don't Work', 2015, p. 6.
[153] Ibid., p. 10.   [154] Sikka et al., 'Reforming HMRC', p. 4.

corporations deployed transfer pricing practices, royalty payments, management fees, interest payments on intragroup loans and other schemes to shift profits from the United Kingdom to low or no tax jurisdictions. By 2009, only 600 staff in the Large Business Service were responsible for 700 groups of companies,[155] though avoidance in any one group could be organised in highly complex forms. Banks, in particular, used their privileged offshore position to avoid tax on themselves and to create, fund and sell tax-avoidance schemes to others.[156]

The Public Accounts Committee had already concluded in 2013 that HMRC was outgunned by the large corporations and accountancy firms. Their report pointed out that Deloitte, Ernst and Young, KPMG, and Price Waterhouse Coopers alone had four times as many specialists in transfer pricing as the tax authority supposed to regulate them.[157] In April 2014, a new Large Business Directorate was supposed to deal with the tax affairs of the largest 2,100 businesses in the United Kingdom, and by 2015 two-thirds of these businesses had open inquiries attached to them, inquiries that frequently involved multiple disputes over many years.[158] By February 2016, however, HMRC still had only eighty-one transfer pricing specialists, though an investigation into a single major company required between ten and thirty specialists, with an average case taking up to twenty-two months to conclude.[159]

What select committee and trade union reviews show is that the Treasury's systematic under-resourcing of the inspectorate meant a rising dependence on 'voluntary disclosure agreements' with corporations suspected of tax abuses. Individuals who had not declared their assets could regularise their affairs by paying a fine in return for immunity from prosecution. The Public and Commercial Union Report concluded: 'In effect, voluntary disclosure is a tax amnesty for wealthy individuals with undeclared offshore funds.'[160] As a report commissioned by the then Labour shadow chancellor, John McDonnell, noted,

---

[155] Shaxson, *Treasure Islands*, p. 274. [156] Ibid.
[157] House of Commons Committee of the Public Accounts, 'Tax Avoidance', p. 8.
[158] Sameen Farouk, 'Enforcement Activity of the Large Business Service', Answer to Freedom of Information Request, 16 February 2015.
[159] Prem Sikka, 'The Tories Promise to Be Tough on Tax Evasion: Where's the Evidence?', *The Guardian*, 22 May 2017.
[160] Sikka et al., 'Reforming HMRC', p. 11.

the nature of the system left HMRC open to threats to withdraw altogether from this voluntary code as demonstrated by the case of *UK Uncut Legal Action Ltd v HM Revenue and Customs & Anor*.[161] In the meantime, the small and medium-sized business sector continued to face the full force of the law.

A further 2013 Public Accounts Committee report on tax collection had concluded that HMRC acted inconsistently towards taxpayers, did not use the full range of sanctions at its disposal and used a tax gap measure that failed to capture all the avoided tax it was supposed to collect. The committee also objected to the new tendency in both policymaking and enforcement to consult exclusively with the large corporations and accountancy firms on questions of 'optimal' corporate tax policy,[162] a policy that remains in place at the time of writing. Between 2010 and 2015 there were only eleven prosecutions in relation to offshore tax evasion, resulting in fifteen years of prison time collectively.[163] Despite pledges to increase prosecutions following the committee's criticism, the number of people charged with tax evasion halved between 2015 and 2020, and in 2019–2020 no corporations were charged with corporate criminal offences.[164] Nor has any action has been taken against the big four accountancy companies who facilitate evasion, despite the committee's repeated criticism of their role.

Conclusion

As Lazonick points out, corporations in the post-war era had reinvested most of their profits in productive capabilities, including those of the labour force, to generate innovative products and to develop and integrate new technologies. Open-ended, empirically informed economic analyses had also left plenty of room for debates on how firms could and should evolve. In the neoliberal economies of today, by contrast, deterministic neoclassical analysis has profoundly undermined

---

[161] 'UK Uncut versus HMRC', EWHC 1283 (Admin), 16 May 2013.
[162] House of Commons Committee of Public Accounts, 'HMRC Tax Collection: Annual Report and Accounts 2012–2013', 19 December 2013 (HC 666), p. 4, www.publications.parliament.uk/pa/cm201314/cmselect/cmpubacc/666/666.pdf.
[163] Sikka et al., 'Reforming HMRC', pp. 9–10.
[164] Emma Agyemang, 'UK Tax Evasion Prosecutions Fall by Half in Five Years', *Financial Times*, 21 December 2020.

our understanding of how economic development occurs, a momentous Kuhn-loss. Encouraged by doctrine, those firms most prepared to cut costs to maximise short-term profits have become the epitome of high economic performance, as measured in traded firms through dividend pay-outs.[165] The practical result in the United Kingdom's large-firm sector is an investment famine – chronically late payments to the tens of thousands of SMEs that supply them and extensive precarity in pay and working conditions that hollows out not just low-income but what used to be middle-income work too. When short-term profit maximisation via least investment is the pinnacle of corporate success, an economy is surely in deep social and ecological trouble.

On the face of it, the neoliberal story of jurisdictional competition should have nothing to do with Soviet experience in either theoretical or practical terms. As with the story of outsourcing, however, this policy history is a cautionary tale of what happens when governments assume that enterprises can be relied on to behave 'rationally' and hence constructively in the terms dictated by utopian orthodoxy. By the 1980s, Soviet states were driven to bilateral special pleading with individual state enterprises to keep the basic production system in motion, and by the Brezhnev era the wheels of Soviet enterprise planning were thoroughly greased.[166] The relationship between large corporations and the UK government now bears a striking resemblance to the regulatory bargaining to which the Soviets had retreated when the promise of ever greater economic efficiency and economic progress consistently failed to materialise. Britain's large firms today are consequently thanked for concessions to social responsibility so nugatory they would have been laughed out of the Treasury by the post-war generation of economic ministers and their officials.

In his 2011 Nobel Prize Lecture in the aftermath of the 2007–2008 Global Financial Crisis, Peter Diamond warned against the dominance of axiomatic-deductive models in mainstream economics.

---

[165] William Lazonick, 'Innovative Enterprise and Sustainable Prosperity', Paper presented to the Institute for New Economic Thinking, Edinburgh, 23 October 2017.

[166] Mark Harrison, 'The Fundamental Problem of Compliance: Plan and Compliance in a Partially Centralised Economy', *Comparative Economic Studies* 47 (2) (2005): 296–314, p. 311.

Assumptions that are satisfactory for basic research, for clarifying an issue by isolating it from other effects, should not play a central role in policy recommendations if those assumptions do not apply to the world. To me, taking a model literally is not taking a model seriously. It is worth remembering that models are incomplete—indeed, that is what it means to be a model.[167]

Jurisdictional competition in practice has meant re-regulation in favour of the narrow interests of asset-holders. The result is a bonanza of reckless corporate activity that has transformed the global balance of power between multinational corporations and democratic nation states for the worse. On the political front, tax competition is a policy tailor-made to undermine fiscal consent and trust in democracy. It fulfils none of its developmental economic promises, but as I'll explore in Chapter 9, it adds grist to the populist mill that rejects democracy as a sham – a cover operation for the organisation of unique advantages by the wealthy for the wealthy to the exclusion of the wider society, as aided and abetted by the political class.

As Thomas Piketty has shown, the state, historically, has been the only force that has optimised the social functions of the firm and stood between society and a return to the patrimonial capitalism of the pre-democratic era.[168] The empirical history of the corporation is that it is constituted not just by functional and technological evolution but also through law, and social and political convention and ambition. What that law should say should consequently reflect a public debate grounded in empirics rather than utopian doctrine. As Chapter 8, on climate change, will demonstrate, our basic survival depends on that debate happening now.

---

[167] Peter Diamond, 'Unemployment, Vacancies, Wages', Nobel Prize Lecture, 8 December 2010, p. 313.
[168] Piketty, *Capital*.

8 | *Efficient Markets and Climate Change*, or *Soviet Cybernetics 2.0*

Imagine two worlds: one characterised by risk, another by radical uncertainty. A world of risk would mean we lived in a system already fully constituted – a knowable system in which individual agents could see and understand everything directly. In this world the only limits on our decision-making would be our personal preferences and incomplete information that we could, in principle, complete, or approximate meaningfully. A world of uncertainty, by contrast, is a world in which the future is always 'becoming', in which there is no predetermined political economic space that we can fully apprehend. Here, the present cannot be computed, let alone the future.[1] As I argued in the opening chapters, the first world is a purely theoretical construct. We live and die in the second. By the late twentieth century a threat was emerging in the physical world that was unprecedented, global, intensifying and potentially terminal – a perfect storm of man-made climate change, ocean acidification and the planet's sixth mass extinction event, the first caused by man and potentially the most complete.[2] In this chapter I explore how neoclassical economics understands risk and how this has played out in neoliberal policy.

There is an overwhelming consensus in the international science community and, as of the 2015 Paris Climate Agreement, between 195 governments that temperature rises above 2°C from mid-nineteenth-century levels will be extraordinarily dangerous. Governments consequently committed to pursuing 'ambitious efforts' to limit the temperature

---

[1] Mark Blyth, 'This Time It Really Is Different: Europe, the Financial Crisis, and Staying on Top in the Twenty-First Century', in Dan Breznitz and John Zysman, *The Third Globalization: Can Wealthy Nations Stay Rich in the Twenty First Century* (Oxford: Oxford University Press, 2013), pp. 207–231, p. 210.

[2] Garardo Ceballos, Paul R. Ehrlich and Rodolfo Dirzo, 'Biological Annihilation via the Ongoing Sixth Mass Extinction Signaled by Vertebrate Population Losses and Declines', *PNAS* 114 (30) (2017): 6089–6096, p. 6089.

increase to 1.5°C above pre-industrial levels.[3] The higher temperatures rise, the more complete the threat to global ecosystems and human civilisation. Beyond 2°C the onset of non-linear processes triggered by tipping points, such as the melting of permafrost and the polar icecaps or the collapse of the Amazon rainforest, shift from being probable to certain. These processes have already begun, however, and their tipping points are likely to pitch ecosystems into conditions of unrecoverable loss, or 'ruin', at uncontrollable rates.

As the author of the 2006 UK government-commissioned *Stern Review on the Economics of Climate Change*, Nicholas Stern warned, '[W]e are the first generation that through its neglect could destroy the relationship between humans and the planet, and perhaps the last generation that can prevent dangerous climate change.'[4] Man-made geo-engineering solutions to the ecological emergency are unethical, untested, unaccountable and high risk, however understandable the wish for a technological silver bullet.[5] In short, the natural science tells us that we need a system-wide transition as a matter of urgency – a global mobilisation akin to a war-footing. So why has this yet to happen?

There is no denying the fact that the nature of climate change makes political action difficult. The threat is hard to comprehend because it is total and unparalleled in scale, and environmental degradation has long been understood as a 'collective action problem'. It was famously described by the ecologist Garrett Hardin as the 'tragedy of the commons', whereby individuals who act according to their self-interest within a system of shared resources may diminish or spoil those resources and so undermine the system for all users, including themselves.[6]

Environmental economists in the 1970s tended towards either a strong statism or a radical faith in markets in their hunt for solutions, a dichotomy Elinor Ostrom declared false for ignoring how people's capacity to solve such dilemmas varied from situation to situation.

---

[3] United Nations, 'Paris Agreement', 21st Conference of the Parties, Paris, December 2015.
[4] Nicholas Stern, *Why Are We Waiting?* (Cambridge, MA: MIT Press, 2015), p. xxvii.
[5] Ibid., p. 23.
[6] Garrett Hardin, 'The Tragedy of the Commons', *Science* 162 (1968): 1243–1248.

Ostrom had then used axiomatic-deductive, game-theoretic logic to show that individuals might rationally 'contract' with each other to pursue conservation under certain conditions and so re-establish the commons in a self-regulating form.[7]

From a political economic perspective, however, this dichotomy between bureaucratic centralisation and privatisation is false not only because of Ostrom's potential for local cooperation but because it is ahistorical. Far from having only bureaucratic and centralising options, the democratic state can deploy diverse strategies for mobilising social action: that set out new opportunities, as well as rules, and offer financial and institutional support for adaptation and innovation without dictating it. Since in practice all economic orthodoxies are political orthodoxies that use state power whether they admit it or not, sterile debates about 'how much' states intervene are misleading. The questions we should ask is, 'for whom, and for what, do they intervene?'[8] In the current timeframe, moreover, the state alone has the power to galvanise environmental action on the necessary scale. Thus, to understand why neoliberal political elites continue to respond to an unprecedented global threat with light-touch regulation and market creation alongside the perpetuation of the fossil fuel economy, we need to look in detail at how neoclassical economics thinks about risk.

Approaching the question from Camp 2, Stern observes that climate change is 'the greatest market failure the world has ever seen'.[9] But the closed-system reasoning in Camp 1 has allowed neoliberalism to develop three core principles, and these have formed the foundations of UK climate policy. The first is that agents in all markets, including financial markets, are completely informed and rational in the face of future risk, though this belief is only viable in the fictional world in which risk probabilities can be accurately assessed through a combination of axiomatic deduction and past statistics. The second principle follows from the first, which is that economic forecasting and hence risk management are dependable methodologies. While useful for scenario planning, these methods have come to dominate neoliberal

---

[7] Elinor Ostrom, *Governing the Commons: The Evolution of Institutions for Collective Action* (Cambridge: Cambridge University Press, 2015), pp. 9–12.

[8] Peter Evans, *Embedded Autonomy, States and Industrial Transformation* (Princeton: Princeton University Press, 1995), p. 10.

[9] Nicholas Stern, *The Economics of Climate Change: The Stern Review* (London: HM Treasury, 2006).

policymaking and encouraged the illusion that, informed as we supposedly are, a policy of incremental change will serve. The last principle is that market competition is the source of efficient economic performance, forever and in all circumstances, and so the maximal acceptable role for the state is to ensure corporations give out the necessary information to allow for rational decision-making by all economic agents, from consumers to financial markets. Adjustments will follow that are equilibrium preserving. All three principles require a world free of radical uncertainty, so how have these arguments emerged?

Calculable Risk

Humility in the face of social change was the norm for the classical political economic thought of the eighteenth and nineteenth centuries, from Adam Smith to John Stuart Mill to Carl Menger.[10] In the 1930s and 1940s, economists who disagreed on practically everything else still agreed that we live in an uncertain world. John Maynard Keynes and Friedrich August von Hayek both insisted that we will always be incapable of knowing what will happen next in a robust way, even as they disagreed on what to do about it.[11] For Keynes, markets were so plagued by imperfect information and herd behaviour they would forever require state intervention to stabilise them. Government had to intervene not because it knew more than 'society' but because it had the unique capacity to take precautions against the clear implications of uncertainty.[12] For Hayek, no government could transcend its own lack of complete knowledge to intervene successfully.[13]

By contrast, the neoclassical economics of the late nineteenth and twentieth centuries insisted that the idea of radical uncertainty was unduly defeatist.[14] The British economist Stanley Jevons had started

---

[10] Julia Köhn, *Uncertainty in Economics: A New Approach* (Cham: Springer Press, 2017), pp. 20, 27.
[11] Richard Bronk and Wade Jacoby, 'Uncertainty and the Dangers of Monocultures in Regulation, Analysis and Practice', MPIfG Discussion Paper 16/6, p. 6.
[12] Robert Skidelsky, *Keynes: The Return of the Master* (New York: Public Affairs, 2009), p. 162.
[13] Bronk and Jacoby, 'Uncertainty and the Dangers of Monocultures', p. 6.
[14] Philip Mirowski, *More Heat than Light: Economics as Social Physics, Physics as Nature's Economics* (Cambridge: Cambridge University Press, 1989), p. 218.

this tendency in the 1870s when he asserted that '[t]he Theory of economy... presents a close analogy to the Science of Statical Mechanics, and the Laws of Exchange are found to resemble the Laws of Equilibrium of a lever'.[15] Leon Walras had adopted the mathematics of Newtonian mechanics to support his argument that economic agents have full knowledge or 'certainty' of 'a programmed external economic reality that governed all past, present and future economic outcomes'. In this view, notes Paul Davidson, '[t]he path of the economy, like the path of the planets under Newton's classical mechanics, was determined by timeless, immutable natural laws'.[16] It is this belief that would go on to define the Camp 1 neoclassical understanding of future risk as something open to precise calculation.

What emerged was an argument for calculable uncertainty on the utilitarian assumption that economic agents optimise their trading possibilities based on full and relevant information and that errors in projected probabilities will be random but always within given parameters.[17] But such faith in the accuracy of probability calculation is coherent only within a closed economic system, since it is only in a closed system that you can be rational and optimise, or irrational and predictably lose out.[18] This approach was criticised from the outset, not least by Alfred Marshall, who pointed out that time had the terrible habit of undermining the stability of any actual factors as 'given', and hence the wiser methodological path would be towards economic 'biology'. Mechanical analogies might be easier to handle mathematically, but they were further from complex reality than organic analogies of 'living force and movement'.[19]

As Julia Köhn notes, these debates about uncertainty effectively split economics into two broad schools. On the one hand you had uncertainty purists, such as Keynes, who saw uncertainty as an inescapable challenge in the real economy and a fundamental constraint

---

[15] Stanley Jevons, *The Theory of Political Economy* (Basingstoke: Palgrave Macmillan, 2013), Preface to the First Edition (1871).

[16] Paul Davidson, 'Reality and Economic Theory', *Journal of Post-Keynesian Economics* 18 (4) (June 1996): 479–508, p. 479.

[17] Richard Bronk, *The Romantic Economist: Imagination in Economics* (Cambridge: Cambridge University Press, 2009), p. 68.

[18] Ibid., p. 219.

[19] Alfred Marshall, *Principles of Economics* (New York: Palgrave Macmillan, 2013), Preface to First Edition (1890), xxvi.

on how much we could ever know about how an economy works. On the other there were those neoclassical economists who acknowledged uncertainty but argued that utility-maximising choice on the basis of probabilistic knowledge was the 'scientific' way to manage it. Between 1920 and 1950 the two sides parted, so that from then on neoclassical economists would reinterpret uncertainty as risk and thereby neglect its fundamental significance for the economy, for economics and, by extension, for the planet.[20]

In the decades after the Second World War the analytical focus on uncertainty had waxed and waned under conditions of unusually stable economic growth, in which even downturns appeared relatively manageable. As we know, however, when that economic stability broke down in the 1970s, it was the diagnoses and prescriptions of Camp 1 economists that came to the fore. Their argument was not that free markets were the safest way to manage the inescapable uncertainty of life, à la Hayek, but that 'out there' existed a world of rational expectations, calculable risk, optimising agents, informational certainty and, hence, fully efficient markets if only the state could be rolled back.[21] Never mind that this was a grammar of justification that only made sense in the language of a closed, two-dimensional space.

The Global Financial Crisis

To understand why the Camp 1 framework is a misguided foundation for tackling the ecological emergency we need to look at two of its arguments in particular: for 'rational expectations' and 'efficient markets'.[22] Their continuing dominance in UK climate policy is all the more extraordinary because these theories sat at the intellectual root of the Global Financial Crisis of 2007–2008, and yet they persist in their practical authority. If we review them and the crisis they caused, we can understand their logic more fully and hear their Soviet echo.

The theory of rational expectations was developed by John Muth in 1961 and popularised by the Chicago economist Robert Lucas in the early 1970s. The efficient markets hypothesis (EMH) was developed

---

[20] Köhn, *Uncertainty in Economics*, p. 27
[21] Bronk and Jacoby, 'Uncertainty and the Dangers of Monocultures', p. 6.
[22] Gillian Tett, 'Crisis of Faith for High Priests of Rational Markets', *Financial Times*, 15 June 2009.

from the mid-1960s by the Chicago economist, and student of Milton Friedman, Eugene Fama. Muth's argument for rational expectations asserted that 'the economy does not waste information, and that expectations depend specifically on the structure of the entire system'.[23] The argument is logically compelling within a closed system but utopian in an evolving world of epistemological uncertainty and ontological indeterminacy. In answer to the criticism that neoclassical models were so often out of kilter with observed phenomena, Muth retorted that this was because dynamic economic models did not assume *enough* rationality. The subtlety of Muth's position was that he did not assert that all entrepreneurs would make correct predictions, or that their expectations were identical, but that *average* expectations would be 'accurate' and that since higher profits would accrue to those who made better forecasts, all agents would converge on the 'correct' outlook. The basis of this intuitively pleasing claim, however, was a model of short period price variations in an isolated market with a fixed production lag of a single commodity that could not be stored.[24] The resulting theory of rational expectations is thus another example of how an axiom derived from an economic island of two-dimensional simplicity would morph into a policy doctrine.

As a technical matter, the rational expectations principle is about model consistency: a rational expectations equilibrium imposes the consistency condition that each agent's choice is a best response to the choices made by others in the model. The assumption allows the modeler to tell a story about how agents can make decent probabilistic judgements about the pre-specified and limited point of uncertainty they want to 'test' within that model. The agents' assumed knowledge about the future follows from their total knowledge about the system and, epistemologically speaking, that knowledge is a gift from God, the modeller: it's just there. It follows that all the real-world challenges around information, its limitations, its interpretation and whose interpretations prevail are wished away in that technical assumption.

Drawing on Muth, Lucas's innovation was simply to assume that given sufficient transparency by government about policymaking, *everybody* would adjust their economic behaviour accordingly

---

[23] John Muth, 'Rational Expectations and the Theory of Price Movements', *Econometrica* 29 (1961): 315–335.

[24] Ibid., pp. 316–317.

because they know exactly how the economy works.[25] As John Cassidy explains, Lucas took the Arrow and Debreu theory of general equilibrium and insisted that with slight modifications this was an accurate representation of reality and, by extension, a decent basis for real-world decision-making, something neither Kenneth Arrow nor Gerard Debreu had ever believed. Lucas's assertion had serious implications for Keynesian and interventionist policies in general. His reasoning was that if government cut taxes to encourage higher investment and demand then people wouldn't spend the money but anticipate the later, compensatory, tax hike and save. As Cassidy concluded, 'According to the rational expectations theorists, the government was either powerless or a source of trouble. Insofar as it behaved in a predictable manner, its policies wouldn't make any difference. Insofar as it adapted to this reality by continually surprising the markets, it would destabilize the economy.'[26]

It was via the logic of rational expectations that a new theory, the EMH, came to enjoy the same ubiquity in financial economics rapidly achieved by Lucas's story in macroeconomics. Fama argued that prices in capital markets are always a reflection of their true value and that, contra Keynes, there is no distorting pessimism, optimism or ignorance to lead investors astray. Financial prices are based on fundamental values. In 1970 Fama refined his earlier claims with the idea that there were three forms of efficiency, weak, semi-strong and strong. The efficient market was duly defined as a highly competitive market of rational and informed profit maximisers who vied to predict future market values of individual securities. The EMH assumed prices incorporated all the available information on a market, which included historical financial information (weak form), all new public information (semi-strong form) and all private information regarding a financial asset (strong form).[27]

According to the EMH you could assume that prices in capital markets always reflected true asset values because competitive pressures

---

[25] Robert Lucas, 'Economic Policy Evaluation: A Critique', *Carnegie-Rochester Conference Series on Public Policy* 1 (1976): 19–46.
[26] John Cassidy, *How Markets Fails: The Logic of Economic Calamities* (London: Penguin Books, 2009), pp. 100–101.
[27] Alexanda Gabriela Titan, 'The Efficient Markets Hypothesis: Review of Specialized Literature and Empirical Research', *Procedia Economics and Finance* 32 (2015): 442–449.

forced market participants to make optimal use of available information, avoid systematic errors in their forecasting and update their expectations rapidly in the face of new evidence.[28] Following Muth, the market economy wasted no information. Politically, the EMH legitimised the idea that not only commodity markets but also financial markets were almost perfectly self-adjusting. Deviations of market prices from the underlying fundamentals were merely the product of short-lived noise. It followed that while governments should require informational transparency between market participants, they should otherwise allow markets to play out their wisdom undisturbed.[29]

These theories transformed global financial markets. The EMH instructed governments to weaken financial regulation, because risks had already been integrated into decision-making by the economic agents involved. Buyers could, and would, beware, hence regulation would only add informational noise and create needless costs. Even 'risk management' within a business was rejected as superfluous, since no additional information beyond that given by the market was useful.[30] The EMH encouraged the rise of the passive index funds that, trusting in the 'strong' form of efficiency, bought large baskets of stocks from a given index to replicate the performance of the overall market – a practice that allowed asset managers to drastically reduce their overheads and fees as they no longer had to interpret that market or assess the record of actual companies. For still 'active' funds adhering to the weaker, or semi-strong variant, the EMH powered the rise of quantitative finance: the dependence on complex models that assumed the probability of future losses was calculable on the basis of past data, and it encouraged the belief that such models could achieve high returns for any given level of risk.[31] Camp 1 neoclassical theory had thus encouraged governments and financial and corporate actors to assume the markets assessed risk accurately and set prices that incorporated all available information. Real actors duly began to act as if this was true.

---

[28] Richard Bronk, 'Uncertainty, Modelling Monocultures and the Financial Crisis', *Business Economist* 42 (2) (2011): 5–18, p. 6.
[29] Ibid.
[30] Dave Ingram, Alice Underwood and Michael Thompson, 'Risk Culture, Neoclassical Economics and Enterprise Risk Management', Enterprise Risk Management Symposium, Chicago, 29 September–1 October 2014, p. 5.
[31] Andrew Haldane, 'Why Banks Failed the Stress Test', Marcus-Evans Conference on Stress-Testing, Bank of England, London, 13 February 2009.

That the theories themselves had changed financial behaviour and hence the very nature of the current financial risks appeared to trouble no one. Rational expectations assumptions had encouraged new financial 'derivatives' that were actively misleading in their parcelling and re-parcelling of poor market risks. Since the models used to assess the risks in collateralised debt obligations (CDOs) were built on historical data these innovations alone guaranteed the future could not resemble the past,[32] but intellectual coherence took a back seat to the profits to be made, which were vast. The hegemony of these ideas meant it came as a genuine shock when the crisis in the American subprime mortgage market revealed the over-exposure of the banking system to debts with no realistic prospect of repayment. It wasn't just that the rational expectations and efficient markets hypotheses had been proved wrong. As Richard Bronk points out, the resulting assumptions had caused 'highly correlated "errors" that were anything but random'.[33]

Perfect Indirect Centralisation Revisited...

To see the utopianism of these ideas it helps to recognise them for what they are: the market analogue to the Soviet cybernetic theories of perfect indirect centralisation that emerged in the Kosygin-era debates over optimal planning. The rational expectations theorist Thomas Sargent had actually referred to the 'communism of models', whereby all agents 'inside the model, the econometrician and God share the same model'.[34] Indeed, rational expectations models make frequent use of an assumed 'social planner' as their baseline.[35]

What you find in both is the same mythic function (and logical necessity) that the economic agent has a complete knowledge of the plan/model/market economy in their minds, so that all data can be correctly interpreted, all forecasting errors can be eradicated and any need for the democratic state as an economic referee in an uncertain

---

[32] Bronk, 'Uncertainty', p. 12
[33] Richard Bronk, 'Epistemological Difficulties with Neo-classical Economics', Southern Economic Association Conference Paper, 19–21 November 2011, Washington, DC, p. 4.
[34] George Evans and Seppo Honkapohja, 'Interview with Thomas Sargent', *Macroeconomic Dynamics* 9 (2005): 561–583, pp. 565–567.
[35] Johanna Bockman, *Markets in the Name of Socialism: The Left-Wing Origins of Neoliberalism* (Stanford: Stanford University Press, 2011), p. 174.

world rendered redundant. Under rational expectations, economic agents are, precisely, idealised social planners; they know the structure of the model, the values of the parameters and how any random shock will be distributed. In the EMH they can even converge on an accurate price for future technological potential. All the levels of the economic hierarchy in both theories, Soviet and capitalist, receive all the information they need. In both systems there will be feedback loops that do not waste or distort information but transmit it near perfectly, either through linear programming or through probabilistic calculation in a competitive market within dependable bounds of risk.

Thomas Sargent's only concession to the lack of realism in this argument was to say that

> it is true that modern macroeconomics uses mathematics and statistics to understand behaviour in situations where there is uncertainty about how the future will unfold from the past. But a rule of thumb is that the more dynamic, uncertain, and ambiguous is the economic environment that you seek to model, the more you are going to have to roll up your sleeves and learn and use some math. That's life.[36]

Except, of course, it isn't. The argument is reminiscent of Lenin because it depends on the shared conceit that, given a correct understanding of political economic 'science' – or sufficient mathematics in this case – we can read the world practically straight off the page. Even if the theory were true, so long as those with access to economic reality were limited to economics graduate students the arguments for the existence of informational feedback loops in the economy were going to remain seriously flawed as a representation of what the rest of us know at any time and consequently about how we were likely to behave.

Soviet cyberneticians' dream of the economy as a transparent, dynamic man-machine system, akin to the antimissile systems of the military from which much of the maths was drawn, would never be implemented, as Adam Leeds points out.[37] This suggests that the Brezhnevites operated with a higher level of social realism than the neoliberal governments of the 1990s and 2000s, which is quite the

---

[36] Art Rolnick, 'Interview with Thomas J. Sargent, Thomas Sargent's Rational Expectations', *Hoover Digest*, Number 1, 2012.

[37] Adam Leeds, 'Dreams in Cybernetic Fugue', *Historical Studies in the Natural Sciences* 46 (5) (2016): 633–668, p. 664.

indictment. The Soviet debate at least recognised that for cybernetics to work the whole economy would need to be precisely articulated and integrated within this computation in a dynamic manner. In the EMH, by contrast, it is simply axiomatic that stock prices offer a complete embodiment of all the underlying asset values. Market signals are taken as correct a priori and hence a sound basis for probabilistic forecasts, based on the historical patterns of previous price distributions.

The Soviets had eventually accepted that even cybernetic models would fail to deal with inner-system change: the changing uses of technology and innovation, the intervening layers of human error, partial knowledge, opportunism, institutional adjustment and discovery. They had also conceded that they lacked Godlike foreknowledge, infinite computing power, constant and complete real-time informational access and its perfect, dynamic interpretation and assimilation, and so they had pressed on instead with the imperfect methods of mechanical balance, input–output planning and linear programming. Meanwhile, in the Anglosphere, the EMH and the underlying assumption of rational expectations became the basis of government policy towards financial markets, and as we shall see, it remains the basis of UK government climate strategy.

One might have reasonably expected the Global Financial Crisis to discredit the ideas of predetermined economic mechanics, fully-informed coordinating mechanisms and dependable forecasting in human environments. As Colin Crouch showed in *The Strange Non-death of Neoliberalism,* however, these ideas had penetrated deep into the neoliberal culture.[38] We should consequently expect a neoliberal government to superimpose neoclassical logic onto its analysis of the environment. We can also expect neoliberal governments to argue that private economic agents at all levels, including corporate and financial actors, should be left to self-regulate around climate risk, on the basis that an efficient pricing of risk under rational expectations will prevail. The private sector, including the financial sector, should be protected as a privileged domain, free of government restraint. If climate change becomes more politically salient, then neoliberal governments have

---

[38] Colin Crouch, *The Strange Non-death of Neoliberalism* (Cambridge: Polity Press, 2011); Stephen Wilks, *The Political Power of the Business Corporation* (Cheltenham: Edward Elgar, 2013).

a fallback position, which is that they too can place a high degree of confidence in risk management, in forecasting and in audit. Where the precautionary principle would require they end the known causes of harm as soon as possible,[39] neoliberals instead seek to minimise new state interventions, even as the legacies of past interventions mean the corporate lobbies and structural dependencies attached to fossil fuels, and to other damaging materials and practices, remain strong.

Risk Management

If we go back to the concept of Kuhn-loss and ask, 'what was lost when we forget about uncertainty?' we must include the capacity of diverse social institutions, including the state, to take precautionary and strategic action: to develop new technologies, coordinate expertise and solve problems. Instead, neoliberal societies shifted ever more wholeheartedly towards what Michael Power describes as a 'world level grand narrative of risk management' across multiple areas of policymaking.[40] 'Risk management' has consequently come to be regarded as central to good government,[41] as well as an effective substitute for the precautionary principle and the strategic thinking and active prioritisations that should go with it. The idea of insurable risk has operated effectively for centuries. The principle of insurance is that there are phenomena of such predictability about which we have accurate and reliable data, that an effective market can be built to manage risks through insurances. In insurance systems the premiums paid are used to smooth out future income losses caused by events, such as house fires, that occur with relatively stable frequency. Under neoliberalism, however, the concept of calculable risk has increasingly colonised policymaking arenas characterised by uncertainty.[42]

---

[39] Joseph Norman, Rupert Read, Yaneer Bar-Yam and Nassim Nicholas Taleb, 'The Precautionary Principle (with Application to the Genetic Modification of Organisms', Extreme Risk Initiative, NYU School of Engineering Working Paper Series, 4 September 2014.
[40] Michael Power, *Organised Uncertainty: Designing a World of Risk Management* (Oxford: Oxford University Press, 2007), viii.
[41] Tom Horlick-Jones, 'On Risk Work: Professional Discourse, Accountability and Everyday Action', *Health, Risk and Society* 7 (3) (September 2005): 293–307.
[42] Richard Brooks, *The Triumph of the Bean Counters and How They Broke Capitalism* (London: Atlantic Books, 2018).

Today's climate uncertainty relates not to the likelihood of catastrophic harm, which is certain without action, but to exactly when, in what order and at what magnitude ecological tipping points are likely to occur. This renders a government preference for a risk assessment, forecasting, monitoring, auditing and hence supposedly 'efficient' decarbonisation strategy both over-optimistic and, by definition, behind the curve of damaging cumulative effects. This is not to say that risk assessment is useless. Monitoring and assessment are informative, but risk management is the wrong primary paradigm. As Joseph Norman et al. explain, risk-assessment techniques such as cost–benefit analysis assume that decisions can be made by accounting for the effects of positive and negative outcomes and their probabilities, and they tend to assume that strategies are available to offset losses and mitigate harms. But these are not realistic options in cases of potential ruin.[43] Such approaches are nevertheless consistent with neoclassical reasoning in which no single or cumulative events are capable of shifting the economic world off its axis.

Norman et al. make a vital distinction between damage from innovation that is local and limited and risks under uncertainty that are potentially total, that is, uninsurable risks. In the first situation, risk management and cost–benefit analyses remain useful; the benefit of innovation can be coherently traded off against the risk of structurally recoverable harm. In the second, there is no acceptable trade-off, because losses are potentially total or systematically catastrophic. Climate change is the textbook case for the precautionary principle, precisely because it combines certainties of unrecoverable harm on present courses with uncertainty about the exact timing and trajectory of harm and because there is no institution capable of bailing out the biosphere. Forecasting and audit have nevertheless emerged as dominant climate risk-assessment techniques under neoliberalism, with Integrated Assessment Models (IAMs) and cost–benefit analyses playing a particularly important role.

IAMs combine climate science with the supposed economic impact of ecological change. Widely used for policy evaluation, including by the Intergovernmental Panel on Climate Change (IPCC), they take a standard neoclassical approach to exploring likely effects on aggregate, economy-wide welfare, where the challenge is to

---

[43] Norman et al., 'The Precautionary Principle', p. 3.

figure out the most efficient market solution to a social problem under the given parameters. Like all neoclassical models, they produce radically different outcomes depending on the axioms and values that govern the inputs. IAMs thus upload rational choice micro-foundations that make sense in 'small worlds', where all contingencies might genuinely be foreseen, to conditions of radical complexity and uncertainty.[44] As the Massachusetts Institute of Technology economist Robert Pindyck explains, the 'damage function' in IAMs defines the relationship between an increase in temperature and gross domestic product, but while there is relatively robust physical science to offer probability distributions around climate sensitivity, there is no theory or data to draw on from the economic side. The fact that climate change is known to hold uncertain but accelerating and non-linear risks for most, if not all economic factors, means IAMs tend to systematically underestimate risk because of the tendency to use historical parameter values.[45] IAMs also exclude key dimensions of climate change that cannot be described in neoclassical terms, such as the unparalleled loss of human life and mass extinction of species.[46]

The risks of misdirection and moral evasion are equally high in cost–benefit analysis models if the choices of discounting and inter-temporal values for climate change are again assumed to be the same as those for which investment projects are usually assessed, that is, according to 'steady-state' conditions or historical capital markets trends.[47] The result is status quo bias again, because of the non-pricing of ecologically important factors and the impossibility of pricing in unanticipated ecological interactions. The same problems apply to corporate use of forecasting data: as the current market for 'catastrophe bonds' demonstrates, past data is no longer as reliable as it used to be for the pricing of nature-related risk-linked securities. How *do* you price the probability and likely costs of hurricanes, floods and wildfires under climate collapse?

---

[44] Antony Millner, Simon Dietz and Geoffrey Heal, 'Ambiguity and Climate Policy', Centre for Climate Change Economics and Policy Working Paper No. 28, December 2010, pp. 2–3.
[45] Robert Pindyck, 'Climate Change Policy: What Do the Models Tell Us?', *Journal of Economic Literature* 51 (3) (September 2013): 860–872, p. 862.
[46] Stern, *Why Are We Waiting?*, p. 148.
[47] Ibid., p. 156–158.

As Power identified in *The Audit Society*, there is a further distinctive danger that arises from risk methodologies, namely that procedural formalism around quantification, monitoring and reporting can easily become a substitute for substantive action. As governments and corporations take up risk management by quantification, more effort can be put into systems of control, or even into systems of 'control of control', than into problem-solving itself. The temptations are great, as risk assessment and audit are cheaper than purposive action and provide 'comforting signals to regulators and politicians',[48] and the history of the Soviet Union shows us how debilitating such formalism can become. For neoliberal governments and businesses alike, the clear risk is that carbon targets, budgets and plans become dead letters the day they are published, and business-as-usual is resumed, as we wait for the wisdom of the market to see us through.

Summary

The more you rely on the assumptions of Camp 1, the more you will favour the wisdom of markets, though markets have historically failed to consider, let alone value, the eco-system, since nature is an unconsidered 'externality'. For Camp 2 neoclassicists minded towards 'liberal environmentalism', such externalities are a market failure to be solved by regulations and new markets that price these 'costs' back in, as if everyone would suddenly define their own utility in terms perfectly consistent with the flourishing of the natural world and within a ceaselessly efficient market. It is outrageous hubris, however, to imagine that the two-dimensional neoclassical thought experiment could represent a dependable governance mechanism, not just for the human economy but, by implication, for the biosphere – that nature's equilibrium and an entirely fictional general economic equilibrium can be made consistent with each other. In conditions of radical uncertainty about tipping points, the placement of all ecological factors into a linear scale of monetary value obscures the enormity – the totality – of the risks.

If we turn now to policy practice, we can see to what extent UK governments have reacted to the climate emergency with assumptions,

---

[48] Michael Power, The Audit Society: Rituals of Verification (Oxford: Oxford University Press, 1999), pp. 114–115.

policies and methods built on neoclassical economics. Based on the discussion so far, we would expect to find the following:

- The presumption of immutable system stability will tend to crowd out the precautionary principle. Neoliberal governments will consequently adopt the view that the private sector is a privileged domain that should be allowed to self-regulate around climate risk.
- Neoliberal governments under political pressure for state action will lean into risk-assessment techniques, cost–benefit analysis and IAMs as forecasting methods, despite their known weaknesses among climate specialists. Given the resilience of the underlying ideological beliefs this reliance is likely to degenerate into procedural formalism, such as non-compulsory target setting for private actors and carbon budgets and targets for governments that go unfulfilled.
- Even more moderate Camp 2 neoliberal governments will limit their interventions to the resolution of specific market failures in existing markets and they will tend to prefer purely market-friendly policy instruments under the illusion that market completion will be biosphere-consistent. Camp 1 governments that inherit such interventions will seek to eradicate these measures as unwarranted in markets that are presumptively rational and competitive. The unwillingness of both camps to intervene against existing markets will sustain the structural advantages held by those polluting producers and practices that continue to cause the ecological emergency.

The next section shows how the paradigm shift we urgently need is thwarted in the United Kingdom by utopian assumptions about the rationality of markets and the idea that risk can be fully calculated, hence modelled, hence forecast and hence fully integrated within existing market mechanisms.

The Politics of Climate Change in the United Kingdom

Before we look at government strategies in detail it is helpful to know the general direction of travel in UK climate politics, though it is important to note that after 1999 the Scottish Parliament, the National Assembly for Wales and the Northern Ireland Assembly also acquired varied responsibilities and some limited devolved powers to set further targets and climate strategies, and Scotland tends to be more ambitious in its renewable energy targets,[49] as well as to reduce its emissions faster.[50] The history of climate policy in Westminster, however, is that of a growing acknowledgement of the threat, the introduction of targeted, 'market-friendly' policies under New Labour and the Conservative–Liberal Coalition and the significant reversal of those policies by the Camp 1 Conservative governments from 2015 to the time of writing.

Margaret Thatcher had accepted the evidence of the IPCC, established in 1988,[51] and her decision to make a rapid switch from coal to gas also gave her a revolutionary victory at home, as the largely unmitigated shock to the UK coal industry devastated the strongly unionised, Labour-voting communities built around it. The 1992 Rio Earth Summit paved the way for the eventual agreement of the Kyoto Protocol in 1997, which committed the ratifying countries to greenhouse gas emissions reductions for 2008–2012. Thatcher's successor, John Major, continued support in principle and the United Kingdom's 'dash for gas' set it on course to deliver its Kyoto commitments for a 13 per cent reduction in carbon dioxide emissions relative to 1990.[52]

New Labour had promised to be 'the first truly green government that Britain has ever seen'. Its 1997 manifesto committed to reduce carbon dioxide emissions by 20 per cent from 1990 levels by 2010 and to 'mainstream' green policies into every department. It offered no policies, however, and the agenda was folded into the party's general promise to champion technological modernisation.[53] It was three years before the Tony Blair Labour government created a Climate Change Programme to deliver the 1997 target, but its measures offered

---

[49] House of Commons Environmental Audit Committee, 'Climate Change and Local, Regional and Devolved Government', 28 July 2008 (HC 225), p. 32, www.publications.parliament.uk/pa/cm200708/cmselect/cmenvaud/225/225.pdf.
[50] The Climate Change Committee, 'Scotland Still Outperforms the UK in Reducing Emissions but Transport and Agriculture Remain Significant Challenges', 24 September 2018, www.theccc.org.uk/2018/09/24/scotland-still-outperforms-the-uk-in-reducing-emissions-but-transport-and-agriculture-remain-significant-challenges/.
[51] Margaret Thatcher, 'Speech at 2nd World Climate Conference', Geneva, 6 November 1990, www.margaretthatcher.org/document/108237.
[52] Jill Rutter, Edward Marshall and Sam Sims, 'The "S" Factor, Lessons from IFG's Policy Success Reunions', Institute for Government, 2012, p. 111.
[53] The Labour Party, 'Because Britain Deserves Better', Party Manifesto, 1997.

only a 10.6 per cent reduction by 2010.[54] What had started as a bold claim for a new form of economic development had immediately been watered down to cohere with the neoclassical notion of 'competitiveness' at the domestic level.

Neil Carter's extensive analysis shows the three main parties merely 'covered their backs' on climate change during the Blair years. The first Blair government (1997–2001) had helped secure the Kyoto Protocol, and the second (2001–2005) signed the United Kingdom up to the European Union's Emissions Trading Scheme launched in 2005. But while Labour led at the international level, it retreated at home in the face of a business community that rejected decarbonising measures on Camp 1 grounds: as a pure cost and competitive disadvantage.[55] Facing continuous business pressure to ignore the climate risks, not least from the Confederation of British Industry, New Labour drove expansions of commercial aviation, road-building and non-intervention in regulatory terms around commercial and domestic buildings.[56] By November 2004, Greenpeace director Stephen Tindale concluded that 'Blair's record on climate change is almost entirely a record of fine words and no action' and leading non-government organisations (NGOs) broke with the government.[57] There was little mention of climate change in Blair's 2005 election campaign speeches and little pressure from the Conservative Party on an issue now avoided by both as 'bad politics'.[58]

It wasn't until public concern over climate change began to grow, in 2006, that political parties began to compete over policy and lead from the front. Higher public awareness had been achieved by a wider dissemination of the science. Media coverage grew around the *Stern Review* of 2006 and, a year later, the 'Report of the Fourth International Panel on Climate Change'. Crucially, the *Stern Review* had challenged the complacency of industry, business and finance,

---

[54] Oliver Ilott, Joe Randall, Alex Bleasdale and Emma Norris, 'Making Policy Stick: Tackling Long-Term Challenges in Government', Institute for Government, 2016, p. 17.
[55] Neil Carter, 'Combatting Climate Change in the UK: Challenges and Obstacles', *Political Quarterly* 79 (2) (2008): 194–205, p. 198–199.
[56] Ibid., p. 200.
[57] Marie Wolf, 'Greens Declare War on Blair for "Failures" over Climate Change', *The Independent*, 19 November 2004.
[58] Carter, 'Combatting Climate Change', p. 197.

though by no means eradicated it.[59] Encouraged by polls that showed some 80 per cent of the population felt 'some concern', mainstream political parties shifted to a 'preference shaping' strategy. Carter shows how David Cameron's election as Conservative leader in May 2005, and his attention to shifting public opinion, forced Labour to focus. Blair's failure to act had mobilised a broad coalition of NGOs and charities to call for a Climate Change Bill. When Cameron signed up in its favour it was a political coup. As his advisor Nick Boles put it, a strong stance on climate change would give the Conservatives a necessary 'eye catching yank into a new place',[60] and the Labour government came under further pressures as the Liberals joined too. In October, Environment Secretary Ed Miliband declared the government would introduce a Bill and instruct a new unit, the Office of Climate Change (OCC), to change the course of policymaking. All three major parties whipped in favour, and the Climate Change Bill became law in November 2008.[61]

The Climate Change Act projected three carbon budgets to set out reductions in emissions: a 28 per cent reduction on 1990 levels through 2008–2012; a 29 per cent reduction through 2013–2017 and a 35 per cent reduction through 2018–2022; it further set a target for 2050: for an 80 per cent reduction on 1990 levels. It also committed governments to pass further budgets in the future. The 2050 target was defined as a legal duty: a world first. The Act required governments to publish plans to meet those commitments and drove a major investment in institutional capacity in the form of a politically independent and multi-disciplinary expert Climate Change Committee (CCC) to ensure targets were evidence-based and independently assessed. The CCC would establish 'the vision and the strategic direction' of policy and an Adaptation Sub-committee to advise on climate risks and assesses progress and would report to Parliament on the progress.[62] To help organise action the government

---

[59] Neil Carter, 'The Politics of Climate Change in the UK', *WIRE's Climate Change* 5 (3) (2014): 423–433, pp. 425, 427.
[60] Institute for Government, 'Policy Reunion on the Climate Change Act (2008)', Institute for Government, London, 6 October 2010, p. 115.
[61] Ilott et al., 'Making Policy Stick', p. 19.
[62] The Climate Change Committee, 'The UK Climate Change Act', www.theccc.org.uk/wp-content/uploads/2020/10/CCC-Insights-Briefing-1-The-UK-Climate-Change-Act.pdf.

also established a new Department for Energy and Climate Change (DECC) to consolidate energy and climate change issues into one leading organisation.

The Act's focus was strikingly narrow, however. Climate change mitigation was not embedded into any wider sustainable development objectives – a serious omission given the interdependent losses in global biodiversity and the growing threat of resource scarcity. Even more significantly, the Act understood the role of government in Camp 2 neoclassical terms. Government was there to correct market failures and otherwise rely on markets to be 'guided' via targets and market incentives. Beyond the establishment of new energy markets, it tended to eschew statutory requirements or direct channels of public investment, decisive regulatory intervention or funded empowerment of local authorities.[63] Lauded as radical, the Act epitomised the neoclassical Treasury playbook at its most interventionist: scenario planning, economy-wide targets and performance monitoring, with government action limited to making markets or to imitating them via targets and quotas.

By autumn 2008, the Global Financial Crisis had struck, and the financial sector bailout and the challenges of economic recovery became paramount. In Coalition after the 2010 election, Conservative interest in the environment was revealed as an electoral expedient to help 'detoxify' the Conservative brand in opposition, and the party now reverted to Camp 1 doctrine as the calculus of political competition changed. Cameron made only two speeches officially labelled as climate-related through his entire first term, and only one of them mentioned 'climate change' and 'global warming'.[64] In the face of the government policy of austerity, climate change would peak as the sixth most important issue facing the United Kingdom in 2007 until the late 2010s.[65]

As one of only two major policy departments with a Liberal secretary of state, the DECC had initially survived the 2010 austerity

---

[63] Sam Fankhauser, Alina Averchenkova and Jared Finnegan, 'Ten Years of the UK Climate Change Act', Grantham Research Institute on Climate Change, LSE, April 2018.

[64] Simon Bushell, Mark Workman and Thomas Colley, 'Towards a Unifying Narrative of Climate Change', Grantham Institute Working Paper, Number 18, April 2016.

[65] Carter, 'The Politics of Climate Change', p. 427.

cuts; indeed, it increased its headcount by 40 per cent.[66] In 2011 the Fourth Carbon Budget was set at a 50 per cent reduction of 1990 levels through 2023–2027, in line with CCC advice. As Carter and Ben Clements show, however, although the Coalition implemented some important measures, on which more later, these were driven by the Liberals in the teeth of hardening Conservative resistance. In 2008, a third of Conservative MPs had questioned the validity of climate science, and by 2010 that hostility was open, and George Osborne reset the government line.[67] That the chancellor was determined to enact Camp 1 policy would prove lethal to climate realism given the Treasury's fiscal authority and Cameron's deference to Osborne on political strategy.[68] Conservatives increasingly played climate change for its potential to divide voters in their favour, a 'positional' issue. The Conservative right would duly designate climate change a socialist-conspiracy-by-stealth,[69] in line with Camp 1 logic.

In October 2011, Osborne told the Conservative Party Conference that 'we're not going to save the planet by putting our country out of business' and promised to stop the United Kingdom from cutting emissions more quickly than its European counterparts in a direct appeal to the principle of jurisdictional competition.[70] In February 2012, 101 Conservative MPs wrote to the prime minister to call for dramatic reductions in subsidies to wind power.[71] Osborne wrote to the energy secretary that summer demanding that unabated gas continue to play a core role in electricity generation to at least 2030, that government should set no 2030 target for electricity emissions and that a cap should be set on those decarbonisation policy costs financed

---

[66] Ilott et al., 'Making Policy Stick', p. 19.
[67] Neil Carter and Ben Clements, 'From "Greenest Government Ever" to "Get Rid of All the Green Crap": David Cameron, the Conservatives and the Environment', *British Politics* 10 (2) (2015): 204–225, p. 209.
[68] Francis Elliott and James Hanning, *Cameron: Practically a Conservative* (London: Fourth Estate, 2012), p. 423.
[69] Carter and Clements, 'From "Greenest Government Ever" to "Get Rid of All the Green Crap"', p. 222.
[70] Greg Philo and Catherine Happer, *Communicating Climate Change and Energy Security* (Abingdon: Routledge, 2013), p. 3.
[71] Patrick Hennessy, '101 Tories Revolt over Wind Farms', *The Telegraph*, 4 February 2012.

through energy bills.[72] By November 2013, Cameron had moved from declaring that the Coalition would be 'the greenest government ever' to privately 'going round Number 10 saying: "We have got to get rid of all this green crap".... "We used to say, 'Vote Blue, Go Green', now it's 'Vote Blue, Get Real'"'[73] – a statement that demonstrates how confused the concept of 'realism' had become.

In 2014, the European Union set targets of a 40 per cent carbon cut and a 27 per cent share of renewables by 2030.[74] At the start of 2015, a bipartisan agreement was brokered by the Green Alliance think tank and supported by Christian Aid, The Catholic Agency for Overseas Development, Greenpeace, the Royal Society for the Protection of Birds and the World Wildlife Fund in anticipation of the year-long negotiations in the run-up to the Paris Summit in December. Under renewed media attention, the three main party leaders David Cameron, Ed Miliband and Nick Clegg pledged 'To seek a fair, strong, legally binding, global climate deal which limits temperature rises to below 2°C; To work together, across party lines, to agree carbon budgets in accordance with the Climate Change Act; To accelerate the transition to a competitive, energy efficient low carbon economy and to end the use of unabated coal for power generation'.[75] Starting in May 2015, however, Cameron's second, now standalone, Conservative government enacted comprehensive policy reversals, explored later. In June 2016, Cameron resigned over the failure of his 'Remain' position in the Brexit referendum, and Theresa May replaced him as the Conservative prime minister.

May abolished DECC on her second day in office and moved climate change responsibilities into the new Department for Business, Energy and Industrial Strategy (BEIS).[76] The Fifth Carbon Budget was

---

[72] Matthew Lockwood, 'The Political Sustainability of Climate Policy: The Case of the UK Climate Change Act', *Global Environmental Change* 23 (2013): 1339–1348, pp. 1340–1341.

[73] Andrew Sparrow, 'Did Cameron Tell Aides to "Get Rid of All the Green Crap"?', *The Guardian*, 21 November 2013.

[74] European Commission, '2030 Climate and Energy Framework', https://climate.ec.europa.eu/eu-action/climate-strategies-targets/2030-climate-energy-framework_en.

[75] Climate Change Committee, 'CCC Welcomes Climate Change Agreement', 16 February 2015, www.theccc.org.uk/2015/02/16/ccc-welcomes-climate-change-agreement/.

[76] Ian Johnston, 'Climate Change Department Closed by Theresa May in "Plain Stupid" and "Deeply Worrying" Move', *The Independent*, 14 July 2016.

set at 57 per cent reduction on 1990 levels through 2028–2032, again, in line with the independent advice of the CCC. However, in its 2017 progress report, the CCC warned that neither the Fourth nor the Fifth Carbon Budgets would be met, as existing strategies and policy had been insufficient since 2015. By 2017, most of the success in reducing emissions had come from sharp reductions in the power and waste sectors but there was a critical lack of progress elsewhere: in agriculture, private housing (reductions in public and commercial buildings were deemed hardly to have begun), industry, transport and fluorinated gases (e.g., refrigerants). The CCC also warned that since much of the policy driving environmental improvements came from the European Union, Brexit would mean domestic replacements were urgently needed. It concluded that 'by 2030, current plans would at best deliver around half of the required reduction in emissions, 100–170 MtCO2e per year short of what is required by the carbon budgets'.[77]

The 2017 Conservative manifesto, 'Forward Together', made no proposals on climate change and the first of its 'Five Giant Challenges' was to create a strong, high-growth economy.[78] It also pledged continued support for the oil and gas industries and for fracking, though fundamentally incompatible with the United Kingdom's international commitments. In October 2017, the now minority Conservative government revealed a much-delayed Clean Growth Strategy, which promised to combine transition to a low-carbon economy with increased economic growth while insisting that '[e]very action to cut emissions must be taken while ensuring our economy remains competitive'.[79] The CCC concluded that 'even taking account of the Strategy's aspirations, a gap in meeting the fourth and fifth carbon budgets remains. Urgent policy development is therefore required'.[80]

---

[77] Climate Change Committee, '2017 Report to Parliament: Meeting Carbon Budgets – Closing the Policy Gap', 29 June 2017, Executive Summary.

[78] The Conservative and Unionist Party, 'Forward Together: Our Plan for a Stronger Britain and a Prosperous Future', Party Manifesto, 2017.

[79] HM Government, 'The Clean Growth Strategy: Leading the Way to a Low Carbon Future', October 2017, pp. 10, 43, https://assets.publishing.service.gov.uk/government/uploads/system/uploads/attachment_data/file/700496/clean-growth-strategy-correction-april-2018.pdf.

[80] Climate Change Committee, 'An Independent Assessment of the UK's Clean Growth Strategy', January 2018, p. 5, www.theccc.org.uk/wp-content/uploads/2018/01/CCC-Independent-Assessment-of-UKs-Clean-Growth-Strategy-2018.pdf.

When the Conservative government was supposed to develop the strategy further with 'A Green Future: Our 25 Year Plan to Improve the Environment in 2018', it spoke in Panglossian terms of development that produced 'environmental net gains' while 'ensuring economic growth and reduced costs, complexity and delays for developers'.

Both May administrations in practice endeavoured to shut down key mitigation policies dating from the Climate Change Act. They also supported a massive expansion of UK aviation, as documented in 'Aviation 2050: The Future of UK Aviation'.[81] From 2019, the governments of Boris Johnson were more rhetorically green even as they threw climate policy more completely into reverse with support for a new coal mine, the issuance of new licences for oil and gas exploration, the halving of overseas aid, slashed incentives for electric cars, the closure of the green homes grant and support for airport expansion.[82] By 2021 the CCC was trenchant in its criticism of his government's inaction.[83]

In sum, as the leaders of explicitly 'modernising' movements within their parties, both Blair and Cameron had squandered their opportunities to change the narrative. Instead, when faced with domestic political risks they had taken the path of least resistance as defined within the neoclassical paradigm. With the exception of the Camp 2 efforts of 2006–2010, what followed was a restoration of the Camp 1 conceptual framework. No British government has attempted to build a political consensus for a substantial, rapid and potentially hugely positive institutional and social transition towards a green political economy.[84] Two major programmes of climate action had

---

[81] Department of Transport, 'Aviation 2050: The Future of UK Aviation', December 2018 (CM9714), www.assets.publishing.service.gov.uk/government/uploads/system/uploads/attachment_data/file/769695/aviation-2050-web.pdf.

[82] Fiona Harvey, 'Boris Johnson Told to Get Grip of UK Climate Strategy before COP 26', *The Guardian*, 12 April 2021.

[83] Climate Change Committee, '2021 Progress Report to Parliament', 24 June 2021, www.theccc.org.uk/publication/2021-progress-report-to-parliament/.

[84] The Grantham Institute, 'Climate Change Communication: Taking a Leaf from the Brexit Book', 10 June 2016, Grantham Institute, Imperial College, London, www.granthaminstitute.com/2016/06/10/taking-a-leaf-from-the-brexit-book-what-climate-change-communicators-can-learn-from-the-eu-referendum-campaigns/.

been established – the Climate Change Programme of 2000 and the Climate Change Act of 2008 – but both were fatally weakened by subsequent governments. As one senior policy analyst commented in the Grantham Centre's ten-year review of the Climate Change Act, 'the [Theresa May] government may support the Act, "but they got rid of almost all the policies designed to implement it"'.[85] If we run through the detail of UK climate policy, we see how the already narrowly conceived Climate Change Act was effectively overridden by the Camp 1 dogma of market rationality.

The Privileged Domain

The contradiction at the heart of neoliberal policy is that if economic actors were, in fact, rational in the face of future risk, we would not be where we are. The United Kingdom's corporate and financial sectors have nonetheless been designated privileged domains, as predicted. There are no legal requirements for corporations to address long-term climate-related systemic risk, and their fiduciary duties remain around the maximisation of shareholder value. At the time of writing, the policy debate has been stalled between government, Parliament and the regulatory authorities on the question of whether climate-related financial risk *reporting* should remain voluntary or mandatory – codified or ad hoc.

The Companies Act 2006 and further 2013 regulations required the Directors' Business Report of traded financial or non-financial firms to include the environment, but in reporting terms only. The report must include the main trends and factors likely to affect the future development, performance and position of the company's business and information about (1) environmental matters (including the impact of the company's business on the environment), (2) the company's employees and (3) social and community issues.[86] Further 2013 regulations added greenhouse gas (GHG) emissions to this list. New regulations in 2016 added more environmental impact reporting for traded, banking and insurance companies, and 2018 additions introduced obligations to report on energy use in large unquoted companies and limited

---

[85] Fankhauser, Averchenkova and Finnegan, 'Ten Years', p. 26.
[86] Companies Act 2006, Section 417. www.legislation.gov.uk/ukpga/2006/46/section/417/2007-10-01?view=plain.

liability partnerships.[87] But no external verification is required around the quality of this reporting, and investors can respond as they choose.

In 2020, the law firm Client Earth reviewed the annual reports of the largest 250 companies listed on the Main Market of the London Stock Exchange and found that only 4 per cent made a clear reference to climate change-related factors in their financial accounts. Some 40 per cent of companies referred to climate among their principal risks and uncertainties, but only 31 per cent disclosed a target to reduce emissions. Despite improvements, the overall picture was of rising rhetorical attention, low clarity about strategies for change and a significant gap in accountability and enforcement.[88] These trends should be understood in the context of financialisation, discussed in Chapter 7, and they were also mirrored internationally.

At the international level a Financial Stability Board had been founded in 2009 in response to the Global Financial Crisis. It brought together senior policy makers from finance ministries, central banks and supervisory and regulatory authorities from the G20 countries plus Hong Kong, Singapore, Spain and Switzerland. Its remit was to 'promote global financial stability by coordinating the development of regulatory, supervisory and other financial sector policies'.[89] At the request of the G20 in 2015, the board established a private sector, industry-led Task Force on Climate-Related Financial Disclosures (TCFD), with a mandate to develop consistent, comparable, clear and reliable disclosures around climate-related financial risks for companies, which they did. However, despite several members fighting for mandatory rules, the resulting disclosure framework was voluntary. By 2018, only 15 per cent of Financial Times Stock Exchange (FTSE) companies reported in line with TCFD requirements and hydrocarbons were the standout sector: 100 per cent of FTSE 100 electricity, gas and oil companies were fully aligned with the TCFD recommendations.[90]

---

[87] HM Government, 'Environmental Reporting Guidelines: Including Streamlined Energy and Reporting Guidelines', March 2019, p. 26, www.gov.uk/government/publications/environmental-reporting-guidelines-including-mandatory-greenhouse-gas-emissions-reporting-guidance.

[88] Client Earth, 'Accountability Emergency: A Review of UK Listed Companies Climate Change-Related Reporting (2019–2020)', February 2021, Executive Summary.

[89] Financial Stability Board, www.fsb.org.

[90] Eco-Act, 'The Sustainability Reporting Performance of the FTSE 100', 10th Annual Report, 23 September 2020, p. 18.

The most destructive companies on earth thus remained fully compliant with international best practice.

On the finance side there are no legal requirements on fund managers, sell-side researchers, credit rating agencies or investment consultants to review corporate disclosures around environmental risks or to advise their investors on the implications for their portfolios. The dominant culture of maximising the ratio of profit to investment (as distinct from thinking of the sustainability and potential of the combined assets) continued to dominate. By June 2021 the world's leading index fund, Blackrock, controlled assets under management of some $9.5 trillion worldwide, or roughly equivalent to the entire global hedge fund, private equity fund and venture capital fund combined.[91] The EMH had provided the rationale for passive funds, but their ecological record has been dismal, with a clear tendency to vote against shareholder resolutions for improved scenario planning and risk reporting.[92] In 2021 Blackrock's CEO, Larry Fink, had made great play of declaring that CEOs should report how they would transform their businesses to become compatible with net zero,[93] but his fund retained $85 billion worth of investment in coal companies a whole year after its January 2020 pledge to disinvest.[94] Blackrock's former head of sustainable investing-turned-whistle blower, Tariq Fancy, concluded in the same year that nothing would steer Wall Street from short-term profit maximisation at any cost until corporate carbon emissions were taxed.[95] In 2022 Blackrock announced it would reject most shareholder resolutions on climate change in the coming financial year on the basis that they had become too extreme or too prescriptive.[96]

---

[91] Robin Wigglesworth, 'The Ten Trillion Dollar Man: How Larry Fink Became the King of Wall Street', *Financial Times*, 7 October 2021.
[92] Attracta Mooney, 'Blackrock and Vanguard's Climate Change Efforts Are Glacial', *Financial Times*, 15 October 2017.
[93] Larry Fink, 'Larry Fink's 2021 Letter to CEOs', www.blackrock.com/us/individual/2021-larry-fink-ceo-letter.
[94] Jasper Jolly, 'BlackRock Holds $85 Billion in Coal Despite Pledge to Sell Fossil Fuel Shares', *The Guardian*, 31 January 2021.
[95] Andrew Brown, 'ESG Whistle-Blower Calls Out Wall Street Greenwashing', *New Economy Daily*, Bloomberg, 2 October 2021.
[96] Brooke Masters, 'Blackrock Warns It Will Vote against More Climate Resolutions This Year', *Financial Times*, 22 May 2022.

British investment funds in general ranked worst in Europe by 2017 for climate change impact and for assessing the investment risks of global warming,[97] a situation unlikely to improve as UK investors shifted towards the passive funds, led by Blackrock.[98] The EMH had assumed that competitive pressures forced all market participants to make optimal use of available information and update their expectations in the face of new evidence, but in practice it has been used to justify an emerging oligopoly of asset management firms that now leverage their exceptional market power to slow the climate transition. The upshot is a regime of asset control that cleaves ever more towards its Soviet shadow: a growing concentration of corporate control justified by a fiction of universal rationality. The Soviet system too had demanded enterprises exceed their annual targets regardless of their environmental impact, and that too had marched on, heedless of the devastation it caused.

When it became apparent that even pension funds were tending to ignore climate-related risks, the United Kingdom's Environmental Audit Committee ran an inquiry into Greening Finance. This concluded that the structural incentives for short-termism constituted a significant systemic risk and proposed that 'government should clarify in law that pension schemes and company directors have a duty to protect long-term value and should be considering environmental risks in the light of this'. In November 2018, the Conservative government refused the committee's recommendation to make climate risk disclosures mandatory and insisted on the sufficiency of corporate choice, though no environmental group agreed. On the contrary, those groups pointed out that given the multiple intermediaries down the asset chain, from asset owners, asset managers, asset consultants and legal advisors to accountants, at minimum the TCFD standards needed to be locked into legal contracts throughout that chain, a position agreed by the committee but, again, rejected by the government.[99] At the same time,

---

[97] Attracta Mooney, 'British Companies Rank Worst in Europe for Climate Change Impact', *Financial Times*, 15 November 2017.

[98] The Investment Association, 'Asset Management in the UK 2015-2016', The Investment Association Annual Survey, September 2016 and September 2018 editions.

[99] House of Commons Environmental Audit Committee, 'Greening Finance: Embedding Sustainability in Financial Decision Making', 23 May 2018 (HC 1063), p. 41, www.publications.parliament.uk/pa/cm201719/cmselect/cmenvaud/1063/1063.pdf.

neither the Financial Reporting Council (responsible for the oversight of statutory audit) nor the Financial Conduct Authority (responsible for the oversight of corporate governance) has appeared willing to clampdown on failures to disclose information even within the weak existing rules. Recall that even the EMH insists that governments must enforce corporate informational transparency, but UK policy operates at sub-EMH standards when it comes to climate-related financial risk reporting. Moreover, the Camp 2 solution of a shift to mandatory and codified risk reporting remains a utopian solution. Though a positive step in itself, it is still an EMH conceit to believe that a reduction in the marginal cost of collecting information must cause market prices to adjust to reflect true asset values, and that all financial actors will respond accordingly.

Public Finance

When it comes to financing new technologies, the cost of borrowing tends to increase with the project's perceived riskiness, with the options for equity stakes in the firms involved, and the creditworthiness of the borrower. The more established the technologies, such as fossil fuels, the cheaper their finance.[100] Public financing is consequently vital for a green transition since states can borrow at the lowest interest rates of all. In UK policy, however, this fact was pushed aside by doctrine. Following hard on the heels of the Climate Change Act, the new Coalition government had acknowledged that green technologies played at a disadvantage and established a Green Investment Bank (GIB) with initial investment capital in 2012. From its launch, and for the duration of 2015–2016, the GIB was wholly publicly owned. Its remit was to aid investment in green infrastructure, mobilise private sector capital and support projects that would otherwise lack funding. By 2015 the GIB had invested £2.3 billion of public money into sixty projects with a total value of over £10 billion.[101]

In line with Camp 1 reasoning, however, the next Conservative government announced the GIB's privatisation, in June 2015. The business

---

[100] Stern, *Why Are We Waiting?*, p. 66.
[101] House of Commons Environmental Audit Committee, 'The Future of the Green Investment Bank', 16 December 2015 (HC 536), p. 4, www.publications.parliament.uk/pa/cm201516/cmselect/cmenvaud/536/536.pdf.

secretary, Sajid Javid, argued that privatisation would provide better access to capital, though the inadequacy of private finance was the reason the bank had been created. The Environmental Audit Committee ran an inquiry into whether privatisation could deliver improvements, only to conclude that more capital could have been achieved by public sector borrowing and that the privatisation was happening 'without due transparency, publication of relevant evidence, consultation or proper consideration of alternatives'. The inquiry also noted that once privatised, the bank would invest in areas that would undermine its role.[102] The government also ignored warnings that the preferred bidder, Macquarie Group Limited, would asset-strip the GIB, and the bank was sold to Macquarie in August 2017.

The sale was part of a wider £20 billion privatisation drive that included stakes in Lloyds Banking Group and Bradford & Bingley and the government's largest-ever sale of student loans.[103] The government insisted the GIB sale made '£186 million profit for the taxpayer', but this was a short-term saving in the context of a structural shortfall in investment for the energy transition and the imminent Brexit-induced loss of European Investment Bank support for renewables. Although another function of a public investment bank is to lower the risk premium on private capital by signalling a long-term policy commitment, the GIB sale did the opposite. Macquarie immediately declared its plans to offload some of the bank's early stage green investments in deals approaching £230 million in the first instance.[104] The National Audit Office concluded that the sale price was too low and that while officials had secured some commitments from Macquarie to continue its green goals these were not legally binding.[105]

The approach to green public finance found little improvement after Brexit. In 2021 Chancellor Rishi Sunak announced the creation of a new National Infrastructure Bank that would invest significantly less per year than the European Investment Bank had done. On a more positive note, the first post-Brexit budget also established a new mandate

---

[102] Ibid., p. 3.
[103] Gill Plimmer and Jim Pickard, 'Green Investment Bank Sold to Australia's Macquarie for £2.3 Bn', *Financial Times*, 20 April 2017.
[104] Ben Martin, 'Macquerie Denies Asset Stripping Plan as It Buys Green Investment Bank for £2.3 Billion', *The Telegraph*, 20 April 2017.
[105] Adam Vaughan, 'Green Investment Bank Sold Too Cheaply, Watchdog Says', *The Guardian*, 12 December 2017.

for the Bank of England that said monetary policy must 'reflect the importance of environmental sustainability and the transition to net zero'. The measure was likely to alter the bank's asset purchases and foster market creation in keeping with Camp 2 reasoning. The 2021 budget also promised a £15 billion green gilt issue, where the money raised from the bonds would be earmarked for green investments, although the functionality of this measure would depend on the money going to wholly green investment and on the repayment of the bonds coming from profits from green activities. Sunak also declared a new green saving instrument on National Savings and Investments, though there was no detail on how those funds would be spent.[106]

These measures were the sum of Sunak's strategy, however, and this budget confirmed his rejection of more direct state intervention in favour of financial market stimuli. Here was a Camp 2 nudge to help the City of London develop as a centre for green investment but within the assumption of the privileged domain, and with no limits on 'dirty' finance. Just weeks before the government was to host, and hence supposedly lead, the COP26 climate summit, Sunak's 2021 October budget *reduced* air passenger duty on domestic flights and froze fuel duty for the twelfth year in a row, while making no mention at all of the climate crisis. The investment stimulus was welcome but wholly inadequate to the emergency at hand. To draw a Conservative analogy, it was as if Winston Churchill had assessed the looming threat of invasion in July 1940 and resolved to organise a limited stimulus to the market for Spitfires.

Forecasting, Carbon Budgets and the Rise of Procedural Formalism

It is worth reiterating that forecasting models per se can be helpful in scenario planning and even monitoring, when used in an ecumenical way. Where models involve long-range, contingent factors with poorly understood inter-relationships, however, like the feedback loops from climate change, they offer governments a dangerous illusion of prediction and control. Hence it matters how forecasts are used and whether they are allowed to morph into the main basis of policymaking.

---

[106] Joshua Oliver, 'UK Plans One of Europe's Biggest Green Bond Issuance Programmes', *Financial Times*, 3 March 2021.

The CCC has used updated IAMs for its major assessments, but it has always highlighted their limitations, and their model-derived documents are peppered with caveats around the incomplete nature of the estimates and the inability of models to capture potentially important non-linear shifts in climate or their compound effects.[107] The committee's five UK carbon budgets are similarly upfront about the contingency of projecting forward to likely carbon prices and emissions pathways and any 'cost effective' path forward. The CCC consistently uses IAMs but highlights the precautionary strategies that ought to be taken. The fact remains, however, that by choosing carbon budgets and their internal economic forecasting as the core strategic instrument, and by seeking to achieve those budgets through market-making or market-imitating strategies, UK governments have used a governmental toolkit that makes sense only in a stable, closed-system world to solve the unprecedented collapse of biological systems.

The real politics of climate policy could be hidden from the start via the accounting system used in the carbon budgets themselves. The United Kingdom's carbon budget targets, and hence the pace of decarbonisation, have been reduced by limiting its formal, as distinct from its actual, liabilities via discrete accounting decisions decided in the Paris Agreement. Paris decided that countries should account for the emissions produced on their territory. But the United Kingdom's consumption footprint is larger than its territorial footprint, and the result is a reduction pathway that systematically underestimates its real responsibilities. The use of production rather than consumption accounting means, for example, that we have poor accounting for the United Kingdom's proportion of international shipping and aviation, but we also exclude imported products, including clothing, electronics and processed foods. Thus, by 2017, some 46 per cent its consumption footprint remained uncounted for,[108] and government rejected the CCC's repeated calls for shipping and aviation, with their heavy footprints, to be included.

Even before the Conservative governments started to actively reverse many climate policies, DECC's own probabilistic measures admitted that existing strategies under the Climate Change Act offered

---

[107] Climate Change Committee, 'UK Climate Action Following the Paris Agreement', 13 October 2016, www.theccc.org.uk/publication/uk-action-following-paris/.

[108] Climate Change Committee, 'Sixth Carbon Budget', 9 December 2020, p. 345, www.theccc.org.uk/publication/sixth-carbon-budget/.

a 63 per cent chance of *exceeding* 2°C.[109] By 2020 this meant that the UK government emissions pathway awarded itself a carbon budget at least a factor of two greater than its fair contribution to deliver on its Paris commitments.[110] As we shall see, the targets rendered too low by the accounting system were then pursued through largely market-imitating price and quota-based measures,[111] alongside the privileged domain norms in regard to the corporate and financial sectors.

Risk Assessment

The Climate Change Act addressed not just emissions reduction – mitigation – but also resilience – adaptation. It did this by prescribing continuous adaptation planning to accommodate the fact that unforeseen impacts would materialise over time. The Act had mandated a rolling five-year Climate Change Risk Assessment (CCRA). Government submitted the first UK CCRA to Parliament in January 2012, and it exemplified the problems with this process in this context. As the CCRA's consultants noted of their own literature survey, the gaps in evidence were huge, which included identification of potential threshold effects, the limits of adaptation and hence lack of knowledge about real points of vulnerability, effects not scoped and many more not quantified. They noted considerable uncertainty around the risks and impacts that were quantified and challenges on the definitions of baselines, and around the nature and timing of the impacts. The list went on, all the way to the standard observation that different methods would produce different results.[112] The dependence on past data also meant conservatism was baked in. The exercise was further hampered

---

[109] House of Commons Environmental Audit Committee, 'Progress on Carbon Budgets', 8 October 2013 (HC 60), p. 8, www.publications.parliament.uk/pa/cm201314/cmselect/cmenvaud/60/60.pdf.
[110] Kevin Anderson, John F. Broderick and Isak Stoddard, 'A Factor of Two: How the Mitigation Plans of "Climate Progressive" Nations Fall Far Short of Paris-Compliant Pathways', *Climate Policy* 20 (10) (2020): 1290–1304.
[111] Samuel Fankhauser, Cameron Hepburn and Jisung Park, 'Combining Multiple Climate Policy Instruments: How Not to Do It', Grantham Research Institute on Climate Change and the Environment, Working Paper Number 38, February 2011, p. 4.
[112] Paul Watkiss, Alistair Hunt and Lisa Horrocks, 'Literature Review for Scoping Study', Defra Contract GA0208, Metroeconomica AEA Group and Paul Watkiss Associates, 2009, p. 10.

by spending cuts. Discontinuity at the Department for Environment, Food and Rural Affairs (DEFRA), the lead department, was caused by severe budget cuts to the adaptation team. Adaptation Sub-committee membership was also cut back.[113]

In 2014 the Coalition government commissioned the Adaptation Sub-committee to lead CCRA2, presented in January 2017. CCRA2 was designed to escape the worst flaws of CCRA1, not least those imposed by the rigid adherence to modelling requirements at the cost of information. CCRA2 limited itself to the academic literature and expertise instead of creating new 'response functions' for each risk or opportunity, previously outsourced at great expense to private consultancies.[114] The second report had made the uncertainty involved explicit and showed how experts made judgement calls. The operating assumptions in CCRA1 had driven its outcomes and cost £3.2 million. The more intellectually honest CCRA2 cost £650,000.[115] The CCRA was thus improved, but its authors still warned it was 'not designed to act as a basis for making decisions on specific policies or practices to manage the risks or opportunities described here'. In other words, the need for political leadership and precautionary government action remained.

In their review of the 2008 Climate Change Act, the LSE's Grantham Institute noted how, when it came to adaptation, the Act had focused on processes for monitoring adaptation but set no requirements that the risks themselves be reduced. Ten years on, the Institute struggled to identify any concrete area of adaptation action (as distinct from mitigation) driven by the Act, even for already intensifying events such as flooding.[116] Here was Power's 'empty formalism', as the Adaptation Sub-committee chair, Lord Krebs, warned, as he stood down in 2017.[117]

---

[113] Fankhauser, Averchenkova and Finnegan, 'Ten Years', pp. 28–29.
[114] The Climate Change Committee, '2017 UK Climate Change Risk Assessment: Synthesis Report – Priorities for the Next Five Years', July 2016, www.theccc.org.uk/wp-content/uploads/2016/07/UK-CCRA-2017-Synthesis-Report-Committee-on-Climate-Change.pdf.
[115] Rachel Warren, Robert Wilby, Kathryn Brown et al., 'Advancing National Climate Change Risk Assessment to Deliver National Adaptation Plans', *Philosophical Transactions*, 28 (June 2018): 1–19, Section 4: Discussion.
[116] Fankhauser, Averchenkova and Finnegan, 'Ten Years', p. 29.
[117] Lord Krebs, 'Lord Krebs Letter to Rt Hon Andrea Leadsom', 24 January 2017, www.theccc.org.uk/publication/letter-lord-krebs-writes-to-the-rt-hon-andrea-leadsom-as-he-steps-down-as-asc-chair/.

Market-Making and Competitiveness

The introduction to CCRA3 in 2022 stated that '[c]limate change is happening now', but you would scarcely detect this from the evolution of UK policy.[118] Camp 2 neoclassical thought recommends that insofar as the state acts, it should intervene to resolve specific market failures and ideally in a 'market-friendly' form. The flaws in this way of thinking range from the anti-investment bias that comes with the typically narrow interpretation of competitiveness as short-term cost reduction to the implicit assumption that no new market failures will emerge within the new market or 'market-like' architecture supposed to resolve the failures identified.

New Labour policies had tended to follow Camp 2 theory: the difficulties renewables had faced to break through in energy markets were treated with targeted, market-making remedies such as quota-setting within new regulatory frameworks. Labour governments nevertheless proved unwilling to intervene in any ways that could be seen as restrictive of existing businesses, for example in agriculture, aviation or, as it turned out, fossil fuels. Under the Coalition and the Conservative majority governments that followed, the United Kingdom has seen a more complete shift towards the reduction of any short-term financial costs to business as the overriding concern. This is in line with the standard neoclassical assumption that state-imposed costs represent a distortion of prices that would otherwise tend towards competitive equilibrium, as if the costs to business from increasing environmental breakdown will not be terminal. If we walk through the key dimensions of policy, we can see how this has played out.

Regulation

Ministers have required a justificatory 'business case' for regulation ever since the advent of New Public Management, and to construct these cases officials use Treasury guidelines rooted in neoclassical theory. With the return of Camp 1 economic policy after 2010 one of its most dogmatic applications arose in the form of the One In, One

---

[118] HM Government, 'UK Climate Change Risk Assessment 2022', 17 January 2022, p. 3, www.assets.publishing.service.gov.uk/government/uploads/system/uploads/attachment_data/file/1047003/climate-change-risk-assessment-2022.pdf.

Out, or 'OIOO', rule introduced by the Department for Business, Education and Skills (BEIS) under the Coalition in 2011. OIOO was based on the Treasury Green Book and the Impact Assessment Toolkit. The grounds for OIOO decisions were impact assessments rooted in cost–benefit analysis. The premise of the new OIOO methodology was simple, and it applied to *all* central government departments and all executive agencies. The objectives of the new rule were, and I quote, to:

- Bear down on the cost and volume of regulation in the economy.
- Encourage departments to implement regulation only as a last resort, having first considered the use of non-regulatory alternatives.

Key principles for this new methodology were as follows:

- The initial scope of OIOO includes any new UK legislation that imposes a direct annual net cost on business or civil society organisations (IN).
- For any direct net cost imposed on business and civil society organisations, departments must identify and remove existing regulations with an equivalent value (OUT).
- Departments will be asked to identify compensatory OUTs at the same time that INs are cleared by the Reducing Regulation Sub-committee.

Measures for which OUTs have not been identified will normally be delayed:

- To ensure the smooth operation of the OIOO rule, officials need to think about identifying OUTs early in the policymaking process.
- Departments will be required to report on direct net costs to business and civil society organisations.[119]

OIOO was too technical to make headlines, but it reduced the state's capacity to intervene where social or environmental harms needed consideration above those of short-term business gain. There were exceptions: taxes, including environmental taxes, were out of scope, as were the results of court or tribunal decisions. In all other areas,

---

[119] Department for Business, Innovation and Skills, 'One-In, One Out Methodology', July 2011, (URN 11/761), p. 3, www.regulation.org.uk/library/2011_oioo_methodology.pdf.

however, the rule put an immediate chill on the government's ability to manage the deepening ecological crisis.

Lorenzo Marvulli was an academic participant observer in DEFRA through 2010–2011 and witnessed how, under OIOO, the Equivalent Annual Net Cost to Business became the decisive factor in policy debate. Treasury guidance was there to help the department's economists decide how to monetise factors that lacked a market price, but the result was a deepening tension between policy officers with sectoral knowledge, their economic advisors and the economists of the new, pan-departmental, Regulatory Policy Committee whose job, according to a senior officer, was to 'thwart and delay regulation'. Whereas policymaking debates prior to OIOO had focused on the wider consequences of government action, DEFRA's policy officers now found environmentally related initiatives 'side-lined, delayed or simply abandoned on the basis of economic considerations'. To illustrate, Marvulli describes a discussion about how to manage the United Kingdom's increasing water scarcity. Though the chair had noted the water market suffered 'imperfections', the economists rejected state intervention because of the unclear financial incentives for utility companies to buy into the problem. The result – and recall the financialisation of utility firms discussed in Chapter 5 – was that the utilities should be encouraged 'to think about it'.[120]

By 2012 the policy was strengthened to One In, Two Out. Thereafter, no new regulation could be introduced without the prior removal of two calculated to operate at twice the costs to business. The government also placed a 'marketing freeze' on all advertising, sponsorship or information campaigns. This halted DEFRA's information campaigns around environmental sustainability. Under a new 'Red Tape Challenge', policy officers learned that the requirement was 'to consider regulatory policy options only as last resort'.[121] BEIS had effectively foreclosed environmental action by a pan-governmental methodological rule that only made sense in Camp 1 terms. But, by 2014, those departments ranked highest for stripping out regulation

---

[120] Lorenzo Marvulli, 'Towards Sustainable Consumption: An Ethnographic Study of Knowledge Work and Organizational Action in Public Policy Development and Implementation', doctoral thesis, University of Cardiff, 2017, pp. 210–216.
[121] Ibid., p. 314.

by cost to business were the Department for Work and Pensions and the Department of Energy and Climate Change. DEFRA came fifth.[122]

Marvulli's study is a testament to the mindless rigidity of 'governance by numbers'[123] – as if the only role of government was to sustain cost competition within some hypothesised competitive equilibrium, a theory conceived in purely logical, as distinct from historical, time,[124] let alone the living environment. To conceive of competitive production as maximum output from a given input with no distortionary 'regulatory' costs ignores the challenge of how to sustain those inputs in an era of ecological collapse. In 2016 Secretary of State for Business Savid Javid raised the 'better regulation' rule to 'One in, Three Out' (OITO). Under OITO, new regulations could not be submitted until three were removed of equal financial impact, and arguments about the benefits of the regulation could no longer be submitted as a trade-off in the justification process. By 2016 the methodology concerned costs alone, and costs were taken to include policy costs (e.g., arising from compliance), one-off costs (e.g., staff training), financial costs (e.g., new taxes) and administrative costs (e.g., book-keeping).[125] In the wake of the Grenfell Tower disaster, 700 organisations signed a letter to the prime minister that said OITO had played a central part in that wholly avoidable tragedy. At the time of writing, the policy still prohibits the development of regulation around the climate crisis that cannot be shown to actively promote short-term business financial gain.

Taxes and Levies

Rather than a direct, steadily rising carbon tax or carbon price floor, New Labour preferred to design consumption taxes and levies as a

---

[122] Department for Business, Innovation and Skills, 'The Ninth Statement of New Regulation: Better Regulation Executive', December 2014, Table 3, https://assets.publishing.service.gov.uk/government/uploads/system/uploads/attachment_data/file/397237/bis-14-p96b-ninth-statement-of-new-regulations-better-regulation-executive.pdf.

[123] Alain Supiot, *Governance by Numbers: The Making of a Legal Model of Allegiance*, translated by Saskia Brown (Oxford: Hart Publishing, 2017).

[124] Joan Robinson, 'Time in Economic Theory', *KYKLOS* 33 (1980): 219–229.

[125] Report by the Comptroller and Auditor General, 'The Business Impact Target: Cutting the Cost of Regulation', 27 June 2016, www.nao.org.uk/wp-content/uploads/2016/06/The-Business-Impact-Target-cutting-the-cost-of-regulation.pdf.

Taxes and Levies

form of price-signalling to encourage presumptively rational and fully informed firms and households to adjust their behaviour accordingly.[126] But, as discussed in Chapter 7, Camp 1 doctrine understands taxes as anti-competitive within a *given* set of endowments, particularly in tradeable sectors such as manufacturing. As a result, the few environmental taxes put in place following the Climate Change Act have been steadily reduced by Camp 1 Conservative chancellors since 2010. The first New Labour government had announced a Climate Change Levy (CCL) in 1999. As David Pearce explains, the CCL was effectively an indirect, single-stage sales tax on energy consumption and it was levied on industry, including agriculture and the public sector. It used the tax system to alter the price signal to industry, and households were formally exempted because of Labour's concerns about regressive taxation, not to mention the political backlash that had greeted the previous Conservative government's addition of value-added tax to household energy bills. The levy thus applied to all non-household use of coal, gas electricity and non-transport liquefied petroleum gas.

In a sophisticated design, revenues from the CCL were significantly recycled back to CCL-paying industries as reductions in employer contributions to social security taxation so you could discourage hydrocarbon energy while encouraging employment.[127] A portion of revenues was also used to subsidise energy efficiency schemes coordinated through the new Carbon Trust – a mentor organisation to help organisations adjust. Energy-intensive industries could gain an 80 per cent discount on the CCL if they took efficiency measures to achieve targets based on government criteria, namely Climate Change Agreements (CCAs).[128] Businesses that failed to achieve their agreed targets would lose their tax discount.

What ensued was a discrete but substantial weakening of the CCL. Policy-defeating concessions were present from the start. In contrast to a pure carbon tax there was no differentiated price between coal

---

[126] Alex Bowen and James Rudge, 'Climate Change Policy in the United Kingdom', Centre for Climate Change, Economics and Policy, Policy Paper, August 2011, pp. 16–17.

[127] David Pearce, 'The Political Economy of an Energy Tax: The United Kingdom's Climate Change Levy', *Energy Economics* 28 (2006): 149–158, pp. 152–157.

[128] Stephen McGinness and Grahame Danby, 'The Climate Change Levy', House of Commons Research Paper, 99/93, 24 November 1999.

and gas because of concerns about the ongoing viability of the UK coal industry.[129] Confronted with opposition from the energy-intensive industries, Labour governments kept CCL rates flat through 2001 to 2007.[130] The 2007 National Audit Office report on the levy and agreements noted that both were designed to encourage energy efficiency rather than reduce absolute emissions. It also noted the formal constraint that 'carbon savings should be promoted without harming competitiveness'. The National Audit Office observed that industry had influenced the design of the CCAs and that the 'targets have been flexed by various means which reduce the effectiveness of Agreements in terms of cutting absolute emissions'.[131] Government, in other words, had designed a complex policy on the basis that indirectly taxing consumption rather than directly taxing carbon production would educate rational consumers and then retreated when that policy was gamed.

The CCL was finally allowed to rise gradually when Gordon Brown became the prime minister, under the 2010–2015 Coalition. By 2015, however, a new Conservative government was in power and in that summer's budget Osborne removed CCL exemptions from renewable electricity with less than a month's notice, creating a shock in the investment market for UK renewables. The move ended the effective tax exemption for organisations that turned to renewables and left few tax incentives for industry to make a forward-thinking choice.[132] Levy rates were raised in the 2016 budget, but the discount rates available to carbon-intensive industries were also increased, protecting them from the higher rates. In 2017 the CCL rate was set to increase only in line with the Retail Price Index.

Where the CCL had specifically targeted industry and agriculture, further schemes following the Climate Change Act had also been 'levy funded' to encourage the development of low carbon energy sources. Under these various schemes, government obliged energy suppliers to

---

[129] Pearce, 'The Political Economy', p. 154

[130] Environmental Audit Committee, 'Reducing Carbon Emissions from UK Business: The Role of the Climate Change Levy and Climate Change Agreements', 10 March 2008 (HC 354), p. 12, www.publications.parliament.uk/pa/cm200708/cmselect/cmenvaud/354/354.pdf.

[131] National Audit Office, 'Review for Environmental Audit Committee: The Climate Change Levy and Climate Change Agreements', 1 August 2007, p. 6, www.nao.org.uk/wp-content/uploads/2012/11/climate_change_review.pdf.

[132] Pilita Clark, 'Summer Budget: End of Climate Levy Relief Undermines Drax Shares', *Financial Times*, 8 July 2015.

increase their renewable energy sources and cover the upfront costs. They could then claw back those costs from customers: the 'levy' in question.

When Osborne became the Coalition chancellor in 2010, however, his Treasury created a Levy Control Framework (LCF) to set a cap on those costs. The LCF required the governing department – DECC, later BEIS – to take early action to reduce costs if *forecasts* exceeded this cap, with urgent action required if forecasts exceeded a 20 per cent 'headroom' above the cap. If the concern was to reduce consumer costs, the LCF was incoherent. It neither monitored nor capped the full range of levy costs, which included the Warm Home Discount, the Energy Company Obligation for energy efficiency and the Capacity Market (largely a subsidy to fossil fuel technology).[133] Nuclear funding also appeared to have its own, far from transparent, funding pot, despite its massive expense.[134]

As it turned out, the LCF forecasts were also badly 'off', though for reasons that remained unclear because of the Treasury's coyness around their methodology.[135] In early 2015 the DECC had predicted that costs in 2020–2021 would be £500 million beneath the cap, but by June 2015 the department projected costs to be £1.5 billion over the cap: a £2 billion swing.[136] The LCF thus forced DECC to make abrupt changes to the levy-supported schemes to cut costs: a huge policy decision effectively forced by a methodological rule. The Renewables Obligation relating to onshore wind and solar photovoltaic projects was closed a year early. DECC also removed guaranteed rates of support for certain solar photovoltaic cells, biomass co-firing and biomass conversions stations,[137] and it imposed new limits on the amount of renewable electricity feed-in tariffs would support by setting a lower tariff. In November 2015 the

---

[133] House of Commons Energy and Climate Change Committee, 'Investor Confidence in the UK Energy Sector', 23 February 2016 (HC 542), p. 24, www.publications.parliament.uk/pa/cm201516/cmselect/cmenergy/542/542.pdf.

[134] Emily Cox, Phil Johnstone and Andy Stirling, 'Understanding the Intensity of UK Policy Commitments to Nuclear Power', SPRU Working Paper Series, 2016-16.

[135] Report by the Comptroller and Auditor General, 'Controlling the Consumer-Funded Costs of Energy Policies: The Levy Control Framework', 18 October 2016 (HC 725), p. 10, www.nao.org.uk/wp-content/uploads/2016/10/Controlling-the-consumer-funded-costs-of-energy-policies-The-Levy-Control-Framework-1.pdf.

[136] Ibid., p. 8.

[137] Matthew Lockwood, 'The UK's Levy Control Framework for Renewable Electricity Support: Effects and Significance', *Energy Policy* 97 (2016): 193–201, p. 196.

government cancelled its £1 billion competition for carbon capture and storage technology only six months before it was due, which was an urgent priority according to the CCC and a 2015 Conservative manifesto pledge.[138] In the meantime, ministers had begun to fast-track fracking in the midst of this 90 per cent cut of the subsidy for solar installation.[139] Between 2015 and 2016 the UK position on the Renewable Energy Country Attractiveness Index duly fell from eighth to thirteenth. The 'big six' top energy suppliers, the UK energy industry's trade association, renewable energy trade organisations, energy market analysts, opposition MPs and the National Audit Office all called for greater transparency around the LCF and its assumptions, but to no avail.[140]

In November 2015, more of the burden of paying for framework schemes was shifted onto consumers to make the energy-intensive industry exempt from some costs, a decision expected to add £5 to the average household bill from 2017–2018 onwards, and to void the short-term savings achieved by the cuts.[141] The climate and cost perversity of the decision was picked up by the National Audit Office, which pointed out that the low carbon support schemes under the framework would have reduced energy costs and that the government's own internal forecasts showed average annual energy bills had fallen by £268 in under two years.[142]

The CCC noted that even if there was overspend this was proof of greater deployment of renewables within an urgent strategy for the deployment of renewables. As it was, the cuts created a stop–start investment profile that hindered cost reduction and industry development, undermined investor confidence, increased the cost of low carbon generation and thwarted essential projects.[143] The LCF had

---

[138] Damian Carrington, 'UK Cancels Pioneering £1Billion Carbon Capture and Storage Competition', *The Guardian*, 25 November 2015.

[139] Damian Carrington, 'UK Government Is Going into Reverse on Clean Energy, Says Former Environment Agency Head', *The Guardian*, 15 December 2015.

[140] Simon Evans, 'Levy Control Framework: The Unanswered Questions', Carbon Brief, 25 January 2016.

[141] Comptroller and Auditor General, 'Controlling the Consumer-Funded Costs', HC 725, p. 29.

[142] Ibid., p. 9

[143] Climate Change Committee, 'Budget Management and Funding for Low-Carbon Electricity Generation', Briefing Note, 14 September 2015, www.theccc.org.uk/publication/technical-note-budget-management-and-funding-for-low-carbon-electricity-generation/.

also shifted the control of a DECC policy to the Treasury. In so doing it switched the policy driver from the fulfilment of the carbon budgets to the satisfaction of Osborne's fiscal hawkishness,[144] with the result, according to the chair of the Energy and Climate Change Committee, that DECC had become 'pennywise and pound-foolish for today. They see all investment today as costs and that's a huge problem'.[145] It is also, of course, a pure expression of Camp 1 reasoning. The CCC concluded that damage to investor confidence could be limited if the LCF into the 2020s was clarified as soon as possible.[146] Instead, in the 2017 autumn budget, Osborne's successor Philip Hammond announced there would be no new low carbon electricity levies until 2025 beyond the money already committed. A later document said new levies would be considered only once the total cost of support was falling.[147]

Seen in total, environmental tax revenue as a percentage of total tax and social contributions peaked in 1998.[148] There has been no greening of the tax regime, and the impulse towards it spurred by the Climate Change Act was actively reversed under Conservative chancellors from 2010 to the time of writing.[149] As shadow chancellor, Osborne had made great play of deploring the Treasury's historical position on climate change as 'at best indifferent, and at worst obstructive' and promised that '[u]nder a Conservative Government the Treasury will no longer be the cuckoo in the nest'.[150] By 2015 he had promised to review the environmental taxes faced by businesses and an explicit end to the 2010 manifesto commitment to increase environmental taxes' share of government revenue.[151]

[144] Lockwood, 'The UK's Levy Control Framework', p. 199.
[145] Evans, 'Levy Control Framework'.
[146] Climate Change Committee, 'Budget Management'.
[147] Carbon Brief, 'Autumn Budget 2017: Key Climate and Energy Announcements', Carbon Brief, 22 November 2017.
[148] Office for National Statistics, 'Environmental Taxes 2014', www.ons.gov.uk/economy/environmentalaccounts/articles/environmentaltaxes/2015-06-01/relateddata.
[149] Treasury Committee, 'Fuel Duty Fiction Clouds Fiscal Forecasts', 23 January 2023, https://committees.parliament.uk/committee/158/treasury-committee/news/175536/treasury-committee-fuel-duty-fiction-clouds-fiscal-forecasts/.
[150] George Osborne, 'A Sustainable Government, a Sustainable Economy', Speech at Imperial College, London, 24 November 2009.
[151] Simon Evans, 'Budget 2015: Key Climate and Energy Announcements', Carbon Brief, 8 July 2015.

There isn't space here to consider the European Union's Emissions Trading Scheme (ETS) in full, but should you explore it you would find another example of how neoliberal doctrine promotes a dysfunctional theatre of markets, and the EU ETS has consequently been revised multiple times. Briefly, the goal in Camp 2 neoclassical terms was to get corporations to stop thinking of GHG emissions as a cost-free 'externality'. The European Union duly established the ETS in 2005 as part of the memberships' commitments to the Kyoto protocols and it became the European Union's flagship climate change adjustment measure. At the time of writing, the scheme covers around 11,000 power stations, manufacturing plants and aviation activities in the EU member states and the European Economic Area. Around 41 per cent of total EU GHG emissions are regulated by the EU ETS. The scheme works by putting a limit on overall emissions from covered installations: a limit reduced each year by a percentage that has risen as the EU revised its targets upwards. Within this limit, companies can buy and sell emission allowances as needed.[152]

Where a predictably escalating carbon tax would have made the rising costs of non-adjustment clear and left firms to decide how much to use and pay each year, the effectiveness of cap and trade depended on the trading element being an efficient market mechanism for raising the price of carbon. By establishing supply and demand for emissions allowances the ETS was supposed to establish an efficient market price for GHG emissions. This would incentivise companies to invest in low carbon technologies, reduce emissions and sell on their allowances to larger emitters, the cap ensuring an aggregate improvement.[153]

Planning the allowances was always going to be hard, however, as well as paradoxical for 'a market', but like public sector outsourcing, it was justified by the model-based illusion that states would set up the market game and then take no interest in how it played out. In practice, the ETS established tradeable allowances under governments convinced by the neoliberal doctrine that restrictive allowances put their companies at a competitive disadvantage, though mutual restriction was precisely the point. 'Cost effectiveness' duly became

---

[152] European Commission, 'The EU Emissions Trading System', https://climate.ec.europa.eu/eu-action/eu-emissions-trading-system-eu-ets_en.
[153] David Hirst, 'Carbon Price Floor (CPF) and the Price Support Mechanism', House of Commons Briefing Paper, Number 05927, 8 January 2018.

a euphemism for rigging the market for allowances to avoid action altogether, and there were further problems with financial fraud.[154] The market-imitating mechanism proved no less political than the tax would have been, just less transparent, and it was only as the scale of the climate emergency started to sink in, and the European Union committed to reduce allowances between 2019 and 2023, that the carbon price started to rise through 2018. Up until this point, however, and through a policy that proved more bureaucratic than a tax, Europe witnessed a dash for coal, with Germany being the standout case.[155] In effect, the government failure in the new carbon trading quasi-market to solve the market failure in wider markets all historically co-constructed by states encouraged investment in high carbon production until re-regulation forced up the price, as if government must constantly surprise itself by its own non-neoclassical behaviour in frameworks that require it.

How did carbon pricing play out in the United Kingdom in this context? The persistent failures of the EU ETS had prompted the United Kingdom's Conservative–Liberal Coalition, still in its initial flush of activism, to announce the introduction of a carbon price floor (CPF) from 1 April 2013 in its 2011 budget. The CPF was meant to rise every year until 2020 to reach a price of £30/tCO2, but this commitment lasted a year, reversed by lobbying from the Confederation of British Industry and the Engineering Employers Federation. In the 2014 budget, Osborne capped the CPF component at a maximum of £18/tCO2 from 2016 to 2020 on the basis that raising the minimum price floor disadvantaged UK businesses because of their comparatively higher energy bills. The freeze was extended to 2025 in the 2017 Conservative budget, with no commitments to adjust it if the EU ETS price changed and with no plans for carbon pricing post-Brexit.[156]

---

[154] Tim Laing, Misato Sato, Michael Grubb and Claudia Comberti, 'Assessing the Effectiveness of the EU's Emissions Trading Scheme', Grantham Research Institute on Climate Change and the Environment, Working Paper, Number 106, 2013.

[155] Dieter Helm, 'Energy and Climate Policy after Brexit', Energy Futures Network, Paper 21, 10 October 2016, p. 3.

[156] Bob Ward, 'Treasury Freeze of Carbon Price Support Rate Could "Endanger" UK 2030 Emissions Targets – Response to Autumn Budget Announcement', Grantham Research Institute on Climate Change and the Environment, LSE, Press Release, 22 November 2017.

Government Spending

Published UK government spending data is split into Environmental Protection and a fluid category under the broad theme of 'decarbonisation'. Environmental Protection Expenditure (EPE) is relatively transparent and includes all activities whose main purpose is the prevention, reduction and elimination of pollution or any other degradation of the environment, such as sewerage, waste management and treatment of exhaust gases and protection of natural landscapes. UK EPE as a percentage of total government spending has stayed essentially unchanged since 2000 and ranged from 1.2 per cent to 2.2 per cent at its highest (2001–2002) even as environmental challenges have increased. In 2018, for example, EPE stood at 1.7 per cent and waste management constituted some 80 per cent of that total, with spending on education, research and development and administration all reduced from the previous year.[157] Between 2010 and 2021, funding for the Environment Agency, the monitoring and enforcement agency for environmental regulation, was cut by two-thirds. Justified as deregulation in Camp 1 terms, these cuts were a green light to corporate malpractice. That the Environment Agency cuts were a false economy was demonstrated beyond doubt by the late 2010s when, to take just one example, multiple private water utilities were found to have not only routinely discharged untreated sewage into English waterways but done it at the rate of 200,000 times in 2019 and 400,000 times in 2020.[158]

Government financial data does not exist on 'decarbonisation' in so clearly disaggregated or comparable form, however. Transparency has been hampered by changes in accounting categories, not least when DECC was folded into BEIS, which then further changed its categories to leave only piecemeal public sources. It is consequently far harder than it should be to track ongoing public subsidies around energy. The Camp 1 view says that government subsidy distorts producer and consumer behaviour and so damages social welfare. Subsidies are modelled for the 'deviation' they create in terms of the prices and quantities of goods exchanged from a hypothesised perfect equilibrium market

---

[157] Office for National Statistics, 'Environmental Protection Expenditure: UK 2018', www.ons.gov.uk/releases/environmentalprotectionexpenditureuk2018.
[158] 'The Times View on Utility Companies Discharging Sewage into Rivers and Seas: Water Works', *The Times*, 23 December 2021.

price. Rather than use the state to drive a comprehensive energy transition away from fossil fuels, however, neoliberal governments have preferred to continue existing subsidies for the least sustainable forms of energy production.

By 2015, the scientific evidence was pointing to the conclusion that to avoid a higher than 2°C rise it was necessary to keep a third of oil reserves, half of gas reserves and over 80 per cent of current coal reserves globally in the ground and unused before 2050.[159] The only responsible government support was consequently around de-commissioning and employment consequences. Nevertheless, beyond carbon pricing and a commitment to phase out unabated coal-fired power stations by 2025, UK governments have still offered no specific policies to phase out fossil fuels despite having made rhetorical commitments to phase out fossil fuel subsidies every year since 2009. Indeed, the United Kingdom lags behind other European governments in neither reporting nor publishing any inventory of fossil fuel or other environmentally damaging subsidies.[160]

This lack of transparency raises a barrier to public scrutiny, and a 2013 report by Parliament's Environmental Audit Committee objected to the Coalition's lack of clear analysis and statistics for energy subsidies; to its blurring of the boundaries of subsidy definition in its support for fracking and nuclear, despite manifesto commitments not to use public money for new nuclear power and to move away from fossil fuel use; and, finally, to the continuation of high subsidy for fossil fuels both domestically and through international financing support and aid operations. The committee concluded that 'energy subsidies in the UK are significant, cover all types of energy technology and run to about £12bn a year. Much of this is directed at fossil fuels'.[161] By 2020, an International Monetary Fund working paper put implicit and explicit UK fossil fuel subsidy at £17.5

---

[159] Christopher Glade and Paul Elkins, 'The Geographical Distribution of Fossil Fuels Unused When Limiting Global Warming to 2 °C', *Nature* 517 (January 2015): 187–190.

[160] Laurie van der Burg and Matthias Runkel, 'Phaseout 2020: Monitoring Europe's Fossil Fuel Subsidies: The United Kingdom', Overseas Development Institute, September 2017, p. 2.

[161] House of Commons Environmental Audit Committee, 'Energy Subsidies: Volume 1', 2 December 2013 (HC 61), p. 3, www.publications.parliament.uk/pa/cm201314/cmselect/cmenvaud/61/61.pdf.

billion.[162] Despite the constant use of neoclassical rhetoric against state intervention, the United Kingdom's neoliberal governments have thus continued to subsidise fossil fuels at a significantly higher rate than renewables, a policy that is lose-lose. It diverts investment from low carbon and renewable technologies while directing high volumes of investment towards assets that cannot be exploited without catastrophic effects.[163] The subsidies are lethal if the fuels are used and create an enormous financial bubble through the overvaluation of hydrocarbon assets if they are not.

Conclusion

According to the IPCC the 'action gap' between the Paris Agreement and current policy internationally puts us at a worst-case-scenario risk of a 4.4°C temperature increase by 2100 relative to 1850–1900 levels.[164] We remain on a credible path to global ruination and dramatically off track to secure the best-case scenario. Although the reasons for this gap vary by country, the hegemony of the neoclassical economics of risk has demonstrably played a significant role. Faith in the neoclassical utopia has rendered neoliberal governments blind, not just to the dynamic realities of the capitalist economy but also to the total dependency of all human agents, economic or otherwise, on the health of the biosphere.

Faced with existential threat, a reasoning government would mobilise all the useful institutions of its political economy, but the United Kingdom's neoliberal governments have kicked the can of necessary action down the road in the belief that self-regulating markets will best perform whatever job of governance is required: through rational expectations, efficient financial markets and 'competitiveness' conceived of in terms that are only coherent in the timeless world of neoclassical logic. Worse, the empty formalism identified by Power

---

[162] Ian Parry, Simon Black and Nate Vernon, 'Still Not Getting Energy Prices Right: A Global and Country Update of Fossil Fuel Subsidies', IMF Working Paper, September 2021, WP/21/236.

[163] Elizabeth Bast, Alex Doukas, Sam Pickard, Laurie van der Burg and Shelagh Whitley, 'Empty Promises, G20 Subsidies to Oil, Gas and Coal Production', Overseas Development Institute, December 2015, p. 12.

[164] Adam Vaughn, 'Earth Will Hit 1.5°C Climate Limit within 20 Years, Says IPCC Report', *New Scientist*, 9 August 2021.

in *The Audit Society* has been instrumentalised by Conservative governments since 2015, in particular in the service of an intense 'greenwashing' – a pretence of action through target-setting and continued reporting that diverts public attention from their substantive reversals of policy. In the meantime, these same governments have continued to support fossil fuel production and quite obviously unsustainable corporate and financial practices that bear no resemblance to the promises of orthodoxy.

While most policy domains benefit from a compromise between the patterns we know about and those we can imagine, the unprecedented challenges around climate change should shatter our complacency about the predictability of the economic world that we have made. The reality is that when a Camp 1 economist tells government to relax around climate change because markets are rational and a climate scientist tells government to comprehend the total nature of the climate emergency and act now, the economist is dreaming and the climate scientist is reporting. Only the natural scientists' conclusions are based on the application of the scientific method over a century of multi-disciplinary investigation and counter-investigation, anchored by dependable laws of thermodynamics, which is why the fossil fuel industry suppressed the warnings of its own scientists for over three decades.[165] Without the transformative greening of our production and consumption regimes, the global political economy will bear ever less resemblance to the past as we become subject to devastating threshold effects, tipping points and unparalleled conflicts for resources within failing ecosystems.

Where scientific thinking in the physical sciences continuously evolves in the light of new evidence, Camp 1 neoclassical orthodoxy has apparently become the useful idiocy for the most regressive corporate and financial actors in the British economy and their political allies who have side-lined strategic thinking in policymaking in favour of axioms already proved foolhardy by the Global Financial Crisis for which the public is still paying. Today's school children grasp the ecological reality that neoliberal governments do not – that when faced with a non-zero probability of ruin, the only sensible, ethical basis for policy is the precautionary principle.

---

[165] Shannon Hall, 'Exxon Knew about Climate Change Almost Forty Years Ago', *Scientific American*, 25 October 2015.

The survival of a habitable world requires that we reject the dangerous illusions of the neoclassical utopia and replace them with reflexive analyses that integrate multiple values, of which ecological renewal is the most important for the foreseeable future.[166] The policy instruments available are many: they include the setting of clear and dependably rising carbon taxes and the introduction of game-changing sustainable technologies such as tidal energy for the island United Kingdom, which is currently stalled in the absence of the necessary investment in engineering infrastructure. Government could also look to public banks and horizontal industrial policies to drive the transition and the parallel cessation of public subsidy for fossil fuels beyond de-commissioning, retraining and developmental investment for the communities affected. Further options include a spectrum of changes in company law and fiduciary duties that range from compulsory long-range financial reporting on carbon footprints and value at risk to new legal obligations around investment decisions, the relegation of shareholder primacy to include ecological values and stakeholders and strict rules on best available technologies (as already exist in environmental pollution legislation). In the meantime, an altogether different paradigm of prosperity *with degrowth in energy and material throughputs* needs to be justified, encouraged and institutionalised wherever possible.[167]

A common neoliberal accusation is that environmental action is a Trojan horse for socialism and centralisation, as if Britain's neoliberal governments have not been the most centralising and bureaucratic in its history. But decisive action does not require state centralisation, only the rejection of the fantasy that markets inexorably tend towards the universally correct pricing of future risks in a world of stable endowments. The history of political economy teaches us that the virtues of markets and states are more or less available depending on their mutually disciplinary effects, and governments can intervene to enable sustainable corporate and financial actors to thrive, and dirty finance to disappear, confident that they break no natural laws when they

---

[166] David Fleming, *Lean Logic: A Dictionary for the Future and How to Survive It* (White River Junction: Chelsea Green Publishing, 2016), pp. 184–185.

[167] See, for example, Tim Jackson, 'Prosperity without Growth: The Transition to a Sustainable Economy', Report of the Sustainable Development Commission, 2009.

do so. The insistence by neoliberal governments that their economic assumptions are good for all times is fatally wrong and potentially for all time, everywhere. As Norman et al. point out, 'We have only one planet. This fact radically constrains the kinds of risks that are appropriate to take at a large scale... Push a complex system too far and it will not come back.'[168] The current prospect of unrecoverable ruin should be enough to make a responsible government act.

---

[168] Joseph Norman, Rupert Read, Yaneer Bar-Yam and Nassim Nicholas Taleb, 'Climate Models and Precautionary Measures', The Black Swan Report, 15 May 2015.

PART III

The Rise and Fall of the Neoliberal 'Movement Regime'

9 | *Neoliberalism*
The Brezhnev Years

British governments since 1979 have based their statecraft on the utopian assumptions of neoliberal economics: the free-market counterpart to its Soviet foe. When it came to policymaking in the Soviet system, the utopian ideology had generated three clear tendencies. First, every move towards the 'pure' form of production was embraced as a step in the right direction. Second, actual measures were pushed far beyond their pragmatic variants and prolonged long after their failures. Third, the utopian blueprint caused all steps in the opposite direction to be treated as regrettable, temporary concessions – as retreats to be reversed at the earliest opportunity and ideally eliminated through revolutionary completion.[1] As Part II has demonstrated, these same tendencies have characterised British neoliberalism. What concerns me here is the impact this has had on the evolution of the British party-political system and on the quality of its liberal democracy.

Leninism was enforced through violence and repression. Neoliberalism was adopted by Britain's established democratic political parties and supported in free and fair elections in one of the most open civil societies in the world. We could consequently expect the affinities between Soviet communism and neoliberalism to end here, in the political realm. As this chapter shows, however, the neoliberal transformation of Britain's political economy has produced a clear political analogue to the Soviet experience: a trajectory of ideological revolution, retreat and attempted reform, neo-traditionalist acceleration and, finally, systemic crisis.

Britain's Conservative, Labour and Liberal parties adopted neoclassical economic analyses as their own. The differences were those between the utopianism of Camp 1 and the technocratic utopianism

---

[1] Włodzimierz Brus, 'Utopianism and Realism in the Evolution of the Soviet Economic System', *Soviet Studies* 4 (3) (1988): 434–443.

of Camp 2, but not of fundamental doctrine. By narrowing the political imagination to the utopian prescription, it also undermined the capacity for adaptive learning that is the peculiar virtue of democracy. In structural terms this consensus instigated the creeping capture of the state by corporations, a condition historically associated with developing economies under authoritarian regimes or their aftermath. It also had a devastating effect on the capacities of the political parties to renew themselves, and for the utopian right in particular, on their standards of conduct in political office. It follows that the history of Soviet politics illuminates far more of the British political experience than one would ever have imagined possible in the 1970s.

The world's first neoliberal government was the Chilean civil-military dictatorship of General Augusto Pinochet in 1974. Neoliberalism had answered Pinochet's political needs, namely, how to achieve economic growth, how to satisfy his backers in the property-owning classes and how to keep American support while undermining the labour movement and the opposition.[2] The argument I put forward here is that even if, by contrast, a neoliberal revolution begins in a democracy, that democracy may not survive the damage that a hegemonic neoliberalism must bring to both its political institutions and its political culture.

The Polish dissident and historian Adam Michnik wrote, '[T]here is no such thing as a non-totalitarian ruling communism. It either becomes totalitarian or it ceases to be communism.'[3] In British neoliberalism, the longer the mainstream parties persisted with the neoliberal project, the more they confronted the problem of political justification in the face of its practical failures. The public bailout of the financial sector after 2010 was initially used as cover for radical austerity measures, but as the 'emergency' justifications of that period started to wear thin, successive Conservative leaders have had to increasingly detach their political rhetoric from their actions. It follows that, between 2010 and 2022, the governments of David Cameron, Theresa

---

[2] Raewyn Connell and Nour Dados, 'Where in the World Does Neoliberalism Come From?', *Theory and Society: Renewal and Critique in Social Theory* 43 (2) (2014): 117–138.

[3] Adam Michnik, 'On Resistance: A Letter from Białołęka', in *Letters from Prison and Other Essays,* translated by Maya Latynski (Berkeley: University of California Press, 1985), p. 47.

May and Boris Johnson had placed a greater narrative emphasis on social conciliation – on the 'Big Society',[4] on 'fairness, opportunity and certainty',[5] and on 'levelling up'[6] – even as they implemented policies of ever more extreme economic liberalisation. The choice of the fanatical economic libertarian Liz Truss as Johnson's successor would usher in a positively manic attempt at revolutionary completion.

In a still representative political system, chronic state failures, increasingly extreme social inequality and the steady loss of real investment and innovation should have prompted a sober debate within all parties about the integrity of the dominant orthodoxy,[7] if not before the Global Financial Crisis then most certainly after it. In this spirit the Labour Party in 2015 had seen its members reject its Blairite record in favour of Jeremy Corbyn, a backbencher from the party's now far left. What was more significant in our context, however, was the choice of John McDonnell as shadow chancellor, since McDonnell set about a policy review that identified financialisation, corporate governance failures, tax havens and climate change as deepening systemic risks in need of urgent attention.[8]

Though McDonnell's economic programme was based on the empirical research of contemporary Camp 3 political economists, the Conservative government and its supporting media would decry it as an unreconstructed return to the statist socialism of the 1970s. This blank dismissal was made easier as both Corbyn and McDonnell were activists from that period, and it was unclear how much Corbyn's vision had, indeed, changed. But McDonnell's policies were new. They combined compelling empirical diagnoses of the United Kingdom's developmental failure with largely innovative and notably green policies designed to rectify them for the wider social good. It was striking, then, that the Conservatives could only invoke the 'bureaucratic Leviathan' language of the 1980s to avoid engaging with their arguments.

---

[4] David Cameron, 'Big Society Speech', 19 July 2010, Cabinet Office, www.gov.uk.
[5] 'Theresa May's Victory Speech outside Number 10', BBC News, 9 June 2017.
[6] The Conservative and Unionist Party, 'Get Brexit Done: Unleash Britain's Potential', Party Manifesto, 2019.
[7] David Sainsbury, *Windows of Opportunity: How Nations Create Wealth* (London: Profile Books, 2020).
[8] Labour Party, 'For the Many Not the Few', Party Manifesto, 2017.

Following Corbyn's electoral defeat in 2019, the Labour Party under Sir Kier Starmer would suffer a notable crisis of identity. While Starmer fought hard to sustain constitutional and moral norms in the face of the Johnson government's increasingly authoritarian strategies, an underlying risk was that the resurgent Blairites within the party would regroup on the economic and environmental front, as if the more critical economic turn under McDonnell had never happened. From the perspective of this analysis, however, any return to Camp 2 neoclassical technocracy can only relegate the party to an organisation of socially conscientious, law-abiding stretcher-bearers within an increasingly destructive hyper-capitalism: an intellectually inert position for the party-political heir to the British radical tradition. It was the Conservative Party, however, that by the early 2020s had essentially completed its self-destruction as a democratic entity. In the run-up to the 2016 Brexit referendum the 'Leave' campaign had claimed, falsely, that the United Kingdom could exit the European Union but retain the full benefits of membership,[9] and Conservative Brexiteers had denied any intention to withdraw the country from the Single European Market (SEM).[10] It follows that we must explain why, having won at last, the same Conservative Brexiteers would then insist upon the hardest Brexit possible. What could possibly have compelled Britain's historically self-identifying 'party of business' to withdraw the economy from all European forms of market integration – not just from the SEM but from the European Free Trade Area, the European Economic Area and even the EU Customs Union? What had made it necessary, in their view, to revoke the United Kingdom's bespoke membership deal in the world's richest and most practically frictionless free trade zone? Here was a decision to become the lone outcast, economically, in the widest possible European space, and it was interpreted internationally as an unfathomable act of national self-harm.[11]

---

[9] Andreas Musolff, 'Having Cake and Eating It: How a Hyperbolic Metaphor Framed Brexit', *LSE British Politics and Policy Blog*, 13 February 2020, www.blogs.lse.ac.uk/brexit/2020/02/13/having-cake-and-eating-it-how-a-hyperbolic-metaphor-framed-brexit/.

[10] Kylie MacLellan and William James, 'UK Will Retain Access to the EU Single Market: Brexit Leader Johnson', *Reuters*, 26 June 2016.

[11] '"Something Resembling Hell": How Does the Rest of the World View the UK', *The Observer*, 4 August 2019.

The answer offered here is that Brexit had always been a project of the party's most committed materialist utopians. The choice to 'liberate' Britain from as many regulatory constraints as possible, including the Single Market's Camp 2 regulations on standards that made free trade in complex goods and services possible, was consistent within its own Camp 1 ideology. In fact, it can only be understood in these terms. When we look at how the Conservative Party's hard Brexiteers fought this battle, we can see how closely the political strategies of late-stage neoliberalism resemble those of the Soviet project in its final years.

In his seminal 1970 essay, 'Development versus Utopia in Communist Policy', Richard Lowenthal argued that it was not simply the pressures of realpolitik and changing leadership personalities that had forced the Soviet regime to adapt. The post-revolutionary Union of Soviet Socialist Republics (USSR) had seen the utopian dreams of the ruling party fade as the regime confronted its own system failures and the reality of its corruption and managed decline.[12] By 1983, the general secretary of the Communist Party of the Soviet Union, Yuri Andropov, had confessed to the Central Committee plenum that '[w]e do not sufficiently know the society in which we live and work, [we] have not fully revealed its inherent laws, especially economic'.[13] In what follows I set out how, after forty years of unanticipated policy failures, the refusal of British Conservative governments to offer an equally honest admission would ultimately drive them to inflict not just an unprecedented crisis on its own political economy but an existential crisis of the United Kingdom as such.

It is in the nature of the closed-system logic of the neoliberal utopia that it is precisely as total in its scope as its Soviet counterpart. The political pursuit of perfect allocative efficiency, whether through the free market or the socialist state, amounts to an equally unrealistic rejection of the challenges of time, space and meaningful individual subjectivity. As we will see, the Brexit vote would force into the open the confrontation between the neoliberal utopia and Britain's

---

[12] Richard Lowenthal, 'Development vs. Utopia in Communist Policy', in Chalmers Johnson, *Change in Communist Systems* (Stanford: Stanford University Press, 1971).

[13] Quoted in Adam E. Leeds, 'Administrative Monsters: Yurii Yaramenko's Critique of the Late Soviet State', *History of Political Economy* 51 (2019): 128–151.

political economic reality, even as it elevated the Conservative's most extreme libertarians to power. To understand why the right wing of the Conservative Party was prepared to sacrifice British democracy on the altar of a God that had already failed, however, it is important to understand how estranged from society the entire British party-political system had already become even by 1979 and how, instead of creating new institutional attachments between parties and people, neoliberalism had only tended to weaken them further.

The End of Embedded Liberalism

By the 1970s, modernisation, technological shifts and the achievements of the welfare state had transformed the social, occupational and religious basis of the mass membership parties of the post-war era. Across Western Europe the partisan, programmatic parties of that period were now compelled to develop more 'catch-all' electoral strategies,[14] and Otto Kirchheimer warned that as parties loosened their ideological commitments to appeal to more diverse constituencies, this growing flexibility might cause a loss of moral purpose for the sake of electoral success. With hindsight, the crises of the 1970s represented a critical juncture wherein a new political economic orthodoxy that prioritised public and private investment and post-industrial renewal might have re-embedded Britain's parties within its society and created new, constructive ties.[15] What happened instead was the neoliberal turn, and with it the accelerated 'professionalisation' of party politics, and henceforth parties would cleave to the unsafe certainties of the new 'science'.

As the era of mass parties came to an end, political scientists would describe the emerging forms as 'cartel parties',[16] 'electoral

---

[14] Otto Kirchheimer, 'The Transformation of the Western European Party Systems', in Joseph La Palombara and Myron Weiner, *Political Parties and Political Development* (Princeton: Princeton University Press, 1966), pp. 177–200.

[15] John Gerard Ruggie, 'International Regimes, Transactions, and Change: Embedded Liberalism in the Postwar Economic Order', *International Organization* 36 (2) (1982): 379–415.

[16] Richard Katz and Peter Mair, 'Changing Models of Party Organisation and Party Democracy: The Emergence of the Cartel Party', *Party Politics* 1 (1) (1995): 5–29, p. 9.

professional' parties,[17] and 'modern cadre' parties.[18] What these concepts indicated in common, however, was that Western Europe's party governments by the 1980s faced growing tension between the expectations of their declining memberships, the rising instability of their wider electoral support and the constraints imposed on their policy options by deepening public debt. Part of their shared solution was to prioritise the party in public office over their grassroots organisations, but the programmatic differences between parties also narrowed as they tried to stabilise competition between organisations now 'socialised' by long periods in government.[19] Neoliberalism offered a most tempting proposition in this challenging context: a strategy to convert the challenges of democratic government into a technical question of 'governance' via neoclassical economic expertise. Like Lenin, Margaret Thatcher's genius was to add a heroic political narrative to this pseudo-scientific materialist frame.

Thatcherism projected the principles of 'personal responsibility' rather than the raw calculation of neoclassical thought as the leading value of this revolution. A brilliant strategy, it bestowed an equal dignity upon everyone: an egalitarianism of high expectations and perfect, free agency, and it did so at the very point the left was in crisis. Thatcher thus repeated the neoclassical shibboleth that if we put our shoulders to the wheel, we are the masters of our fates within the limits set only by taste, technology and the material resources that we can simply choose to build through the application of our own rationality. That this promise ignored how in reality individuals must navigate complexity, unforeseen calamity, relative economic powerlessness and the hidden and overt injuries of class,[20] race and sex followed from the circularity of the economic argument that underpinned it.

While Thatcher was strongly influenced by Friedrich August von Hayek it was only neoclassical economics that offered policy solutions,

---

[17] Angelo Panebianco, *Political Parties, Organization and Power* (Cambridge: Cambridge University Press, 1988).
[18] Ruud Koole, 'Cadre-Party, Catch-All or Cartel? A Comment on the Notion of the Cartel Party', *Party Politics* 2 (1996): 507–534.
[19] Peter Mair and Richard Katz, 'The Ascendancy of the Party in Public Office: Party Organizational Change in Twentieth-Century Democracies', in Richard Gunther, José Ramón Montero and Juan Linz, *Political Parties: Old Concepts and New Challenges* (Oxford: Oxford University Press, 2002), pp. 113–136.
[20] Jonathan Cobb and Richard Sennett, *The Hidden Injuries of Class* (Cambridge: Cambridge University Press, 1988).

and if you subscribe to an ideology that depends for its 'truth' on a form of perfect universal rationality and agency, at some point you have to assert those either exist or can be achieved. Like Lenin again, Thatcher had duly declared that a transformation in the material order would bring people to their 'true' consciousness. As she told the *Sunday Times* in 1981, 'If you change the approach, you really are after the heart and soul of the nation. Economics are the method; the object is to change the heart and soul.'[21] If the phrasing is oddly familiar it may be because the statement is a hair's breadth from Joseph Stalin's invocation of the 'engineers of the human soul', though Stalin was referring to writers, not economists.[22]

'New' Labour had emerged in the aftermath of Thatcher's second landslide electoral victory in 1983 – first with the rejection of the 'militant' left under Neil Kinnock and then, following the sudden death of his successor John Smith, with the Labour Party being moved more decisively to the economic right by Tony Blair from 1994. Blair had concluded that Labour could no longer win on a left-wing platform. A convert to Camp 2 neoclassical reasoning, he argued that the only way to appeal to the middle classes in the aftermath of Thatcherism was through the same pro-market and low-tax agenda as the right but with clear emphasis on equality of opportunity and choice, as distinct from the party's post-war commitments to actual equality.[23]

Blair's intention was not to roll the state back but to bring the market virtues presupposed in the neoclassical view to bear within it, so that the resulting 'efficiency gains' would allow Britain to transcend the conflicts of its past. In this more overtly technocratic approach, markets were still to be prioritised but on the understanding the state should retain a role to mend market failures at their microeconomic source. This was an interpretation of the political economy from the 'second-best-world' positions of Camp 2, and hence, wittingly or otherwise, New Labour had adopted the illusion that once mended, the market would tend towards the first-best world of general equilibrium. If you could mend capitalism, you would not have to fight it, and

---

[21] Ronald Butt, 'Mrs Thatcher, The First Two Years', Interview, *The Sunday Times*, 3 May 1981.
[22] Joseph Stalin, 'Speech at Home of Maxim Gorky', 26 October 1932, *Collected Works*, Vol. XIII, p. 410.
[23] Jonathan Hopkin, *Anti-system Politics* (Oxford: Oxford University Press, 2020), p. 123.

politically this seemed to liberate the Labour Party from the Leviathan-building slanders of the Thatcher era. The left's shift to the economic right was supported by business and finance. For the large corporate sector in particular, the continuing deregulation of the financial market, the birth of an expanding public services markets and the collapse of the political veto on the shedding of corporate social responsibilities heralded a future of unprecedented financial opportunity. New Labour's three successive administrations from 1997 to 2010 would thus slow the rate of increase in social inequality but not reverse it. In fact, the top 10 per cent in the income distribution would grow its share of pre-tax income from 18.4 per cent in 1997 to 42.6 per cent by 2007.[24]

As the smaller Liberal Party also proceeded to split between camps 1 and 2, Britain's mainstream parties no longer offered the electorate the substantive economic choices that had characterised post-war politics. Even as poverty and inequality climbed, successive British governments continued to reduce the tax burden on the rich and retrench spending on social policies and infrastructure, though survey evidence continued to show British voters believed in redistribution and in the necessity of a welfare state.[25] In England most of all, the political parties substantially reconfigured the economic arena of electoral competition into a debate about the transformation of the state – to the question of who was most competent to oversee the New Public Management and who would benefit from it.

By the 1990s, a rising generation of politicians, not just in Britain but beyond, saw themselves less as representative agents of society than as professional agents of the state.[26] In Britain this meant a state that was itself an increasingly corporate-oriented entity. As Peter Mair put it, voters retreated to their particularised spheres of interest and political leaders withdrew into the closed world of the governing institutions. Both were 'cutting loose', and this was damaging to political parties as the primary agents of representation in the democratic system.[27] In the context of a strengthening neoliberal orthodoxy, party membership also become largely symbolic – valued

---

[24] Ibid., p. 121.   [25] Ibid., p. 122.
[26] Katz and Mair, 'Changing Models', pp. 20–21.
[27] Peter Mair, *Ruling the Void: The Hollowing of Western Democracy* (London: Verso Books, 2013), Chapters 2 and 3.

by political elites for its contribution to the legitimising myth of a party over genuinely informational or representational roles.[28] The result was a technocratic politics around the managerial state that was significantly less expressive of the underlying needs and hopes of the electorate than the often passionately fought moral and substantive political economic debates of before. Following the three Devolution Acts of 1998 for Scotland, Wales and Northern Ireland there remained the potential for a return to some ideological variation in the devolved parliaments, and this would become particularly marked in Scotland. Here the Scottish National Party found it could pivot to the left of New Labour on economic and social policy, and by the early 2020s the threat to Labour in Scotland from the Scottish National Party had become a rout.

As we have seen in Part II, both New Labour in government and the left of the Liberal Party in the 2010 Coalition were open to policy experimentation, and they effectively agreed on the increased use of private finance initiatives, public sector outsourcing and quasi-markets in welfare and only marginally stronger regulation in finance and corporate governance than their Camp 1 Conservative opponents. To compensate for the loss of their economic radicalism, Blairite Labour had emphasised its far greater social liberalism and its internationalism, although this would become a muscular humanism that would ultimately persuade Blair's second government to undertake an illegal war in Iraq as an ally of the United States.[29]

The growing factions of Camp 1 parliamentary Conservatives and Liberals in the meantime preferred the state's continued withdrawal wherever feasible, and the Conservative–Liberal Coalition from 2010 would massively expand Labour's experiments in private finance initiatives, outsourcing and, in a less mediating spirit, quasi-markets across the board. It would also make historically unprecedented cuts in local government spending and income transfers, all continued apace by the Conservative governments that followed, including under the minority government of May. Though Conservative MPs by the late 2010s held diverse views on everything from Britain's place in Europe, religion, family values, sexual equality and city versus rural interests, by 2020 their economic beliefs as a body were

---

[28] Katz and Mair, 'Changing Models', p. 18.
[29] 'Iraq War Illegal Says Annan', BBC News, 16 December 2004.

far to the right of even their own councillors and party members, let alone of the wider electorate.[30]

The neoliberal turn had effectively narrowed the political economic imagination of the governing mainstream elite to the spectrum allowed within the neoclassical utopia, from Camp 1 to Camp 2. Britain's political parties had adopted this panacea in the face of intensifying developmental dilemmas only for those dilemmas to deepen, as neoliberal policies failed to work as anticipated. From the 1980s, however, those policy failures had fallen upon a party system more organisationally separated from voters than at any point since the Second World War, with party membership in steady decline from the 1970s and more sharply so from 1997.[31] Political sociologists had duly monitored the rise of 'consumer democracy',[32] as well as how, from the Thatcher era onwards, parties were coming to depend in organisational terms on the same professional, corporate networks that supported business.[33]

As the mainstream parties came to think of themselves more as firms that operated in volatile markets, the purely transactional conceptualisation of parties invented by public choice theory increasingly became an institutional fact. Meanwhile, the legal, accountancy, consultancy and public relations firms and corporate-funded think-tanks that now circulated around parties had no interest in undermining the business model in which they thrived.[34] These new fields of business focused their efforts instead on the quest for successful consumer branding:[35] for new forms of increasingly personal political appeal that could mask the self-imposed limits of the real political 'offer', so long as neoliberal orthodoxy held. While this is particularly true for the Conservatives, the organisational networks around Labour, though tempered by

---

[30] Tim Bale, Aron Cheung, Philip Cowley, Anand Menon and Alan Wager, 'The Social and Economic Values of MPs, Party Members and Voters', *The UK in a Changing Europe*, June 2020, Section 7.

[31] House of Commons Library, 'Membership of UK Political Parties', *Research Briefing*, 9 August 2019.

[32] Richard Sennett, *The Culture of the New Capitalism* (New Haven: Yale University Press, 2006), Chapter 3.

[33] Margaret Scammell, *Designer Politics: How Elections Are Won* (London: Palgrave Macmillan, 1995), pp. 233–268.

[34] Chris Bick, 'Political Professionalisation and Representative Crisis: Ideational Infrastructure and Party fields in the United Kingdom', Paper presented at the SASE Meeting, 8–11 July 2022, Amsterdam.

[35] Margaret Scammell, 'Politics and Image: The Conceptual Value of Branding', *Journal of Political Marketing* 14 (2015): 7–18.

more critical think-tanks, trades unions and social and environmental non-governmental organisations, had also become dominated by single-issue organisations whose concerns could still be spoken to in the market failure logic of Camp 2, and it begged the question of how either party would renew its wider vision given the profound failures of the basic paradigm.[36]

Having leaned so heavily into their identities as managerial agents of the state, Britain's party leaders over four decades had offered up their competence in that role as the primary reason to vote for them. The neoliberal revolution itself was to be the source of social renewal and, insofar as government had any role left to play, it was to produce better government that cost less. Consider, then, how completely this new social contract would prove a hostage to fortune. It required that the neoclassical strategies built from abstract assumption be open to near-complete realisation in practice. Short of the end of time, space and three-dimensional human agency, however, this development could only place British politics on a collision course with social reality. Political parties committed to this agenda had thus doomed themselves to fail in their representational and expressive functions, a failure most disenfranchising of all for those most vulnerable to exploitation and neglect within an ever more weakly mediated capitalism. The Global Financial Crisis revealed the basic sterility of neoliberal reasoning. So long as they remained confined within doctrine, the political parties could not begin to honestly account for it, nor for the deepening social and economic stagnation that the country had already endured.

As Mark Blyth and Jonathan Hopkin noted, the shift from catch-all parties to party cartels and the bid to sell leadership on its technocratic skill and personal charisma had not only brought with it the downsizing of constituent expectations, the externalising of policy commitments into 'the marketplace' and the separation of party from any defined constituency. It created parties 'whose purpose is precisely not to govern'.[37] As a close colleague of Cameron admitted to his biographers, if the new Conservative prime minister had not inherited the post-crash justification for radical austerity in 2010,

---

[36] Chris Bick, London School of Economics Ph.D. thesis, forthcoming.
[37] Mark Blyth and Jonathan Hopkin, 'The Global Economics of European Populism: Growth Regimes and Party System Change in Europe', *Government and Opposition* 54 (2) (2019): 193–225, p. 205.

it had been far from clear what he was going to do instead. 'I don't think people have got any idea', they concluded, and 'that's a problem for the longer term'.[38] It was indeed. The declining ability to form a cross-class electoral coalition in a majoritarian electoral system presented the Cameron government with a serious political quandary, namely, how *do* you sustain a failing neoliberal revolution via other narrative means?

Brexit: Nationalist in Form, Libertarian in Content

The Yugoslav dissident Milovan Djilas said of the communist system in 1959: 'The heroic era of communism is passed. It is at the height of its power and wealth, but it is without new ideas. It has nothing more to tell the people. The only thing that remains is for it to justify itself.'[39] In the run-up to the Brexit referendum, British neoliberalism stood at the height of its structural power, but the chronic non-fulfilment of its promises now drove the Conservative's most radical neoliberals away from the explicitly economic appeals of the preceding decades and, like their Soviet counterparts, towards nationalism.

The USSR's transnational policy of 'national in form and socialist in content' had almost certainly been inspired by the passage of the *Communist Manifesto* that read: 'Though not in substance, yet in form, the struggle of the proletariat with the bourgeoisie is at first a national struggle.'[40] In keeping with his critique of imperialism, Lenin had attacked Tsarism's Greater Russian nationalism as the exploitative chauvinism of a colonising power,[41] and colonial peoples in the Leninist view had become 'the global equivalents of the western working class'.[42] In the absence of revolution in a more advanced capitalist

---

[38] Francis Elliott and James Hanning, *Cameron: Practically a Conservative* (London: Fourth Estate, 2012).
[39] Milovan Djilas, *The New Class: An Analysis of the Communist System* (New York: Praeger Publishers, 1959), pp. 54–55.
[40] Friedrich Engels and Karl Marx, *The Communist Manifesto* (London: Electric Books Company, 2001) (first published in 1888), p. 24.
[41] Veljko Vujačić, *Nationalism, Myth and the State in Russia and Serbia: Antecedents of the Dissolution of the Soviet Union and Yugoslavia* (Cambridge: Cambridge University Press, 2015), p. 161.
[42] Yuri Slezkine, 'The USSR as a Communal Apartment, or How a Socialist State Promoted Ethnic Particularism', *Slavic Review* 53 (2) (Summer 1994): 414–452, p. 421.

state, however, the Bolshevik victory had turned Russia into the vanguard proletarian nation, and hence no longer a colonising power but the leading socialist society.[43] It followed that appeals to an adapted greater Russian pride 'in the socialist sense' could be deployed as both revolutionary tactic and propaganda, and the Russian Party would return to such appeals again and again in times of crisis, most dramatically in the Second World War under Stalin but also under the conditions of deepening economic stagnation under Leonid Brezhnev.[44]

The wider manipulation of nationalist sentiment had to varying degrees remained subordinate to the socialist cause across the Soviet space, but the formal rights to 'self-determination' held by the Soviet Socialist Republics were highly circumscribed by the higher interests of 'the proletariat', and these were defined by the democratic-centralist party headquartered in the Russian vanguard.[45] In the dying years of these regimes the increasing substitution of socialist with nationalist content by hard-line Soviet and Yugoslav communists would have tragic, bloody consequences.[46] Even decades later these practices would return in Vladimir Putin's invasion of a sovereign Ukraine: a vainglorious resurrection of a now zombie Greater Russian state nationalism, the most obvious function of which was to divert domestic attention from the regime's authoritarian kleptocracy and failing economy.

Leninism in practice had always operated as an unstable combination of scientific rationalism and charismatic politics.[47] As the sociologist Veljko Vujačić observed, as the credibility of the communist scientific blueprint had started to collapse through the 1970s and 1980s these charismatic elements were driven to the fore. Thus:

When communist regimes enter a period of terminal systemic crisis, leading 'conservative' in the communist party *apparat* activate the heroic and

---

[43] Vujačić, Nationalism, p. 162.
[44] Walker Connor, The National Question in Marxist-Leninist Theory and Strategy, Memorial Edition (Boston: Asia Research Associates, 2019), pp. 487–496.
[45] Vujačić, Nationalism, p. 171.
[46] Veljko Vujačić, 'From Class to Nation: Left, Right, and the Ideological Roots of Post-Communist "National Socialism"', East European Politics and Societies 13 (3) (2003): 359–392.
[47] Kenneth Jowitt, New World Disorder: The Leninist Extinction (Berkeley: University of California Press, 1992), pp. 8–9.

charismatic components of their ideological worldview. Since appeals to class struggle are no longer viable, and the existing ideological corpus does not provide answers to new challenges, ideologically defensive postures are gradually replaced with a growing commitment to alternative but potentially equally charismatic notions more typical of the 'nationalist right' ... the political circle captured by the phrase *les extremes se touchent* is closed and a new form of national socialism is born...

In organisational terms, the defence of the state or the nation becomes a substitute 'combat task' that can potentially restore the institutional integrity of the party by providing the cadres with a new sense of mission and well-defined institutional targets in a radically changed social environment. For the more orthodox cadres deeply steeped in a combat ideological ethos, such a struggle against 'external enemies' and 'internal traitors' is, in any case, just a continuation of 'the revolution' in a new historical context... desperately needed popular support is simulated, manipulated, and partially created, new opportunities are opened for deflecting the responsibility for the economic failures of late socialism from the proletarian vanguard itself to various external and internal enemies. The newly manipulated consensus that is thus created can serve to substitute, in Jowitt's excellent phrase, the national unity of elite and citizens[48] for the real political equality between them.[49]

We tend to forget that the radical economic fervour of Thatcher in 1979 was both alien and alienating to many of the parliamentary Conservative Party's still largely One-Nation Tory MPs, and it was Britain's victory in the Falklands War and Thatcher's subsequent 1983 electoral landslide that had consolidated her leadership. It was a military victory that enabled Thatcher to entrench neoliberal economics as the party's core value, but in these first decades a sizeable faction of One-Nation traditionalists such as her successor, John Major, his chancellor, Kenneth Clarke, and their supporters had remained at the left of the party. In opposition through the Blair years, however, a younger generation of social liberals and Camp 1 economic liberals had come in to sit at their right, and it was this generation that came to the fore in the 2010–2015 and 2015–2016 governments, led by Cameron and his chancellor, George Osborne. Cameron and Osborne were both open admirers of Blair's political acumen and even identified themselves as

---

[48] Kenneth Jowitt, 'Soviet Neo-traditionalism: The Political Corruption of a Leninist Regime', *Soviet Studies* 35 (July 1983): 295–197, p. 291.

[49] Vujačić, 'From Class to Nation', pp. 382–384.

'children of the Blair years'.[50] While they thus held to the greater social liberalism of their generation, they would nevertheless accelerate the neoliberal transformation of the increasingly centralising state with a single-mindedness that far surpassed their predecessors.

What distinguished the Cameron governments was not any critical re-evaluation of neoliberal economic orthodoxy, only their willingness to soften the political narrative that accompanied it. Cameron had replaced Thatcher's insistence that 'there is no such thing as society' with a concession that 'there is such a thing as society, it's just not the same thing as the state',[51] but the shift was essentially rhetorical. Charities were encouraged to participate in the provision of public services, but they tended to be crowded out by corporate players. Massive cuts to local authority funding made a mockery of the promise to enhance local self-government. Having proved empty, Cameron's core slogan, 'the big society', was quietly dropped by the end of the Coalition.[52]

Not content with these positions, however, a group of Camp 1 militants had emerged in the parliamentary party who apparently determined that economic liberty was more important than liberal democracy, in accord with the theoretical economic constitutionalism outlined in Chapter 3. Here was the British version of the faction led by the Republican Newt Gingrich in the United States who, as Speaker of the House of Representatives (1995–1999), had rejected the postwar conventions of bipartisan policymaking in favour of a winner-takes-all approach to government and its institutions. In Gingrich's narrative, the Democrats were no longer to be seen as a legitimate opposition or government, as fellow Americans under one constitution, but as implacable enemies of the neoliberal republic understood in the relentlessly pro-corporate terms of Camp 1. In Britain it was this group, together with the Conservative Party's more nationalist-authoritarian leaning MPs, who, from the 1990s, would mobilise for Brexit under a strategy of 'nationalist in form, libertarian in content'. Fatally, it was Cameron's conviction that he could use a referendum

---

[50] BBC Documentary, *The Cameron Years: The Best Is Yet to Come* (Episode 2), first broadcast on 26 September 2019.

[51] Margaret Thatcher, Interview with *Women's Own*, 23 September 1987, www.margaretthatcher.org/document/106689; 'In Full: Cameron's Victory Speech', BBC News, 6 December 2005.

[52] 'Society and the Conservative Party', BBC News, 9 January 2017.

on EU membership to outflank the nativist UK Independence Party (UKIP) that would elevate the party's most extreme Camp 1 faction to government.

The 2017 LSE Growth Commission had found that after the Global Financial Crisis the United Kingdom had experienced fast employment growth, but no growth of the typical worker's pay. Median real wages were lower in 2016 than they were in 2006. Between 2008 and 2014 real wages fell by 8 per cent, a drop unprecedented in post-war history. The relative real wage growth data for 2007 to 2015 placed the United Kingdom twenty-seventh out of twenty-eight countries, surpassed only by Greece. Low standard employment had become a core characteristic of the British political economy and for the youngest generation most of all. The country had entered a 'high employment low pay' syndrome in which deregulation and the shrinking of the safety net had abandoned a steadily growing proportion of the population to precarious work for meagre wages.[53] In 2015 England saw life expectancy at birth level off for the first time since Office for National Statistics records began (1980) and decline for men and women in Scotland and Wales and for men in Northern Ireland.[54] Here was the ringing alarm of developmental decline, as well as the indicator often cited in the 1980s as definitive evidence of Soviet failure.

In this situation the Conservative Party risked losing both voters and members who sat either to the left of the Cameron Coalition on distributional politics or socially and politically to its more authoritarian right. Such defections could open the way for Labour victory by splitting the Conservative vote.[55] According to the British Election Study, all income groups by 2015 viewed spending cuts as having gone too far and by the highest margin – some 40 per cent – among the lowest income quintile.[56] The result within the parliamentary party was a deepening disagreement between the government and the

---

[53] 'UK Growth: A New Chapter', LSE Growth Commission, Centre for Economic Performance, 2017, pp. 19–27.

[54] 'National Life Tables 2015–2017', Office for National Statistics.

[55] Paul Webb and Tim Bale, 'Why Do Tories Defect to UKIP: Conservative Party Members and the Temptations of the Populist Right', *Political Studies* 62 (2014): 961–970.

[56] Alexandre Afonso, 'To Explain Voter Intentions, Income Is More Important for the Conservatives than for Labour', *LSE British Politics and Policy Blog*, 25 April 2015, https://blogs.lse.ac.uk/politicsandpolicy/to-explain-voting-intentions-income-is-more-important-for-the-conservatives-than-for-labour/.

Conservative MPs to its right. Where the government preferred a strategy to protect economic doctrine through softer rhetoric and socially liberal legislation such as the equalisation of marriage rights to same sex couples (2013), the party's economic libertarians embraced the absolutist strategies of their American colleagues.

As a faction, the Conservative Party's hard economic right had formed by following Thatcher, a leading architect of the SEM through the mid-1980s, when she turned against the SEM as it became apparent that for less neoliberal European governments the creation of a liberalising trade zone would require a commensurate monetary and perhaps even fiscal and social integration to manage its consequences. These MPs had answered Thatcher's fierce opposition to the ensuing Maastricht Treaty with the creation of the European Research Group (ERG) in 1993.[57] Years later, in *Statecraft* (2002), Thatcher had concluded that the European single currency was an attempt to create a 'European super state' and one that would fail economically, politically and socially,[58] as public choice theory dictated it must. What duly became the ERG's obsession with Britain's exit from the European Union would eventually launch the entire country on a wild odyssey towards the neoliberal mirage.

In January 2013, Cameron finally caved to the constant pressure from the MPs to his right and announced that were the Conservatives to win the 2015 election the government would hold a referendum on the United Kingdom's EU membership. On the face of it this seemed to kill several political birds with one stone, although a more socially observant leader would have recognised them as canaries. In the first place it was hoped a referendum in which the 'Leave' side lost would quash the internecine debate that had raged within the party since the United Kingdom had joined the European Economic Community in 1973 – a battle that threatened to derail Cameron's leadership as it had derailed Thatcher from her left and Major from his right. In the second, it was hoped that by calling a referendum the Conservatives could render the encroaching UKIP redundant and gain the allegiance of its voters.

If we consider the first of these birds, the essential question within the party, though not expressed in these terms, was whether Conservatives

---

[57] Margaret Thatcher, 'Maastricht', *The European*, 8 October 1992.
[58] Margaret Thatcher, *Statecraft: Strategies for a Changing World* (New York: Harper Perennial, 2002).

should continue to fight the Camp 1 corner within a Europe Union that operated in predominantly Camp 2 terms or whether they should lead Britain out of the Union to complete the Camp 1 revolution supposedly unencumbered. As such it was a dispute akin to that between Bolshevism and Menshevism at the outset of the Russian Revolution, only this time as if revolutionary Bolshevism had only been pursued after a gradualist Menshevism had been tried, tested and proven to fail, continuously, for three and a half decades. However, precisely because it was an inner-party dispute between more or less pragmatic Camp 1 neoliberals about an increasingly discredited and unpopular body of beliefs, this debate could never be conducted in public within the real terms that motivated and, indeed, financed it.

Both Cameron and Osborne were keen to 'remain' in Europe as neoliberals who accepted the adequacy of Britain's opt out from the Eurozone and preferred to act as a deregulatory voice within the SEM, the world's largest free market built on Camp 2 neoclassical lines. The SEM operated not through the abandonment of regulations and government standards but via their deliberate harmonisation to reduce transaction costs in cross-border trade, in accord with Camp 2 reasoning around informational barriers and market failures. For the Conservative's most fervent economic libertarians, and what would become the Vote Leave campaign group, however, this position was a betrayal of a purist Camp 1 belief in the wisdom of the marketplace in the *absence* of the state. For the European Research Group, Brexit promised an escape from the continuing dynamics of EU state-building into a purportedly frictionless space of true global freedom, unchecked by regulations, standardising or otherwise, or by de-commodifying state interventions more generally. That the Brexiteers could only ever define what this future would look like in purely negative or wholly abstract terms was an artefact of the goal itself: the creation of a harmonious two-dimensional world built on superhumanly rational agents in the neoclassical vein or, for its more Hayekian advocates, a free and equally melodious land ordered through the natural selection of 'social traditions', the wisdom of the price mechanism and the enforcement of property rights.

The real aftermath of Brexit was always going to remain decidedly earthbound, however. It would be one in which any new trade deals that Britain could make anywhere would still impose regulations and standards. Sheer geography would also dictate that Britain would continue to trade with its nearest and richest neighbours – in Europe – only now it would do so as a third-party regulation-taker and hence on far costlier and significantly more bureaucratic terms of trade. Britain would be forced to negotiate new international trade agreements as a single economy rather than as a beneficiary of the European Union's unrivalled negotiating leverage as the world's largest trading bloc.

Exit from the Customs Union and the SEM would mean the erection of a customs border either between the Republic of Ireland and Northern Ireland or down the Irish Sea to protect the integrity of the SEM, now that the Republic would become the European Union's external border. Both of those options had an awful potential to undermine the courageous, hard-won peace in Northern Ireland as secured through the 1998 Good Friday Agreement. As for the other advantages of mutual rights of travel, work, residency, education and professional recognition; the flowering of cooperation and exchange in scientific research; the joy and mutual understanding created through the sharing of arts and culture and the apparently forgotten point about the prevention of catastrophic wars between neighbouring countries, these were all removed from the balance. In Brexiteer logic, a correct interpretation of liberty would tell you these losses were trivial compared to the gains to be had. Such insouciant faith in laissez-faire was duly noted by those interests not embedded in the real, productive British economy, and over three-fifths of the Leave campaign was funded by five men, four of whom made their fortunes in financial services.[59]

As for the second canary, Cameron had hoped the referendum would steal UKIP's thunder. What this failed to acknowledge was that UKIP's appeal had grown as a symptom of the neoliberal project itself. The distinguishing feature of populist parties is their claim that they alone represent the 'real' and implicitly pure people against the corrupt elite who only work for themselves,[60] a narrative that flowed all too easily from the neoliberal assertion that the democratic state was an instrument of exploitation when left in the hands of anyone but neoliberals.

---

[59] Caroline Mortimer, 'Brexit Campaign Was Largely Funded by Five of UK's Richest Businessmen', *The Independent*, 24 April 2017.
[60] Jan Werner Müller, 'The Rise and Rise of Populism?', *Open Mind*, www.bbvaopenmind.com/wp-content/uploads/2018/03/BBVA-OpenMind-Jan-Werner-Muller-The-Rise-and-Rise-of-Populism-1.pdf.

Indeed, outflanked by Blair on the economy, William Hague had unsuccessfully resorted to nativist, authoritarian and Eurosceptic values by the late 1990s, as the leader of the Conservative opposition.[61] But UKIP too would translate the traditional 'socialist' and 'bureaucratic' enemies of Thatcherism into an unspecified new class of governing 'cosmopolitan liberal elites' and claim that this elite were as happy to feed from the trough of the European Leviathan as 'the left' had been from the post-war state at home. UKIP duly charged the United Kingdom's socioeconomic failures to the account of a self-serving and bureaucratic European Union, to corrupt mainstream parties at home and to excessive immigration and cultural change. UKIP was also openly Islamophobic. Under cover of its relentless chauvinism, however, it too operated with economically libertarian policies. It sold nostalgia for post-war certainties even as it rewrote the history of the post-war state.

The UKIP manifesto in 2015 promised lower and flatter tax rates, the abolition of inheritance tax and an end to 'politically correct' but unspecified spending programmes. It promised to cut the size of the House of Commons and abolish multiple departments including the Department for Energy and Climate Change, the Department for Overseas Development and the Department for Culture, Media and Sport.[62] Though Brexit was sold as a form of political time machine, UKIP's rendition of British history was an exercise in selective amnesia, and its social conservatism was reactionary even by post-war standards. UKIP made constant reference to the courage of the armed forces throughout the Second World War but said nothing of the fight against Nazism and fascism. The deaths, the devastation, the grief and the post-traumatic stress of those who had fought Britain's wars were forgotten, though the reverberations were still felt through the generations. UKIP narratives assumed their voters knew nothing about the real post-war political economy: its Keynesianism, the nationalised industries and the top rates of income tax that averaged 90 per cent through the 1950s to the 1960s.

As Adam Michnik observed, it was a peculiarly devastating feature of communism that it drove public discourse away from nuance and observable fact and enforced division between those who did and

---

[61] Tim Bale, *The Conservative Party from Thatcher to Cameron*, 2nd ed. (Cambridge: Polity Press, 2016), pp. 123–235.
[62] UK Independence Party, 'Believe in Britain', Party Manifesto, 2015.

did not understand 'the scientific truth', as signified by whether you supported or opposed its self-appointed custodians. Now the Brexit campaign insisted that you were either for the 'real' people or against them, and the result was a bitter dialogue of the deaf, not least because both official campaigns were nearly equally bound to direct the debate away from Britain's own developmental model and its failures. EU membership as a topic of high public salience was barely on the political map before the referendum itself was announced, but it became a proxy vote for all the stresses and frustrations of the political economic regime even as the official campaigns avoided their debate. According to the British Social Attitudes Survey, public opinion in favour of leaving the EU as a general position had climbed slowly from 10 per cent to 22 per cent from 1992 to 2015. The high point in that period was the 30 per cent support recorded in 2012. It was only in 2016 the issue rose to prominence via the Conservative referendum promise, when 41 per cent favoured exit. Britain emerged from the referendum more sceptical about the European Union than it had ever been before. By the time polling took place on 23 June 2016, three in four voters felt that Britain should either leave the European Union or that if it stayed the institution's powers should be reduced.[63]

In charge of the Leave campaign were the Conservative Party's leading economic libertarians Michael Gove, Jacob Rees Mogg, Member of the European Parliament (MEP) Daniel Hannan and, in a notoriously last-minute decision, Johnson.[64] As if to prove Marx's famous citation of Georg Wilhelm Friedrich Hegel, that all world historic personages appear, as it were, twice so that 'history repeats itself… the first as tragedy, then as farce',[65] the Leave campaign's chief strategist was Dominic Cummings, an alleged admirer of Lenin.[66] As with Lenin's tactical promotion of the right to self-determination,[67] Cummings deployed straightforwardly nationalist propaganda as a foil

---

[63] John Curtice, 'The Vote to Leave the EU: Litmus Test or Lightening Rod?', in *British Social Attitudes* 34 (London: NatCen Social Research, 2017), p. 172.
[64] Jessica Elgot, 'Secret Boris Johnson Column Favoured UK Remaining in EU', *The Guardian*, 16 October 2016.
[65] Karl Marx, *The Eighteenth Brumaire of Louis Bonaparte*, translated by Saul Padover (Moscow: Progress Publishers, 1937), Chapter 1.
[66] Nicholas Watt, 'Dominic Cummings and the Battle for Downing Street', BBC News, www.bbc.co.uk/news/extra/09jpSjVUpQ/dominic_cummings_battle_for_downing_street.
[67] Vujačić, *Nationalism*, p. 10.

for the campaign's real economic goals. The Leave campaign used a heightened culture war rhetoric, particularly around immigration and EU 'oppression', and there is no denying the skill of the exercise. That the utopian economic purpose of Brexit was successfully conflated with an act of national liberation from tyranny was a product of charismatic politics and a polarised social media landscape driven by a newspaper media powerfully biased to the right. That it managed to pass off the intended, final evisceration of Britain's post-war democratic developmental state as the return of the Dambuster Spirit was a truly remarkable political achievement.

There was not the slightest chance that the moment of communal effervescence could be sustained, however. It is one thing for the first-generation devotees of a materialist utopia to believe their ends justify any means, as the process of educating the population in their supposedly true natures has just begun. It is altogether more arresting that four decades into this systematically floundering project, Conservative libertarians were still convinced that a dream-fulfilling economic rabbit could be pulled from this nationalist hat. Even if we assume an idealistic motivation on their part, they were content to engage in a shocking level of public deceit about the nature of their dream. What Brexit consequently exposed was that neoliberalism in its purest form contains no civic republican values, no respect for the norms of liberal democracy as sacrosanct. The reason for this would have been clear to anyone who had read the economic constitutionalism that underpinned these ideas, since this explicitly identifies liberal democracy as the essential source of trouble. Just as Leninism and Stalinism had stripped out the radical democratic republicanism of Marx, so too neoliberalism picks liberalism clean of its nineteenth- and early twentieth century ethical debates about the nature of republican virtues.[68] Here the marketplace alone is the sphere of true freedom: the only republic. It follows that at this potentially decisive moment of doctrinal struggle, the very institutions of Britain's liberal democracy would be regarded as fair game.

For the Remain side, led by Cameron, it was near impossible to make a popular case for the protection of the economic status quo, and

---

[68] Adam E. Leeds, 'From the Soviet Republic to the Planned Economy: Lenin, Socialism and Cold War Modernity', Guest Lecture, Jordan Centre, New York University, 26 February 2020.

the official campaign was fatally detached from the daily lives of multiple constituencies and most obviously from those on low incomes. The official campaign talked up the benefits of EU membership and how it allowed the country to retain its influence in the world, but this could only ring hollow for voters who for too long had lived with precarious employment and financial insecurity. What was the purpose of such influence, these voters could reasonably ask. Influence for whom? Ranged against such blithe disregard stood a Leave movement that combined nationalist populism and insurgent, optimistic zeal about an entirely idealised future. The vacancy around the realistic basis of future prosperity was filled with the pitch-perfect promise that with Brexit 'the people' would 'take back control'.

There was nevertheless candour if you looked for it. In *What's Next? How to Get the Best from Brexit*, the widely acknowledged 'brains behind Brexit', Conservative MEP Daniel Hannan, had written: 'Here is our chance to create a free-trading, deregulated, offshore Britain – an entrepôt trading with the EU and the rest of the world, working for the reciprocal dismantling of tariff and non-tariff barriers wherever possible, but being prepared to reduce its own barriers unilaterally if necessary.'[69] The future was 'free trade, tax cuts, low regulation, localism and direct democracy', the latter a direct reference to the withering away of the central state. *What Next* conjured the libertarian Fata Morgana of purely harmonious human enterprise and frictionless trade – the free market unbound by the state and unsullied by the dynamics of economic power at any level. Hannan's intellectual references were explicit. In 2010 he had written an homage to Hayek called *The New Road to Serfdom: A Letter of Warning for America*, that notorious bastion of socialism.[70] A similar call for concerted free market radicalism, *Britannia Unchained*, had been written in 2012,[71] and four of its five authors – Priti Patel, Kwasi Kwarteng, Liz Truss and Dominic Raab – would go on to serve as senior ministers in the second Johnson administration. In September 2022, following the

---

[69] Daniel Hannan, *What Next? How to Get the Best from Brexit* (London: Heads of Zeus, 2016).
[70] Daniel Hannan, *The New Road to Serfdom: A Letter of Warning for America* (New York: Harper, 2010).
[71] Kwasi Kwarteng, Priti Patel, Dominic Raab, Liz Truss and Chris Skidmore, *Britannia Unchained: Global Lessons for Prosperity and Growth* (Basingstoke: Palgrave Macmillan, 2012).

ignominious collapse of that government, Truss would be appointed prime minister through a poll of Conservative party members, and she would appoint Kwarteng her chancellor.

The lead economist for Leave, Patrick Minford, had argued that the British economy would grow rapidly after Brexit through the increased trade it would inspire by a unilateral abolition of all import tariffs, even as it continued to pay all external tariffs. Here was an argument for 'libertarianism in one country' and a surreal echo of Stalin's vanguardist policy of 'socialism in one country' that had justified the violent industrialisation of Russia as its contribution to the world-historical struggle.[72] Minford's theory of 'Britain alone' was far more abstract, however; indeed, it was built on Camp 1 logic of a most spotless form – specifically, that small changes in trade costs would have enormous effects on volumes of trade because in his operating model each country would purchase from the lowest cost supplier.[73] A review of this argument by Thomas Sampson et al. noted first that 'theories should be grounded in facts, not ideology' and then, with barely concealed frustration, proceeded to explain:

> In reality, everyone does not simply buy from the cheapest supplier. Products are different when made by different countries and trade is affected by the distance between countries, their size, history and wealth (the 'gravity relationship'). Trade costs are not just government-created trade barriers. Product differentiation and gravity is incorporated into modern trade models – these predict that after Brexit the UK will continue to trade more with the EU than other countries as it remains our geographically closest neighbour. Consequently, we will be worse off because we will face higher trade costs with the EU.[74]

Given Minford's public statement that Britain's unilateral abandonment of all trade protections would 'effectively eliminate manufacturing in the UK',[75] it is clear why Vote Leave preferred to keep such arguments under wraps and instead to place what turned out to be an entirely false promise of renewed National Health Service funding on the side of the campaign bus and to spread the lie that the

---

[72] Vujačić, *Nationalism*, p. 179.
[73] Thomas Sampson, Swati Dhingra, Gianmarco Ottavanio and John Van Reenan, 'Economists for Brexit: A Critique', Centre for Economic Performance: Brexit Analysis, Number 6, p. 1.
[74] Ibid.   [75] Ibid., p. 2.

European Union's 'free movement of persons' was about to be applied to Turkey. When it came to the vote, Conservative voters would prove the most divided of all party supporters,[76] but a new electoral coalition had effectively, and indeed literally, been forged.

There is evidence that the referendum enabled a protest vote, but that was not the whole picture. According to the British Attitudes Survey those most likely to vote Leave were:

- Those with no formal education qualifications (78 per cent) or whose highest qualifications are CSEs or O-levels (61 per cent).
- Those with an income of less than £1,200 per month (66 per cent).
- Those in social housing provided by a local authority (70 per cent) or housing association (68 per cent).[77]

Those from ethnic minority groups were much less likely to vote Leave. Regional differences were significant: those in the East and West Midlands and the Northeast were significantly more likely to vote Leave than those in London, Scotland and Northern Ireland.

The subjective accounts – how people described their own attitudes – suggest a strong component of real and perceived relative deprivation. Those most likely to vote Leave were:

- Those finding it difficult to manage financially (70 per cent of those who voted) or just about getting by (60 per cent).
- Those who believed Britain has got a lot worse in the last ten years (73 per cent).
- Those who think things have got worse for them rather than other people (76 per cent).
- Those who perceive themselves as working class (59 per cent).
- Those who see themselves as English rather than British (74 per cent) or more English than British (62 per cent).[78]

To these constituencies, built by decades of neoliberalism, the Leave campaign suggested that national, if not nationalist, solidarity was the way out, and voters could project their diverse attachments to country onto the promises of Britain's resurrection. The Leave campaign

---

[76] Curtice, 'The Vote to Leave the EU', p. 175.
[77] Kirby Swales, 'Understanding the Leave Vote', NatCen Social Research, December 2016, pp. 2–7.
[78] Ibid., pp. 2–7.

promised the return of status and pride, a restoration of the dignity so hard to find in the stagnating and inhumane political economy of 2016. This was confirmed by Sascha Becker, Thiemo Fetzer and Dennis Novy, who found that education profiles, historical dependence on manufacturing employment, low income and high unemployment to be the key determinants of voting Leave. At the level of wards within cities they found those areas with deprivation in terms of education, income and employment were more likely to vote Brexit.[79]

Using interviews, focus groups and local news sources to investigate why lower income communities had voted against their apparent economic interests, Kira Gartzou-Katsouyanni, Max Kiefel and Jose Javier Olivas Osuna likewise showed that at the local level a combination of relative economic decline, the spread of low value-added business models, the declining quality of infrastructure and public services and the ensuing disruption of formerly proud and cohesive communities had played a determinant role. These losses had driven profound political unhappiness and created a natural nostalgia for the lost era of community. The Leave campaign would blame the absence of renewal on 'outsiders' and the evils of the European Union.[80] But Britain had been the leading voice for neoliberalism in Europe as a whole, and by elevating the Conservative Party's most extreme economic liberals to government, Leave voters would only intensify this revolution at home, not end it.

There was, however, a distinct but corresponding logic to voting Leave for the winners of neoliberalism. As William Davies notes, those who worked at senior levels in the extractive economy could expect to benefit further from more radical deregulation and privatisation under neoliberal governments released from EU constraints on environmental, financial and labour standards.[81] Those on the receiving end of financial rents would also benefit – those older, wealthier voters who had retired as owners of valuable property and

---

[79] Sascha Becker, Thiemo Fetzer and Dennis Novy, 'Who Voted for Brexit? A Comprehensive District Level Analysis', *Economic Policy* 32 (92) (2017): 601–650.

[80] Kira Gartzou-Katsouyanni, Max Kiefel and Jose Javier Olivas Osuna, 'Voting for Your Pocketbook but against Your Pocketbook? A Study of Brexit at the Local Level', *Politics and Society* (2021): 1–41.

[81] William Davies, 'England's New Rentier Alliance', *New Stateman*, 1 August 2019.

shareholding portfolios and who also hankered after the post-war social order.[82] The result was a 'rentier alliance' between those who had benefited from neoliberalism's extractive dynamics and those on far lower incomes persuaded that to escape 'European bureaucracy' was the only way out of the dead-end of disinvestment and neglect. Far from cultural identity and economic conditions being opposing contributory factors, they were clearly interdependent, and nobody understood this better than the Leave campaign itself. The country voted 48 per cent to remain and 52 to leave the European Union, while majorities in both Northern Ireland and Scotland voted to stay.

There was one aspect of economic libertarianism that the Brexiteers had been willing to emphasise, however, and that was trade. Contrary to the tide of commentary that declared Brexit an exercise in nostalgia for the Empire, the historian Robert Saunders has shown how the 'histories' told by the Brexiteers set out to establish 'a heroic vision of the past that was global, rather than imperial… of a small island that had always punched above its weight: of a "swashbuckling", "buccaneering" people, winning out against the odds'.[83] By uploading the Thatcherite emphasis on individual enterprise to the international level, Leave would project Britain as an agent uniquely endowed with its spirit. It appealed to the Commonwealth, and in particular Australia and New Zealand – the liberal 'Anglosphere' – as Britain's natural home, as against the confining, 'foreign', bureaucratic space of 'Europe'.

At the inaugural conference of Commonwealth Trade Ministers in 2017 the Brexiteer and international development secretary Priti Patel hailed the Commonwealth as 'an exemplar' of 'free markets, private enterprise and liberal economics', as if what bound the Commonwealth together was a shared enthusiasm for Milton Friedman rather than the search for constructive relations in the aftermath of Britain's violent, exploitative past. Here, in other words, was a form of organised historical forgetting to match the elisions of the economics itself: a vision of Britain's historical trading dominance detached from the imperial power structures and racist brutality that

---

[82] Ibid.
[83] Robert Saunders, 'Brexit and Empire: "Global Britain" and the Myth of Imperial Nostalgia', *The Journal of Imperial and Commonwealth History* 48 (6) (2020): 1140–1174, p. 1144.

had made it possible, not to mention the liberation struggles for decolonisation that had brought it to an end.[84]

Soviet communism too had taken to periodically extolling the virtues of the Great Russian nation as bearers of the liberation theology of communism to the former territories of its empire,[85] and here was British history now rewritten in counterpart form. As Saunders put it, the Brexiteers cast 'the Britain that ruled the waves, not as a coercive military empire but as a champion of "free trade"; and in so doing, rendered entrepreneurialism – rather than empire – the golden thread connecting past and present'.[86] The Brexiteer's turn to the Commonwealth thus promised to domesticate globalisation by recasting it in the light of Britain's long-vanished supremacy.

The Conservative Party versus Reality

The pressures towards constant review and self-critique in a democracy must ultimately become an affront to governments ideologically wedded to a materialist utopia. It follows that once the terms of justification available within that utopia have lost their credibility, a government that refuses to change course will be forced to turn more completely towards narrative mysticism. From its inception, the Central Committee of the Communist Party of the USSR had declared the unprecedented achievements of the socialist system. But by the Brezhnev era, otherwise known as the Era of Stagnation, these pronouncements had scant connection to political economic realities. Far from communism being largely achieved by 1980, as Nikita Khrushchev had promised, it became necessary to invent an entirely new, hitherto unsuspected phase in the trajectory of historical materialism. The era of 'Developed Socialism' was proclaimed in 1971 at the Twenty-Fourth Congress of the Communist Party of the Soviet Union as the stage through which the USSR would have to pass for an unspecified period before it could reach the age of communist abundance – now officially behind schedule. For Britain, Brexit was the functional equivalent of developed socialism: a new, artificial horizon to prolong the life of an already failed and corrupted political economic regime.

---

[84] Ibid., p. 1154.   [85] Connor, *The National Question*, pp. 486–491.
[86] Saunders, 'Brexit and Empire', p. 1154.

What these parallels suggest is that the only leadership that can sustain a materialist utopia in its inevitable crisis is one that is willing to obfuscate and flat-out deny the experiences that daily crash in on the citizenry itself. This is the tipping point that Vujačić identified when the hard-line right of both the Russian and Serbian communist parties abandoned the no longer viable appeals to the economic struggle and replaced them with the charismatic narratives of the nationalist right and evocations of their respective martial traditions.[87] The result in the British public domain was a growing cognitive dissonance between Conservative government narratives and observable reality that would only intensify through the early 2020s, when the devastating consequences of Brexit and the Covid pandemic would start to play out, not least through a fire sale of now-undervalued UK assets.[88] In the years between the 2016 referendum result and May 2021, when the final Brexit Trade and Cooperation Agreement came fully into force, Conservative government speech would more completely transition from promises that were merely ideologically incoherent under May to the systematic deployment of lies, evasions, fabrications and denials by the Johnson governments that followed.

The Brexit campaign and the social polarisation it exposed had put the parliamentary Conservative Party at war with itself, and this could already be seen in May's 2017 Conservative manifesto 'Forward Together'. This spoke the inclusive language of One-Nation Conservativism even as it called for fiscal conservatism, 'the lowest possible taxes', less regulation and 'free trade', whatever the latter was now supposed to mean. Given the collapsing 'promissory legitimacy' of neoliberalism,[89] the political personality of the 2017 manifesto was necessarily split, and the party now had little choice but to talk of the good that government can do, but this was a tortured confession from a party so essentially committed to Camp 1. 'Forward Together' consequently also insisted on the 'threat' to firms and households from a 'government's thirst for their cash' even as it spoke of 'recruiting the best and brightest graduates' into the civil service and renewing

---

[87] Vujačić, 'From Class to Nation', p. 382.
[88] Daniel Thomas and Peggy Hollinger, 'UK Plc Up for Sale as Overseas Buyers Eye Bargains', *Financial Times*, 1 March 2021.
[89] Jen Beckert, 'The Exhausted Futures of Neoliberalism: From Promissory Legitimacy to Social Anomy', *Journal of Cultural Economy* 13 (3) 2020: 318–330.

the physical estate of the National Health Service and rewriting the contracts of both general practitioners and hospital consultants. The manifesto was necessarily silent on the institutional and financial principles by which that might happen.[90]

The threat to British democracy always immanent in neoliberalism would finally arrive when the stoic and procedurally traditionalist May was replaced by Johnson, a man with a childhood ambition to become 'World King'.[91] The failure of May's 2017–2019 minority government to find an inner-party consensus on the Brexit deal's content marked the final victory of the Brexiteers within the parliamentary Conservative Party. As their opportunistic leader, and in keeping with the mobilising tactics of the Leave campaign, Johnson then embraced many of the governing strategies of the nationalist-authoritarian right. In neoliberalism as in Soviet communism, therefore, it appears that nationalism is the 'last stage'.[92] Bereft of credible solutions to the multi-dimensional problems of the British political economy, the Johnson governments would sally forth with the entirely fallible notion of an infallible nation.[93]

Johnson's entire journalistic and political career had been built on the picaresque: on his ability to tell fantastical, outrageous stories with himself as the loveable rogue at their centre, only to be repeatedly sacked for his dishonesty, first by *The Times* and eventually by Michael Howard as leader of the Conservative Party. It consequently tells us a great deal about the party's existential crisis that by 2019 a majority of Conservative MPs and members preferred to select Johnson as the prime minister than to review what it was about the existing economic regime that made a notoriously amoral fabulist the party's best electoral hope. Johnson's ascendency is a case of 'cometh the hour, cometh the man'. Unfortunately for the country, the hour was that of a materialist utopia as it collapsed under the weight of its own contradictions and its advocates sought to defend the project by whatever means necessary. It is in this context that

---

[90] Abby Innes, 'The Political Economy of the Conservative Manifesto', *British Politics and Policy Blog*, 24 May 2017, https://blogs.lse.ac.uk/politicsandpolicy/the-political-economy-of-the-conservative-manifesto-the-state/.
[91] 'Boris Johnson: The Boy Who Wanted to Be World King', BBC News, 24 July 2019.
[92] Adam Michnik, 'We Are Bastards of Communism', *Der Spiegel*, 31 July 2013.
[93] Eric Jarosinski, *Nein: A Manifesto* (Melbourne: Text Publishing, 2015), p. 125.

Johnson selected a cabinet that for its inexperience, ideological zealotry and lack of intellectual heft would have been inconceivable in any other period of the Conservative Party's modern history.

The signs that Johnson would seek to free both himself and his government from the systems of democratic accountability were there from the start of his premiership. Even before he had won an electoral mandate in the December 2019 election, Johnson removed the Conservative whip from twenty-one of the party's longest serving and most respected and largely One-Nation MPs, including two former chancellors and numerous ex-ministers. The twenty-one had shown a dogged tendency to insist on the rule of law, but the pretext for their removal was that they had joined a cross-party vote against a 'no deal' Brexit in September 2019 – a prospect that Johnson himself had earlier declared unthinkable. Those expelled included Rory Stewart, who had emerged as the only leadership challenger to Johnson in July 2019 clearly determined to remake the party in the spirit of a democratic and empiricist centre-right. The unprecedented purge was an early sign of Johnson's willingness to 'manage' democracy rather than admit he had bet the country on the most extreme economic fantasy of the twentieth century. Another was buried in the party's December 2019 election manifesto, which declared, 'After Brexit we also need to take a look at the broader aspects of our constitution: the relationship between the government, parliament and the courts, the functioning of the Royal Prerogative.'[94]

Johnson's contempt for parliamentary accountability and the rule of law would become clearer with each passing month. For the Internal Markets Bill in 2020, the government legislated to break international law in order to override parts of the EU withdrawal agreement to which it was a signatory, a disregard that led the head of the Governments Legal Service to resign in protest.[95] In the final Brexit Treaty Bill itself, some 1,200 pages of complex legal agreements with the European Union were placed before parliament on 30 December, with only twelve hours of scrutiny, to be completed twenty-four hours before the Act was to be enforced. Buried within the Treaty text was a

---

[94] The Conservative and Unionist Party, 'Get Brexit Done', p. 48.

[95] Sebastian Payne, George Parker and Jim Pickard, 'Top UK Government Lawyer Quits over Brexit Withdrawal Agreement Changes', *Financial Times*, 8 September 2020.

powerful 'Henry VIII' clause that empowered the executive to reinterpret existing domestic laws without recourse to parliament if justified as necessary for the implementation of the EU deal.[96] Johnson himself would take to misleading parliament and refusing to correct the record.[97]

The coronavirus pandemic exposed the unwillingness of the Brexit libertarians to use the state for the public good, and not least because it would tend to remind voters of that basic capacity. The Johnson government locked the country down too late and reopened it too early, not just once but repeatedly, though the chancellor was eventually forced to make huge fiscal interventions to prevent a complete economic collapse. These measures were nevertheless set to be reversed as soon as possible.[98] Covid laid bare the fragmentation and de-funding of the state, and of the social care sector in particular. It exposed the incompetence and extractive practices of the public service industry firms to whom the government turned, even now, for the procurement of vital protective clothing. It laid bare the ease of corruption, when the cabinet established a VIP lane for covid procurement contracts, which fast-tracked those firms with links to the party, however fraudulent or incompetent. Now, practically everyone experienced the disconnect between headline-grabbing government promises and the clear lack of state capacity to carry them out. The pandemic also showed how high the vocational commitment of people who work in public services continued to be.

The pandemic and its development through 2020 would also demonstrate with unerring tragic force the fault-lines of British socio-economic inequality.[99] Measured between 2016 and 2018, fully half of the total aggregate wealth in Britain was held by just 12 per cent of households. Where the top three wealth deciles held 76 per cent of aggregate wealth the bottom three wealth deciles put together held a

---

[96] Eleni Courea, 'Warning of Sweeping Powers Rushed Through in Treaty Bill', *The Times*, 30 December 2020.

[97] Lizzie Dearden, 'Every Misleading Statement Boris Johnson Has Made to Parliament since the General Election', *The Independent*, 19 April 2022.

[98] See Institute for Fiscal Studies, 'Spring and Autumn Budget Reviews', 21 March 2021 and 28 October 2021, www.ifs.org.uk/collections/autumn-budget-and-spending-review-2021.

[99] Richard Blundell, Robert Joyce, Monica Costa Dias and Xiaowei Xu, 'Covid-19 and Inequalities', The IFS Deaton Review, Institute for Fiscal Studies, 11 June 2020.

mere 2 per cent.[100] By 2018, the Office of National Statistics declared UK household debt to be higher than at any time on record,[101] and this social inequality was translated directly into health inequality.[102] Britain by the close of 2020 had suffered the highest death toll per capita in the world and the deepest economic recession of any country in Europe.

It was a notable feature of late Soviet regimes that their Central Committees had combined individuals of vaulting ambition alongside ministers distinguished by nothing but their ideological conformity. It had required either powerful opportunism or blind faith to seek to sustain the Soviet system at the height of its dissipation. After the revolutionary intelligence of the Thatcher cabinets, the relative moderation of Major, the Khrushchevian technocratic optimism and relative social inclusiveness of the Blairites, the illusions of technocratic continuity in the Cameron years and the already defensive nationalism but relative probity of the May administration, the Johnson cabinets from 2019 stepped up to the plate as the United Kingdom's true neoliberal Brezhnevites. As the sociologist Ken Jowitt concluded of the USSR: 'Brezhnev's novelty seems to have been to take the Party's organizational corruption and elevate it to the status of an organizational principle.'[103] Insofar as Johnson had a strategy to manage the confrontation between the Brexit fantasy and its real economic consequences, it was to proclaim that everything would be for the best in the best of all possible worlds and to engage in straightforward nihilism around standards of conduct in public life.

By 2022 the 'salami tactics' deployed by Johnson to entrench executive power included the criminalisation of peaceful protest, concerted legislative efforts to undermine civil service neutrality and judicial review,[104] the abuse of public revenues as campaign finance, most notably in the highly politicised allocation of 'levelling up' funds, and a short march through the institutions in which formerly independent

---

[100] Office for National Statistics, 'Total Wealth in Great Britain: April 2016 to March 2018', Statistical Bulletin Released December 2019, Section 6.
[101] Philip Inman, 'Household Debt in UK Worse than at Any Time on Record', *The Guardian*, 26 July 2018.
[102] Blundell et al., 'Covid-19 and Inequalities'.
[103] Jowitt, *New World Disorder*, p. 237.
[104] Graham Cowie and Joanna Dawson, 'Judicial Review Reform', House of Commons Library, 1 April 2021.

pillars of civil society such as the BBC were tied to the government through political appointments or, in the case of the independent and commercially successful Channel 4 public broadcaster, put up for privatisation. In April 2022, a new Elections Act allowed ministers to determine the remit of the formerly independent elections regulator, the Electoral Commission. It also allowed for a governing majority on the parliamentary committee that oversaw it.[105] The Act stripped the Electoral Commission of its powers to prosecute criminal offences against election rules and changed the law to require ID cards, though electoral fraud in the United Kingdom was negligible and the more obvious effect would be to disenfranchise some of the poorest cohorts, least likely to vote Conservative – a direct imitation of contemporary Republican voter suppression legislation in the United States. Taken together these tactics imitated those of the corrupt, nativist neoliberal, Viktor Orban in Hungary, and they heralded the use of increasingly blunt political force to retain power. They also allowed government to gain more outright control over the corporate brokerage opportunities produced by neoliberal policies.[106]

The inexorable ideological introversion identified by Václav Havel in communism was now apparent in the leadership battle that followed Johnson's resignation as the prime minister on 7 July 2022. The stream of financial and sexual scandals and the palpable sense of chaos emanating from Downing Street had flowed steadily since Johnson's election, but it was only once Johnson had clearly become an electoral liability that his own cabinet ministers had started the avalanche of parliamentary party revolt. There followed no moment of critical self-reflection within the party, however. To the contrary, in the teeth of a devastating cost-of-living crisis, a collapsing National Health Service, an exodus of essential workers from the public sector, public sector pay strikes, spiralling energy costs and water shortages unchecked by regulators, and a summer marked by unprecedented heatwaves, floods, wildfires and drought, the party's emerging leadership contenders differed only in the timing of their 'revolutionary' commitments to resolve all these issues by shrinking what was left

---

[105] House of Commons, 'Elections Act 2022', https://bills.parliament.uk/bills/3020/publications.
[106] Abby Innes, 'Hungary's Illiberal Democracy', *Current History*, 11 March 2015; Cornel Ban, Gabor Scheiring and Mihal Vasile, 'The Political Economy of National Neoliberalism', *European Politics and Society*, 10 August 2021.

of the state in favour of, by now, demonstrably mythical market virtues. That, and the frequency with which they invoked the name of Thatcher, whose personal inconsistencies and tactical pragmatism, like those of Lenin, were now brushed aside.

Having won that leadership contest in September 2022 by a narrow majority of the party's largely older, wealthier, southern, male, white membership, Truss became the fourth Conservative prime minister in six years. She appointed a cabinet of committed small state, anti-climate action Brexiteers, with nine ministers drawn from the ERG. Now making an explicit virtue of their ideological zeal, Truss and her chancellor, Kwarteng, determined to complete the Camp 1 revolution, but in economic conditions that shone a glaring spotlight on the utopianism of their beliefs. The new government was appointed amidst collapsing living standards and double-digit inflation. The lack of resilience in the UK energy system had left it unusually vulnerable to Putin's leveraging of energy prices through the war on Ukraine, and the population faced a winter in which unpayable energy bills threatened millions with destitution and businesses with bankruptcy. Within three weeks of coming to power, Truss and Kwarteng's answer was to declare radical deregulation, the largest tax cuts in fifty years, including the abolition of the top rate of income tax, and 'free enterprise zones', but they combined this with an unprecedented, open-ended, taxpayer-funded payment of those energy bills instead of a windfall tax on the exceptional profits of the energy companies. The strategy was to ride out the immediate energy crisis through borrowing, while taking a blind leap towards the revolutionary frontier, on the basis that only a more completely Camp 1 Britain would produce 'growth, growth, growth'.[107]

The result of this strategy was a collapse in the value of sterling to its lowest rate against the dollar since 1971, sliding market confidence in UK government bonds and intensifying pressure on the Bank of England to raise interest rates significantly in a country with historically unprecedented levels of private debt. In less than a month at the helm, Thatcher's most devoted disciples had thrown the UK economy into a full-blown re-enactment of the long economic crises of the 1970s, only now amidst shocking social inequality, collapsed public trust in government and a state hollowed out from within. In this single, calamitous

---

[107] Liz Truss, 'Prime Minister's Speech', Conservative Party Conference, Birmingham, September 2022.

political act, Truss and Kwarteng paraded the gulf between theory and reality, between logical and historical time. They demonstrated the impossibility of achieving a small state utopia in the real world in which even financial markets steeped in neoclassical reasoning would refuse to throw billions of pounds at a project where growth strategy, public spending, borrowing and the future tax revenues to pay for it no longer had the slightest credible relationship. As the Resolution Foundation's Torsten Bell concluded on social media: 'Just because you believe in markets, doesn't mean that markets believe in you.'

The political result was a near total and immediate disintegration of electoral support for the Conservative government, as the cost of living and the cost of borrowing soared in a country that had lived beyond its means for decades. Kwarteng was summarily sacked as chancellor by Truss for the diligent implementation of her intentions, and Truss was ousted only days later. The new chancellor, Jeremy Hunt, immediately embarked on a programme of tax increases and public spending cuts to calm the financial markets. With the Camp 1 Brexiteer Rishi Sunak quickly installed as the prime minister, an agenda of harsh austerity and culture wars returned as Conservative 'realism', though it guaranteed only deeper social misery and further developmental decline. Instead of a freer society within a harmonious marketplace for people with ever less need of politics, British neoliberalism had reduced one of the richest, most stable democracies in the world to something dangerously close to political and economic chaos.

Corruption

As Vujačić concluded of the late Soviet and Yugoslav regimes, the shift rightwards, to national socialism, typically came at the price of the Communist Party's collective decision-making, which was increasingly replaced with more personal, charismatic rule. Over time, the legitimacy and organisational coherence of the party could become both subordinate to and dependent on the leader's charisma, or person. And as Vujačić pointed out, 'Once the continued enjoyment of the "spoils of office" becomes a matter of the leader's discretion, the road is open to the kind of political corruption that was the source of so much rot already in the "neo-traditional phase" of late socialism.'[108]

---

[108] Vujačić, 'From Class to Nation', p. 386.

Far from there being a viable social contract, the nexus between the Brezhnev regime and Soviet society had become that of a protection racket, as the Communist Party lost any remaining impulse to renew the revolutionary 'combat task' of the state. Instead, party elites and their enablers in the security forces and the shadow economy had merely intensified their parasitic practices within the failing system. Once Khrushchev's reforms were abandoned, the Communist Party of the Soviet Union retightened its monopolistic lock on political power and socio-economic privilege as it mouthed the traditional platitudes about the sunlit uplands to come.[109] Likewise, the economic theories of Camp 1 have also become an alibi: the ideological pretext in this case, for an outright rentier capitalism now characterised by open cronyism and clientelism at the top. The rise of systematic corruption and political cronyism within neoliberalism is a feature, not an aberration, as it was under the Soviet system.

'Corporate state capture' is the high point of corruption whereby private interests subvert legitimate channels of political influence and shape the rules of the legislative and institutional game through private payments to public officials.[110] The dynamic towards capture in materialist utopias is rooted in the fact that their ideologies privilege the interests of one social group as its political vanguard. In neoliberalism it is business, rather than the industrial proletariat, that is taken to exemplify the idealised rational economic agent and hence 'business' is endowed with the 'leading role' in society. Corporations are sacralised as the bearer of true consciousness. If we take representative democracy in Abraham Lincoln's formulation as 'government of the people, by the people, for the people', then such an idealisation of any one group implies the fundamental disruption of that inclusive principle. The exceptional access given to corporations in British policymaking in everything from agenda-setting and policy development through to its delivery, audit and review has enabled corporate state capture and all the conflicts of interest that attend. In *Statecraft* Thatcher had argued, 'Those who think they know, but are mistaken, and act upon their mistakes, are the most dangerous people to have in charge.'

---

[109] Jowitt, *New World Disorder*, pp. 223–226.
[110] Joel Hellman, Geraint Jones and Daniel Kaufmann, 'Seize the State, Seize the Day: State Capture, Corruption and Influence in Transition', World Bank Policy Research Working Paper 2444, 2000, pp. 2–3.

The political practices of late-stage British neoliberalism suggest that in this, at least, she was right.[111]

To be clear, such creeping corporate state capture need not be intentional from the outset to develop in the neoliberal state. But since no neoliberal policy or administrative strategies work in the terms by which they are justified, informal connections and practices must emerge to manage the unintended consequences that result. When you combine an economic orthodoxy that insists on self-regulation as an article of faith, a corporate culture dominated by financial extraction over investment and a political culture in which the younger generations of neoliberal MPs have been schooled in the primacy of self-interest, there is nothing that obviously intervenes to stop those informal practices from becoming corrupt practices. In the absence of meaningful regulation, the stage is well and truly set for corporations themselves to become the de facto planning agents, but those corporations are planning for private profit, and not for the public interest.

The failure to stop corruption and corporate state capture is a case of deliberate 'regulatory drift' in the face of dramatic institutional change. Regulatory drift occurs when formal rules are knowingly held constant in the face of major shifts in context, so that outcomes change.[112] Britain's neoliberal governments have insisted that the historical norms of 'self-regulation' be maintained by politicians around abuse of function, money laundering, trading in influence, prohibited political contributions, lobbying abuse, consultancy, cronyism and revolving doors of corporate-government appointments, even as the opportunities to abuse those powers have increased enormously from those available in the more Weberian post-war state. The result is that none of these behaviours are covered by the Bribery Act, and only partially and inadequately by other legislations, and with weak transparency and enforcement mechanisms. Cronyism, nepotism and revolving door abuses are covered by no legislation at all.[113]

---

[111] Thatcher, *Statecraft*, p. 104.
[112] Jacob Hacker, Kathleen Thelen and Paul Pierson, 'Drift and Conversion: Hidden Faces of Institutional Change', in James Mahoney and Kathleen Thelen, *Advances in Comparative Historical Analysis* (Cambridge: Cambridge University Press, 2015).
[113] Nick Maxwell and Ben Cowdock, *Corruption Laws: A Non-lawyers' Guide to Laws and Offences in the UK Relating to Corrupt Behaviour* (London: Transparency International, 2016), p. 3.

The United Kingdom's cross-party Committee on Standards in Public Life, the Public Administration and Constitutional Affairs Committee and the Public Accounts Select Committee have repeatedly called on government to tighten all these rules, only to be rebuffed in all their substantive requests. To take just one example, the 2017 report on the Advisory Committee on Business Appointments (ACOBA) by the Public Administration and Constitutional Affairs Committee concluded that the regulator was 'toothless'.[114] But all the recommendations to give ACOBA real powers, made after multiple inquiries by both the Committee on Standards and the Public Accounts Select Committee, have been rejected, despite the repeated governmental statements of concern in public. In 2010, for example, Cameron had made great political play of decrying the laxity of rules around lobbying.[115] But, in March 2021 it emerged that Cameron himself had worked as a paid advisor for Greensill Bank and lobbied the chancellor and two Treasury ministers to secure Bank of England Covid-19 loans for the financial firm before it collapsed.[116] Voters were still nevertheless expected to believe that Cameron had been recruited for his judgement.

For neoliberal governments to have set up regulations that kept pace with the growth in the political power of large firms would have violated many of the core assumptions of the neoliberal project: that unfettered business activity is the route to general equilibrium, that self-regulation is always superior to state action, that rational self-interest confers no unacceptable social losses. The result is that these assumptions have become a convenient fiction as corporate state capture intensifies. By 2015, in Britain there were some 4,000 people working professionally in the United Kingdom's £2 billion lobbying industry, which made it the third largest lobby in the world.[117] While the sociologists of New Labour's 'Third Way' had insisted the state

---

[114] House of Commons Public Administration and Constitutional Affairs Committee, 'Managing Ministers' and Officials' Conflicts of Interest: Time for Clearer Values, Principles and Action', 24 April 2017 (HC 252), p. 3, www.publications.parliament.uk/pa/cm201617/cmselect/cmpubadm/252/252.pdf.

[115] Andrew Porter, 'David Cameron Warns Lobbying Is the Next Political Scandal', *The Telegraph*, 8 February 2010.

[116] George Parker, 'David Cameron Lobbied Matt Hancock on Greensill's NHS Pay Scheme', *Financial Times*, 11 April 2021.

[117] Elizabeth David-Barrett, *Lifting the Lid on Lobbying: The Hidden Exercise of Power and Influence in the UK* (London: Transparency International, 2015).

was in the process of organically withering away,[118] it is clear the corporate sector has never been under any such illusion.

The public almost certainly underestimate the opportunities for abuse and corporate exploitation in the neoliberal state even if, on balance, the evidence before 2019 was that most MPs and the vast majority of civil servants, that is, those not parachuted into senior positions from the private sector, continued to resist those temptations for a variety of reasons: a stubborn ethos of public service; adherence to the guidelines on appropriate conduct as disciplined by critical media scrutiny and, last but not least, the history of political careers cut short by scandal. It is equally clear, however, that this inherited political culture of self-restraint had been weakening with each new intake of MPs: in 2019 a fifth of the Conservative's new MPs had a background in lobbying or public relations.[119] Most dangerously of all, the second Johnson government proceeded to destroy this culture from the top. Throughout the pandemic one cabinet minister after another breached the Ministerial Code,[120] and then the law, but in a complete break with post-war practice, no resignations followed.[121] When Truss became the prime minister she appointed Matthew Sinclair, former CEO of the Taxpayer's Alliance, a libertarian think tank of notoriously murky funding, as her chief economic advisor.

What had tended to get lost in the noisy scandals of each breach in the Code was that the clientelist practices of the second Johnson government were not simply a result of the prime minister's personal delinquency: they were completely consistent with the right of the party's ideological convictions, and the most vivid illustration of this came in November 2021. When the Standards Committee agreed on a thirty-day suspension of a leading Brexiteer, Owen Paterson, MP, for lobbying violations, Johnson's response was to place a three-line whip on Conservative MPs to abolish the committee, and the vote was passed.[122]

---

[118] Anthony Giddens, *Modernity and Self-identity: Self and Society in the Late Modern Age* (Redwood City: Stanford University Press, 1991).
[119] Adam Ramsay, Caroline Molloy and Tamasin Cave, 'Tory MPs Have Worked as Lobbyists', *Open Democracy*, 21 December 2019.
[120] 'Priti Patel: Bullying Inquiry Head Quits as PM Backs Home Secretary', BBC News, 20 November 2020.
[121] Anoosh Chekalian, 'Gavin Williamson, Matt Hancock and Michael Gove Acted Unlawfully: What Next?', *The New Statesman*, 15 June 2021.
[122] Richard Vaughan and Emily Ferguson, 'Owen Paterson: The Lobbying Row Explained after Tory MPs Voted to Rip Up Anti-sleaze Rules', *The Independent*, 3 November 2021.

The public outrage that greeted this decision forced Johnson to retreat, and Paterson to resign, but his ministers had supported the strategy and Paterson himself was arguably sincere, in his own ideological terms, when he claimed he held his integrity 'very dear'.[123] As Alain Supiot points out, 'From the perspective of the total market... society is simply a swarm of contracting particles whose relations to each are based purely on calculated self-interest. Calculation – and hence the contract – thus comes to occupy the space previously assigned to the law as a normative reference.'[124] Here was the amorality that matched the narrowly transactional worldview of the neoliberal utopia. Its politics had turned the once broad church of the democratic Conservative Party into a corporate brokerage agency, a development that Truss would seek only to consolidate.

Colin Crouch had it right when he described the neoliberal state as a 'semi-permeable membrane' in which doctrinaire governments refrain from intervening in the private sector but enable ever greater business access to public authority and revenue.[125] The extraordinary feature of corporate state capture under neoliberalism is that it is gifted as a matter of *policy*. Successive UK governments have both consciously and inadvertently built opportunities for the abuse of public powers for private gain that elsewhere you would have to blackmail or bribe, if not kill for. It is a peculiarly tragic outcome for a country that hitherto had suffered low rates of political corruption and a comparative integrity in public life achieved only after centuries of reform.

Conclusion

Ideologies matter in democracies because they structure the debate within a given set of institutions. In totalitarian systems, or in revolutionary regimes that aspire to a monologue of power, ideas matter absolutely because they define all institutions and the doctrine under which they operate. Neoliberalism in its hegemony has pushed to the margins what should have remained a continuous debate about Britain's real political economic dynamics, and by now these dynamics

---

[123] Heather Stewart and Aubrey Allegretti, 'MP Owen Paterson Resigns from "Cruel World" of Politics', *The Guardian*, 4 November 2021.

[124] Alain Supiot, *Governance by Numbers: The Making of a Legal Model of Allegiance*, translated by Saskia Brown (Oxford: Hart Publishing, 2017), p. 5.

[125] Colin Crouch, 'The Paradoxes of Privatization and Public Service Outsourcing', *Political Quarterly* 86 (December 2015): 156–171, p. 165.

are of stagnating investment, market concentration towards monopoly, financialisation and corporate rent-seeking from the state, precarious employment, stark social inequality, stalling innovation, rising corruption, a trashing of Britain's 'soft' power, globally, and, most pressing of all, the ecological emergency. None of these problems can be solved through markets alone, if at all.

In the aftermath of the Global Financial Crisis, Chantal Mouffe identified the illusory nature of consensus under neoliberalism. She warned that the vision of a 'post-political' future so internalised it now passed for 'common sense' was actively dangerous. It failed to acknowledge the continuity of social disagreement under capitalism: of conflicts of interest that could only be reconciled through a political competition that sought to express the interests of all sides and to offer effective strategies for their amelioration, as framed by a clear social purpose. Mouffe warned that the progressives who argued for a 'second modernity' in which 'individuals liberated from collective ties can now dedicate themselves to cultivating a diversity of lifestyles, unhindered by antiquated attachments' had excessive faith in individual rationalism and a desire for a world 'beyond left and right, beyond hegemony, beyond sovereignty and beyond antagonism', that is, beyond politics. She concluded that this delusion would only exacerbate 'the antagonistic potential existing in society'.[126]

At the root of this impulse to escape politics is the aspiration to replace it with a supposedly dependable economic science, but as Richard Bronk points out, the need to 'write out' complexity is embedded in the DNA of neoclassical economics, enforced by the idea that values exist along a single plane of utility and hence there will always be one right answer in any trade-off or decision to be made. Quite apart from the epistemological impossibility of knowing what the outcomes of such decisions must be, such a conception must strip decision-making of its three-dimensionality and of the ethical complexities better understood as an inalienable feature of human society.[127]

While there are clearly multiple ways in which the neoliberal imaginary violates democratic conventions, the most glaring is this: that in laying claim to scientific infallibility, neoliberalism contradicts the basic democratic principle that voters are sovereign and can change their values and

---

[126] Chantal Mouffe, *On the Political* (London: Routledge, 2011), Introduction.
[127] Richard Bronk, *The Romantic Economist: Imagination in Economics* (Cambridge University Press, 2009), pp. 263–264, Chapter 7.

their priorities over time, including about the state that serves them. It is difficult to do this, however, without critical narratives that allow us to reflect on our conditions from outside the dominant paradigm and to imagine alternatives.[128] It is made even harder when alternatives are derided as 'parochial' – as unscientific and hence 'wrong' as distinct from simply representative of a different constituency or moral perspective.

It is this question of alternative perspectives that throws into relief one of the most important political *differences* between the Soviet and neoliberal systems. It was in the nature of Soviet central planning that every single person's life was touched daily and explicitly by the state's machinations. When the state failed everybody knew how it failed. When the Soviet state was reformed, everybody knew from their own experience how inadequate those reforms were. This 'undeniability' helps explain why, as soon as it became apparent under Mikhail Gorbachev's leadership that not even revolutions for democracy in Central Europe would be repressed, the result was a domino effect across the entire territory of the former USSR. It is arguably here, at this time of late-system crisis, that neoliberalism may actually prove more tenacious in its forms of governance. In this light the blazing zeal of Truss – her unquestioning faith in markets and her open rejection of the redistributive role of the state – at least had the virtue of ideological honesty.

The effects of state failure in Britain have been dispersed, to name only the most obvious differences, by age and income level, by source, form and level of education and by employment sector, region, ethnicity and sex. Despite the best efforts of neoliberal governments to convince us that all the major problems we confront in our lives are our own, and we alone are responsible for them, we may nevertheless know of, and aspire to, alternative diagnoses and prescriptions in principle. But until one, and ideally all, of the major parties repudiates this governing dystopia, none of these new interpretations will have the authority of 'high', national, political expression, nor the resources to support them. Until the paradigm shift comes from the top, from the party system itself, Britain risks a deepening political fragmentation and narrative chaos in which it may be relatively easy for neoliberalism's Brezhnevites to cling to power.

---

[128] Jonathan White and Lea Ypi, 'On Partisan Political Justification', *American Political Science Review* 105 (2) (May 2011): 381–396, pp. 385–386.

10 A Politics for the End of Time

Britain's neoliberal transformation was a revolution in the strict sense – that new political and economic institutions were designed to replace the old. The resulting regime has proved anything but stable, however. The founders of this revolution assumed that if you shrank the state and brought business practices into what remained you would get the best of states and markets: a lean, more efficient bureaucracy and dynamic, innovative enterprises. What Britain's neoliberal governments created in practice was the worst of both 'regimes': an organisationally fragmented, and yet rigidly bureaucratic, public sector beset by conflicts of interests and a private sector dominated by large corporations that abandon investment in favour of short-term financial extraction. Neoliberal governments have reproduced many of the pathologies of Soviet statecraft, only now in capitalist form. My question was 'why'?

Eric Jarosinski has jokingly defined ideology as the mistaken belief that your beliefs are neither beliefs nor mistaken, but my argument has never been against political ideology per se.[1] On the contrary, we need political ideologies to provide us with well-founded diagnoses of society's problems from different perspectives and agendas of potential solutions that may or may not require the interventions of the state in some form. In addition, political parties are not simply one mechanism among others that make liberal democracies 'work'. Historically, parties have been the principal and most practical way to transmit the concerns of the electorate to those state agencies able to drive real social change.[2] When organised around clear social values, as distinct from a utopian blueprint, political parties have been vital for effective political expression in societies that are inescapably argumentative

---

[1] Eric Jarosinski, *Nein: A Manifesto* (Melbourne: Text Publishing, 2015), p. 122.
[2] Peter Mair, *Ruling the Void: The Hollowing of Western Democracy* (London: Verso Books, 2013), p. 21.

and prone to conflict. This is why a bipartisan consensus on a materialist utopia could only prove destructive to democratic politics.

It is only in totalitarian systems that a single doctrine aspires to define all institutions, the one governmental logic under which they should operate, and the 'correct' rationality for the citizenry itself, and we have seen how neoliberalism is totalitarian in this strict sense. Indeed, the political science distinction between totalitarian and authoritarian regimes lies precisely in this transformative, rather than opportunistic, use of power. In the case of neoliberalism, the resulting philosophy is phenomenally harsh, both in its theory and in its practice. To be three-dimensionally human – fallible, vulnerable and generous – in a neoliberal society is to be an ontological freak. But as Cornelius Castoriadis pointed out,

> To treat a person as a thing or as a purely mechanical system is not less but *more* imaginary than claiming to see him as an owl; it represents an even deeper dive into the imaginary... Primitive societies always seem to preserve a certain duplicity in these assimilations [of people with other things], but modern society in its practice takes them literally, in the most brutal ways.[3]

If today you worry that you have failed to 'invest' enough in yourself, in your education, in your relationships or in your productivity, if you pause to wonder whether you are truly 'living your best life' and, if not, which of your own inadequacies has caused your lack of self-optimisation, you might reasonably ask when such 'efficiency' became an all-consuming requirement. It becomes a political act to refuse to occupy the binary narrative spaces that a late-neoliberal regime would prefer us to inhabit, as winners or wasters,[4] patriots or traitors. In truth, it is the insistence that a superhuman calculator is the ideal human subject that is so strange, and so alienated from our nature, although it makes it altogether less surprising that narcissistic cynics emerge as the charismatic defenders of late-neoliberal systems built on this image.

While it is surely unsettling to admit that the art of government will always remain uncertain, whatever our powers of reasoning or computation, to acknowledge this is not to suddenly know nothing. It is only to accept that evidence-based analyses, a pluralist debate about

---

[3] Cornelius Castoriadis, *The Imaginary Institution of Society*, translated by Kathleen Blamey (Cambridge, MA: MIT Press, 1998), pp. 99–100.

[4] Wendy Brown, *Undoing the Demos: Neoliberalism's Stealth Revolution* (New York: Zone Books, 2015), Chapter 1.

the nature of justice and a common empathy within the framework of a democratic constitution are likely to prove far more socially beneficial and sustainable than imagining that the human economy is logical, and we know how that logic works. As George Shackle pointed out, 'Only when novelty is eliminated and all is known can reason be the sole guide of conduct.'[5] It follows that a democratic political programme can never be more than provisional, but the founding ideas behind the neoliberal revolution were never democratic by nature. They never operated in its spirit of contingency.

The Book of Laughter and Forgetting

By the close of 2020, a debate had arisen in the United States about President Donald Trump's use of the Nazi strategy in which a revolutionary political force tells a 'big lie' in order to seize power and exclude opponents. The historian Timothy Snyder argued that Trump's insistence that he had won the election he lost was just such a device, and one with the potential to destroy reasoned public argument through the creation of a parallel universe of 'alternative facts'.[6] In the British case, the Leave campaign's determined misrepresentation of the European Union and of Britain's constant victimhood within it might also fall into this category, but we should notice that the arguments made against the European Leviathan were simply a repetition of the deeper falsehood on which neoliberalism is based. The big lie at the heart of neoliberalism is the accusation that the democratic state, and by extension the European Union, is inescapably no more and no better than a self-serving bureaucratic Leviathan. But this was always an assertion based on ideological assumption rather than history, and nothing has proved more fictitious than the replacement utopia.

It was a characteristic of late Soviet socialism that since the party's promises had been gradually reduced to a ridiculous posture, a culture of dark satire was one of the few forms of political agency that

---

[5] George Shackle, *Epistemics and Economics: A Critique of Economic Doctrines* (New Brunswick: Transaction Publishers, 1992), p. 96.
[6] Timothy Snyder, '10 Things You Need to Know about the Big Lie That Threatens to Tear Apart Our Democracy', *Blog Gen*, 13 January 2021, https://gen.medium.com/the-10-things-you-need-to-know-about-the-big-lie-that-threatens-to-tear-apart-our-democracy-58070db279f3.

remained for the population to enjoy.[7] I think it no coincidence then that the crisis of neoliberalism in an open society such as Britain produced in Boris Johnson an antic prime minister who embodied both the promissory posturing itself and an awareness that this posturing is fatuous.[8] It has likewise followed that the political theatre of the cruel and absurd has become the last redoubt of those governments determined to avoid any shift in the economic paradigm.

Johnson's rise to power and the governmental chaos induced in his time in office were a symptom, rather than the cause, of the crisis in British politics. The more the Conservative Party had internalised neoliberal values, the more narrowly transactional its political culture had become, the smaller was the space that survived within it for moral seriousness and integrity beyond the corrupting logic of the quid pro quo. As the poet and former communist Stephen Spender had warned, '[T]he intellectual Communist… puts his faith in an automatism of history which even if it is achieved by bad men by bad means will eventually make men good.'[9]

In a democracy, the language of politics must deal in observable fact for the electoral cycles of mandate, policy and accountability to function, but the temptation for neoliberal governments in crisis is to embrace the anarchy of political affectation and misdirection, to make promises they know they cannot keep, to start political fires they know to be diverting and, when push comes to shove, to simply make stuff up. What alternative strategy do they have, in fact, when reality becomes a constant source of embarrassment to their politics? To take just one example, in March 2021 the government published the findings of a Johnson-appointed Commission on Race and Ethnic Disparities that argued against the existence of institutional racism in Britain, a conclusion it reached by the simple means of ignoring the evidence submitted to it.[10]

---

[7] Alain Supiot, *Governance by Numbers: The Making of a Legal Model of Allegiance*, translated by Saskia Brown (Oxford: Hart Publishing, 2017), p. 15.

[8] Edward Docx, 'The Clown King: How Johnson Made It by Playing the Fool', *The Guardian*, 18 March 2021.

[9] Stephen Spender, in Arthur Koestler, *The God That Failed* (London: Hamish Hamilton, 1950), pp. 229–273, p. 237.

[10] See Nosheen Iqbal, 'Business Chiefs Say Their Advice Ignored in No 10's Race Report', *The Guardian*, 3 April 2021; Gareth Iacobucci, 'Healthcare Leaders Reject "Damaging" Denial That Institutional Racism Exists', *The British Medical Journal* 373 n. 911 (2021).

As A. J. Polan noted in *Lenin and the End of Politics*, '[T]he advent of a society in which the economic grounds for conflict have been removed is also the advent of a society where there is no possibility of political disagreement and debate.'[11] As the Soviets had known from the start, when politics refuses to disappear it must be disappeared, so that it no longer poses a threat to the new order. It is thus the peculiar fate of materialist utopias built on closed-system reasoning that the more completely the doctrine is applied, the greater the misrepresentations of the social and institutional order must become, and the more implausible, fabricated and deliberately divisive the explanations for the deepening crises in the real political economy. When the necessarily imperfect government of people is replaced with a 'science' of the allocation of things, the result is bound to be a growing detachment of public political language from social reality, and any government of committed materialists must eventually embrace the cult-like qualities of these ideas in full, retain the show of it to sustain the power they have acquired or abandon their faith completely. The literature on exactly this phenomenon in the Soviet system thus becomes relevant.

By the early 2020s, Johnson and his cabinet ministers were consistently to be found declaring that under their government failure was success, that the things that had happened had not happened, that the problems that were getting worse were getting better and that the United Kingdom was about to become the most innovative country in the world, or, as the chancellor, Rishi Sunak, put it at the 2021 Conservative conference: 'the most exciting place on the planet'.[12] A government comprised of ministers apparently impervious to basic social and scientific facts had found that their only political option was to invite an electorate hungry for hope and meaningful allegiances to believe in both joyful fictions and perfidious enemies as a patriotic act.

In Arthur Koestler's chilling novel about the nihilism of purely instrumental reasoning, a senior Bolshevik, Rubashov, is required to denounce himself so that he may offer himself up as the scapegoat

---

[11] Anthony Polan, *Lenin and the End of Politics* (London: Methuen Ltd, 1984), p. 176.
[12] George Parker, 'Sunak Warns Excessive Public Borrowing Is "Immoral" and Hints at Tax Cuts', *The Financial Times*, 4 October 2021.

'saboteur' in a show trial, indeed, to do this as his last political act. Rubashov must destroy himself to fulfil the function assigned to him by the logic of the ceaseless revolution, and it leads him to a terrible realisation. He says, 'I no longer believe in my own infallibility. That is why I am lost.'[13] Under the government of Johnson such trials of self-abnegation through faith were not nearly so lethal, but they were likewise to be found at the top of the governing party. In the aftermath of Brexit, it became clearer with each passing news day that a willingness to repeatedly humiliate yourself intellectually, morally and in public was a necessary condition for being a member of the Johnson cabinet, if not of the parliamentary Conservative Party itself, as it more completely abandoned its basic decency, the last vestiges of its Burkean pragmatism and its respect for evidence and the law.

In *The Captive Mind*, the Polish Nobel Laureate Czesław Miłosz had explored the psychological costs to those who chose to surrender their capacity for independent thought – to those who clung to the belief that there was an inexorable natural mechanism at work that justified the daily moral outrages or organisational absurdities they had witnessed, if not perpetrated themselves. Miłosz cited the novel *Farewell to Autumn* by the novelist Stanislaw Witkiewicz, an allegory in which traders appear in a stylised Poland peddling the 'pill of Murti-Bing'.

A man who used these pills changed completely. He became serene and happy. The problems he had struggled with until then suddenly appeared to be superficial and unimportant. He smiled indulgently at those who continued to worry about them. Most affected were all questions pertaining to unsolvable ontological difficulties. A man who swallowed Murti-Bing pills became impervious to any metaphysical concerns... He lived in the midst of his compatriots like a healthy individual surrounded by madmen. More and more people took the Murti-Bing cure, and their resultant calm contrasted sharply with the nervousness of their environment.[14]

Miłosz, a poet, examined these temptations with sympathy. He acknowledged that to abdicate your critical intelligence in favour of a panacea is a relief from the constant effort of hope and rebellion in an unceasingly uncertain world. He nevertheless concluded that the price

---

[13] Arthur Koestler, *Darkness at Noon*, translated by Philip Boehm (1941) (London: Vintage Classics, 2020).
[14] Czesław Miłosz, *The Captive Mind* (1953) (London: Penguin Books, 1985), p. 6.

any of us pay when we do that is a dislocation of the self: a necessary splitting off from one's own capacity for critical reason. In Richard Crossman's 1949 collection of essays by penitent former communists, Koestler also explained how difficult it became for one side to persuade the other once the debate was polarised between a politics based on an observable reality and a politics based on utopia. Thus, 'To the psychiatrist, both the craving for Utopia and the rebellion against the status quo are symptoms of social maladjustment. To the social reformer, both are symptoms of a healthy rational attitude.' As for his own conversion to the materialist cause, Koestler says:

I learned to distrust my mechanistic preoccupation with facts and to regard the world around me in the light of dialectic interpretation. It was a satisfactory and indeed blissful state; once you had assimilated the technique you were no longer disturbed by facts; they all automatically took on the proper colour and fell into their proper place.[15]

In communist Czechoslovakia, Václav Havel, then a dissident playwright, had written an essay in 1978 called 'The Power of the Powerless' in which he confirmed these experiences of communist life.

To wandering humankind it offers an immediately available home: all one has to do is accept it, and suddenly everything becomes clear once more, life takes on new meaning, and all mysteries, unanswered questions, anxiety, and loneliness vanish. Of course, one pays dearly for this low-rent home: the price is abdication of one's own reason, conscience, and responsibility, for an essential aspect of this ideology is the consignment of reason and conscience to a higher authority.[16]

In the era of Brexit these observations have become ever more relevant, and we can see why, when politicians and their supporters are caught within the utopian mind-set, the well-founded criticism of opponents are disregarded as false consciousness, as not motivated by empirical facts, or the wisdom or pain of experience, or analytical expertise in any given arena. The experts explicitly despised by the Conservative minister Michael Gove during the Leave campaign in 2016 could consequently be dismissed as mere products of the old system they sought to defend, their arguments implicitly derided as a thin veneer for their material

---

[15] Koestler, *The God That Failed*, p. 34.
[16] Václav Havel, 'The Power of the Powerless', (October 1978), translated by Paul Wilson, *East European Politics and Societies* 32 (2) (2018): 353–408, p. 357

self-interest.[17] This temptation to pour scorn on your critics without respectful reflection on their analyses is a risk in any ideological position, but it becomes a Manichean fight in an ideology that understands itself as the one true science. In 1928, Joseph Stalin had likewise run a campaign that encouraged 'a healthy lack of faith in the specialists', specifically those in the economic and educational bureaucracies, in an effort to silence expert opposition to the scale of the first five-year plan.[18] There was no question of Gove terrorising anyone, but the implication that he and his supporters had access to a higher knowledge was no less arrogant.

In the 1979 essay 'Maggots and Angels', written from a Polish prison, Adam Michnik considered how absolutist ideas must brutalise human discourse, as nuance and sympathy are replaced by claims of purity versus impurity. In an observation that also resonates with the bitter arguments of the Brexit campaign, Michnik warned that this same toxic condition would spread to the opponents of an oppressive dogma. Thus, in the context of late communism's still active repressions, he wrote,

[The dissident] who perceived conformists as resembling slaves found in himself and his friends the pathos and tragedy of the romantic heroes. Seeing maggots in the cowed population, he 'angelized' himself and his friends... The 'angelic' character of the picture he had of himself led him – often subconsciously – to assign himself special rights.[19]

In 'On Resistance', Michnik acknowledged that resentment was the natural response to a humiliating system that had deprived so many individuals of their own subjectivity, their community, their ideals and their language, but he warned that they would be left alone with their hate, 'which spells helplessness'.[20] He concluded that Poland would never transcend the vicious politics of its twentieth century without

---

[17] Henry Mance, 'Britain Has Had Enough of Experts, Says Michael Gove', *Financial Times*, 3 June 2016.

[18] See Jeremy Azrael, *Managerial Power and Soviet Politics* (Cambridge, MA: Harvard University Press, 1966), pp. 55–57; Robert William Davies, 'Economic Aspects of Stalinism', in Alec Nove, *The Stalin Phenomenon* (London: Weidenfeld and Nicolson, 1993), p. 55.

[19] Adam Michnik, 'Maggots and Angels', in *Letters from Prison and Other Essays*, translated by Maya Latynski (Berkeley: University of California Press, 1985), pp. 169–199, pp. 195, 198.

[20] Michnik, 'On Resistance: A Letter from Białołęka', in *Letters*, 41–64, p. 51.

empathy and mutual respect and 'an unceasing struggle for reform and evolution that seeks an expansion of civil liberties and human rights'.[21]

In the aftermath of the monologue of communist power, these dissidents of Central Europe were elected to government only to find they faced a legacy of historical relativism and proliferating conspiracy theory. Because everyone had lived under a pseudo-scientific doctrine of life that had proved profoundly misconceived and exceptionally prone to manipulation and corruption, the political inheritance was one of widespread public distrust in everything associated with those decades, including in political parties, the state and in science itself. The result was the high circulation of conspiratorial accounts of what would happen next and who was *really* in power.[22] These theories took the same narrative form as the rejected ideology: that of total explanation unmoored from observable reality. In this light it is understandable that political mistrust and conspiratorial discourses had become rife in Britain by the early 2020s.

So where does all this leave the British neoliberal state? Soviet regimes had evolved from 'combat' governments who fought the old system and the class enemy, to consolidating regimes that secured Communist Party power, to 'inclusion' regimes which tried, and failed, to create a centrally planned economy that could fulfil the Edenic promises of the ideology. They ended, over decades, with economic stagnation, corruption, and the instrumental use of a divisive, nationalist politics.[23] It is usually unwise in comparative politics to look for neat synchronicity in how political regimes play out in different countries, but such synchronicity is surely inevitable in the histories of closed-system materialist utopias. Open-ended social reality must force them to proceed through revolutionary idealism, failure, doctrinaire remedial action, resilient failure and on to decadence and systemic crisis. The sorry punchline, however, is that Britain's neoliberal revolution has produced a state far closer to the hyper-centralised, arbitrarily intervening, bureaucratically rigid and captured mercenary behemoth of the original public choice fever dream than its post-war state, however imperfect, *ever* was.

---

[21] Michnik, 'A New Evolutionism', in *Letters*, 135–149, p. 143.
[22] Shari Cohen, *Politics without a Past: The Absence of History in Post-Communist Nationalism* (Durham: Duke University Press, 1999).
[23] Kenneth Jowitt, *New World Disorder: The Leninist Extinction* (Berkeley: University of California Press, 1992), Chapter 3.

Not only has the British state singularly failed to wither away, it cannot, so long as the electorate continues to insist that the democratic state – the state supposed to operate for the people – can defend them from the enormities of contemporary capitalism. But, under neoliberalism, the state's capacity to act in the public interest has been substantially undermined. The neoliberal revolution has proved an exercise in high modernism,[24] but what passed for intellectual innovation in late British neoliberalism only demonstrated how the country had condemned itself to a game of 'Grandfather's Footsteps', unaware, apparently, that Grandad was a Red.

In June 2020, Gove delivered a speech on 'The Privilege of Public Service' as the Annual Ditchley Lecture. His purpose was to set out the government's agenda for the next stage in the radical reform of Whitehall. Widely regarded as having been at least co-written by Dominic Cummings, many of its aspirations might have been lifted from the Soviet debate on cybernetic planning. Its leading argument was that 'government needs to evaluate data more rigorously' and to do this it needs to hire more mathematicians, statisticians, data scientists and others from the physical sciences. Why? Because

> so many policy and implementation decisions depend on understanding mathematical reasoning. That means we need to reform not just recruitment, but training. We need to ensure more policy makers and decision makers feel comfortable discussing the Monte Carlo method or Bayesian statistics, more of those in Government are equipped to read a balance sheet and discuss what constitutes an appropriate return on investment, more are conversant with the commercial practices of those from whom we procure services and can negotiate the right contracts and enforce them appropriately.[25]

Mathematics was presented here as the discipline – the enchanted craft – that would optimise all these decisions and relationships and render them efficient. The emphasis on comprehensive measurement in 'The Privilege of Public Service' was positively nostalgic. Gove declared that government must prove that money is well spent, that

---

[24] Michael Moran, *High Modernism and the British Regulatory State* (Oxford: Oxford University Press, 2007).

[25] Michael Gove, 'On the Privilege of Public Service', Annual Ditchley Lecture, 1 July 2020, Cabinet Office, www.gov.uk/government/speeches/the-privilege-of-public-service-given-as-the-ditchley-annual-lecture.

improvements must be measurable; he asked for 'hard, testable data' on how each policy has worked and suggested that 'randomised control trials' should be used for comparative quality control. He argued that by collecting more information, data analysts would learn the 'valuable lessons that lie buried in our data', as if the ontological question of how to interpret that data was already solved. Here was the agenda for perfect indirect centralisation reborn, but now, so Cummings enthused elsewhere, with the possibility of 'real time data',[26] as if the existence of astonishing quantities of contemporaneous information must make you suddenly omniscient about what it all meant.

The Cyberneticians' dream of government as an orderly machine, with inputs, outputs and feedback loops, was thus resurrected. The potential abuses of such powers were immense, as demonstrated in the Soviet system, but now with an altogether higher technological capacity for personal surveillance with little to nothing by way of an increase in wisdom to show for it. Forty years in, and the leading edge of Conservative statecraft was to reinvent the Soviet strategies of the 1960s, as they too had prayed that mathematics would resolve the institutional maze their doctrinaire predecessors had created. 'The Privilege of Public Service' opened with a quote from Antonio Gramsci, but it was Lenin who haunted this text, opposed by Gramsci insofar as he insisted on reading Marx as a determinist.

The Ratchet Effect of Failure

As Joan Robinson wrote in 1977, 'historical time moves from the dark past behind it into the unknown future in front', while the purely 'logical' time of neoclassical models 'can be traced from left to right on the surface of a blackboard'.[27] In practice, governmental prescriptions based on diagnoses made in logical time build in a ratchet mechanism for failure in historical time. Doctrinaire projects of state

---

[26] Dominic Cummings, 'On the Referendum #33: High Performance Government, "Cognitive Technologies", Michael Nielsen, Bret Victor, & "Seeing Rooms"', *Dominic Cummings Blog*, 16 June 2019, www.dominiccummings.com/2019/06/26/on-the-referendum-33-high-performance-government-cognitive-technologies-michael-nielsen-bret-victor-seeing-rooms/.

[27] Joan Robinson, 'The Labour Theory of Value as an Analytical System', in *Collected Economic Papers*, Vol. 5 (London: Basil Blackwell and Oxford, 1977), p. 57.

transformation built on utopian economic blueprints contain the seeds of their own undoing, sown in their lack of analytical humility. When confronted with the developmental failures caused by policy, the more ideologically committed the government, the more the closed-system reasoning in neoliberalism dictates a doubling down on action in the belief that, if not now, it must be at the point of revolutionary completion that the programme would be proven right.

This same tendency towards governmental introversion Havel identified in communism exists more fiercely in neoclassical economics, and consequently in the politics it justifies, because neoclassical economics is more completely de-historicised. The promise of convergence towards ever greater market efficiency is an artefact of logical reasoning, not of history. But in one of the most important political economy works of the twentieth century, *The Great Transformation*, Karl Polanyi had demonstrated that, to the contrary, economic development was inescapably politically contingent. Polanyi showed how periods of laissez-faire orthodoxy had been pushed by the more politically powerful economic forces of wealth-holders who wished to operate without constraint, but their actions had invariably produced social dislocation on such a scale that a remedial wave of social protection had tended to follow. He refers to this reaction as the 'double movement' from liberalisation and commodification, through social dislocation, to social mitigation. As a result, not only could Polanyi famously conclude that '*laissez faire* was planned' but that the constant evolution of markets and states should be understood as coterminous and in constant socio-political dialogue. The idea that markets exist by natural, as distinct from human, law was flatly contradicted by historical experience. Markets were made by the state.[28] It is consequently one of the more fundamental intellectual ironies of the supply-side revolution that the neoliberals have only one instrument at their disposal for the making and mending of markets, and it continues to be the state.

Given persistent failures within their marketised machinery of government, committed neoliberals will only offer remedies from a necessarily fixed repertoire of privatisation, outsourcing, less regulation,

---

[28] Karl Polanyi, *The Great Transformation: The Political and Economic Origins of Our Time*, 2nd ed. (Boston: Beacon Press, 2001) (first published in 1944), p. 147.

re-regulation in favour of capital, lower taxes, new targets, new plans, iterations of 'the corrected managerial line', tighter budgetary ceilings, more recruitment from business, new production measures and ever more synoptic forms of regulatory oversight. But it follows that the disruptive energy of these doctrines becomes fully unwound only once the dysfunction, corporate state capture, inequality and disorder they create have spread to every part of the polity, that is, when the entropy is total. In the autumn of 2022, as the accelerationist government of Liz Truss imploded in under one month, the United Kingdom came extraordinarily close to that moment.

The neoliberal prescription is held to be scientific, though it is nothing of the kind in methodological terms. On closer inspection, the argumentation tends to be more obviously religious in quality. This is politics as revealed prophecy, and the potency of neoliberal thought is not least that of a quasi-religious philosophy given fully institutionalised power – another direct parallel with Soviet communism. When the core axioms are proved wrong or unreliable, but their advocates refuse to adjust their views, we enter another territory much surveyed in the most insightful anthropology and dissident literature of the Soviet system. As Koestler said of communism,

> From the psychologist's point of view there is little difference between a revolutionary and a traditionalist faith. All true faith is uncompromising, radical, purist; hence the true traditionalist is always a revolutionary zealot in conflict with pharisaian society, with the lukewarm corrupters of the creed. And vice versa; the revolutionary's Utopia, which in appearance represents a complete break with the past, is always modelled on some image of the lost Paradise, of a legendary Golden Age. The classless Communist society, according to Marx and Engels, was to be a revival, at the end of the dialectical spiral, of the primitive Communist society which stood at its beginning. Thus, all true faith involves a revolt against the believer's [real] social environment, and the projection into the future of an idea derived from the remote past. All Utopias are fed from the sources of mythology; the social engineer's blueprints are merely revised editions of the ancient text.[29]

As Tony Judt elaborated in *Thinking the Twentieth Century*, Leninism was strategically designed to substitute for organised religion, 'complete with hierarchy, elite, a liturgy and catechism'. Where Marxism told us the story of 'a lost world that we might regain' Leninism

---

[29] Koestler, *The God That Failed*, p. 16.

embraced the new theory of human destiny and, with it, a new narrative of 'necessary sacrifice' in the services of the revolution.[30] It managed to evoke not just the innocence of life before the Biblical Fall but also, and lethally, the 'last battles' depicted in Revelations, in which a rider on a white horse will lead the armies of heaven against those of the false prophet, Satan, and all will be judged on their works and those found wanting must be thrown into the fire.[31]

The British have tended to think of Leninism as entirely foreign to the 'common sense' we historically and complacently ascribe to ourselves, but in the meantime, we apparently swallowed whole a strategy for government that fails to integrate the most basic social realities, such as the existence of time, technological change, cooperative behaviour, culture, empathy, uncertainty, ethics and imagination. In neoliberalism too you see the appeal to the religious impulse that could be proclaimed to the public as redemptive prophecy, and adorned with homilies, only this time about the evils of 'socialism'. As Margaret Thatcher declared in 1975,

Something vital has been lost, which we must restore...[but] we are still the same people. All that has happened is that we have temporarily lost confidence in our own strength. We have lost sight of the banners. The trumpets have given an uncertain sound. It is our duty, our purpose, to raise those banners high, so that all can see them, to sound the trumpets clearly and boldly so that all can hear them. Then we shall not have to convert people to our principles. They will simply rally to those which truly are their own.[32]

Both Soviet and neoliberal materialist doctrines insist that man can stop being the 'object of history' as Marx put it, and hence no longer gripped by false interpretations as he comprehends the 'truth'. As Leszek Kołakowski said of Marxism, '[T]he riddle of history is solved, man's alienation is ended.'[33] The expectation in both cases is that their uniquely scientific revolution will abolish the contradictions of past society and usher in a golden age. But as Kołakowski warned, even

---

[30] Tony Judt and Timothy Snyder, *Thinking the Twentieth Century* (New York: Random House, 2012), pp. 82–85.
[31] Revelations 20 (King James Version).
[32] Margaret Thatcher, 'Speech to the Conservative Central Council', 15 March 1975, www.margaretthatcher.org/document/102655.
[33] Leszek Kołakowski, 'The Devil in History', in George Robert Urban, *Stalinism: Its Impact on Russia and the World* (London: Wildwood House, 1982), p. 247.

'Christianity does not claim that God's justice will prevail in our life in this world – that merit will be rewarded, and wrongdoing punished. It holds that God's ways are inscrutable – that we cannot comprehend them by intellectual cognition alone... Communism, by contrast, claims to be offering a scientific and empirically verifiable explanation of the whole of reality.'[34] But, he added elsewhere, 'it is a caricature and a bogus form of religion, since it presents its temporal eschatology as a scientific system, which religious mythologies do not purport to be'.[35]

The political economic orthodoxies of the post-war West had accepted our imperfection and the deep fallibility of human foresight: our 'original sin' if you must. In stark contrast, Leninists and neoliberals have insisted that thanks to them alone we were no longer sentenced to see through a glass, darkly,[36] and the authority ascribed to neoclassical economics has come to resemble that asserted by Leninism. But the authority ascribed to such orthodoxy and its practitioners is better understood as cultural more than scientific, for theirs is the presumption of a 'clerisy': the currently assigned specialists in cognition, legitimation, salvation and ritual, the monopoly-seeking seers, who claim access to a higher order of knowledge, so that they may define a supposedly unifying 'doctrine'.[37]

By demonstrating how Britain has reproduced so many of the pathologies of the Soviet system I hope this book might contribute, somehow, to a more empirically informed debate about the principles of good government, but when I began this research, I had no idea that the historical comparisons would run so deep. No imaginable conspirator, of the plutocratic libertarian right who wanted to dismantle the state and see all but its powers of law and order rescinded, or of the revolutionary Marxist left who longed for the end times of capitalism, could ever have masterminded such an elaborate and comprehensive cock-up as the developments investigated in the pages of this book. But if the history of communism teaches us anything, it is that whatever governments do, whatever means they believe to be justified by the utopian end, you cannot make these materialist fantasies real.

---

[34] Ibid., p. 249.
[35] Leszek Kołakowski, *Main Currents of Marxism*, Vol. 3 (Oxford: Clarendon Press, 1978), p. 1208.
[36] 1 Corinthians 13 (King James Version).
[37] Ernest Gellner, *Plough, Sword and Book: The Structure of Human History* (Chicago: Chicago University Press, 1989), pp. 17, 73.

I hope it has always been clear that I reject a moral equivalence between the deliberately violent means–ends savagery of Stalinism and the aspirations of the great majority of neoliberal free-marketeers, whether they were committed pro-Brexit economic libertarians, Machiavellian billionaires, technocrats at the leading edge of academic economics or formerly moderate, centrist conservatives, liberals and social democrats who were sincerely persuaded that neoclassical economics and our increasing powers of computation might finally mean the elimination of market failures and risks. Yet, while Britain's neoliberal politicians perpetrated nothing remotely akin to the terror imposed by the Soviet system, neoliberal policy has corrupted a comparatively functional state and proved both immiserating and demoralising for millions of its citizens.

Long before the pandemic, whole regions of Britain had been left at the mercies of an increasingly exploitative capitalism, and countless individuals might have lived altogether happier, safer, less troubled lives had the country's post-war public institutions been renewed, rather than ceaselessly disrupted and asset-stripped, and had the private sector been encouraged to understand itself as an integral part of the wider social fabric. Stephen Spender had emphasised in *The God That Failed* that 'for the intellectual of good will, Communism is a struggle of conscience. To understand this, explains many things'.[38] No doubt the same case can be made for neoliberalism, but as Spender pointed out, the question nevertheless becomes that of how much human suffering, incompetence and corruption you are willing to inflict on your society in the name of your beliefs before you concede they might have been wrong after all.

Conclusion

The Leave campaign in 2016 had shared much in common with the 1979 Conservative election manifesto. Both had evoked the threat of a bureaucratic super-state and something approaching a conspiracy of that state against the public. Both had promised to rescue a Greater Britain from the oppressive forces that supposedly were holding it back. Both campaigns were a misdiagnosis of the real crisis at hand. By the early 2020s, however, the country faced a crisis of ungovernability

---

[38] Spender, *The God That Failed*, p. 240.

far worse than that of the 1970s, with a dysfunctional and analytically myopic central state, depleted and restricted local government and an altogether more divided society. Britain's neoliberal revolution in practice has been centrifugal: those who cannot thrive under its doctrines have been flung aside as private failures in what is better understood as a common tragedy. The Camp 1 purists behind Brexit then made exactly the wrong diagnosis of the country's condition. It was their idea of a cure that would prove most damaging to the British body politic. As Evsei Liberman wrote of the USSR in 1970, 'When one encounters so many people making mistakes, it is necessary to look for the reason not only in their individual qualities, but in that system.'[39]

At this point, the existential threat is not simply to the United Kingdom as a liberal democracy but to its existence as a Union of four nations. The Johnson governments that came to power via the strategy of English 'nationalist in form, libertarian in content' were singularly ill-equipped to acknowledge, let alone resolve, the growing alienation of the Scots, Welsh and Northern Irish from Westminster. The final two contenders for the Conservative leadership that followed Johnson, Truss and Sunak, had only competed in their disrespect for national devolution. But as Scotland and Wales continue to suffer the relative deprivations of the financialised economy that systematically favours the South-East, and as Northern Ireland begins to thrive, economically, as the only part to remain within the Single European Market, drawing it closer to Ireland, the United Kingdom itself may yet be broken on the neoliberal wheel. For a country that historically prided itself on its immunity to ideological 'enthusiasms' it is an astonishing fate, and perhaps the clearest testament to how completely the 'Conservative and Unionist' party has forgotten itself.

The isomorphism in the practices of the Soviet and neoliberal state has proved profound. Both revolutions empowered a specific cohort of political economic agents: the proletarian *nomenklatura* of the Communist Party versus the large business sector in neoliberalism. Both groups were the presumed bearers of revolutionary consciousness, but they became a grotesque parody of workers' solidarity and of innovative enterprise respectively. In neoliberalism, as in Soviet

---

[39] Evsei Liberman, *Economic Methods and the Effectiveness of Production* (1970) (New York: International Arts and Sciences, 1972).

communism, these privileged cadres have sought to consolidate their structural privileges through rent-seeking behaviours that bear the most tenuous relation to the productive, inclusive wealth-building expected of them. The capacity for remedial action in both systems is likewise blindsided by analytical monoculture and doctrinal hubris. Both systems develop forms of economic growth doomed to completely undermine themselves in developmental terms: via nineteenth century Prussian heavy industrialism for Leninism versus financialisation and rentier state capitalism for neoliberalism.[40] The neoliberal revolution in the United Kingdom has carried huge, and largely negative, implications for the capacity of the democratic state to deliver the mandates of governments, for its basic functionality as an agent of public authority and as an honest custodian of public funds. As if the Fates had conspired to call the country to a reckoning, Queen Elizabeth II, the country's longest-reigning monarch and its exemplar of public service, constitutional duty and dignity in office, respected even among republicans, died in the week that Truss was appointed.

The Sovietologist Robert Tucker described the potential of revolutionary 'movement regimes' to remain in power long after they had become functionally extinct.[41] In post-Brexit Britain, as in Brezhnev's USSR, such an 'extinct movement regime' can now be found in the succession of Conservative governments that have proved incapable of moving the country forward except within the terms laid down by an already failed orthodoxy, but entrenched against the pent-up public demand for political and social reform based on empirics.

As Polanyi remarked, 'To suppose that there exists some smoothly functioning automatic mechanism of adjustment which preserves equilibrium if only we trust to methods of *laissez-faire* is a doctrinaire delusion which disregards the lessons of historical experience without having behind it the support of sound theory.'[42] With the benefit of hindsight, it is clear that if you institutionalise a high modernist script of the political economy as a predictable machine, citizens as hyper-rational and society as amenable to codification, quantification,

---

[40] Brett Christophers, *Rentier Capitalism: Who Owns the Economy and Who Pays for It?* (London: Verso, 2020).
[41] Robert Tucker, 'Towards a Comparative Politics of Movement-Regimes', *American Political Science Review* 55 (2) (1961): 281–289.
[42] Polanyi, *The Great Transformation*, p. 32.

managerialism and target-setting, and if you insist on selling this to the electorate not as utopian revolution but as the un-improvable technological frontier of 'scientific' progress, then you should expect to hear the mordant laughter of Soviet ghosts.

Both systems promised to relieve us of our ethical duty as citizens to think about what might be prudent, practical and socially just, as distinct from automatically 'true' or allegedly inescapable within the terms of trans-historical 'natural' economic laws. Both doctrines contain a completely dehumanised attitude to suffering, and both operate with an increasingly lethal hubris in relation to the natural world. The disunited Kingdom is currently governed by the last believers in a corrupted utopia at the very point when our socioeconomic and ecological crises demand we apply the precautionary principle and some basic humanist ethics in public policy. Kołakowski called radical uncertainty 'the metaphysical horror', but he insisted it was better to teeter on the brink of that horror with your eyes wide open than to live in flat-out denial of its existence.[43]

The paradigm shift we need requires a renewed willingness by governments to test policies in development against historical precedents, known risks, observable social facts and moral values, but we must add something else: a willingness to advance immediate, radical but non-utopian solutions to the ecological catastrophe at our door. You cannot wish away the difficult choices. An instant, absolute application of precautionary principles would crash, rather than adapt, the economy. The costs of avoiding *any* carbon emissions and pollutions on day one of this essential transition would be too high under any assumptions, but this fact should direct comprehending decision-makers in politics, business and the wider society to find immediate win-wins at scale and as fast as humanly possible, pathways to system-wide transformation. Transition should be driven by the precautionary principle as the dominant strategy, along with the effective mitigation of the social costs of transformation to enable the changes to continue apace. In the cradle of the industrial revolution, these necessities could open the door on a fresh, popular and inclusive democratic politics for any political party with the wit and moral foundations to grasp the nature of the task.

---

[43] Leszek Kołakowski, *The Metaphysical Horror* (Chicago: Chicago University Press, 1988), p. 54.

Since this is a book about production regimes, I want to close by highlighting the concept of the 'circular economy'. Happily, the circularity in question here refers not to the delusion of our own omniscience but to our need to tread as lightly as possible on the natural world. Based on three principles, a circular economy is a production regime that designs out waste and pollution, keeps products and materials in use and regenerates natural systems.[44] Like all such ideas it can be co-opted by the defenders of the status quo, but taken seriously it could be transformative and reignite the innovative potential of the British political economy. For a country newly cut off from so many of its existing supply chains, and with its small and medium-sized enterprises sector suffering a multi-dimensional crisis from monopsony buyers, Brexit trade restrictions and supply-chain shortages, any British government worthy of the name could embrace these ideas as part of its escape strategy from the negative-sum logic of rentier capitalism to a positive-sum logic of sustainable prosperity.[45] The British government's mobilisation of policies to this end might begin to fill the political and social void that we have made. We already have the technologies to enable a radical reduction in energy and material throughputs. What's needed is the political will to apply them.

In Britain today there are powerful corporate and financial interests who will oppose any such paradigm shift, and they depend upon late-stage neoliberal governments to prevent it for them. There is consequently no time like the present to remember that political engagement and institution-building for the public good are not just legitimate but necessary activities in a society that wishes not just to thrive but, in our current predicament, to survive. We can no longer, and most of us never could, afford a utopian politics in which kindness, cooperation, ecological respect and social justice are regarded as anti-system values. It follows that we have to rebuild the ideas of the social, and the public, as we review what it means to be a 'realist' in a world on the edge of irreversible environmental collapse.

This is not to say that neoclassical economics has nothing to offer, only to admit that it has overreached itself entirely and that its

---

[44] See, for example, the work of the following organisations: the Ellen McArthur Foundation, Forum for the Future and the New Economics Foundation.
[45] Tim Jackson, 'Prosperity without Growth: The Transition to a Sustainable Economy', Report of the Sustainable Development Commission, 2009.

determinism is dangerous. If you remain convinced that freer markets to the point of general equilibrium are the only way forward, you are assuming that an economic doctrine with no basis in human history will nurture your children more than clean water, food, shelter and a climate compatible with natural life. Both Soviet and neoliberal economics equate politics with the achievement of a form of being – of perfect universal rationality – rather than with the management of the human struggle. As Polan said of Leninism, it is 'a politics for the end of time'.[46] So, too, is neoliberalism, but by continuing to drive the destruction of the living planet, the last champions of deregulated markets are currently set to accelerate the real end of human history by other means.

The solutions are political, but as Kołakowski concluded,

> We do not need crazy dreams of a society from which all evil temptations have been removed or dreams of a total revolution which all at once will bring us a bliss of final redemption in a world devoid of conflict. What we need [are political ideas] that will help us find our way in the complex reality of the brutal forces that operate in human history, [political ideas] that will strengthen our readiness to fight poverty and social injustice. We need [political] traditions conscious of [their] own limitations, because the dream of final redemption is despair dressed in the cloak of hope, the greed for power clothed in the gown of justice.[47]

---

[46] Polan, *Lenin*, p. 182.
[47] Quoted in Michnik, 'Conversations in the Citadel', in *Letters*, p. 328.

Index

Ackerman, Frank, 26, 69
agencification, 115, 160–170
   affinities with Soviet planning, 163–167
   formal criteria for, 161–163
   performance of, 165–169
   rejection of, 170
Austrian school, 16, 95–101
   critique of Soviet planning, 37
   disputes with neoclassical economics, 23, 55
   knowledge, theory of, 107
axiomatic deduction, 12–16, 29–34, 74, 79, 133, 274

Blair, Tony
   Iraq war, 336
   shift to New Labour, 130, 193, 330, 334, 336, 342, 360
Bockman, Johanna, 24, 36, 58
Brexit
   affinities with 'developed socialism', 345, 355, 388
   referendum decision, 343–348
   social structure of the Brexit vote, 352–354
   utopianism of, 119, 330–332, 339–343, 350–352, 387
   Vote Leave campaign, 330–332, 345–352, 373
   Vote Remain campaign, 345, 349–350
Brezhnev, Leonid
   Brezhnevite tendencies in neoliberalism, 153, 270, 283, 327–370
   'Era of Stagnation', 3, 142
   neo-traditionalism, turn to, 68
Bronk, Richard, 6, 10, 28, 118, 369

Brown, Gordon, 130, 194, 250
Buchanan, James, 81, 85–87, 98–101, 227
bureaucracy
   Leninist critique of, 88–91
   as necessary feature of modernity, 102
   neoliberal practice, 371
   public choice critique of, 79–93, 118–120
   Weberian, rational-legal view, 101–104
Burke, Edmund, 79, 376

Cameron, David
   lack of new ideas under, 341–342
   political challenges facing, 329, 339, 350
   reasoning on Europe, 343–345
Carillion, the collapse of, 146, 151–153
circular economy, 390
climate breakdown, 272–273, 321, 391
climate policy
   carbon accounting, 303–305
   carbon budgets, 288, 291, 294–296, 303–305
   carbon taxes, 310–317, 322
   Climate Change Act, 290–292, 297, 305, 306
   Climate Change Committee, 295–296, 304
   Climate Change Levy, 311–312
   Climate Change Risk Assessments, 284–287, 305–306
   Environmental Protection Agency, 318

Index

EU Emissions Trading Scheme, 316–317
  forecasting, 2, 275, 280–288, 303–306, 313–314
  Levy Control Framework, 313–316
  neoclassical economic theories behind, 275–288
  regulatory regime, 307–310
  subsidies, 318–320
  Task Force on Climate-Related Risks, 298–299
  utopianism of, 287–288, 320–323
closed-system versus open-system reasoning (explained), 8–19, 28–36, 52
Cold War, 23, 51–52, 80, 89
Commonwealth, The, 355
communism, 4, 40, 47, 60, 64, 89, 90, 243, 328, 361, 385
  last stage of socialism, as, 95, 118, 355
Communist Party of the Soviet Union
  ideological decay of, 46–48, 331, 340–341
  Menshevism versus Bolshevism, 38, 345
  revolutionary 'leading role', 15, 89–90
Conservative Party and conservatism
  One-Nation, 341, 356–358
  post-war, 79, 173
  Thatcherism, 109–120, 174, 332–334, 341–345, 354, 360, 362–363
  versus reality, 355–363
contract theory, 137–139, 148, 182–189, 198
Corbyn, Jeremy, 329–330
corruption, 363–368
  corporate state capture, 265–266, 364–368
  Covid-19 procurement, 152
Covid-19 pandemic, 359–360
critical realism, 4–15, 28–30, 32–33, 105
Crouch, Colin, 283, 368
Cummings, Dominic, 348–349, 380–381

determinism, the problem of, 15–16, 49, 52, 391
  in neoclassical economics, 34–35, 59
  in Soviet economics, 37–40
Devolution Act, The, 336
devolved powers in
  Northern Ireland, 249, 289
  Scotland, 289, 336
  Wales, 289, 336
dirigisme, French, 77–78
Dunleavy, Patrick, 91–92

economic constitution, the ideal
  contrast with liberal democratic ideal, 93
  Hayek, in, 95–98
  in Leninist thought, 93–95
  public choice theory, in, 98–101
education policy
  Academy programme, history of, 190–197
  accountability, legal and parental, 179, 195, 197, 208–213, 216–217
  Camp 2 neoclassical policy, as, 175–178, 180
  education finance, 200–207
  Education Funding Agency, 207–214
  Local Education Authorities, 189–190, 215
  Multi-Academy Trusts, 198–199, 204–207, 218
  quasi-markets in education, theory of, 175–189
  Regional School Commissioners, 213, 218
  regulatory instability in, 207–214
  related-party payments, 187, 204–206, 219
  Soviet affinities in, 184–187, 197, 210, 217–220
Ellman, Michael, 37, 41, 46, 67
Empire, the British, 262, 354–355
epistemological uncertainty, 10–12, 34, 278
epistemology, the problem of, 4–20, 37–45, 48
European Union, 3, 84, 224, 344, 347, 353, 354, 374

Fama, Eugene, 277–279
Financial Crisis, the Global, 24, 258–259, 271, 277–281, 283, 292, 321, 329, 338, 343
financial sector, the, 73, 234, 242, 247, 257–259, 262, 284, 292, 297–301, 328
firms
  agency theory of, 237–242
  corporate governance, 145, 154, 158, 237–242, 254–256, 329, 336
  financialisation of, 146, 154, 157, 159, 237–244, 253–256, 260, 309, 329, 368–369, 388
  index firms, passive, 240–242, 280
  maximisation of shareholder value, 145, 154, 237–242, 254, 297
  monopoly, 77, 79, 82–85, 91–92, 110, 130, 135, 139, 146, 154–157, 160, 206, 369
  monopsony, 135, 390
  oligopoly, 135, 139, 244, 300
  public service industry firms, 140–153, 188, 359
  small and medium sized, 136, 245, 269, 270
Fleetwood, Steven, 105, 181
forgetting, organised, 105–109, 133, 181, 218

Gove, Michael, 194–195, 213–214, 218, 348, 378
governing science, 3

Hannan, Daniel, 348, 350
Havel, Vaclav, 362, 377, 382
Hayek, Friedrich August von
  ideal constitution, on the, 95–100, 112
  philosophy of knowledge, on the, 37, 55, 57, 173, 275–277
  utopianism in thought, 109, 119, 334, 345
Her Majesty's Revenue and Customs, 150, 263–269
heterodox economics (Camp 3), 32–33, 75, 109, 113, 223, 225, 329
historical institutionalism, 18
hypothetical deduction. *See* scientific method, the

imagination as disruptive social fact, 11, 119, 328, 337, 384
individualism
  neoliberal subject, the, 28, 49, 110, 118–119, 332, 372, 375–379
  Soviet subject, the, 48, 375–379
inequality, social, 9, 219, 329, 335, 360, 363
innovation failures
  in neoliberal practice, 115, 142, 165, 224, 230, 235, 244, 253, 257, 263
  in Soviet practice, 45, 47, 64, 65, 149, 164
insurance and insurable risk, 284
investment
  performance in neoliberal practice, 134, 145, 154, 157–159, 169, 174–175, 201, 238–242, 252–259, 261–265, 270, 300–303, 315, 317, 320, 365, 371
  performance in Soviet economy, 62–68
  theoretical challenge, as a, 46, 54, 109, 113, 172, 184, 188, 221–224, 228–237, 279, 286, 307, 332, 380

Johnson, Boris
  affinities with late-Soviet rule, 373–381, 387
  Brexit, role in, 349
  function for the Conservative Party, 356–358, 360–362
  institutional vandalism of, 4, 151, 359, 367–368, 381
  policy direction, 296, 329

Kant, Immanuel, 7, 38
Kantorovich, Leonid, 65–66
Keynesian economics, 71, 77, 82, 85, 232, 235, 266, 275–277, 279, 347
Khrushchev, Nikita, 61–65, 149, 360, 364
Kołakowski, Leszek, 43, 384–385, 389, 391
Kornai, Janos, 44–46, 140–144, 149
Kosygin, Alexei, 63, 149, 281

Index

Kuhn, Thomas
  'Kuhn losses', 108, 270, 284
  normal scientific progress, on, 108
  paradigm shifts in science, 5–7
Kwarteng, Kwasi, 351, 362–363

Labour Party, the, 193, 329–330, 334–335
law, the rule of, 83, 96, 246, 248, 359
Lawson, Tony, 29–34, 52
Lazonick, William, 133, 253, 270
Le Grand, Julian, 177–181, 183, 185–187, 192–194, 204, 207, 209
Lenin, Vladimir Ilyich, and Leninism
  'bad philosopher', as, 38–44
  bureaucracy, on, 88–91, 113
  circular reasoning in, 45, 52, 59–61, 100, 107, 115, 118, 122, 170–171, 246, 381
  cult of, 362
  democracy in socialism, on, 349
  leading role of the party, on the, 14–15
  liberal democracy, on, 104
  nationalism, and, 339–341
  ontology and epistemology of, 1–3, 38–44, 49, 59–61, 171–172, 282
  religious qualities of, 94–95, 383–385, 391
  socialist revolution, on the, 339–341
  'withering away of the state', on the, 79, 93–95
Leontief, Wassily, 65, 232–233
Liberal Party, the, 335–336
Lucas, Robert, 111, 277–281

Mair, Peter, 333, 336
Major, John, 249, 289, 341
Marx, Karl, 89, 171, 348, 383
  Leninism, contrasts with, 14, 37, 40, 43, 47, 349, 381, 384
  tensions within his writings, 38
mathematics, limitations of, 17, 25–36, 64, 74–75, 119, 231, 276–277, 282, 381
May, Theresa, 194, 294, 329, 336, 356–357
McDonnell, John, 269, 329
Michnik, Adam, 328, 348, 378–379

Miłosz, Czesław, 376–377
Mirowski, Philip, 26, 28, 30
models, nature of economic, 10, 70–72, 105–109, 221, 229, 236, 271, 278
movement regimes, 388
Muth, John, 277–281

nationalism
  deployment in neoliberal practice, 113, 342–343, 350, 357
  deployment in Soviet practice, 339–341
  nationalist in form, libertarian in content, 349, 352–355, 387
  nationalist in form, socialist in content, 340
neoclassical economic theory
  Camp 1 (first-best world) defined, 32–36
  Camp 2 (second-best world) defined, 32–36
  closed-system reasoning in, 24–36
  competition, concepts of, 27, 35–36, 49, 53–58, 80, 133–136, 175–176
  computational general equilibrium (CGE) models, 232–236, 241, 256–257
  dynamic stochastic general equilibrium (DSGE) models, 72, 232, 236, 242
  efficient markets hypothesis (EMH), 240, 277–284, 300–301
  general equilibrium, 27, 51–76, 100, 105, 112, 172, 221–237, 243, 279, 335, 366, 391
  market failures, 16, 32–36, 82, 101, 133, 137–139, 147, 192, 223, 224, 288, 292, 334, 386
  partial equilibrium, 106, 227
  physics, metaphors from, 25–27, 29, 70, 75, 82
  rational expectations, 111, 236, 277–284
  rationality, 2, 23–36, 48, 79, 82, 90, 117, 118, 127, 137–138, 278, 288, 334, 372
  representative agent, 71–72, 91, 231, 236

neoclassical economic theory (cont.)
  risk, calculable and incalculable, 275–277, 284
  Sonnenschein, Mantel and Debreu, 69–70
  time, logical versus historical, 29, 53, 62, 118, 310, 363, 381
neoliberalism, the emergence of, 16–19, 75, 84, 110–114, 118–120, 222, 275, 283, 328, 332–339, 373
New Public Management (NPM) in theory, 114–117, 127–131
Niskanen, William, 81–82, 85, 88–93, 111, 116, 171

ontological indeterminacy, 29, 34, 278
ontology, the problem of, 4–16, 29, 107
ordoliberalism, 18, 23, 77
Osborne, George, 131, 256, 292–294, 313–315, 342, 345
  austerity, 153, 170, 214, 262, 292, 329, 339
outsourcing, 127–153
  contract, problems of, 137–140, 182–189
  coordination failures in, 116, 218
  factors missing in the theory of, 133–137, 181–182, 270
  high costs of, 131–133, 200–207
  increased uses of, 128–131, 170, 337
  Soviet-type pathologies in, 140–153, 184–187
  state capacity, loss of, 220
  Strategic Suppliers, 144–145

Pareto, Vilfredo, 15, 47, 55, 56, 73
Paris Climate Agreement, 273, 294, 305
party system change
  cartel parties, 333
  catch-all parties, 332, 339
  corporate brokerage parties, 368
  democratic functions of, 93, 118, 335–339, 342–343, 372
  mass parties, 333
Polan, Anthony, 44, 375, 391
Prague Spring, the, 68

privatisation
  affinities with Soviet planning, 154
  financialisation in privatised utilities, 157–160
  regulatory failures in, 156–160, 318
  tensions in theory of, 128, 153–157
procedural formalism, 287, 303–307
public choice theory, development of, 79–88, 101, 107, 112, 117–120, 171, 187, 338

racism, institutional, 165–166, 333, 374
regulatory competition, 222, 227, 263–269
regulatory drift, 365
regulatory rule, one-in-three-out, 307–310
religion, neoliberal and Soviet affinities with, 94, 100, 383–385
rentier state, 3, 82, 84, 153, 188, 369, 388
Republican Party, 342, 361

scientific method, the, 11–16, 48, 104, 108, 172, 321, 332, 369, 375–381
Scottish National Party, 336
Shackle, George, 10, 373
Single European Market, 223, 330, 344, 346, 387
Smith, Adam, 25, 111, 275
socialist calculation debate, 37, 54–55, 232
Soviet central planning
  balanced plan, 51–52, 59–76
  closed-system reasoning in, 13–16, 36–50, 59–76, 115, 118, 154
  corruption, 47, 270, 364
  cybernetics, 63–68, 74, 234, 281–284, 381
  developmental achievements, 45
  evolution of, 37–47, 95, 220, 283
  hoarding, 46, 63
  information problems, 36, 44–51, 63–72, 166, 210, 282
  innovation, weaknesses of, 45–47, 163
  input-output planning, 65–69, 221, 232–236
  linear programming, 65–68, 282
  material balances, 62, 65, 67

New Economic Mechanism, 63
New Economic Policy, 42
perverse incentives in, 153, 167, 184–187
rationality requirement in, 2, 44–46, 50, 90, 116–118, 372, 391
shadow economy, 242, 364
soft-budget constraints, 140–145
Stalin, Joseph, and Stalinism
economic strategies, 2, 15, 42–45, 47, 49, 52, 59–63, 118, 163
experts, on, 151, 378
politics of, 47, 334, 351, 386
Starmer, Keir, 330
Stewart, Rory, 358
Sunak, Rishi, 302–303, 363, 375, 387

tax policy
corporate tax rates, 221
corporate taxation regime, evolution of, 248–252
investment, in theory and practice, 227, 229–230, 232–248, 252–259
macroeconomic models, problems of, 231–236, 256–259, 271
neoclassical theories of tax competition, 222–237
regulatory bargaining, Soviet, 270
regulatory laxity, 246–247, 265–269

tax havens, 59, 234, 242–245, 247, 251, 263–265, 329
Tiebout hypothesis, 31–32, 225–227
Thatcher, Margaret. *See* Conservative Party and Conservatism: Thatcherism
think tanks, 110–111, 215, 242
transaction costs, theory of, 137–138, 168, 183, 345
Treasury, Her Majesty's, 120, 234, 252, 257, 265–266, 269, 270, 292–293, 307–310, 313–314, 315
Truss, Liz, 329, 351, 363, 368, 370, 383, 387–388

United Kingdom Independence Party (UKIP), 344–347
utilitarianism, 26–27
utopia, definition of, 123

Vujačić, Veljko, 339–341, 356, 363

Weber, Max, 101–104, 129, 161–162, 170, 365
welfare state, 85, 92–93, 335
post-war era, 84, 174, 332
quasi-markets, 175–189
social investment state, 174
Windrush scandal, 165–166

Printed in Great Britain
by Amazon